The Diary of ... William Windham, 1784 to 1810. Ed. by Mrs. H. Baring

William Windham

THE
RIGHT HON. WILLIAM WINDHAM'S
DIARY

THE RIGHT HON. WILLIAM WINDHAM'S DIARY

GLORIA
DEO IN

THE DIARY

OF THE

RIGHT HON. WILLIAM WINDHAM

1784 TO 1810

EDITED BY

MRS. HENRY BARING

LONDON
LONGMANS, GREEN, AND CO.
1866

PREFACE.

THE 'Diary of the Right Honourable William Windham' was given to me by my brother William Windham, a short time before his death, in December, 1854.

It is in truth chiefly a record of Mr. Windham's health and feelings, made for himself alone, which can hardly be supposed to possess much general interest; but there are many passages interspersed in it, strongly indicative of his character, which I trust I shall be forgiven for wishing to rescue from oblivion.

No portion of this Journal of any consequence has ever been made public, with the exception of that which relates to the last moments of Dr. Johnson, which Mr. Croker included in his edition of Boswell's account of his life. The records of several years are wanting, having been unfortunately mislaid long since. A life of Mr. Windham, prefixed to his speeches, was published by Mr. Amyot in 1821.

The political career of Mr. Windham is part of the history of his country, nor is it my purpose to discuss it. It brought him ultimately into connection with both the great parties of the State during many eventful years, but even in the heat of those times, no one ever doubted for a moment that his course was guided by the highest principles and the nicest sense of honour. On this subject I gladly transcribe the eloquent language of the late Earl Grey in his speech in the House of Lords at the time of Mr. Windham's death: 'It was his misfortune,' he says, 'at different times to differ from that distinguished and regretted character; yet in the heat of political disagreement he never ceased to admire his many and splendid virtues. He was a man of a great, original, and commanding genius, with a mind cultivated with the richest stores of intellectual wealth, and a fancy winged to the highest flights of a most captivating imagery, of sound and spotless integrity, with a warm spirit but a generous heart, and of a courage and determination so characteristic as to hold him forward as the strong example of what the old English heart could effect and endure. He had, indeed, his faults, but they seemed, like the skilful disposition of shade in works of art, to make the impression of his virtues more striking, and gave additional grandeur to the outline of his character.' *

If therefore, after much consideration, I determine to submit these pages to the press, it is not with a view to enhance the fame of the writer, but to preserve some portions of a relic consigned to me (φιλάδελφα κάτω νέκρυ' εἰδομένη), before time shall have obliterated all names and traces of the former possessors of Felbrigg, and whilst there are still living those who cling with fondness to its memories.

* The late Lord Lansdowne, when last at Felbrigg, in the year 1861, remarked, that Mr. Windham had the best Parliamentary address of any man he had ever seen, which was enhanced by the grace of his person and the dignity of his manners.

It appears that the task which I have undertaken was at one time committed to the able hands of the late Mr. George Ellis, and it is indeed much to be regretted that it was not performed by so intimate a friend of Mr. Windham, and so accomplished a scholar. Mr. Ellis had written a preface to his intended publication, which forms part of the present volume, but he had gone very little way in arranging the extracts for publication.

From the brevity with which every event is recorded, and the length of time which has elapsed since their occurrence, allusions will, no doubt, be found to persons now forgotten, and to incidents which the Editor is unable to explain; but it is possible that, by a comparison with other memoirs of the time, these papers may contribute to elucidate some of the important transactions of the age in which Mr. Windham lived.

CECILIA ANNE BARING.

11 Berkeley Square:
January 1, 1866.

GENEALOGY

OF THE

WINDHAM FAMILY.

It may be well to attach to this memorial some history of the ancestry of the Windham family. Soon after the Norman Conquest, Alwardus, an eminent Saxon, became possessed of lands in the county of Norfolk, and resided at Crownethorpe Castle, in the parish of Wymondham, and assumed his surname from that place.

Felbrigg was purchased in 1461, by John Wyndham, of the trustees of Sir Simon de Felbrigg, *alias* 'Bigod,' who was a descendant of a younger branch of the Earls of Norfolk. Sir Simon was standard-bearer to Richard II.; and his brass, one of the finest in England, is now in the church at Felbrigg. He was one of the first Knights of the Garter. John Wyndham was at the battle of Stoke, near Newark, in 1487, and was knighted for his valiant behaviour. He was a correspondent of Paston.

He became afterwards engaged in the interests of the House of York. Lord Bacon, in his 'History of Henry VII.' gives the account of the King's jealousy of Edmund de la Pole, Earl of Suffolk; whereupon he says, 'W. Courtenay, Earl of Devonshire, and Sir John Wyndham, were taken into custody, and Sir John was beheaded on Tower Hill, 6th of May, 1503. Sir John Wyndham was page to the first Howard, Duke of Norfolk, and married his daughter. Their motto, *au bon droit*, was assumed at this time.'

His descendants were men of energy and consideration; one was Vice-Admiral of England, and fought under his uncle, the Earl of Surrey; and others in the next generation rose to eminence at the bar. Sir Thomas Wyndham, of Felbrigg, was a distinguished naval commander, who attended Henry VIII. at the conferences between Guisnes and Ardres.

In the days of Queen Elizabeth the eldest, or Norfolk, branch of the Windhams became extinct, and the property of Crownethorpe and Felbrigg went into possession of a second son of Sir Thomas Wyndham, settled in Somersetshire. He was Sir John Wyndham, who married Joan Portman, of Orchard Portman, from whom descended, first, the Egremonts, second the Windhams of Felbrigg, Wadham, Salisbury, Dinton Askrigg, Clearwell, Cromer.

There is in the church of Felbrigg, a monument to the memory of Thomas, third son of Sir Edmund,* who died unmarried, on December 20th, 1599, erected by his cousin and heir, John Wyndham, of Orchard, county of Somerset.

Livest thou, Thomas? yeas: where? with God on high.
Art thou not dead? yeas, and here I lye.
I that with men on earth did live to die,
Died for to live with Christ eternallie.

Sir John Wyndham, of Orchard, succeeded, therefore, to the estate of Felbrigg. His sons, during the Civil Wars, were attached to the Royal cause, and Colonel Francis Wyndham, his fourth son, is memorable for conducting Charles II. to his seat at Trent, after the battle of Worcester, when he entertained the King with the following remarkable passage of his father, Sir John Wyndham, calling his sons together before his death and saying to them: 'I commend you to honour and obey our gracious Sovereign, and in all things to adhere to the Crown, and though

* The will of Sir Edmund Windham is given at length in Collins's 'Peerage.' He wishes that 'his son Edmund should have the manors of Felbrigg, Aylmerton, Metton and Runton, Sustead and Barningham; and that they should find an honest priest to sing in the churche of Felbrigg for my soule, and for my wife's soule, and for my fader and mother soules, and all my friends' soules.'

the Crown should hang upon a bush, I charge you, forsake it not.'

It may be well to say, after this somewhat long digression, that Thomas Wyndham, who married the daughter of Sir John Lytton, of Knebworth, was the direct ancestor of the last Right Honourable William Windham, from father to son. William married the daughter of Sir Joseph Ashe, of Twickenham, a staunch Royalist. His portrait, and that of his wife, are at Felbrigg. Miss Ashe, sister to Mrs. Windham, married the (Restoration) Lord Townshend. Ashe Windham was born in the family coach on the high road, but although he came hastily into the world he remained in it to the age of 77. He represented the county of Norfolk in the days of Queen Anne, and died in 1749. His son William was a very remarkable man, and took more after his uncle Charles, a handsome, dashing naval officer, captain of the 'Kent,' one of the finest 74's of that day. He fought a good action off the coast of Barbary, the picture of which is in the north drawing-room at Felbrigg, and his own portrait is in the dining-room.

Colonel Windham quarrelled in early life with his father, and lived much abroad, having entered the Hungarian hussars in the days of Marie Theresa.

He was a beautiful horseman and swordsman; very handsome in person, slightly made, but athletic; fond of adventures, and in company with Pococke, in 1741, penetrated some of the higher valleys of the Alps, and ascended Mont Blanc. He delighted in theatricals: Garrick and others were his constant guests. He was a very good classical scholar, besides being well acquainted with French, German, and Spanish.

There is now at Felbrigg, or there ought to be, a MS. of his upon the art of war, which proves that he had studied the theory, both ancient and modern, to good effect.

He hunted the hounds from Felbrigg to London, and married Sarah Hicks, the widow of Robert Lukin* of Dunmow, who was

* The Lukins, or Lykyns, are an old Essex family, the direct ancestors of Geoffry Lukin, of Chignall Castle, in Essex, the ruins of which may still be seen. They lost all their property in the Civil Wars.

possessed of great beauty, good sense, and determination, as may be judged from the fact of her having been able, at the age of 41, to captivate one of the most admired Cavaliers of his day.

She came of a good family, but was left by her husband in very reduced circumstances.

From these parents sprang William Windham, the author of this 'Diary,' and the last of his branch of the Windham family. He was born in Golden Square, London, on the 3rd of May, 1750, and died 3rd of June, 1810.

From great personal love to the late Admiral Lukin, his nephew by half blood through his mother, he left him the whole of his property, on the condition of his taking the name of Windham, and then left the property, in remainder, to the head of his family, the late George O'Brien, Earl of Egremont. Admiral Windham had six sons: the eldest married Sophia, youngest daughter of the first Marquis of Bristol. They had one son, by whom the property has been sold.

PREFACE BY MR. ELLIS.

THE public life of Mr. Windham may be considered as having commenced in the year 1783, when he undertook the office of Principal Secretary to Lord Northington, appointed Lord-Lieutenant of Ireland; and it happened by a fortunate, though, probably, accidental coincidence, that he began, in the same year, that series of Diaries which will furnish the most amusing and interesting part of this narrative. It was not, indeed, without much hesitation, that the writer of that narrative was induced to abstain from the publication of the original documents, in the exact state in which they have been left by their author, with the suppression only of the very few passages which it might be deemed imprudent to draw from their concealment.

But it appeared, on a careful examination, that merely to suppress what was only interesting to Mr. Windham himself would by no means be sufficient; that many things which, at the moment they were consigned to paper, might have been well worth noting, had, by the lapse of time, been rendered wholly unimportant; that much which was once clear had become obscure; that some mode of illustration would, therefore, be absolutely necessary; and that the chain of events being frequently imperfect, the intermediate links must, after all, be supplied by the biographer. On these grounds it was thought more convenient to employ the materials furnished by Mr. Windham in the shape of extracts, so as to be connected, but not confounded, with the texts, than to fatigue the reader by an irksome reference to occasional notes, the effect of which would be to multiply the calls on his attention at those moments when, from the barrenness of the story, it was most exhausted and torpid. Whether this opinion be justly formed will best appear from a short account of the motives by which the Journal in question seems to have been dictated, of the purpose which it was intended to answer, and of the mode in which it was conducted.

It is not improbable that the project of undertaking this troublesome task may have been suggested to Mr. Windham by his friend, Dr. Johnson, to whose advice he always listened with reverence, and whose example he was ever disposed to follow. The reader will have frequent occasion to remark that the species of mental discipline to which Mr. W. was so anxious to subject himself was, even in many minute particulars, exactly conformable to the practice of Dr. Johnson. To establish the empire of reason over imagination was their common object; and with a view to acquire the power of continued thought undisturbed by the intension of fancy, they imposed on themselves the same exercises; accustoming themselves to occasional composition in the learned languages, converting Greek into Latin epigrams, and taxing the memory by long mental calculations. An English translation of Thuanus was, as Mr. Boswell relates, frequently meditated by Dr. Johnson, and has been partly executed by Mr. Windham, with that sort of reluctant diligence which would be almost unaccountable if, in undertaking the task, he had been solely guided by his own predilection for the voluminous historian. Dr. Johnson wrote, in two quarto volumes, a diary of his own private life, and strongly recommended to his friends the adoption of this practice.

'The great thing to be recorded (said he) is the state of your own mind, and you should write down everything that you remember; for you cannot judge at first what is good or bad: and write immediately, while the impression is fresh, for it will not be the same a week afterwards.'*

There is, indeed, an apparent allusion to this advice amongst the minutes of a conversation with Dr. Johnson, which Mr. Windham has preserved, and which took place, as Mr. Boswell relates, when Mr. Windham, 'before he set out for Ireland, as secretary to Lord Northington, then Lord-Lieutenant of Ireland, expressed to the sage some modest and virtuous doubts, whether he could bring himself to practise those arts which, it is supposed, a person in that situation has occasion to employ.'† The heads of Dr. Johnson's answer were, as appears by Mr. Windham's notes, 'I have no great timidity in my own disposition, and am no encourager of it in others. . . . . Never be afraid to think yourself fit for anything for which your friends think you fit. . . . .

'You will become an able negotiator; a very pretty rascal. . . . .

'No one in Ireland wears even the mask of incorruption. No one professes to do for sixpence what he can get a shilling for doing. . . . .

* Boswell's 'Life of Johnson,' vol. ii. p. 75, 8vo. edit. 1793.

† Ibid. vol. iii. p. 453.

'Set sail; and see where the winds and the waves will carry you. . . . .

'*Every day will improve another. Dies diem docet, by observing at night where you failed in the day, and by resolving to fail so no more!*'

It may, perhaps, be considered as some confirmation of the conjecture here advanced, and as a proof of Mr. Windham's deference to his friend's admonition, that he actually began his 'Diary' in July 1783, the conversation just cited having taken place in the beginning of June.

The work itself is also, as the reader will presently observe, exactly conformable to Dr. Johnson's advice. It is wholly devoted to the purpose of self-examination. The employment of time is punctually brought to account, and severely scrutinised; and many pages are filled with expressions of regret for the valuable hours unprofitably wasted; with lamentations over those habits of indolence from which neither the bustle of business nor the tranquillity of solitude was found to be a sufficient preservative; and with resolutions of future amendment; resolutions, however, which, when recorded, only served to awaken new remorse, because they were constantly succeeded by fresh avowals of repeated negligence.

The severity of self-reproach with which Mr. Windham accustomed himself to contemplate his own omissions, though such as the generality of mankind are in the habit of considering as most venial, was probably encouraged by the example or precepts of his friend; and it affords a curious instance of practical coincidence between two persons whose dispositions were, in many respects, extremely dissimilar, and even opposite. But the habit certainly originated in a strong impression made on Mr. Windham's mind during his illness at Bury in the year 1780, and which appears to have produced a considerable effect on his character and conduct during the whole remainder of his life.

That a man in the bloom and vigour of life, already distinguished by his various attainments, ambitious of every kind of distinction, and conscious that all were within his reach, should contemplate, with no common alarm, the prospect of being arrested in his career by a disease which, without much hastening his death, might deprive life of all its enjoyments, is perfectly natural. It is not less natural that, feeling himself responsible for the due use of his talents, and persuaded that the preservation of them depended on regular and active exertion, he should deplore, with sincere contrition, the frequent instances in which he had inadvertently resigned them to intervals of dangerous inaction. The corroding anxiety which had thus fastened on his mind, explains that sudden air of dejection which was sometimes observable even in his gayest moments, that 'dread of competition, and habitual distrust of his own abilities,' of which he often expresses his consciousness, and that hesitating indecision which formed such a singular contrast with the general firmness of his manly and intrepid character.

It will also sufficiently account for a peculiarity in the Diaries, which, for the purpose of guarding the reader against any future disappointment, it may now be proper to notice.

Mr. Windham was in the habit of registering, day by day, the names of all the persons whom he met at the tables of his friends and acquaintances, as well as of the guests whom he invited to his own; and, indeed, there are many volumes of his Journal which contain very little else. He has thus furnished us with a muster-roll of his contemporaries, comprehending, probably, every individual with whom he associated during a long series of years; but a muster-roll unaccompanied, in almost any instance, by the slightest comment. Such a list, it is true, was a sufficient aid to his memory, since the names of persons who were familiarly known to him could require no further designation. Yet it may seem strange that he, who, though shrinking from dispute and controversy, was particularly fond of rational discussion, and who, at the hours of study, delighted to unravel whatever appeared most entangled in subjects of science or of literature, should suddenly dismiss from his mind the topics with which it had been so strongly occupied in society. It may be thought odd that, whilst employed in committing to paper much that was certainly trivial, he should, in scarcely any instance, attempt to perpetuate the scenes in which he had received both amusement and instruction. It may excite some surprise that, whilst many of his intimates were dropping into the grave, he was not induced to sketch, for his own satisfaction, some memorial of those whom he had been accustomed to meet with pleasure, but could hope to meet no more. The answer is, that the daily toil which he had imposed upon himself was a daily conflict with all his natural propensities. Whilst occupied in tracing the waste of a life which he considered as unusually precarious, dissatisfied with his past exertions, and looking with melancholy forebodings to the future; it was not likely that his mind should be directed to any extrinsic objects, or that his feelings should be much awakened to sympathy.

But, although the following extracts from the 'Diary' may possibly fail to satisfy all the expectations which the public may have formed, they will at least be found to exhibit such a minute and impartial description of the writer as no other pen could possibly furnish.

Unexceptionable materials for biography must be of rare occurrence; because few persons are disposed to examine their own conscience, and fewer still are, like Mr. Windham, aware that to draw up a faithful and dispassionate record of such an examination, requires no common portion of candour and sagacity.

'What a pity it is (says he, in an article of his 'Adversaria') that a man cannot, for a while, stand at a distance from himself, and behold his own person, manner, behaviour, and character, with the eyes of a stranger! What a pity that no one can see himself as he is seen by everyone else! It is from this impossibility that one meets people every day, who are as perfect strangers to their own characters as a man would be to his own countenance who had never seen the reflection of it in a mirror. In this latter predicament few can be found; art, incited by vanity, having furnished us with such ready means of viewing our own persons. But there is no mirror that can, at one view, give us a distinct image of our characters. That image is only to be formed like the map of some of the planets, from the result of observations made with pain and difficulty, and at various times. For this reason few people ever form it at all, but remain in such total ignorance of the appearance of their own characters, as seen from without, that nothing is more common than to hear a man arraigning in others the very failings for which he is himself most notorious, and treating his own favourite follies, the very vices of his own bosom, with as much severity as if he had not the smallest kindred or relation with them!'

It was such an image of his own mind that Mr. Windham was desirous of delineating for his own improvement; and if that image be, as it certainly is, extremely different from the idea of him impressed upon the memory of his friends, it is only because he was able to discover, and disposed to exaggerate, defects which were invisible to any other observer.

The first entry in the 'Diary' informs us, that having left Dublin on the 8th of July, 1783, he arrived in London on the 13th. His return from Ireland was rendered necessary by the ill state of his health; and this compulsory abandonment of his post was the more distressing, because he was aware that the state of public affairs did not admit of delay, and that his protracted convalescence would be likely, at that busy moment, to occasion much inconvenience to Lord Northington. Whilst thus harassed by disease and anxiety, he seems to have been utterly incapable of any mental exertion; but having fortunately found in his friend Mr. Pelham (the present Earl of Chichester) a successor to whom he could safely delegate the duties from which he had withdrawn himself, he soon began to regain his health and spirits, and to revert to his usual occupations. He complains, indeed, in his Journal—which he seems to have resumed as soon as he was able to hold a pen—that his powers of bodily exertion were still very imperfect; that a drowsiness which he was unable to overcome often interfered with the progress of his studies; and that to complete a common letter of business required a succession of the most strenuous efforts. But the tranquillity of his residence at Oxford—a place which he always visited with delight; the gaiety, or the air, or the waters of Tunbridge Wells; gentle exercise, and frequent change of air and of company, had, before the end of the year, completely restored his strength, and enabled him to encounter the fatigues of an election. He set off for Norwich on the 19th of December, having then learned the dismissal of the Coalition Ministry, and commenced an active canvass with a view to the dissolution of Parliament, which was expected to follow almost immediately. That measure, however, the new Ministers deferred till the 24th of March, 1784, during which interval, though unable effectually to resist the two great parties united against them in the House of Commons, they rapidly acquired an unexampled ascendency in the affections of the people. A large majority of the nation declared their determination to support the legitimate prerogative of the Crown, against what they deemed the unjust and arrogant claims of their own representatives; and Mr. Windham tells us on the 21st of January, that 'the Corporation of Norwich have been voting an address to the King on the appointment of the new Ministry, and the freedom of their city to Mr. Pitt.' Yet he writes this in London, to which place he had returned on the last day of the preceding year, and which he did not quit till the end of February, so confident was he that the favour attached to his private character would counterbalance the unpopularity of his political principles.*

The events recorded in the 'Diary' at this time are, in general, such as every man must have to tell who mixes in the extensive society of London; and consequently stipulates to accommodate his own habits and occupations, and modes of life, to those which he finds established by fashion. But a regular commentary on the moral and physical effects of this state of hurried existence, consigned to paper at the moment, could scarcely fail to amuse by its novelty, even if it were not rendered interesting by the talents and character of the writer; and this consideration has led to the selection of the following extracts.

* And he was accordingly returned to Parliament for the city of Norwich on the 5th of April, 1784, after a long contest, at the end of which the numbers on the poll were as follows:—Sir Harbord Harbord, 2305; W. Windham, Esq., 1297; Hon. H. Hobart, 1233.

MATHEMATICAL NOTES BY MR. WINDHAM,

EXTRACTED BY MR. ELLIS.

To explain the reason of the common operations respecting numbers,—in other words, to the common rules of arithmetic,—a beginning must be made by explaining the principle of the notation of numbers according to the methods now in use; the connection between which and the rules of arithmetic is so direct, that those rules have, for the most part, nothing else in view than to exhibit, in that notation, numbers which are already known and defined.

When it is proposed to multiply or divide any number by another, nothing more is required than to exhibit the product or quotient of those numbers according to the notation now in use; for, in fact, the quotient or product required is just as much defined, and often as satisfactorily so, by being the quotient or product of the given numbers, as it can be when exhibited in any other form. Five times seven is as good a description of thirty-five as three tens and five, and so of any other operation. It is not here, as in many other cases, that you are wanting to ascertain whether the number in question is, or is not, given.

To judge of rules, therefore, that have for their object the exhibiting of numbers according to a certain form of notation, we must consider what that form of notation is, and how it is effected that, by means of nine simple marks, and one to denote the absence of all marks, the power is possessed of expressing all possible numbers.

To begin with the most general conception. If there be a series of cells or places, each of them capable of containing a certain number, no matter what, of units; if this series may be extended without end, it is plain that, in such a series, beginning at one extremity and adding places or cells as occasion may require, any possible number may be disposed of.

It will obviously make no difference as to this possibility, though the capacity of these cells, and the number of units capable of being contained in each, should have any proportion one to the other, that may be thought proper.

Let it be supposed, then, that each succeeding cell, proceeding from one end, should be capable of containing just ten times the units capable of being contained in the one preceding it.

If to this you add the condition that, in distributing your numbers through these cells or places, as soon as any cell is filled, and that a number equal to a ninth part of what it contains is further collected, you discharge the whole into the cell next behind it, you have the principle that will guide to the exhibition of any number according to the notation now in use.

For, beginning with a first or lower place, as soon as ten are collected, which is all that the first place can contain, and a ninth part besides, you discharge the whole into the place next following, marking the whole so discharged as one in the second place. You repeat this operation till you have filled the second place, that is, till the number of these wholes discharged into it is nine, marked as nine units of the second place; and till you have collected one whole more; then, agreeably to the principle laid down with respect to all places generally, you discharge the whole of what you have collected into the next or third place.

The two former places are then empty, and capable of admitting a repetition of the whole of what is above described; which may, accordingly, be repeated till the third place shall in like manner overflow by the collection of one unit of the third place more than the third can contain; when the whole ten units of the third place shall be transferred to the fourth as one unit of the fourth place.

It will not fail to be observed that these successive wholes or unity of the several places, and successive discharges, all arise from the continued accumulation of units in the first place. It is the addition of one that completes the supernumerary or tenth unit of the second place, and thus produces a necessity of transferring the whole to the third place. The same accumulation of one in the first place again fills the second place, and causes the necessity of a new transfer to the fourth place. In general, the continued accumulation of units in the first place produces the units of the second place; these again produce the units of the third place; the units of the third place those of the fourth, and so on through all possible numbers; there being no reason why the operation should ever stop while there is the power of adding indefinitely new places behind.

Conceive, as an illustration of this, that all the places up to a certain extent are completely filled. The addition of one in the place of units, or the next one added to the number already so collected, will have the effect of emptying all these places, and transferring their contents, with the one added, to count as a unit in the place next behind.

For since the place of units has, by the supposition, as many as it can contain, the addition of one forms, with the number so collected, what is to be transferred as a unit to the second place; and since the second is, in like manner, supposed to be full, the addition of what is a unit of that second place produces a number that must, in like manner, be transferred as a unit to the third, and so on till you get to the place first beyond those at first supposed, and which, being wholly unoccupied, can receive and retain all that it is wanted to put into it; which is the thing that was to be shown.

All the preceding places of course remain empty, and are ready to receive whatever intermediate numbers shall be added, till they are again filled, and that the addition of one beyond what shall be necessary to fill them shall occasion the same operation to be repeated, and transfer another unit (of the new and higher denomination) to the place next beyond those originally supposed.

It was above observed, that the law regulating the proportion of the capacity of these places with respect to one another, made no difference as to the possibility of disposing in them all possible numbers; supposing the number of these places to be capable of being increased without limitation, it will still less make any difference whether, when the size or capacity of these places is supposed continually to increase, it increases by one proportion or by another.

In the notation now in use they increase in a decuple proportion; so as that each place will contain just ten times what is capable of being contained in the one preceding, the progress being always from right to left: or that each unit in the succeeding place should be equal, precisely, to ten units of the preceding; or, what is obviously the same thing, should be equal to the nine units already contained in that preceding place, with one unit of the same value added to them, in which way we have spoken of these comparative values in some of the paragraphs preceding.

But it is plain that the principle of the notation, and its fitness to express all numbers, could be the same, though the proportion between the capacity of the contiguous places, or the value of the units contained in them, was different, as a sextuple, for instance, or any other; only it must be observed that, in this case, viz. of a sextuple proportion between the value of the units, the number of units capable of being set down in each place must be five: and generally, that whatever be the proportion settled between the capacities of the contiguous places (the proportion being throughout the same), or the value of their respective units, the number of units, capable of being set down in each place, must be one less than the number expressing that proportion.

Example.—Where the proportion is ten, the number of units capable of being put in each place must be ten, one, or nine; where the proportion is nine, must be eight; where six, must be five.

The reason of which is that, in order to ensure the power of expressing all numbers by means of a few marks having certain relative values, according to the places in which they are put, the addition of a unit in each place (having the value which belongs to it in that place) to the units already put there, supposing the place full, must constitute a unit such as belongs to the place following: this of course it can only do when the number of the units, capable of being contained in each place, is one less than those that would constitute a unit of the value of those in the place next following; so as that the addition of one shall make the whole equal to one of those of the place following, *i.e.* counting from right to left.

Were no recourse to be had to the expedient of expressing the numbers in each place by the same marks having different values, the above restriction would not be necessary; whatever the proportion was of the capacity of the places, nothing would be required but to go on to the succeeding places after you had filled those that went before.

But, for the sake of the above contrivance, by which, through the means of only a few marks, all possible numbers may be expressed in a manner to make them known with perfect ease and precision, it is necessary, as was before said, that no more units should be contained in each place than with the addition of one more will constitute a unit of the place succeeding.

That a series, such as those above described—such, namely, as that the value of a unit increases according to a stated proportion in each succeeding place; and that the number of units capable of being put in each place is one less than the number expressing that proportion, is capable of expressing all possible numbers, may be otherwise shown, thus:—

Since the value of the units in the assigned proportion, by taking more and more terms or places, may be increased without limitation, a place may always be found the unit of which shall be greater than the number assigned, whatever that number may be. Find the place next below it in which the unit shall not be greater than the assigned number, and calling this place A, deduct the unit of A from the assigned number as often as it shall be contained in it. The numbers of times of its being so contained cannot be greater than nine, otherwise A would not be the highest place (or the first in descending) in which the unit was not greater than the supposed number.

If it measures the proposed number, or is contained in it a certain number of times exactly, nothing is necessary but to set down the figure denoting that number of times, which, by the observations just made, can always be done; and the whole of the proposed number will be expressed in the place A. If there be a remainder, that remainder must be less than the unit in A, and an enquiry must be again made in the places below A, for the first in which the unit shall not be greater than the number now remaining: let that place be called B, which may be the next below A, or not, as it may happen, and the same process will be again to be repeated with a less number, and with fewer remaining places; that is to say, it must be considered how many times the unit B is contained in the number now under consideration: the figure expressing that number of times must be set down in the place B, and an enquiry must be made what place next below will contain a unit not greater than this new remainder.

As it is plain that the number of places to which these successive enquiries relate is limited, and is continually decreasing, if the operation does not previously stop, by the occurrence of some remainder that is measured exactly by the unit of a term or place preceding the last, you must come, ultimately, to the last, or place of units; that is to say, you must have a remainder which is measured only by units; and by being less than the unit in the next place above, or ten, must contain not more than nine units, and which can, of consequence, be expressed in the last place. This, therefore, being the only remaining part of the proposed number, has been expressed, which is what was required to be shown.

It is to be observed that, by an inadvertence, what is here said has been accommodated only to the case of the decuple notation, though capable of being easily transferred to any other.

Otherwise, as it is plain that this process can never stop while there is a remainder, and while a term can be found, the unity of which is not greater than that remainder, and as such a term must always be found in the last term or place of units, it follows that, if the process is not previously stopped by the completion of the work, and the entire expressing of the number proposed, such completion must take place when the only term, the unity of which is not greater than the remainder, is the place of unity itself. For the remainder, then, being less than ten, or, in the case of any other proportion, less than the unity of the last place but one, must be capable of being expressed in the last place; which last place, by the principle before described of the series, may contain any number that is not equal to the unit of the last but one.

Thus we are led, equally, to the same conclusion, viz. that in a series such as has been described, any proposed number whatever may be expressed.

Before we proceed to apply the consideration of this series to the explanation of the operations of arithmetic, it may be well to make one or two general remarks; the first of which may be that, the form of the lines being everywhere the same, that is to say, each term having exactly the same relation to the term preceding it, the relation will be the same between all terms. Taking two and two, which are equivalent, from each other; for each relation will consist of an equal repetition of the relation subsisting between contiguous terms, which we have just observed is everywhere the same. Whatever the relation is between one and ten, the same will be the relation between 1,000 and the term next above it; that is, between 1,000 and 10,000. And, therefore, whatever relation there is between one and the next term but one, that is, between one and 100, the same will be between 1,000 and 100,000.

The lowest term, therefore, of any two, in whatever part of the series taken, may always be considered as one; and is, in fact, one with respect to the terms above it. For one is anything that we choose to consider, without reference to any quantity less than it; and which is contained in it a certain number of times. Thus, with respect to

10,000 or 100,000, 1,000 is *one*. Though, with respect to a quantity contained in it a thousand times, it is a thousand. In considering, therefore, the terms of a series such as has been described, whenever I am looking only to the relations which any term chosen has to those above it, I may consider myself as at the beginning of the series, and proceed just as I should if the term chosen were actually the first. Thus, if the term which presents itself in the course of an operation be the fifth from the bottom, or that of which the units are each equal to 10,000, and that I am merely considering its relation to any term or terms above it; I have no occasion to consider it otherwise than as one, and may throw out of my mind its character of 10,000, which it possesses only with reference to the first of the series, or fifth term below it.

With these observations in mind, let us proceed now to the consideration of the several rules of arithmetic, describing the nature of each operation as it occurs.

The first and simplest is *Addition*; the object of which is, to express in a prescribed form of notation, viz. in that which we have been considering, the number which results from adding together any two or more proposed numbers, exhibited each in the same form of notation in which it is required that the whole should be expressed.

The first step for this purpose is to arrange the series in which these are severally expressed in such a manner as that like parts may be under like; that done, and beginning with the column containing the lowest places, you arrange in your mind the sum of the units there found, according to the proposed method of notation; setting down, as the result of your operations so far, whatever figure may be found in that sum in the place of units. The figure so set down, with the remainder of the sum, which you carry in your mind, makes the whole of the first column; and as the remainder, which you carry, contains no place of a lower denomination than tens (for whatever was found in the place of units has been set down), add this remainder to whatever is contained in the second column, which is, in fact, a column of tens, but which you have no occasion to consider in performing the operation otherwise than as a column of units; that is (agreeably to the observation made some time since), otherwise than with relation to the columns that follow it to the left hand, taking care only that the lowest figure (0, or otherwise) of the number so collected, shall be set down in the place which will give it its proper value, that is, in the second column. In this manner you will have got rid of the second as well as the first column; that is to say, the figures set down with the remainder, which you are to carry, will be the amount of these two columns, and, being added to the remaining columns, will give the amount of the whole.

The same process then recurs; you add the remainder, if there has been one, to the third column, and set down the amount, if it can be done, under the third column; otherwise, so much of it as can be set down, and add the remainder when you take the sum of the fourth column, If there is no remainder, you take the sum of the fourth column by itself, and set down the whole, or as much of it as can be; that is, the last figure of it, if it has more than one place, under the fourth; and so on, for as many columns as there are. Should the sum of the last column, with or without any remainder that may have been carried to it, amount to more than one place, the last place is that which will correspond in denomination to the last column; and the others must, accordingly, be placed below it.

In general, beginning with the lowest column, you take

the sum of each column, setting down, underneath, the figure of the sum that is in the place of units. The figure of the sum that remains, and comes next, if there is any other figure, is a unit of the next column, to which next column the whole remainder of this sum may be added, considering it as a number, the lowest term of which is of the same denomination with the second column; and the last figure of the sum resulting is, in like manner as before, to be set down under the third column. The process will be repeated for as many columns as there are; setting down, as before, the last figure of the sum formed from the last column under the last column, and any other figures of which that sum may consist, in their proper order. As an example take the one adjoining:—

```
  5 7 3
  2 5 0
  1 9 2
  2 9 3
  0 8 4
  0 9 0
  0 9 2
  1 8 0
  1 7 0
  2 6 1
  0 9 2
  1 9 0
  0 7 2
-------
2 5 3 9
-------
```

Here, the amount of the first, or lowest column, is 19, when thrown into the form of the established notation, of which I set down 9 in the place of units, and carry the remainder 10, which may be considered as one in the place of tens, to the next column, which, with the one so carried, produces 103, *i.e.* 103 tens. Setting down, then, the 3 in the place of tens, I carry the 10 to the column of hundreds; the amount of which is 15, which, added to (the hundred tens remaining of the 103 tens, or) the 10 hundreds remaining of the 10 hundreds and 3 tens, makes 25 hundreds (2,500), and, together with the number before set down, makes 2,539: the sum of all the columns, or of all the numbers, the sum of which was proposed to be taken.

Subtraction is the rule for expressing the difference between two numbers, or the number which arises by taking the less from the greater. Here, the same condition is to be observed of putting like parts under like, the number to be subtracted, and which is, of consequence, the least number, being put underneath.

In this state, were all the parts of the upper number to be subtracted, nothing would be necessary but to subtract these latter parts from those above them; and the sum of these remainders, each by the place it was put in having its proper value, would be the remainder of the whole taken from the whole.

The only difficulty arises from this, that while the number above is, upon the whole, greater than the number below, some of its parts may not be greater than the parts of the lower number corresponding to them. To understand the mode of proceeding in this case it must be recollected that one, in any place, is, by the very formation of the series, greater than the whole collection of units that can be disposed in all the places below it; consequently, that if one number is, upon the whole, greater than another, it must be greater in the highest place; moreover, that one, in any place, is equal to the whole of what can be contained in any number of places below it, viz. to the result of nine, put in each of those places, together with the unit of the last of those places.

Supposing, therefore, that in subtracting one number

from another, I find that the subtracted, though necessarily less upon the whole, is greater in that particular place which I am about to subtract, than the upper number, I borrow one from the next place above in the upper number, in which there is a significant figure, and conceive the one so borrowed to be distributed between the place of the upper number, from which the subtraction is to be made; and, in the intermediate places (if any there are) in such a manner as to allot nine to each of the intermediate places, and ten to the place in question, so as to dispose of the whole (agreeably to the second remark made not long since) of the one so borrowed. The ten so allotted to the place in question, together with the number previously belonging to it, if there was, in fact, any number, and the place was not occupied by an 0, must be greater than the number to be subtracted, which, from the nature of the series as before set forth, can never be greater than nine; but as that number was, by the supposition, greater than the number above it, in the place in question, when this greater number is subtracted from the other, augmented by ten, the remainder must be less than ten, and, of consequence, may be set down in its proper place; inasmuch as any number up to nine inclusive, *i.e.* any less than ten, may be so set down.

MISCELLANEOUS EXTRACTS.

One does not understand how anger should enter the mind, except through the medium of pain or opinion. A certain degree of anger, however irrational, may thus arise towards anything by which we are hurt: as a child will show a desire of beating an object against which it has struck its foot. But if no pain be felt nothing can be a just occasion of anger, but the conviction of certain qualities and dispositions existing in the object of our anger. No one, therefore, could naturally feel angry against things not affecting him with uneasiness, and of the nature of which he was entirely ignorant; yet instances of anger, so applied, every day occur; and, in fact, all that hostility by which classes of men are incited against each other is, in the greater part of those who feel it, of that sort. But the same is observed in men standing singly; and in these enmity is found to operate so capriciously that one would suppose that people had the power of creating to themselves objects of resentment out of anything they thought proper, without the least natural connection between the object and the passion. As some sounds are naturally significant of the things which they express, and others significant only by compact, so some things may be said to be naturally objects of resentment, and others to become so only by arbitrary association. When such an association is once established men will grow angry at the mention of particular subjects, as they would grow hungry at the sound of a dinner-bell. On some minds, even without such an association, particular subjects seem formed to produce such effects: as, on the minds of many Tories, the mention of Whiggism will operate like the sight of anything red upon a turkey-cock.

'God has made the intellectual world harmonious and beautiful without us; but it will never come into our heads all at once; we must bring it home piecemeal, and there set it up by our own industry, &c.'*

It seems as if great knowledge of the system of things

* Locke, 'Conduct of the Understanding.'

was never the effect of single views, or intuitive and simultaneous perception. The portion that can be seen at once is never sufficient to determine the general law. The laws of nature, therefore, seem to be known to our minds only as a curve is, by the assignment of its points; the assignment of which points, in nature, is a matter of painful investigation and subtle invention, of nice and difficult examination, and operose comparison of minute particulars.

Every important discovery of the nature of things has been the result of deduction following deductions, of which the several parts have been performed by minds not communicating with one another, and of which no one has seen more than the part immediately before him.

It appears sufficiently in the orations of Demosthenes to what a horrid pitch the practice was carried, among the Athenians, of applying torture, as a means of discovering truth. It seems to have been the ordinary process whenever a slave was to be examined, and to have been applied at the instance of either party. Of the dreadful cruelty and injustice of such a practice nothing need be said; the wonder is, how a practice should have become so general that seems founded in absolute absurdity. How is it that suffering is connected with speaking truth? Why must those declarations be true that are made in moments of extreme pain? Pain and truth of declaration have certainly no physical and necessary connection, so as to make it true of every being that, at a certain degree of pain, he must speak truth. The connection between pain and truth is established on no other principle than between pain and any other act in the power of the person suffering, namely, that which will subsist whenever the performance of the act can be made the condition on which the pain shall cease. If, therefore, torture is inflicted in order to extort confession of a truth, which would be known for such as soon as confessed: as if, for example, a man were required to discover where he had hidden his treasure, or such other fact as carried its own proof along with it, whatever other objections there might be to the use of such means, they would, at least, answer their purpose. The condition above stated may then be applied; because the sufferer, knowing that the truth, when declared, will produce a cessation of torment, will be urged by his sufferings to declare it. But why should a man under torture, either greater or less, be inclined to speak truth rather than falsehood, if he has no reason to suppose speaking truth to be a readier way of putting an end to his pain? The operation of the torture must be to make him speak, not that which is true, but that which he conceives most likely to be taken for truth; and, as in innumerable cases, those two may be very different, it will, of consequence, happen, in innumerable cases, that the application of torture will produce the very reverse of what is intended.

In reading anything mathematical, particularly any enunciation or definition, I think I have observed it to be the best way to examine completely every step as you advance, and not to endeavour at getting a general idea of the whole previous to the consideration of parts. There is danger in the last method of getting an erroneous idea which may mislead you throughout.

One is seldom aware of the number of arrangements that may be made upon a few words. Let the following sentence be taken as an example :—

'One must consider, therefore, the knowledge of this as most useful in all situations of life.'

The number of words here is sixteen; but considering those as one word only which must always be contiguous, and in the same order with respect to one another, the number will be reduced as follows:—'One must consider' =1—'therefore'=1—'the knowledge'=1, 'of this'=1, 'as most useful'=1, 'in all situations of life'=1, making in all six; upon which, therefore, the number of arrangements will be 720. For the facility of reckoning these, call them respectively by letters of the alphabet, and perhaps there is not one of the 720 but might be suffered without great violence to the construction.

It might be useful, as well as curious, to examine the extent of the benefit which may be derived from abbreviations of expression in matters of reasoning. The advantages of the language of infinitesimals in mathematics, and of technical expressions in all arts, are instances in point. Whoever attends to the work of ratiocination will perceive of what advantage it is to the mind to express its reasonings in least terms, and to review them in their most succinct form. A great part of the operation of reasoning is directed to no other purpose, and is no more than a skilful abridgment.

DIARY

OF THE

RIGHT HON. WILLIAM WINDHAM.

1784.

January 1*st.*—I had returned to town the night before from Norwich, where I had been from the 19th ult. in consequence of the expected dissolution of Parliament. The Ministry had received the King's message on the night preceding, that is to say, Thursday the 18th.

2*nd.*—Came down a little after eight. Resumed mathematics about ten. Fisher* called, and continued with me more than an hour.

12*th.*—Great day in the House of Commons, viz. the first day after the adjournment; I stayed till the first division, about half-past two, in which the Opposition divided, 232 against 193. House did not break up till past seven.†

19*th.*—Came home to dress a little after six. Went immediately after to see Dr. Johnson; sat about an hour and a half with him. Went after to the Club with Mr. Ryland.‡ Spent the remainder of the evening alone with

* John Fisher, Bishop of Salisbury, 1809; died 1825.

† It was the debate on Mr. Fox's motion for resuming the 'Committee on the State of the Nation,' immediately after the formation of Mr. Pitt's administration.

‡ John Ryland, Baptist minister, kept an academy, and officiated to a

him; learnt some anecdotes of Dr. Johnson's life. Walked home.

21*st.*—Spent some time at Robson's, who had put out a catalogue, and bought Doletus' 'Comment. Ling. Lat.' vel. 5*l.* 5*s.*; Themistius' 'Orations' by Petavius, and Theodor. in Libr. Laur. Valla. Did not get to the ice till past two. About eight I set out for Dr. Johnson's, who not being well enough to admit me, I called at the Pay Office. Soon after came home, having just time to write a letter to Norgate: the corporation of Norwich have been voting an address to the King for the appointment of the new Ministers and the freedom of the city to Mr. Pitt.

22*nd.*—Did not rise till an hour after I ought. Got to the ice between one and two; pleasant skating. Called on my way home on Lady Cornewall. Dined at Coleman's—company, Mr. Elliot, Dr. Wharton, and Thom: Dr. King, Sir Joshua. Went afterwards to the Club—Dr. Brocklesby, Mr. Cook, Mr. Allen, Daines Barrington. Went to Brookes's and supped—Fox, Fitzpatrick, Hare, Sheridan, and, late in the evening, G. Selwyn.

23*rd.*—Skated in the morning. Went afterwards to Legge's, and went afterwards to Brookes's, where I stayed till the House of Commons broke up between two and three in the morning. Called on Lord Palmerston relative to a borough mentioned to me the evening before by Fox. Was in great health and spirits all day.

25*th.*—Dined alone. Between eight and nine drove with Dr. Horsley* to see Johnson, on whom I had called the day before, but with no better success than now, he not being well enough either time to admit company. Went home with Horsley; sat with him till twelve.

27*th.*—Went out, a matter of necessity, that I might not be too late as usual, for some books that I had

congregation in Northampton: he was much esteemed by Dr. Johnson and other eminent men.

* Dr. Samuel Horsley was Bishop of St. David's in 1780.

marked in Payne and White's catalogue; did my business with the former; but falling in with Sir Gilbert Elliot, went with him to Fox's, and afterwards, by myself, to the Duke of Portland's.

29th.—Went in the evening to the pit with Mrs. Lukin. Mrs. Siddons, I think, in 'Mrs. Beverley.' The night of Lady Buckingham's rout, I had gone out, if I recollect right, early in the morning in order to see Miss Kemble, and had breakfast with Sir Joshua Reynolds.

31st.—Went with Horsley to the Club: this was the morning, I believe, of my going with Steevens to see Romney and Hamilton's picture of Mrs. Siddons. The same was the time of Horsley's finding out the notes in my Stanley's 'Æschylus,' while in Theobald's hand.

February 1st.—In the morning went to Mrs. Siddons to settle about play in the evening; the part, 'Isabella.' Mrs. and Miss Kemble and I went together. This was the day for moving the address in the House of Commons.

4th.—Steevens called just after breakfast; went with him to Sir Joshua and Burke's, to settle engagement. Went with D. Burke to Kensington Gardens to skate, and stayed there with unusual satisfaction till near three, when I was obliged to come away, having engaged to dine with Steevens at Wood's, to go afterwards to the pit. 'Measure for Measure.' After the play, went with Miss Kemble to Mrs. Siddons' dressing-room: met Sheridan there, with whom I sat in the waiting-room, and who pressed me to sup at his house with Fox and G. North.

5th.—Went to the Club: present, Horsley, Poore, Dr. Brocklesby, Cook, Mr. Allen. Went afterwards to Westminster meeting.

7th.—Did not rise till past nine; from that time till eleven, did little more than indulge in idle reveries about balloons. About twelve, went out; called on Mrs. Siddons, afterwards on Fox. Burke, Horsley, Sir Joshua Reynolds, to dine with me; they went, except Horsley, before nine;

and Mrs. Siddons and Miss Kemble came, &c. Have not seen Dr. Johnson since 19th ult., *i. e.* to the present day inclusive, nineteen days.

8th.—From the commencement of this account, January 1, to the present day, February 8, a space of five weeks and four days, it appears that, excepting one morning, viz. 2nd, and that for about an hour, not an attempt made to resume mathematics; no Latin written, little read; no Greek even looked into, no translation; no progress made in any author; nothing but a little odd information collected, of history, physiology, and biography.

Debated whether I should go out; at last resolved in the affirmative, intending to call at Lord Townshend's, and thence to proceed to Dr. Johnson. The determination against my present liking, particularly in the first article; let this instance show the advantage of acting now and then against the present impression. I called on Lord T.; let in; stayed there till eleven o'clock, much pleased at what I had done, and enjoying myself more than I had done for a long while. In the latter part of the evening the Spanish Ambassador, Signor del Campo, came in, and, with his secretary accompanying him with his voice and guitar, sang several Spanish airs. At eleven o'clock I went away with Jack Lee,* and called at Sheridan's, where there had been a meeting about some Westminster business.

9th.—My old practice, a practice at least established since the year 1779, of rising as soon as I waked, I have only discontinued since my leaving Tunbridge in November last; nor had I for many months before that maintained it regularly. I have tried it this morning for the first time for more than these two months, and the effect I find in exciting a disposition to employment, as well as furnishing the time and conferring the capacity, is quite equal to what I have been accustomed to lay it at.

* Jack Lee, Solicitor-General in 1782; Attorney-General in 1783. He was noted for his jokes and his honesty.

10*th*.—Went about half-past five to the pit; sat by Miss Kemble, Steevens, Mrs. Burke, and Miss Palmer.*

11*th*.—Don't recollect what I did to-day.

12*th*.—Went out pretty soon; called on Mrs. Siddons; sat there a good while: pleasant. Steevens came in; went with him, and had a good deal of discourse about the picture. Afterwards to the ice.

13*th*.—Went out soon; called on Lady T. and Mrs. Beresford about box; proceeded to Drury Lane; thence to Dr. Fordyce to consult about balloon. Just able to dress and dine for the play—part, 'Mrs. Beverley;' stayed the farce also. Finished Baker's 'Reflections on Learning;' it should rather be called, I think, Baker's *Reflection*, for it seems to me to contain but one, and that a very poor one.

14*th*.—Day of Westminster meeting in the Hall; business not over till two. Stayed in very earnest conversation with Mrs. Byng† till half-past five.

15*th*.—Employed (with a slight interruption) in reading the first vol. of Petavius,‡ with such other matter as grew out of that; not dissatisfied with my morning.

Began this morning some historical collections not intended to be preserved in the present copy, but to serve as an experiment of a work of that sort that may hereafter be made more complete.

16*th*.—Vandeput § called. Argument with George ‖ about the propriety of the law which discharges a bankrupt from his debt on the condition of his surrendering his all.

* Niece to Sir Joshua Reynolds. Married to Lord Inchiquin.

† Daughter of Commodore Forest. Sister to Cecilia, afterwards Mrs. Windham. Married to the Hon. John Byng.

‡ Rationarium Temporum.

§ Sir George Vandeput, who stood for Westminster, 1751.

‖ George Lukin, his half-brother on the mother's side, afterwards Dean of Wells. He married Miss Katharine Doughty, of Hanworth, who is frequently referred to in this Diary, as Mrs. Lukin.

During the hour or two that I was in my own room while they were in Duke Street, went on with the sacred history, and read the twenty-second chapter of Numbers in the Greek containing the story of Balaam. Afterwards sat down to the continuation of the account in 'Adversaria:' 'Mirari, aliquando, subiit,' &c.; but could not satisfy myself about a sentence I was attempting; at last went off into a reverie about an air balloon.

17*th*.—Did not get up till ten minutes past ten. The first effect of what is here stated is, that I have two hours less in the day, at least that my day begins two hours later. Are there not also other losses? Are not the two hours which I should so gain, better than any other? Would not every other hour be improved by additional health and spirits? And might not the advantage gained in the application of my time be more than in proportion to the time added? There is great reason to think that all this difference would be found, and if so, the conduct is very unwise that sacrifices the hopes of such advantages, either from the pleasure of continuing an hour or two in bed between sleeping and waking, or from the uneasiness of shaking off sleep before it has left me of its own accord. I will continue this conduct no longer, but to-morrow morning revert to the practice of rising as soon as I wake. Dined at the Club; conversations about balloons, at which Sir Joseph Banks chose to take offence, and exposed himself most completely. Went with Burke for a short time to Brookes's.

18*th*.—Did not go out till I went with Mrs. Lukin to the play, Mrs. S. in 'Belvidera;' met Steevens there by appointment. Mrs. S.'s performance very happy, and the whole pleasant.

19*th*.—Day remarkably fine. Went out early with intention of skating, but, after calling in Leicester Fields for the purpose of proposing to Mrs. Siddons to go, and passing a quarter of an hour with Sir Joshua, proceeded to

Grosvenor Square. A little before nine went to Sheridan's, where stayed till near three. The first meeting of the Club: present in the course of the evening, Lord Fitzwilliam, Lord Fred. Cavendish, Lord Robert Spencer, Fitzpatrick, G. North, Tickell, Richardson, Adam, and General Burgoyne; the six last only stayed.

20th.—Called on the Duke of Portland; dined at home between five and six. Evening spent by myself; have gone on with Petavius; continued, though slowly, an article in the 'Adversaria;' time employed in it about two hours; not in bed till near two.

21st.—Rose not till half-past nine. Steevens below, who continued with me about an hour. Wrote to Sheridan, as per list, urging him to apply in time to Coleman about Miss Kemble. After reading for a little while in Petavius, took up continuation of article in 'Adversaria,' and continued it with little intermission till four. The time employed in continuation of article in 'Adversaria' has been about two hours.

It appears by a list that I have not wrote a letter since the beginning of this month, at least, that is to say, three weeks; there are three or four that have been upon my mind for at least that time, and by the neglect of which great inconvenience may be sustained.

The continuation of the article in the 'Adversaria' happened on the 16th. This might furnish an article against the use of Latin, it being certain that this would have been despatched in much less time in English, probably in a few hours, and that my return to mathematics has been delayed on this account.

29th.—About six in the evening left London in company with George and Mrs. Lukin. Experienced the feeling not unusual to me upon those occasions of indecision and want of preparation. Walked down, before I went, towards St. James's, in order to learn the particulars of the disturbance that had happened the night before between the chairmen at Brookes's and Pitt's mob. Dined in my way back with Tickell: during dinner a strong paroxysm of mental malady.

March 1*st.*—On the journey we slept the first night at Hockrill, the second at Thetford, not arriving at Norwich till the third day; when George and Mrs. Lukin proceeded to Felbrigg, and I prepared for the celebrated meeting at the Swan.

25*th.*—Went over to Norwich; met the account of the dissolution of Parliament.

April 5*th.*—Day of the election.

14*th.*—Day of the county election.

20*th.*—Came to Felbrigg. In the morning had breakfast with Dr. Parr, who lent me, to take in the chaise, a treatise of Andronicus Rhodius, **Περὶ Παθῶν**, as also one of Pletho.*

29*th.*—Set off for town in order to vote for Fox. Slept at Barton Mills, having left Hanworth, whither I had gone the preceding night between twelve and one. During my stay, I have spent my time more satisfactorily I think, upon the whole, than for the same time at any former period, the causes of which are to be sought for in the exertions of the month that has preceded. I have made some progress and laboured not unprofitably in the 'Arith. Univ.,' and have missed, or seemed to miss, no opportunity of going on with Thu[s]. [Thuanus], yet I cannot find that I have sat down to it more than once.

Of books taken up at odd times I have read some sermons and other treatises, lent to me by Dr. Parr. Among the rest Cibber's letter to Pope, and 'Remember Sawney's Fate.' I am going on with the historical volume of Petavius; when I was here last I read through Phædrus.

May 2*nd.*—Left town with Lord Derby, who was going

* George Gemistus, surnamed Pletho, Platonist phil. A.D. 1400.

to Newmarket. Arrived there about five, and passed the evening by myself.

3rd.—After seeing a greater part of the sport, went on my way to Norwich and arrived at Cossey* about eleven o'clock. The Prince and the Duke de Chartres were at Newmarket. I dined at Barton Mills, and was in the next room to Lord Orford.

4th.—On my way to London, viz. when I went up to the Westminster election, read Petavius, very diligently. On my return, after quitting Lord Derby, had no book, and thought chiefly what I was to do at the Swan.

Left Felbrigg, with little prospect of returning for a long while. Got to Norwich before nine o'clock; sat some time with Dr. Parr. Arrived in London, having come by the diligence in time to be at Covent Garden before the poll of that day was over.

14th.—Saw a tight battle at the corner of Russell Street.

15th.—Rose early in order to attend the office in Lichfield Street, on the part of Pat Carney, taken up on the charge of being concerned in the riot when the constable was killed. Breakfasted with Baker; went thence to Colonel North. Dined at three with Dr. Brocklesby; present, Dr. Johnson, Colonel Vallancey, William Smith (Member for Sudbury), Deveynes (the apothecary), Boswell, Murphy, and somebody else. After dinner, took Johnson an airing over Blackfriars Bridge, thence to the Club; present, Boswell, Murphy, Brocklesby, Berry, Mr. Bowles, Hoole and his son, and a son of Dr. Burney; he that was expelled Cambridge.

May 18th.—Parliament met.

June 23rd.—Play at Aylsham, bespoke in my name. Slept at Hanworth.

24th.—Arrived at Felbrigg. On my way down I read

* Cossey Hall, Norfolk, seat of the Jerningham family.

* Cossey Hall, Norfolk, seat of the [illegible]

very diligently (except when I slept) in the article 'Cebes' Table,' which I had not read since my being at Glasgow; a volume of the 'Monthly Review;' Petav. Rat.; and a good deal of Rousseau's 'Confessions.'

27*th*.—Rose about eight. Walked before breakfast near the house, taking with me Horace, and reading and repeating an ode, 'Mercuri nam te.' Returned about one from church, from three to four going on with memorandums, and working a logarithm or two.

July 3*rd*.—Doughtys* supped with me, the whole party having taken before a pleasant ride by the Beacon, and through Aylmerton Field. The country beautiful, the appearance of the company gay.

4*th*.—Left Felbrigg. All the way in the chaise I read very earnestly Petav. Rat. vol. i. Dined at Fakenham, drank tea at Swaffham, and slept at Brandon, where I did not arrive till past eleven. The last stage very pleasant; the moon shone, the country looked wild, and the slow progress of the chaise gave me an opportunity often to walk.

My stay at Felbrigg was very satisfactory; I made considerable progress in mathematics, and felt that if I could have stayed, I should have made more. At the first, from an opinion of my strength, I indulged myself more than was prudent in the thoughts of the place, and quickly found reason to repent of the indulgence. Let this be a caution against next time. Suppose I come now to the

* The Doughtys of Hanworth were unquestionably one of the oldest families of country gentlemen in England at the time of the Conquest. They were owners of the manor and demesne of Hanworth, and continued in unbroken succession till the year 1819. The records of this family, which in consequence of their connexion with the Royal Manor were very perfect, were formerly kept in the great chest in the church of Hanworth; but in the sixteenth century they were taken away by the Earl of Northampton, and have never since been found.

The old mansion was burnt down in the reign of Henry VIII. The present house was built in the end of the seventeenth century. They intermarried with the *Bullein*, or Boleyn.

resolution, that, for the first week after my next return to Felbrigg, the thoughts of the place, while I remain within the house, shall not, if possible, be admitted into my mind.

5*th*.—When I came, the House of Commons was just up. But the Hatters' business, which I came to attend, viz. an application from them to prohibit the exportation of rabbits' wool, had been compromised.

July 12*th*.—Having been ill in the night from some accident that caused a sickness in my stomach, did not get up till past ten. After breakfast, Mr. Steevens came; sat with me till half-past one. I believe, my mind clear, and his visit pleasant. After he went, a long conversation with the man upon the Hat tax, in which I experienced the same clearness of faculties noted above. At nine, went to Coleman's to be present at Miss Kemble's first appearance in the 'Guardian;' after the play went to Bolt Court to leave my compliments with Johnson, and wish him a good journey. I am sorry to find that he continues far from well.

16*th*.—Read Pitt's India Bill. Royds called. *Feel very strong and distressing*. Great feeling of weakness while I was reading the Bill; also during my conversation with Royds. Went down to the House; third reading of the India Bill. Went out during the debate, and rode a good deal. Wrote articles 14th, 15th, and 16th.

17*th*.—Called in at Beckett's to settle a party going to Putney, where Mr. Canning* was to give the Club supper. Agreed with Richardson and Sir James Erskine to meet in the Park at half-past eight, and to go by water. After some debate took a boat, though the tide was against us; near half-past nine when we set off, half-past eleven when we arrived; passage not unpleasant. Found at Canning's only Sheridan and Mrs. Sheridan.

* Father of the present Viscount Stratford de Redcliffe.

Carried in Sheridan's coach into Fulham town, thence I walked to Legge's, and was in bed about four.

18*th.*—Have foolishly suffered the morning to pass, with little or nothing done, though I had brought down materials for employment in 'Adversaria' and 'Arith. Univ.'

19*th.*—Note to Miss Kemble; read article in 'Lex. Mercatoria.' The fortnight that has elapsed since my return to town, 'July 5th,' is certainly a proof that the progress made in study of any kind is much slower here than in the country. During the latter part of my stay in Felbrigg, more was done every day in mathematics than in the whole time since I left it; in fact, excepting a few hours one evening, that, namely, in which I supped afterwards with Shore at the Thatched House, I don't know that anything has been done. In the same period spent at Felbrigg, considering the rate at which I was going on, there can be no doubt that the advancement would have been very considerable; yet I cannot charge myself with mismanagement or neglect, with having missed many opportunities of being at home, or misapplying those which I had.

20*th.*—The greater part of the time, till now, one o'clock, spent in foolish reveries about balloons. Went early to the House of Commons, to attend a business of Lord Milton's.

21*st.*—Rose a little before eight with the intention of going out before breakfast and doing my business at the Custom House. Bad morning. Stayed at home with very little interruption till four. Employed almost the whole time in mathematics; application pretty close but not very satisfactory.

22*nd.*—Too late for going, as I intended, to the Custom House. Thought I felt a want of air and motion, and walked out first to Sir Sidney Meade, where I found only a servant of the Sardinian Ambassador exercising a horse. Thence to Fozard.

23rd.—Called at Lord Northington's; walked with Courtenay, afterwards, without going home, to the House of Commons, and about seven came out, and taking a boat, rowed about for nearly an hour. Went to Mulgrave's: present, Lord Longford, Charles and Augustus Phipps; walked home part of the way with Lord Longford.

24th.—Kent called while I was at breakfast; immediately afterwards set out for the Custom House; took boat at Whitehall; walked home from the Custom House, endeavouring all the way to fix my thoughts on something, and utterly unable to accomplish my purpose.

25th.—In the morning began by putting up and taking account of my books that I had got from the Custom House; sat down by way of repose to open the leaves, and read a little in a new publication, pretending to be the 'Memoirs of Voltaire.' After that lounged a little over Barry's pamphlet that he has just sent me. I had but little time then to take mathematics before dinner came. After dinner finished Dodington.* On this occasion one or two remarks are to be made; the day being observable for being passed wholly in the house, is an argument that such instances are not frequent. Being passed in the manner above described, yet not very ill passed, it shows how very unprofitably one's time is in general disposed of.

27th.—Dined with Lord Palmerston:† present, Lord Northington, Sheridan, Sir Ralph and Lady Payne, and Lord North.

28th.—Was to have dined with Lord North; went to the House of Commons; did not come home till half-past twelve. Burke spoke much about India matters;‡ it was

* Dodington's Diary.

† Henry Temple, second Viscount Palmerston, born 1739, died 1802.

‡ The debate on the third reading of Mr. Pitt's India Bill. Mr. Burke rose at 11 P.M., and spoke with great vehemence against the Bill. In this

upon this occasion that he made the happy comparison between the delinquents in India and the malefactors in Newgate; a good deal of *feel*, if I recollect.

August 1*st.*—Went to Tickell's at Hampton to dinner, drove down in my phaeton; pleasant day with him and his wife; particularly enjoyed the situation. Returned in the evening to Legge's, at Fulham, calling in the way at Mr. Canning's, where was Sheridan.

2*nd.*—Instead of attending the House, went to see the wager rowed on the Thames. After passing some time at home, in preparation for my journey, resolved to defer it a day longer.

6*th.*—At Cossey, and engaged in Norwich; dined very pleasantly at the Bishop's.* Sir William Jerningham, Sir Thomas and Lady Beauchamp, Lady Loughborough, present. After dinner Nichols took me, with Mr. Gooch the chaplain, into his room, which was calculated to inspire the most delightful ideas of monastic life.

9*th.*—Upon getting to Hanworth, found Mr. Bulwer's family there, and dinner over. Nearly bedtime before I got home.

11*th.*—At home all the morning till I went to Hanworth to dinner. In great spirits before I set out, in consequence of being satisfied with my morning's work; but before I got to Hanworth found myself sick, and, before dinner was over, was obliged to go out.

14*th.*—Rode out early, taking a round through Aylmerton Field. Employed in the translation of a Greek epigram; remained at home till about seven.

16*th.*—Rode before breakfast with Mrs. Lukin. After Doughtys went away, George and I played three games

speech he broke out into the famous apostrophe, beginning with 'Forgive me, O Newgate! if I have thus dishonoured your inhabitants by an odious comparison.'—The Bill was read a third time, and passed.

* Lewis Bagot, Bishop of Norwich, 1783 to 1789.

of draughts, out of which he beat me two; after which I read till bedtime Cardinal Bentivoglio's 'Memoirs.'

18*th.*—Much debate, both this morning and over night, about the method to be pursued relative to my leaving the country. Soon after I got up, Kent came, which was a new circumstance to complicate the deliberation. I accordingly set out on horseback, leaving my horse afterwards at Aylsham, and proceeded from thence in a chaise; in my way met Lady Buckingham, with whom I had a good deal of conversation. Got to Norwich about dinner, and called upon the Bishop, who would not ask me to dinner; dined at Taylor's;* drank tea, and passed two hours with Parr. Taking my horse again at Aylsham, arrived at Hanworth by supper, and got home by eleven.

Sufficiently satisfied with the employment of my time during my stay at Felbrigg. I had brought with me from Ipswich a problem taken from the 'Ladies' Magazine,' which I had met with there; this I set myself to solve, and completed during my stay (*vide* 'Adversaria'). Now for the material fact, that this is perhaps the only Latin verse I made or attempted to make, since the verses wrote the first year after my leaving Eton (that is to say, seventeen years ago), sent to George from Scotland. After such an instance of neglected talent, can I wonder at any deficiency of power or acquirements, or can I be surprised, as I have sometimes been inclined to suppose, I should be incapable of doing what it now appears I have not attempted for seventeen years. The fact, however, was this — I did not find myself at all incapable, but executed what I undertook with a degree of facility that I had no right to expect; let this be a reason to inquire at least whether I shall not find that half the things of which I supposed myself incapable, I have never attempted.

* A zealous Whig, and a cordial supporter of Mr. Windham.

Other employment during my stay at Felbrigg was, I think, going on with Petav. vol. i. Much satisfaction in reading Cardinal Bentivoglio's 'Memoirs;' Lucan also gone on with.

Part of the time applied to the solution of the problem was rather unprofitably spent; and, in general, I am of opinion that the endeavour to make out solutions, unless very vigorously pursued, is the least advantageous part of mathematical study; without great care, it quickly degenerates into musing. My object is to preserve in my mind, as much as possible, a continued series of connected thoughts, which cannot easily be done where the next idea proper to follow, or the idea sought, cannot from the nature of endeavour always be found. The mind is then very apt either to pause in perfect suspense or to fly off to extraneous matter.

19*th.*—Left Felbrigg; went in the phaeton; from thence to Holkham, with Doughty in his carriage.

20*th.*—In the morning we all rode about on horseback; the place finer than I expected; nothing more just, in my opinion, than Coke's ideas of laying it out. Coke accompanied me after dinner in his chaise to Lynn.

21*st.*—Walked about the town all the morning with Rishton; first time of my ever having been there; much disappointed at the want of all those appearances which usually characterise a trading town.

22*nd.*—Left Wisbeach immediately after breakfast; arrived at Peterborough in time to see the cathedral before dinner.

23*rd.*—Rose early, and debated long whether I should breakfast before or after seeing Burleigh; my determination right at last, that I would breakfast first. Spent full two hours there very satisfactorily. Late before I got to Leicester; overturned by the way.

30*th.*—Arrived, after seeing Lord Vernon's house by the way, in good time at Ashbourne.

Johnsonian Memorandum of Conversation.

The credit due to the first translators of Greek authors.

The principal of all amusements is to beguile time, and fill the interval between active thought and perfect vacuity.

Grævius and Benedictus give the palm to Sir Thomas More,* among all the translators of Lucian.

The three whom Scaliger declares himself to envy, Politian, Picus Mirandula, &c.

The source of everything in or out of nature that can serve the purpose of poetry to be found in Homer; every species of distress, every modification of heroic character, battles, storms, ghosts, incantations, &c. Dr. J. said he had never read through the 'Odyssey' completely in the original.

Anecdote of his first declamation at college; that having neglected to write it till the morning of his being to repeat it, and having only one copy, he got part of it by heart while he was walking into the hall, and the rest he supplied as well as he could extempore.

Description of himself as very idle, and neglectful of his studies.

His opinion, that I could not name above five of my college acquaintances who read Latin with sufficient ease to make it pleasurable; the difficulty of the language overpowers the desire to read the author; that he read Latin with as much ease when he went to college as at present. Attention to the language overpowers the regard to the matter; rather not know the contents than dig them out of Latin.

That a year or two elapsed between his quitting school and going to college.

* Sir T. More appears to have appended some translations from Lucian to his 'Utopia.' Ed. Basil, 1563, 8vo.; Oxon. 1663, 8vo.

His opinion of that fact of Sir Thomas Hearne, that he had never been in London.

Recommended the reading the 'Fasti' of Ovid; also, Watton and Wood on Homer.

Commended Ovid's description of the death of Hercules. Doubted whether Virgil would not have loaded the description with too many fine words, that Virgil would sometimes 'dare verba.'

Opinion that there were three ways in which writings may be unnatural: by being bombastic and above nature, affected and beside it, fringing every event with ornaments which nature did not afford, or weak and below nature; that neither of the first would please long; that the third might indeed please a good while, or at least many, because imbecility, and consequently a love of imbecility, might be found in many.

Barretti had told him of some Italian author who said, that a good work must be that with which the vulgar were pleased, and of which the learned could tell why it pleased; that it must be able to employ the learned and detain the idle.

'Chevy Chase' pleased the vulgar, but did not satisfy the learned; it did not fill a mind capable of thinking strongly.

The merit of Shakespeare was such as the ignorant could take in, and the learned add nothing to it.

'Stat magni nominis umbra,' would construe as 'Umbra quæ est magni nom. h. e. celebrata.'

Τερπόμενος τε νόον ὁ πλείονα εἰδώς—the offer of the Syren to Ulysses. Any man will preserve his respect who can promise this to another; applied to a college tutor.

Opinion of Rowe's translation of Lucan, that it would have been improved if Rowe had had a couple of years to render it less paraphrastical.

Quintilian says of Lucan that he is—

'Declamatoribus potius quam poetis annumerandus.'

'Απέλαυον μὲν ὡς οἰκείων, ἠμέλουν δ' ὡς ἀλλοτρίων.

Approved turn-out of Isocrates,* of whom he was disposed to speak favourably.

Vast change of the Latin language from the time of Lucretius to Virgil; greater than known in any other even the French.

Suspicion that the old grammarians have given us, from an analogy, more modifications of tenses than were ever used. Remember but one instance of second future, viz. εὑρῶ in Josephus; and three of the optative, if I recollect; of the preterite and middle, one of them in Hesiod.

The first female warrior, the Camilla of Virgil, the story of Dido in Ovid's 'Fasti,' also Mezentius; Virgil's invention, therefore, less than supposed. Take from him what is in Homer, what do you leave him?

Conjecture of the passage in Lucan, 'Quis justior induis se,' that it should be read with an interrogation to avoid the indicative after 'quid.' In like manner the conjunctive, a very slippery mood, use doubtful—after 'seu' and 'sive,' 'Seu per incertos' and 'sive tu mavis—sive sub incertas zephyris motantibus,' &c.

Great advantage of a University, that a person lives in a place where his reputation depends on his learning. Argument about that feel, that persons on great heights suppose themselves to have, of a wish to throw themselves down.

Boëthius was translated by Alfred, two of whose translations are extant and in print, by Thom. Aquinas, and by Chaucer. Chaucer translates the poetical parts into prose. Boëthius the classic of the barbarous ages.

The idea of *Delitescence*, one of those that please the mind in a hilly country. *Torpescence*, much of the faculties of mankind lost in them.

* Isocr. Panegyr., p. 56 A. ed. H. Stephens

'*Qui stupet in statuis*,' applied to Jos. Warton's admiration of fine passages; his taste is amusement.

The pretensions of the English to the reputation of writing Latin, founded not so much on the specimens in that way which they have produced, as on the quality of talent diffused through the country.

Erasmus appears to be totally ignorant of science and natural knowledge.

But one Italian writer is mentioned in Erasmus.*

Opinion about the effect of turnpike roads.—Every place communicating with every other. Before these were cheap places, and dear places. Now all refuges destroyed for elegant or genteel poverty. Want of such a last hope to support men in their struggle through life, however seldom it might be resorted to. Disunion of families by furnishing a market to each man's abilities, and destroying the dependence of one man on another.

September 1st.—Left Ashbourne at half-past one, having gone with Dr. Johnson in the morning to prayers, but regretted upon reflection that I had not stayed another day. At Sudbury I suffered myself after dinner to go to sleep, I was then too late for Lichfield; so that the question lay chiefly between staying there for the night and going to Walton. On this I did not decide, till the sight of a guide to take me across the forest, but before I had gone far the difficulties of the way and the uncertainty of his information made me again hesitate, till at last, after a long delay and walking about the end of the forest, I decided upon returning to Yoxall.

3*rd*.—Rose at six; morning delicious, and country not unpleasant.

Arrived at Birmingham, walked about the town, wrote great part of a long letter to Mrs. Siddons, went to the

* Probably Laurentius Valla, whose work on Latin grammar was 'honoured with a paraphrase by Erasmus,' says Hallam, *Literature of Europe*, part I. ch. iii.: whence Johnson conjectures that he did not understand Italian.

play, 'Much Ado About Nothing;' 'Benedick' by Yates. Amazingly satisfied with my day.

4th.—Had some conversation, before I set out, with Lord and Lady Lucan, who had slept in the same inn, on their way from Ireland. After dinner, pleasant drive to Chapel House, reminding me much of my drive through the same country in the year '79.

5th.—Breakfasted at Woodstock, stayed till King* came home and settled to go with him next day to Burke's. Got to Oxford in time to have some dinner prepared for me in college. After writing a letter to Miss Loveday, went to All Souls', where were the Warden, Finch, Vansittart, Sir Joseph Banks, Jenkinson and Topham. Drank tea with the Warden. Went with Finch to Horsman's in search of Price.

7th.—Rode in the morning to Clifden. Should have enjoyed the scene, but for the heat. Lord Inchiquin returned with us to dinner.

9th.—Translation of Thuanus. The design of this was first conceived, if I do not mistake, in the early part of the year 1783, when I was at Felbrigg; but, after about ten days, no more was completed than the first paragraph, with which at last I was so little satisfied as afterwards to cancel it. Still, however, I found even by that imperfect trial, that it would answer very well to my expectations. The work was then not resumed till my being at this place, Oxford, after my leaving Ireland,† at which time I brought down the book from London, bespoke a quantity of paper of a particular size, and planned a course of proceeding for the execution of it.

During the time of my being last at Felbrigg, as at every other time and place where I have had a prospect

* King (Richard), M.A., Oxon, 1774, polemical divine, author of *Abraham Plymley's Letters.*

† Mr. Windham resigned the office of Chief Secretary for Ireland in August, 1783.

of leisure, I have purposed to go on with this undertaking, but have as uniformly suffered it to be deferred from day to day, till the opportunity was past. If the work ever is to be executed, it must be now. The period is arrived of all others the most calculated and destined in my mind for the purpose, nor is there a single circumstance attending it that can furnish me with a pretence for dispensing with my resolution.

10*th*, 11*th*, 12*th*.—At Oxford, usefully and diligently employed: on the last of the above days, being Sunday, dined at Nuneham: present, Mr. Whitehead, Mrs. Macartnay, Lady Mary Fordyce.

13*th*.—Left Oxford about twelve for London. Day excessively hot; notwithstanding which, kept myself well employed, so as to complete the demonstration which I had left off over night of the 6th Proposition of the 'Arithmetica.'

Got out of the phaeton at the top of the hill near Burke's and walked down, and found them all going to London the next day on the same errand as myself, viz. to see Lunardi ascend. Very pleasant during the evening.

14*th*.—Went up in Burke's carriage. Much talk. Dined at his house, and sat till I went to Dr. Fordyce. London appeared as if I had been long absent, though the time was only from August 4th, viz. six weeks.

15*th*.—Lunardi ascended. Dined at Sir Joshua Reynolds's, with Burke, Lord Inchiquin, Dr. Burney, &c.

16*th*.—Dined unexpectedly at Burke's. Uncomfortable rather from want of decision of arrangement. Had long conversation with Fox in the street.

17*th*.—Breakfasted at Burke's. Met a curious man, a Mr. Foster, who had come through the back part of Persia. In great spirits and power all the morning. Employed myself in looking into Calmet's 'History of the Bible,' and getting some lines out of Oppian cited in

Stackhouse's work, which apply very well on the present subject of balloons.*

18*th*.—Walked to Canning's in hopes of meeting Sheridan. From the uncertainty of their coming, viz. he and Tickell, took a boat and proceeded to town.

In the 'Life of Æsop' by Planudes, mentioned in some of the preceding articles, and read during my tour, the number of words of which the meaning was unknown to me was forty-two.

20*th*.—Came to town in the morning, I think, by water; with the waterman, whose phraseology I noticed as a specimen of natural eloquence.

21*st*.—Resumed doctrine of chances after an interval of two years. It was about two months before that period that, being at Carshalton, I had occasion to reflect on the great benefit and pleasure I had derived from that enquiry, and to form new resolutions for the diligent prosecution of it. On my leaving Oxford at the end of October, '82, I quitted the pursuit, just at the moment when I had the greatest encouragement to persist in it.

23*rd*.—*Fulham*.—Driven by shower into grocer's shop, and amused by the wit of gardeners. Set off on foot to town, but taken up by Lord Spencer. Called on Mrs. Siddons, her mother, and Miss E. Kemble there.

27*th*.—Rose early and walked to town with Horsley. Usual effect of a walk before breakfast, viz. great alertness

* οὐ γάρ τι πέλει καθυπέρτερον ἀνδρῶν
νόσφι θεῶν· μούνοισι δ' ὑπείξομεν ἀθανάτοισι.
ὅσσους μὲν κατ' ὄρεσφι βίην ἄτρεστον ἔχοντας
θῆρας ὑπερφιάλους βρότος ἔσβεσεν, ὅσσα δὲ φῦλα
οἰωνῶν νεφέλῃσι καὶ ἠέρι δινεύοντα
εἷλε χαμαίζηλόν περ ἔχων δέμας· οὐδ' ἐσάωσεν
αἰετὸν ἠνεμόεις πτερύγων ῥό·ος, οὐδὲ λέοντα
ῥύσατ' ἀγηνορίῃ δμηθήμεναι· ἀλλὰ καὶ Ἰνδὸν
θῆρα κελαινόῤῥινον, ὑπέρβιον ἄχθος, ἀναγκῃ
κλῖναν ὑπερβρίσαντες, ὑπὸ ζεύγλῃσι δ' ἔθηκαν
οὐρήων ταλαεργον ἔχειν πόνον ἑλκυστῆρα.

OPPIAN, *Halieutica*, v. 10–20.

of spirits. The balloon being again deferred, called on his brother. Afterwards to see Blanchard's balloon. Met Burke and D. Burke; walked with them to Pantheon to see Lunardi's.

Employed in transcribing notes from 'Loci Plani.'

29th.—About nine came to Brookes's, where I heard that the balloon had been burnt about four o'clock. Stayed talking on public matters with the Duke of Portland till eleven. Home, settling argument on the principle of chances.

October 2nd.—Rowed up the river as far as the lock, the longest row I ever took. Reflection on the folly of supposing oneself incapable of that which one has never properly attempted.

Mr. Windham to Mrs. Siddons.

Oxford: October 10, 1784.

I sincerely congratulate you on the victory obtained over malice and brutality the first night of your appearance. From Mr. Lawrence, a friend of Sheridan's, who was present upon the occasion, and who is just come down here, I have received the whole account. Nothing has pleased me more than the style of your address, which completely removed any regret for the necessity of delivering it. It spoke the only language proper for the occasion—the language of innocence, disclaiming favour, and calling only for justice against calumny and outrage. I regret that I was not in the house at the time. You will now resolve, I hope, that the matter shall end, and that nothing shall provoke you to further explanation.

Yours most, &c.,
W. W.

Oxford, October 16th.—For the first time almost since my being interrupted by my mother fourteen months ago, tried an instance of multiplication in my head: the problem required a sum of 4 places into 1 of 3. I executed it without mistake in little less than ten minutes, In comparing this with former attempts of the same kind,

I think I should say that I was improved in continuity of attention, as the time of performance rather shows; but not in strength of conception or retention. The numbers, if I recollect, were 8,352 into 437; the product 3,649,824.*

18*th*.—At Burke's read in Keil the explication of those phenomena which give to the two tropics the names of Cancer and Capricorn: ignorant as a person was likely to appear from a want of this knowledge, and easy as it was to acquire it, I had been content to remain without it till that day. The fact gave occasion for me to reflect on the folly of that practice which refused information on every subject till I could sit down to study it professedly. Most of the knowledge necessary to save a man from the appearance of gross ignorance may be collected without hindrance to any other pursuit, and almost without effort, by the mere use of those opportunities which chance is every day throwing in his way. In fact, that knowledge which it is disgraceful not to have, must from the very condition of it be easily got. How foolish, then, to neglect, much more to decline, such knowledge! yet such has been my practice all my life. In fact, I seem to have treated knowledge like commodities subjected to a duty, which can only be permitted to land at certain places regularly appointed. Thus my information goes no further than my studies, and all that knowledge which is floating in the world, and which to a mind properly prepared affords its chief nourishment, has been wholly lost to me; kept off by negligence on the one hand, and a perverse fancy on the other; and leaving me, like some exotic in a green-house, to the precarious and imperfect supply of art.

27*th*.—In the evening, Fisher being expected, removed into the rooms which I had inhabited during my residence in the university, and to which I now return after an interval *of thirteen years*. Oh! that the intermediate

* **Correctly done by me in six minutes, 11th Oct. 1825; not having looked at the product.—T. Amyot.**

time had been employed in the way in which it now appears to me that the perseverance of a month would always have enabled me to employ it. There is not a period of my past life that would not have been improved beyond all proportion by the very means that were necessary to secure happiness in future. How strange, then, the infatuation that could neglect such means! Other men, if they have been idle, have been happy; others, if they have sacrificed the hopes of future good, have sacrificed them to present enjoyment. To what have I sacrificed them?

29th.—Breakfasted with Chief Baron Yelverton; employed all the morning in going over the University with him. Sat with Burgess,* Crofts, and Schomberg till half-past twelve.

November 5th.—I refused to-day an invitation to dinner at the Warden of All Souls', where I should have met a pleasant party, on the principle of not sparing time. My resolution over night was to devote this morning to the removal of that load of neglect which has been upon my mind, in the whole or in part, I may say, for many months. Only three hours now remain to dinner, one of which I cannot well forbear to spend at the Fencing School. If I could only have prevailed upon myself to begin the work at the time I had proposed, I should have been prepared probably for any vigorous exertion, and it would have qualified me for the full enjoyment of the literary conversation that was to succeed. How different is the state of each period as it actually happened! how useless! how unproductive! how joyless! how unsatisfactory!

8th.—Set off for Sir George Cornewall's.

21st.—Went with Burgess to Caversham.

Fulham, 28th.—Soon after I had done breakfast, a stop

* Thomas Burgess, became Bishop of St. David's in 1803, and remained there till 1825, when he was translated to Salisbury.

was put to any further business, by a message from Burke, which obliged me to go out: from him I went to call on Dr. Johnson.

29*th*.—This morning rose early, disposed to be diligent, but interrupted between ten and eleven by Lord Spencer: by him and consequent business, relative to balloons, together with a visit to Phipps, employed till past four o'clock. Evening passed in a way in which I find few examples in the whole history of my London life. I have sat the whole time at home, and I have employed myself in the same way as at Oxford or Felbrigg. What upon earth has prevented my doing the same thing every second or third night, or for ten nights together?

30*th*.—Proposed to execute the work so shamefully delayed, and so indispensably necessary, of copying the paper which ought to have been sent to Sir John Stuart* two months ago. Found a pretence for employing myself for the time in something else, and accordingly took up Euclid. In consequence of something there, thought I would look (for almost the first time *after about eighteen years'* intention) into Locke, whose opinions I consulted on the subject of infinity. The reading this chapter (which I must finish to-morrow) is quite an epoch in my literary history.

Before this proceeded far Lord Spencer came in, and we soon after proceeded to the balloon, which, after several hours' waiting, we saw from the top of Lord Derby's house. A little before it went up we were joined by Burke. Instead of attending the House, went to see the wager rowed for on the Thames.

December 5*th*.—Upon recollection, that when mention has accidentally been made of Thucydides, I have often found myself at a loss for want of sufficient acquaintance with the style and nature of his work to give any opinion

* General the Honble Sir John Stuart.

upon it; and also that for some months back, viz. since my reading the 'Life of Æsop' by Planudes, in August, I have not read a passage in any Greek author, I determined to sit down to Thucydides for a couple of hours, in which time as much may be collected as to supply the deficiency above stated.

Tuesday, 7*th*.—Ten minutes past two, P.M. After waiting some short time in the adjoining room, I was admitted to Dr. Johnson in his bedchamber, where, after placing me next him on the chair, he sitting in his usual place on the east side of the room (and I on his right hand), he put into my hands two small volumes (an edition of the New Testament), as he afterwards told me, saying, '*Extremum hoc munus morientis habeto.*' He then proceeded to observe that I was entering upon a life which would lead me deeply into all the business of the world; that he did not condemn civil employment, but that it was a state of great danger; and that he had therefore one piece of advice earnestly to impress upon me—that I would set apart every seventh day for the care of my soul; that one day, the seventh, should be employed in repenting what was amiss in the six preceding, and for fortifying my virtue for the six to come; that such a portion of time was surely little enough for the meditation of eternity. He then told me that he had a request to make to me, namely, that I would allow his servant Frank to look up to me as his friend, adviser, and protector in all difficulties which his own weakness and imprudence, or the force or fraud of others, might bring him into. He said that he had left him what he considered an ample provision, viz. 70*l.* per annum; but that even that sum might not place him above the want of a protector, and to me therefore he recommended him, as to one who had will, and power, and activity to protect him. Having obtained my assent to this, he proposed that Frank should be called in, and desiring me to take him by the hand in token of the promise, repeated before him the recommendation he had just made of him, and the promise I had given to attend to it. I then took occasion to say how much I felt, what I had long foreseen that I should feel, regret at having spent so little of my life in his company. I stated this as an instance where resolutions are deferred till the occasions are past. For some time past I had determined that such an occasion of self-reproach should no longer subsist, and had built upon the hope of passing in his society the chief part of my time, at the moment when it was to be apprehended we were about to lose him for ever! I had no difficulty of speaking to him thus of my apprehensions; I could not help, on the other hand, entertaining hopes; but with these I did not like to trouble him, lest he should conceive that I thought it necessary to flatter him. He answered hastily that he was sure I would not; and proceeded to make a compliment to the manliness of my mind, which, whether deserved or not, ought to be remembered that it may be deserved. I then stated that, among other neglects, was the omission of introducing, of all others, the most important, the consequence of which particularly filled my mind at that moment, and on which I had often been desirous to know his opinions. The subjects I meant were, I said, 'natural and revealed religion.' The wish thus generally stated was in part gratified on the instant. For revealed religion, he said, there was such historical evidence as, upon any subject not religious, would have left no doubt. Had the facts recorded in the New Testament been mere civil occurrences, no one would have called in question the testimony by which they are established. But the importance annexed to them, amounting to nothing less than the salvation of mankind, *raised a cloud* in our minds, and created doubt unknown upon any other subject. Of proofs to be derived from history, one of the most cogent, he seemed to think, was the opinion so well authenticated and so long entertained, of a Deliverer that was to appear about that time. Among the typical representations, the sacrifice of the paschal lamb, in which no bone was to be broken, had early struck his mind. For the immediate life and miracles of Christ; such attestation as that of the apostles, who all, except St. John, confirmed their testimony by their blood; such belief as their witness procured from a people best furnished with the means of judging, and least disposed to judge favourably; such an extension afterwards of that belief over all the nations of the earth, though originating from a nation of all others the most despised, would leave no doubt that the things witnessed were true, and were of a nature more than human. With respect to evidences, Dr. Johnson observed, we had not such evidence that Cæsar died in the Capitol, as that Christ died in the manner related.

11*th.*—First day of skating; ice fine. Find I have lost nothing since last year.

Between nine and ten went to Sir Joshua, whom I took up by the way to see Dr. Johnson—Strachan and Langton there; no hopes, though a great discharge had taken place from the legs.

12*th.*—Came down about ten; read reviews, wrote to Mrs. Siddons, and then went to the ice; came home only in time to dress and go to my mother's to dinner. About half-past seven went to Dr. Johnson's, where I stayed chiefly in the outer room till past eleven. Strahan there during the whole time, and latterly Mr. Cruikshanks and the apothecary. I only went in twice, for a few minutes each time. The first time, I hinted only what they had been before urging, viz. that he would be prevailed upon to take some sustenance, and desisted only upon his exclaiming, 'It is all very childish; let us hear no more of it.' The second time I came in, in consequence of a consultation with Mr. Cruikshanks and the apothecary, and addressed him formally. After premising that I considered what I was going to say as a matter of duty, I said that I hoped he would not suspect me of the weakness of importuning him to take nourishment for the purpose of prolonging his life for a few hours or days. I then stated what the reason was, that it was to secure that which I was persuaded he was most anxious about, viz. that he might preserve his faculties entire to the last moment. Before I had quite stated my meaning, he interrupted me by saying that he refused no sustenance but inebriating sustenance, and proceeded to give instances where, in compliance with the wishes of his physicians, he had taken even a small quantity of wine. I readily assented to any objections he might have to nourishment of that kind, and observing that milk was the only nourishment I intended, flattered myself that I had succeeded in my endeavours, when he recurred to his general refusal, and begged that there might be an end of it. I then said that I hoped he would forgive my earnestness—or something to that effect; when he replied eagerly, 'that from me nothing would be necessary by way of apology;' adding with great fervour, in words which I shall (I hope) never forget—'God bless you, my dear Windham, through Jesus Christ;' and concluding with a wish that we might meet in some humble portion of that happiness which God might finally vouchsafe to repentant sinners. These were the last words I ever heard him speak. I hurried out of the room with tears in my eyes, and more affected than I had been on any former occasion.

13th.—In the morning meant to have met Mr. Cruikshanks in Bolt Court, but while I was deliberating about going, was sent for by Mr. Burke. Went to Bolt Court about half-past three. Found Dr. Johnson had been almost constantly asleep since nine o'clock in the morning, and heard from Mr. Des Moulins an account of what had passed in the night. He had compelled Frank to give him a lancet, and had, besides, concealed in the bed a pair of scissors, and with one or the other of these had scarified himself in three places, two in the leg, &c.

On Mr. Des Moulins making a difficulty of giving him the lancet, he said, 'Don't you, if you have any scruples; but I will compel Frank;' and on Mr. Des Moulins attempting afterwards to prevent Frank from giving it to him, and at last to restrain his hands, he grew very outrageous, so much so as to call Frank 'scoundrel,' and to threaten Mr. Des Moulins that he would stab him. He then made the three incisions above mentioned, of which one in the leg, &c., were not unskilfully made, but the other in the leg was a deep and ugly wound, from which, with the others, they supposed him to have lost nearly eight ounces of blood. Upon Dr. Heberden's expressing his fears about the scarification, Dr. Johnson told him that he was *timidorum timidissimus.*

A few days before his death, talking with Dr. Brocklesby, he said, 'Now will you ascribe my death to my having taken eight grains of squills, when you recommended only three; Dr. Heberden to my having opened my left foot, when nature was pointing out the discharge in the right.' The conversation was introduced by his quoting some lines to the same purpose from Swift's verses on his own death.*

It was within the same period (if I understood Dr. Brocklesby rightly) he enjoined him, as an honest man and a physician, to inform him how long he thought he had to live. Dr. Brocklesby inquired in return whether he had firmness to learn the answer. Upon his replying that

* The lines referred to were probably these:—

> The doctors, tender of their fame,
> Wisely on me lay all the blame:
> 'We must confess his case was nice,
> But he would never take advice.
> Had he been ruled, for aught appears,
> He might have lived these twenty years.'

he had, and Dr. B. limiting the term to a few weeks, he said that 'then he would trouble himself no more with medicine or medical advice,' and to this resolution he pretty much adhered.

In a conversation about what was practicable in medicine or surgery, he quoted, to the surprise of his physicians, the opinion of Marchetti, for an operation (I think) of extracting part of the kidneys.

He recommended for an account of China, Sir John Mandeville's 'Travels;' Halliday's 'Notes on Juvenal' he thought so much of as to have employed himself for some time in translating them into Latin.

He insisted on the doctrine of an expiatory sacrifice, as the condition without which there was no Christianity, and urged in support the belief entertained in all ages and by all nations, barbarous as well as polite.

He recommended to Dr. Brocklesby, also, Clarke's 'Sermons,' and repeated to him the passage which he had spoken of to me.

While airing one day with Dr. B., in passing and returning by St. Pancras' Church, he fell into prayer, and mentioned, upon Dr. B.'s enquiring why the Catholics chose that for their burial-place, that some Catholics in Queen Elizabeth's time had been burnt there. Upon Dr. B.'s asking him, during the same airing, whether he did not feel the warmth of the sun, he quoted from Juvenal,

> 'Præterea minimus gelido jam corpore sanguis
> Febre calet sola.'

45 past 10 P.M.—While I was writing the adjoining articles, received the fatal account, so long dreaded, that Dr. Johnson was no more! May those prayers which he incessantly poured from a heart fraught with the deepest devotion, find that acceptance with Him to whom they were addressed, which piety so humble and so fervent may seem to promise!

Dr. Brocklesby made him an offer of 100*l.* a year if he should determine to go abroad; he pressed his hands and said, 'God bless you through Jesus Christ, but I will take no money but from my sovereign.' This, if I mistake not, was told the King through West. That Johnson wanted much assistance, and that the Chancellor meant to apply for it, His Majesty was told through the same channel.

On dissection of the body, vesicles of wind were found on the lungs (which Dr. Heberden said he had never seen, and of which Cruikshanks professed to have seen only two instances), one of the kidneys quite gone, a gall stone in the bladder, I think; no water in the chest and little in the abdomen, no more than might have found its way thither after death.

15*th.*—*Fulham.*—The two days passed there afford a strong example how much more is sometimes done on supposed occasions of idleness than in times professedly devoted to study. Stopping at —— shop and looking into some things in Simson's 'Algebra,' I felt at that moment what an amazing difference would take place in my mind had I employed the years of leisure which had lapsed through my life in making myself master of the subjects then before me. To these reflections my practice so far conformed, that, after going home about eleven o'clock, I sat up till past two employed very diligently in reducing the formula which I had given in the morning. The work since that time has never been resumed; neither that nor any other kind of work has been done. I cannot, indeed, say that all the time has been misspent; much of it has been employed in performing the last duties of respect and affection to the great man that is gone.

But two entire mornings have been taken up, I fear, with little utility of any sort, certainly with none to myself, in attendance on Indian business, and much the greater part of the time dissipated in such avocations as I fear will be for ever incident to a life in London.

16*th.*—Went to business as soon as I got downstairs, without trusting myself to a book.

Went out to dine at my mother's; took with me Scioppius;* returned home about seven, tired; had rather suffered my mind to wander. After reading about an hour during tea in the 'Life of Dion,' recollected the Club in Essex Street, and drove down there.

19*th.*—N.B. On the day preceding, I had dined at Lord Palmerston's: company, Sir Joshua Reynolds, Sir Joseph Banks, Colman, Malone, Langton,† and Dr. Warren.

20*th.*—A memorable day—the day which saw deposited in Westminster Abbey the remains of Johnson. After our return from the Abbey, I spent some time with Burke on the subject of his negotiation with the Chancellor. We dined at Sir Joshua Reynolds', viz. Burke and R. Burke, Metcalf, Colman, Hoole, Scott, Burney, and Brocklesby. Burke, R. Burke, and I went afterwards to Lord Loughborough.

21*st.*—I had only time to call for a moment on Sir William Jerningham, who had just returned from France.

23*rd.*—Never felt so much danger on horseback as in riding down to Fulham, my horse not being frost-shod.

24*th.*—Walked to town. Dined at the Mitre—Horsley Metcalf, Maskelyne,‡ Wilson, Hutton, and Welsh. Went home with Horsley, to whom I showed my idea about balloons; afterwards to Byng's.§

* Gaspar Scioppius, a German writer of great learning, and of as great asperity, born about 1570, died 1649. Author of upwards of 100 different publications, &c., subjects of criticism, religious opinions, Jesuits, Protestants, &c., sent forth under feigned names. He also wrote a Latin Grammar. See Hallam's *Lit. of Europe*, part iii. ch. 1.

† Langton, a very good Greek scholar.

‡ Dr. Nevil Maskelyne, Westminster, and Catherine Hall, Cambridge; a famous mathematician.

§ The Hon. John Byng, afterwards Viscount Torrington.

25*th*, *Christmas Day*.—Sat meditating whether I should undertake with Sadler the enterprise of crossing the Channel; I had before determined against it, and now confirmed the determination.

26*th*.—Looked a little before I came down into Halley's 'Treatise on Annuities,' prefixed to logarithm tables.

28*th*.—In the evening with Sir Joshua to Mrs. Siddons', where were Lord and Lady Palmerston also.

31*st*.—Sat with Mrs. Legge reading Waller, the first poetry of Waller (except possibly one or two pieces), I ever read in my life: much struck with the merit of it. Whilst we were talking, Lord and Lady Willoughby came in. Sat in my bedroom till near one, trying unsuccessfully, though not unpleasantly, at the translation of an epitaph on Æschylus; but I should mention that I first wrote a letter to the mayor of Norwich.

Though I have talked all my life like a man familiar with Locke's writings, and am in fact acquainted to a great degree with their subject and character, yet I don't recollect to have looked into them with attention at all continued more than three times. The one was many years ago at Rainham,* where the book happened to be in the room where I slept, and I read the part relating to association; the other when, about two or three years ago, in consequence of a conversation with Repton, I examined the argument about personal identity; and lastly, in this very month, when a passage in one of Williamson's dissertations made me desirous to read the chapters on the idea of infinity. The first of the above times has been remembered, not as an instance of my reading Locke, but as an example of the great accessions made to knowledge, and the valuable ideas acquired in careless and accidental excursions of the mind.

* Rainham, Norfolk, the seat of Lord Townshend.

The following letter, though anterior in date to the commencement of Mr. Windham's Diary, is inserted in this place, because it throws light on the formation of Lord Rockingham's Administration.

The Right Hon. W. Windham to Mr. Bartlett Gurney, Norwich.

March 25, 1782.

Dear Sir,—After every expression of dislike and reluctance, the bitter draught is at length swallowed, and His Majesty has submitted to the hard necessity of taking for his Ministers the most virtuous set perhaps of public men that ever appeared in this country. About four o'clock to-day Mr. Dunning announced to the House of Commons, in the room of Lord North, who did not choose to come down, that the arrangement known to have been proposed the evening before, was accepted, and that it would be signified in form to the House on Wednesday next. The arrangement is as follows:—First Lord of the Treasury, Lord Rockingham; Chancellor of the Exchequer, Lord John Cavendish; President of the Council, Lord Camden; Privy Seal, Duke of Grafton; Commander-in-Chief, General Conway; Ordnance, Duke of Richmond; Admiralty, Admiral Keppel; Secretaries of State, Lord Shelburne, Mr. Fox. Other appointments are left for further consideration. Every art of evasion and negotiation was put in practice to the last, and it was hardly known what was determined upon till the moment Mr. Dunning came to the House, his message coming to him, as I understood, from Shelburne, to whom it was signified by the King. Lord Rockingham's conduct has been as great in the latter part of this negotiation as in the former. He refused absolutely to abate one jot of his first declaration; at the same time he was willing to sacrifice every private punctilio by which the King hoped to have created a jealousy between him and Lord Shelburne. The first-fruits of this administration will be an exclusion from Parliament of all those who have fattened on the ruins of the country by jobs and contracts, and the destruction of one source of undue influence without doors in the exclusion of the votes of revenue officers. Secondly, the great articles of reform proposed in Mr. Burke's life, will go on with all despatch. With what face will people oppose the appointment of a Ministry, composed of men who have uniformly supported the cause of the country for near twenty years, and who make it the condition of their entering into office, that they should deprive themselves of the means of corrupt influences?

Those who declare themselves enemies to this administration must declare themselves the friends of corruption and enemies of reform. My best respects and congratulations to all friends, and believe me,

Dear Sir,

Your obedient and faithful servant,

W. WINDHAM.

If you see Mr. Armstrong I will be obliged to you to say that I will write to him shortly.

P.S.—A blank was left for the Chancellorship in case Lord Shelburne should have required it for Dunning: but it is said Mr. Dunning does not require it.

1785.

January 1st.—Having come from Fulham the day before, spent the evening by invitation at Mrs. Siddons'; only Miss Kemble, and latterly Signor del Campo. Learnt his 'Seguidilla.'

Mrs. Siddons to Mr. Windham.

Saturday, January 1, 1785.

Dear Sir,—I wish you many happy returns of this day, and hope you will not be engaged this evening to tea, as I am to have a little music; but my party does not exceed two gentlemen, who perhaps you know, with my own fireside. I am sure you would like it, and you can't be to learn that I am truly sensible of the honour of your society. I am flying to rehearsal, and shall flatter myself that you will give me the happiness of seeing you.

I am most truly yours,
S. Siddons.

2nd.—Went for an hour to Horsley's; talked with him about Plato, and the opinion mentioned by him long since as entertained by a person whom I now find to be the Mr. Mitchell that I dined with at the Mitre, of the penetrability of matter, of which opinion I find Mr. Cavendish also is. At my return, in consequence of our conversation, I took down Plato, and read about half of the 'Dialogos' of Meno. In the evening thought I would go to Mrs. Vesey, which I did, but found none there but old Sheridan. After a short stay and calling at Lady Galway's, went to Duke Street, where I stayed with Mrs. Byng and Cecy till near eleven, and found in the satisfactoriness of my visit a sufficient compensation for my absence from home.

4*th*.—Mrs. Siddons in 'Belvidera;' performance happy, but some innovations introduced, in which I at least doubt, and the last scene injured by a failure of voice. I did not feel quite my usual pleasure. After the play deliberated about going to Brookes's; at last went, and finding Fox there, stayed to supper.

6*th*.—*Fulham*.—In the evening Lady Lonsdale; long debate about her coming.

8*th*.—Cholmondeley * arrived from Broadlands.

10*th*.—The last eight days were far from being among the portions of my life that I have spent with least advantage. Nor is that necessarily conveyed in the account given, but this fact is clearly deducible from it, that time so passed affords but little opportunity for the use of books, and will admit of but little advancement in studies requiring continued application. A man may be a poet, an essayist, and a philosopher, who lives in that way, but he cannot be an historian, a philologer, nor a mathematician.

16*th*.—Came to Felbrigg.

18*th*.—In the two days, or day and a half, I was at Felbrigg, was not unemployed. Went on with the seventh book of Euclid, which I began lately. Examined articles (mathematics) in Chambers' 'Dictionary.' Entered things in 'Adversaria.' A great portion of the time was spent in meditating on the fundamental question, whether the idea of proportion belongs primarily to number or to quantity. I am as yet pretty much of my former opinion, which I conceive to be the same as Barrow's. I think I can reduce the question to very narrow limits.

* George Cholmondeley was the son of the Hon. and Rev. Mr. C., who married the sister of Peg Woffington. He was an agreeable, sociable man: he married three wives—one of whom was Miss Francis, daughter of Sir Philip Francis.

One part of my employment at Felbrigg was the examination of some calculations in the 'Transactions' relative to the increase of mankind, which I should formerly have passed over without an attempt to understand them, but which I found, from that cause only, would not have been understood.

19*th.*—Arrived at Bury at six. Rather think that this is the second time only of my having been here since my great illness.*

20*th.*—Set out the next morning before it was well light; stopped at Sudbury; dined at Chelmsford; got to Repton's by tea. Diligent by the way.

21*st.*—Read diligently, but with interruptions from question of going with Sadler: called on Sadler as soon as I came; walked much about. Dined at Legge's: Cholmondeley and Douglas† there: more of *feel than I am now often acquainted with.*

22*nd.*—Up late; literally lounging till twelve or one. Went to Brookes's; the Prince being there, did not go to supper, but sat in the outer room with Lord Foley and Lord Duncannon.

30*th.*—Very little done the last week that can be recollected with pleasure. On the 25th Parliament opened. On the Wednesday I went to see Mrs. Crawford in 'Belvidera,' and found her much as I expected, though her disparity was very great. I can perhaps better conceive the delusion that, aided by a little prejudice and the recollection of Mrs. C. in better times, could hesitate about the preference. The chief faults that I should find would be, that her articulation was cramped and timid, her tones sometimes colloquial and vulgar, her action confined, and her countenance inexpressive. A new man of the name of Pope performed; I pronounced him in my own judgment as inferior, upon the whole, to Brereton.

* A fever, from the effects of which he never entirely recovered.

† Afterwards Lord Glenbervie.

Friday I dined at the Mitre: present—Masères,* Hutton, Mr. Brown, Mr. Atwood,† and Mr. Horsley. Conversation more pleasant than usual, till at last we got to politics, which I have enough of elsewhere.

Dined at the Duke of Portland's, to meet Club. Went to Mrs. Siddons', where were Sir Joshua and Miss Palmer, Sir Charles and Lady Dorothy Thompson, Kemble and Miss E. Kemble; talked, rather than felt, gaily. In the whole week nothing done, though some attempt made; the result, I fear, rather retrograde.

31*st.*—Between January 20th and this day, 31st, read political pamphlet, viz. 'Gleam of Comfort,' which I think written with copiousness and vigour, and conceived at first to be R. Burke's, but am now inclined to think to be O'Brien's. Parr agrees with me in opinion of it, which I hardly expected, the style being perpetually licentious and incorrect. It was the vogue at the Duke of Portland's to call it bad; it did not appear to me there was anyone in the room who could have written it or (Fox excepted) so good a one.

February 1*st.*—The House of Commons having broken up early, went to Club in Dover Street, where I found only Steevens and Colman. Drove to Mrs. Siddons', in order to communicate a hint on a passage in 'Lady Macbeth,' which she was to act the next night. Not finding her at home, went to her at the playhouse.

3*rd.*—Thirteen days since I came to town, a time during which, in any situation such as Oxford or Felbrigg, considerable advance would have been made in some articles of study, or some habit of mental improvement. At the end of this time in London I find myself less powerful in every respect than at the beginning of it. I cannot have the smallest doubt that this would not have happened in the country. In what then does

* Masères (Francis), Cursitor Baron of Exchequer, a mathematician of note.

† G. Atwood, F.R.S., a famous mathematician, educated at Westminster and Trinity College, Cambridge; patronised by Mr. Pitt.

the difference consist? Is it from causes merely mental, occasioned by the difference in the habits of life, or from bodily causes dependent on the temperature of the air and want of opportunities of exercise? This should be ascertained by exact observation. I suspect that enough time might be found for most purposes, both of business and pleasure, if there was no intermediate state, and every moment not wanted for amusement was vigorously employed in business.

5th.—Went between seven and eight to sleep at Kent's. Whether from imagination, or from some other cause, certainly found myself much pleasanter by the time I arrived there. Strongly bent upon having a residence out of town.

6th.—I dined at the Speaker's:* Fox, Lord North, Sheridan, Eden, General Burgoyne, Fitzpatrick, G. North, Lord George Cavendish, Leigh, Lord Surrey, and Welbore Ellis. Supper of the Club, at my house; Brummel, Richardson, Adam, Sir J. Erskine, Canning, Tickell, Dudley, Ellis, Shore, and Lord Fitzwilliam. More of *feel* than of late.

7th.—Went to meeting at Fox's on Westminster business; from Fox's house, where I sat up till past two. Well employed in De Moivre.† Had reason to reflect, as usual, on the folly of not recurring to such studies oftener.

8th.—Drove to House of Commons with Symonds, and in way back saw race between Charles Phipps and Stepney.‡

9th.—Day bright and tempting; rode to Hampstead to call on Steevens. Went to the House and spoke for the first time.§ Not home till seven in the morning.

* Charles Wolfran Cornewall, of Winchelsea, Sussex.

† Abraham De Moivre, born 1667 at Vitry; wrote in the 'Doctrines of Chances;' died in London, 1754.

‡ Sir Thomas Stepney (singular in dress), a Welsh gentleman of fortune.

§ Mr. Windham delivered his maiden speech on the 9th Feb. 1785, on the Proceeding relative to the Westminster Scrutiny.

10*th.*—Rose at twelve and continued at home till dinner, with the *feel* that sufficiently proved the importance of exertion to happiness. My mind was so light, and my powers so active and vigorous, that no undertaking appeared difficult. The activity of the mental powers awakened the feelings also, and made me susceptible of enjoyment, to which I am in general a stranger. It is strange that an exercise of powers of which previously one might have been pretty certain, should have produced such effects; yet certain it is, that life appeared dressed in new colours, and I myself to be endued with new capacities of enjoyment. At five went to dinner at Legge's, where I remained, partaking more of the pleasures of the company and conversation than I can often remember to have done till now. Cholmondeley dined at Legge's, and Ellis and I supped there and carried me home.

15*th.*—Drove from the House of Commons, without dining, to Drury Lane, to Mrs. Siddons in 'Lady Macbeth.'

16*th.*—Went to Sir Joshua's, where were Lord and Lady Harcourt, Mr. Edward and Charles Jerningham, Sir Charles and Lady Thompson, Mrs. Siddons and Miss Kemble, Lord and Lady Loughborough.

February 25*th to March* 18*th.*—Twenty-two days. Penryn Committee.

March 20*th.*—Rode down to Fulham to dinner. I was doubtful whether I should not have returned to town to meet the Club at Canning's, but am well satisfied at having stayed. My brother and William* breakfasted with me this morning, and lastly I read a proposition out of Euclid with William, and have advised his being

* William, eldest son of the Dean of Wells and Mrs. Lukin, and father to the editor; entered the navy in 1781; he commanded at different times the 'Standard,' the 'Doris,' the 'Thames,' the 'Gibraltar,' the 'Mars,' the 'Chatham.' There is nothing to say of him as an officer but that he thoroughly understood and did his duty, and that in Sir S. Hood's action, in 1806, he was prominently mentioned in despatches. He died in Jan. 1833.

sent for some time to stay with me, if the addition of another person in the house is not too inconvenient. I think I shall find my own account, as well as his, in the taking upon me the office of instructing him.

I have now reached the 20th of March, two months since my return to town; for the greater part of the time literary business almost wholly abandoned; faculties, however, not dormant, considering that three weeks were spent on the Penryn Committee.

I am afraid the fact is, that in no equal period my faculties were ever so much excited. Such are the advantages I have lost by delaying so long my entrance into business; and such the reasons of that superiority which men of the world are perpetually to have over men of study. The love of knowledge and general desire of improvement will not produce such exertions as are called forth in the prosecution of business involving present interests and terminating in immediate consequences. What progress might men make in the several parts of knowledge, if they could pursue them with the same eagerness and assiduity as are exerted by lawyers in the conduct of a suit!

How much I might have done in the last three weeks in mathematics, if I would have bestowed upon them every day as many hours as I have spent in the committee room, leaving all the remainder of the day for other purposes or amusements!

What a pity I cannot suppose the place where I am Rhodes, and do that involuntarily for a favourite study which I do by compulsion in a business the most ungrateful!

21st.—Rode out before breakfast towards Wimbledon; fell in with the hounds; morning pleasant. Just in time to go down to the House to attend the presenting of the Norwich petition.

23rd.—Went out in order to attend the balloon in

which Zambeccari and Sir Edward Vernon were to ascend.

25*th*, *Good Friday.* — Breakfasted at Sir Joshua's; morning that —— came in. Reflected while I was there on the strange state of my past life, in which time was either wanting, or supposed to be wanting, for such company as I was then in. From Sir Joshua's to Banks's, thence to Fordyce's for balloon news, thence with a few intervening visits home. Dined in Grosvenor Square, Mrs. Legge's birthday, her 36th year. '*Eheu! fugaces!*' I went away, and after a short visit to Horsley, went home, not feeling sufficiently fresh to go either to Lady Palmerston's or Mrs. Crewe's.

27*th*.—Day cold; snow in the air, and I languid and heavy. A little before seven set out to return to Fulham, but stopped for the best of an hour with Lady Cornewall; very pleasant. The Speaker and his wife were coming to drink tea with her, and perhaps I might as well have sent my carriage back and stayed.

28*th*.—Set out at twelve to ride to Moulsey to see the balloon for the first time. Drank tea with Lady Cornewall. At ten to the Duchess of Portland's; very pleasant.

29*th*. — Cholmondeley breakfasted with me. Went about twelve to Mrs. Siddons'; back to Mrs. Legge; Lady Brudenell there. Went early to the playhouse; Duke of Portland's box; Mrs. S. in 'Desdemona.'

31*st*.—In my way out of town called in Stanhope Street, and finding Lady Cornewall at dinner, was prevailed on to stay. Stay would have been pleasanter but for the old reason, want of determination what to do. From the time of my return till twelve o'clock well employed, having at length, after a delay transcending all credibility, considering what is at stake, begun, and pretty successfully, what I should say on the subject of Reform.

April 2*nd*.—Walked to Duke Street to enquire after

Mrs. Byng, then to Lady Cornewall's to drink coffee, thence to Fulham in the carriage.

From my arrival well employed in preparing for the Reform; success such as to inspire hope, and as ought to have increased diligence.

3rd.—I had settled overnight that I would excuse myself at dinner at Sir Ralph Payne's, where I expected to meet Fox, Lord North, &c., and from Mrs. Siddons in the evening, that by devoting this day to the prosecution of my intended speech I might have some chance of getting ready in time. Many good resolutions were formed for this purpose, and many reflections made on the extreme folly I should be guilty of, were an opportunity thus procured, and thus purchased at this price, in the end thrown away. What has been the state of the fact? 'Tis now past ten at night—twenty-two hours and a half since the time when these resolutions were made. Till one, all that I did besides reading some reviews, which I had no business to look at, was to write three or four notes, and to give some directions. At a little past one, I rode, and taking this opportunity to fulfil a necessary purpose, the calling on Wilberforce, did not return till four to dinner. At dinner thought with effect on work; then from indulgence, necessary or blamable, read reviews; before seven walked, during which, thought, but not on work. Dressed at eight. Liddel to tea, for whose continuance till past ten I am not answerable. It now strikes eleven. All that I can say is, that, bating the failure of my appointed purpose, the day has not been very ill spent.

4th.—Dined at the Whig Club, at the London Tavern; Duke of Portland in the chair. First time of my hearing to any advantage Captain Morris.*

5th.—Rose in good time with *feel* of considerable en-

* Captain Morris was a natural son of the Duke (Jockey) of Norfolk known as a singer and composer of songs.

joyment; but abated somewhat by uncertainty about the disposal of the day. If deliberations like this can harass one's mind, when can it be at rest? Such dubiety may exist wherever choice can exist. The course determined on for the present was to go out on horseback; but no decision was come to, even when my foot was in the stirrup, where I should go to. Thence to Tickell, but, altering my mind, turned from the door. At seven called in Stanhope Street, and having stayed till near eight, sat down, and with assistance of Lady Cornewall, wrote a pretty long letter to Parr. At nine, set out to ride hither. At Walham Green, found a Scotch piper playing, who they told me was the Duke of Atholl's piper, and whom I accompanied for some time, but without feeling from his strains all my usual satisfaction.

6*th.*—This habit of indecision, if some means are not found to stop its progress and abate its malignity, will corrupt and eat away my understanding to the very core; it wastes my time, consumes my strength, converts comfort into vexation and distress, deprives me of various pleasures, and involves me in innumerable difficulties. Some canon must be framed for proceeding in these cases. Let the first resolution be, that from the moment the question is instituted, and the trial commenced, no interruption should be permitted, nor any adjournment take place. The cause should be concluded before the jury go out of court. The methods of conducting it will be the same as in other cases; approaching indeed not so much to the cases usually submitted to courts of judicature, as to cases resolvable under the doctrine of chances. A distribution must be made into the primary modes of action which the question admits; these, again, must be continually subdivided, and all the combination of parts, capable of existing together, be made out and compared. If this work requires to be performed completely, more time than the circumstances will admit, or than its importance deserves; and if the condition above proposed—that, namely, allowing no interval in the discussion—is not found sufficient limitation, some certain period must be allowed, at the end of which the return must peremptorily be made, whether my conscience is made up or not. An adherence to these rules will, I have no doubt, go a great way towards a cure.

The fact on which the above speculation arose was that, till eleven o'clock, I could do nothing, from not having been able to settle in what manner I should dispose of the day; and in consequence, seven of the best hours of the day, viz. from seven till two, without more having been done than the writing of the present article, and thinking loosely on some parts of my work. Half-past three, went to dinner at Kent's; not unpleasant. Quarter-past five, rode, going over wild ground about Wimbledon Common; not unpleasant, but not so pleasant as it might have been. Returned about seven, pleasant and refreshed; from then till bed-time, employed chiefly in thinking on work; latterly in doing, what I have so often thought of and never performed, and of which the trial shows that the neglect is to be severely regretted, namely, in getting by heart parts of Johnson's writings. The present instance was No. 104 of the 'Rambler.'*

7th.—Upon considering in the morning how I should regulate my going to town and dispose of myself there, remembered the resolutions of the day before: returned to Legge's to dinner, to meet Mills, who was just come from abroad. Sat up till past two in my bedroom, settling satisfactorily the plan of speech on Reform.

10th.—Dinner at the Duke of Portland's: present, Burgoyne, Mr. Ladbroke, Powys, Francis, Mr. Stanley, Burke, Sawbridge, Fred. Montague, afterwards Sir Gilbert Elliot. Did not go away till ten. Burgoyne wants me to

* 'The Original of Flattery.'

be nominee on his committee, but I must not on account of Reform. Went from Burlington House to Duke Street, where were Cecy, Malone, &c.

11*th.*—At five, very unwillingly, went to town, but, besides an engagement at Sir Joshua's, wished to hear Erskine on the Report of the Private Committee. Ride not unpleasant; business not come on; felt while I was in the House that I could have rose without difficulty and with perfect possession of myself.

12*th.*—My purpose to have spent some hours in translations, but diverted from it by reading propositions. It was near two before I sat down to it; from then till the arrival of Lady Cornewall tolerably successful. Returned to town in Lady C.'s carriage. Dined at Club: Malone,* Lord Ossory, Sir Joshua, Boswell, Bishop Shipley, Dr. Warren, Fordyce. Stopped at mine own house, and wrote answer to Wildman, declining to be nominee for Mr. Curtis.

14*th.*—After reading the remainder of Matty's 'Review,' returned to Thuanus, and succeeded; doubtful when Lady Cornewall came whether I should go to town; determined at last upon going. I might have done better by staying, and I might not. Drank tea at Sir G. Cornewall's; at Fulham by nine. Had felt much mental disorder during my absence, but was now pretty right; and sat down for the first time since *this day se'nnight* effectually to prosecute my purpose: continued my employment till one, with success more than I deserved.

15*th.*—Put no constraint upon myself as to the time of rising. Read carefully a proposition entered in article in 'Adversaria.' It is now absolutely necessary that I should go to my task. Went to Bensley's. Upon coming in, not finding myself in a state to proceed with my main business, went on with propositions. In my contentions with

* Edward Malone, born at Dublin 1741, died in 1812. An intimate friend of Burke and Johnson.

myself, during the latter part of my walk, strained my mind very much so as to bring on a degree of headache. Surely these states are the effects, not of want of exertion, but of want of method.

18th.—Went to town without a suspicion that I should not deliver some part at least of what I had prepared with so much thought, and to my own apprehension with so much success, on the Parliamentary Reform. The heat of the House disordered my faculties and enfeebled my powers and brought on a state of inability, from which I could never recover sufficiently to venture to rise. I have done very wrong; I was wrong not to use greater efforts to recover myself; I was wrong, I believe, not to make the attempt, even in the state I was.

19th.—Dined with Horsley; went with him to the pit, to 'Macbeth.'

20th.—Met Minching, who applied to me to be nominee for Okehampton; I was too late for the ballot, which was for Burgoyne; remained in the House waiting to introduce Burnard to Fox.

21st.—With Mrs. Byng to the play; 'Othello.' Afterwards to Brookes's, where stayed supper till about three.. Fox there.

23rd.—At Fulham, all day employed in settling notion treated of in page 160 of 'Adversaria,' viz. of those propositions which, instead of giving the proof, seem rather to point out how it may be given. Though I did nothing else during the day, did not succeed in settling that. Sadler called after dinner, and at tea I had the company of Liddel.

24th.—Breakfasted at Kent's. At Chelsea I took a coach. To dinner at Horsley's to meet Lord Monboddo. In the carriage so sick that I fainted.

25th.—Went by appointment to dine at Bensley's; the only person there Dr. Roberts, master of St. Paul's School, very stupid, and I should imagine very illiterate. He said, as we walked home together, that Erasmus had not begun to learn Greek till he was fifty—but could not tell me where he learnt it.

How long after fifty did Erasmus live?

26*th.*—Went to town to attend ballot; was nominee for Lord Spencer. Obliged to go to Bloomsbury to meet Lord Spencer, to hear something of the cause. Dined at Club—Lord Ossory, Lord Palmerston, Fordyce, Boswell, Langton, Banks, Colman, Burney. Went to play, 'Zara.' *

29*th.*—Waked at six. Got up a little before seven. Sauntered, rowed, employed on question in mathematics and metaphysics. My thoughts have rambled, but with this consolation, that they have gone to pleasurable objects. It would have been better however, in the end, even for the interests of pleasure, that they had been kept to their proper object.

May 5*th.*—Went up in balloon.† Much satisfied with myself; and, in consequence of that satisfaction, dissatisfied rather with my adventure. Could I have foreseen that danger or apprehension would have made so little impression upon me, I would have insured that of which, as it was, we only gave ourselves a chance, and have deferred going till we had a wind favourable for crossing the Channel. I begin to suspect, in all cases, the effect by which fear is surmounted is more easily made than I have been apt to suppose. Certainly the experience I have had on this occasion will warrant a degree of confidence more than I have ever hitherto indulged. I would not wish a degree of confidence more than I enjoyed at every moment of the time.

12*th.*—Spoke for the second time in the House for the adjournment of the debate on the Irish Propositions.

* Tragedy by Hill.

† Memoranda copied from pocket-book, one which I had in balloon:—'N. the current which brought us over. The wind N.E. when we came to Rochester. Circumstance of hat falling. Crossed at Tilbury. Direction of wind after descent, contrary to that immediately preceding.'

Felt more possessed than on the former occasion, but thought my performance inferior, and conceived that others thought so too. I have found since that they were inclined to think well of it. They are so good as to be cheaply pleased. It was a mere effusion, and though delivered in a forcible and perhaps graceful manner, contained nothing more than anyone would have thought of in conversation.

16*th*.—Sat long with Mrs. Legge in the morning. Conversation about reasons, for and against, being acquainted with Mrs. Sheridan, whose singing the evening before at Mrs. Crewe's I was extolling.

18*th*.—To Mrs. Siddons' 'Rosalind.' To Brookes's; talked to Fox* about Homer. At twelve to Mrs. Crewe's rout; home not till past two.

20*th*.—Not home from the House till seven in the morning. The debate was on the Irish commercial propositions, &c. Falling in with Burke, dined with him in St. Albans Street; old H. not at home. After dinner we went to the Exhibition, thence to Burlington House, where we drank tea, sitting chiefly with the Duchess, on account of the Duke's accident; not unpleasant. Lord John and O'Brien there. Thought when I left my own house I would return and not go to Mrs. Crewe's; actually did go home, and then at last altered my mind and went to Mrs. C.'s. Not unpleasant there, and doubtful till this moment whether I did wrong.

21*st*.—Rose late. By the time I had wrote a letter to Captain Palmer, Bill Lukin's captain, and one to Mr. Wilkes at Norwich; time to go to balloon.

June 27*th*.—One month and five days since last article. My late stay at Felbrigg appears to have been just fifteen

* Fox said of Mr. Windham, 'He was, indeed, a very singular character, and that he was almost the only man he had ever known who was a thinking man without being a grave man—"*vir gravis et constans*"—a meditating man with so much activity, and a reading man with so much practical knowledge.'

days. I went down with Doughty in the mail coach, and returned in the mail diligence; sufficiently pleased with both journeys. I don't think my time at Felbrigg was spent quite so well as it might. The first cause, suffering myself to be withdrawn from going on with Maclaurin, which I had resumed (and was proceeding in prosperously) by an endeavour to solve a problem occurring accidentally in Pappus. This took me up four days at least and I at last did not accomplish it, and was wholly drawn off from my other pursuits. The want, then, of some stated task on which I might be intent, relaxed my endeavours; yet I cannot accuse myself of having been much absent from my room or of having spent ill the hours passed there. I finished the first volume of Robertson's 'History,' the 'Monthly' and Matty's 'Reviews;' read a sermon or two of Clarke's; translated into Latin a good deal of Lucian's 'Dialogue de ——;' went through with William the second book of Euclid, and twenty propositions of the third. To Thuanus only a single sentence was added.

I tried at first for the division of time, the going out in the middle of the day, but found that besides the objection of the heat, the prospect of going out at the time seemed rather to unsettle me during the morning, nor could I return in time to gain any interval worth having before dinner. Then I took the method of taking my exercise before breakfast. The general objection is, the early unsettling of thought; the advantage may perhaps be secured and the inconvenience avoided, by confining one's walk or ride in narrow bounds.

Had an interruption of above an hour with a man of the name of Wilson, who has a plan for improving the police.

I came back at eight, after dining at my mother's and going to the House, where was some talk about the Scrutiny Bill. Felt how little power I have to supply, by solitary exertion, the effect produced in the mind by a debate; and what immense benefit I should find from the necessity of passing six weeks in such exercise of the understanding as must be practised by those by whom a debate is carried on.

From eight till ten have been completing the conspectus of the books 'De Sectione' till twenty before one; finished with great attention and great comfort the formulæ extracted from Guignée for the construction of quadratic equations.

28*th*.—From breakfast till past three diligently employed in mathematics; from then till past four discussing with Sir Gilbert Elliot some elementary matters in the same science, which he is resuming. He thinks that the impossibilities of two lines having a common segment follows from their not being capable of containing space. I rather think his reasoning not legitimate. His observation upon Williamson's remark on Simson's Corollary to the Eleventh Proposition, is right enough, that he has expressed himself as if Euclid had made a mistake, which is not the case. Simson's Corollary, too, may be established, though not precisely by his means, yet by help of the axiom that says all right angles are equal; but then that will not well answer Simson's purpose, because that axiom itself cannot be admitted unless the point in question, viz. the impossibility of a common segment, be admitted. At half-past four went to dress to dine at Mr. Hamilton's; present, Beresford, Judge Eyre, Courtenay, Sir Godfrey Webster, Andrew Stuart, General Dalrymple.

July 9*th*.—Went to Windsor with Ellis and Munday.

10*th*.—Dined at Chiswick; Mrs. Sheridan and Mrs. Crewe, Sheridan, Crewe, Ellis, Munday, Lord William Russell, Duke of Portland.

11*th*.—Stayed at home till I went to the House of Commons, but did little else than write a letter to Gurney, and meditate on a problem for finding a point in a given diameter where the perpendicular and the line to the extremity should be equal to the diameter. *Vide* 'Adversaria.'

12*th.*—Three o'clock at home, with little interruption; yet, except writing a letter to Norwich, have done nothing but meditate without success on the problem above mentioned. I believe, in my present state of mathematical habits and acquirements, this kind of exercise is the least profitable; the fact is that, after a certain time, one can neither lay it out of one's thoughts, nor yet make it possess them altogether. I must now go to the House.

16*th.*—Went to Beaconsfield; conveyance, Sir Joshua's coach; object of visit, to meet Madame De Genlis. Her manners were what we should call French, but not remarkable either in that or any other respect.

30*th.*—Burke, Beresford, Beresford jun., Malone, Lord Sunderlin, Courtenay, and Boswell dined with me; sat till eleven. Spent an hour at a coffee-house in Conduit Street. Walked a good while, the moon shining bright, in Berkeley Square, enjoying a feel of more happiness than usual.

August 9*th.* — Set out for the North. Dined at St. Albans; saw the Abbey, which I had seen before in tour made with Mulgrave and Colman. Great quantities of Roman brick in structure of church, one twenty-three inches long and about the thickness of a common brick. Church five hundred *plus* feet in length: longer this, I believe, than Peterborough cathedral. The origin of the expression 'dining with Duke Humphrey'* to be re-

* Humphrey, Duke of Gloucester, brother of Henry V., was indeed buried at St. Albans, but the tomb of Sir John Beauchamp, in old St. Paul's Church, was popularly supposed to be that of the Duke. Fuller in his writings says, persons of the better class, who could not afford a dinner, were always welcome at the table of the Duke of Gloucester. When the Duke was dead they often went without a dinner, and they were then said,

ferred probably to the times when the courts of justice were held there, viz. during the plague of Charles I.'s time, when those students who, for want of some place to dine at, were compelled to walk about in the church, were said to dine with Duke Humphrey. This conjecture, if I am not mistaken, I had heard, though I had so totally forgot, that even the mention of the expression on the spot did not recall it to me. From St. Albans proceeded to Stevenage, walking through Lord Melbourne's park and drinking tea at his inn, where I had so often stopped during the days of Ickleford. From this time till the middle of the day thought much of those times, but not so much as I ought.

10*th.*—Went on to Milton without stopping. Some time before we could get dinner; Lord Fitzwilliam not having dined at home.

11*th.*—Rode in the morning to Peterborough and saw the cathedral, attended by the Dean. Remarkable in the building that there are no buttresses. Part near the altar built by Henry VI., I think. Architecture of different ages; Burke thinks four. Tomb of Mary Queen of Scots; removed to the Dean's garden and used as a summer house. Burke's observation, that as it had been a receptacle of dead beauty, so now it was of living—viz. Mrs. Farrant.

Lord Fitzwilliam. Public day. No one remarkable; but a most offensive fellow by the name of ——

In a collection of voyages, translated from an English collection, an account of three voyages in years 1550, 1551, 1552, to the coast of Africa, by Thomas Windham, a gentleman of Norfolk, but removed to Somersetshire, and who is there styled the 'Father of the English navigation to foreign seas.' In the last he died, as is there

mockingly, to dine with Duke Humphrey, to intimate they were the same description of people who formerly dined with him, and unless they got a dinner with him, would have none at all.

represented, by his obstinacy and presumption in acting contrary to the advice of one Pinteado, a Portuguese, in connection with whom he had undertaken the voyage.

12*th*.—Parted with Lord Fitzwilliam after an early breakfasting, we proceeding with our journey, he going a-hunting. At Grantham, where we dined, overtaken by Lord Daer, who with Lord Selkirk was returning to Scotland.

13*th*.—From Newark to Wentworth, through Worksop and Rotherham. Progress slow; walked a good deal. Way over part of Sherwood Forest, which has newly been enclosed. Agreeably surprised by the magnificence of the house and beauty of the place.

14*th*.—Between looking over the house and driving to Wentworth Castle (Lord Strafford's), morning altogether taken up; so but little time was spent in the library, where the goodness of the collection would have induced me to stay more.

15*th*.— Passed through Wakefield and Leeds. Saw Lascelles.

VERSES LEFT AT LASCELLES', BY R. BURKE.

Hail, Harewood! splendid, hospitable dome,
A regal mansion, and a quiet home,
Made to receive our monarchs, when they move
To reap the harvest of their people's love;
Made for the heroes', for the lovers' joy,
Grand as a palace, finished as a toy.

17*th*.—Breakfasted at Richmond. Spent an hour or two in looking at the castle, which is very magnificent. Arrived at Mr. Morrit's to dinner.

18*th*.—Breakfasted with Jack Lee at Staine Thorp. Saw with him Raby Castle and Park. Nothing can be imagined more in the character of ancient feudal grandeur. Thence to Durham. In the same room where I stopped in the year '72.

19th.—Saw Alnwick, and dined with the Duke. Present, Lord and Lady Percy and Mr. Moore, secretary of the Society for the Encouragement of Arts. After dinner, instead of going, as we intended, to Whittingham, to meet our other chaise, were driven, by mistake of the postboy, to the next stage on the north road, twenty miles from the place we proposed. The last stage was a cross road over a moor; for the greatest part of which I walked; feeling great enjoyment, though not so much as I ought to have done.

20th.—Arrived about seven at Minto. Incessant rain all day.

21st.—Passed without any memorial. The pain in my face sufficient to prevent my employment, and to keep me uncomfortable. Uncomfortableness not a little increased by the humour of Lady Elliot of keeping the windows open, and allowing no fire. In the evening, not being able to read, small talk with Lady Harris.

23rd.—Employed for some time in my own room, partly in some algebraic questions. Took a walk with Burke and Sir Gilbert.

24th.—Left Minto. Saw Melrose. Drank tea at Galashiels. It was dark nearly when we passed Dalkeith, but not so much so but that I thought I recollected part of the road. Much pleasure at arriving in Edinburgh, where we were lodged at Duns Hotel.

25th.—Dined with Adam Smith; present, Dr. Robertson, Mr. Cullen, Mr. Erskine (Henry). Don't recollect anyone else.

Dr. Robertson told me that Brantome, though little favourable to what he found in Scotland, speaks of Holyrood House, part of which remains as it was in his time, as of a building not inferior to anything of its kind on the Continent. The modern part was built after James I.'s time, when they had no kings to inhabit there; but there being a surplus of some money, which they feared the

Parliament would lay hold of, they chose rather to apply it in this way. He cited an observation of Lord Holderness', that it was the most commodious of any of the king's houses.

28*th.*—Heard Dr. Robertson preach. Dined at Johnston's. Walked about in the park, of which my recollection was sufficiently correct, as also of Burns' house, which I surveyed only on the outside. Supped in the evening with Principal; only his son present. Sufficiently pleasant.

29*th.*—Left Edinburgh in time to dine at Lord Lauderdale's, where we have stayed the night on our way to Glasgow. Hatton (Lord Lauderdale's); a respectable old house, more commodious and better fitted than I had expected. Style of living good. Present at dinner, Lord Glencairn, Sir William Cunningham and his new wife. The superiority of Southern manners very observable in the latter.

31*st.*—Set off for Glasgow; on the way I had allowed myself to ramble too much from what should have been the subject of my thoughts, viz. the recollection of the period of my first being in this country.* Indulged only in fancies.

September 1*st.*—Ceremony of Burke's admission; none but boys present. Saw the library, and the classes that I had been used to: mathematical class appeared much smaller. *Feel* at the sight of the college, and in general upon arrival here, not so strong as at return to Oxford; reason probably the interval too long, the stay not long enough; the character of the place too, perhaps, not so striking. Dined in the college hall: present, Mr. Meek, Dr. Williamson, Mr. Richardson, Dr. Stevenson, Dr. Wil-

* On leaving Eton in 1766, Mr. Windham was placed in the University of Glasgow, under the tuition of Dr. Anderson and the learned Dr. Robert Simson the editor of *Euclid.* He removed to Oxford in 1767, and was entered a gentleman commoner of University College, Sir Robert Chambers being his tutor.

son and his two sons, Mr. Hamilton (Professor of Anat.), Mr. Arthur, Mr. Young, Dr. Irwin, Mr. Millar and son, Dr. Reid, Dr. Taylor, Lord Maitland, and Burke. I remained among the latest, finding in them so much wish that I should stay, and in myself so much satisfaction in staying, that I was content to sacrifice to that motion time that would otherwise have been spent with Lady Harris. I was soon obliged to go away in order to attend the Committee of Operative Weavers, who were assembled at our inn, in honour of Lord Maitland and Burke. I was obliged to say a few words, which I did in a manner very unsatisfactory. I certainly might have done better, if I could have exerted myself more vigorously to collect my thoughts. From the inn we were conducted in grand and orderly procession ; the windows on each side being lined, and a transparency with different superscriptions carried before us, to Dr. Stevenson's, where we were to sup.

2nd.—When Burke went to the College I took my walk to Hamilton Hill to see Miss ——; so altered that with any assistance from circumstances less than I had, I should not have known her. Alas! how frail and transient is beauty.

3rd.—Breakfasted at Luss. After dinner, long walk to Loch Long. Our boatman had ten and sixpence—would not take a crown for going on to the head of the loch ; so we parted. All our rowers shrewd intelligent men; one had been in the 77th in the time of the mutiny.

4th.—Dined at the inn, ten miles short of Inverary. Had message in the evening from the Duke, with whom we engaged ourselves to breakfast next morning.

5th.—Passed riding about the grounds and the castle : persons there—Lady Augusta Campbell, Lady Derby, Miss Campbell (the same who has travelled with Lady Derby), and a painter who seemed to be an Englishman, and one or two others.

6*th*.—The country magnificently wild before you come to Loch Awe. Stopped at a cottage, where there was an old man who had been wounded at Fontenoy. Good specimen of Highland living. Some melancholy reflections.

7*th*.—Melancholy reflections continued. Country to Killin very fine, particularly from Loch Dochart. Mr. Campbell, Lord Breadalbane's factotum, talked to us on the bridge, and waited upon us afterwards with his son, the most modest, gentlemanlylike man I ever saw in Scotland.

8*th*.—After seeing the Hermitage and Lord Breadalbane's, set off for Blair. A great fool for letting my desire to show Burke the northern lights break up our walk.

9*th*.—To Blair. Could not effect our return to Maclaurin's to dinner. Vexation added to my melancholy; drank tea there; not quite satisfied with myself.

10*th*.—Saw the place (Dunkeld); day unfavourable. Arrived at Perth by dinner; went before dinner to see the scene of the conspiracy, in Gowrie's house. Some time spent by me in the evening, in a bookseller's shop—where I purchased Johnson's 'Poems,' and a small book of astronomy for Miss Morrit.

11*th*.—Followed Morrit, &c., to Lord Kinnoul's place, to my mind one of the finest in Scotland; the reception not the most flattering; no concern of mine. The sycamore tree at Dumblane, proportionate in all its parts, measured three of our spans and a cubit, which at 5 ft. 8 in. for a span would be about 19 ft. 6 in. The sycamore at Dunkeld was, I think, two spans and an arm, and a space of the same size nearly, but neither of these I distinctly recollect—a bad specimen of my memory. At Lord Kinnoul's was a Mr. Erskine, a deformed young man of engaging manners, and whose character H. Erskine says corresponds; and a Mr. Hope, another advocate, of sulky appearance, and self-sufficient, conforming in like manner, as the same authority informs me, to his character. Wrote out verses I had completed before I went to bed:—

As Adam by the bright Archangel led,
Saw life's great span, in destined order spread,
So in these leaves to thee, fair nymph, is shown
The instructive image of a world unknown;
Where thou mayst learn, by trial, yet untaught,
How never happiness by wealth was bought,
There see what ills assail the rich and great,
Nor scorn the blessings of an humbler fate.
Still to this fate with equal hand is given
The choicest bounties of indulgent Heaven,
Untainted joys, the sunshine of the breast,
Love's purest flame, by mutual ardour blest.
To thee, fair charmer, be such joys decreed,
Of worth and beauty, such the precious meed.
Bless with thy charms some fond admiring swain;
Some swain be found, worthy those charms to gain.

12th.—In the morning after breakfast to see the castle, and thence to Hopetown House. Barely got to Hopetown in time to dress. Lord H. absent, on account of Lady Haddington's funeral. A large company to dinner chiefly of retainers of the family; of the rest, Sir W. and Lady Cunningham, Mr. Hope and his wife, of Amsterdam, and her sister. Style of living in the house, though grand from the numbers entertained, not uniform and consistent, nor of the same quality throughout.

13th.—Proceeded to Edinburgh. After dinner walked to Adam Smith's. Felt strongly the impression of a family completely Scotch. House magnificent and place fine. Burke, after riding about with Sir W. Cunningham, proceeded to Edinburgh, where we arrived in time for dinner: after dinner walked to Adam Smith's; found there Colonels Balfour and Ross, the former late aide-de-camp to General Howe, the latter to Lord Cornwallis. Felt strongly the impression of a company completely Scotch. Faculties not clear.

14*th.*—Dined at Adam Smith's; present only a Mr. Skene. After walking with Burke in the Square went home.

16*th.*—Saw in the morning Holyrood House; dined with the Advocate.

18*th.*—All day at Minto.

19*th.*—Dined at Longtown, just in the south of the river—the Esk, I think—that divides the counties. Carlisle—pleasant appearance and pleasant *feel* at approaching it. The North of England more connected in my imagination with old times, than Scotland; and England itself, viewed perhaps with more complacency.

20*th.*—Out by half-past six, attended by a postboy on horseback, to see Eden Hall; * spent an hour there with much satisfaction; five pictures on each side the drawing-room. Thence to Ullswater, from which we returned only to save our daylight. At dinner Lord Surrey came in with a proposal, which we should have probably accepted, but for the most unaccountable of all pieces of stupidity in our servants. They carried us by a tedious journey to Appleby.

21*st.*—From Appleby to Kendal, on a moor, before you arrived at the house where we baited, those stony tracks are to be seen which are called in the country scars, and which are in appearance different from any that I remember to have seen elsewhere. The rock for several acres arises above the surface in small contiguous masses, each consisting of several horizontal lamina, like scoriæ, much detached and some of them loose.

We arrived at Kendal time enough for a late dinner, after which we walked about the town, and had some talk with a dyer whose yard lay by the side of the river.

* Eden Hall, Cumberland, the seat of Sir George Musgrave.

and in whose manners I observed much of that confident familiarity which I think I have observed in the people of the North. It was here, if I am not mistaken, Mr. Burke's bedroom was adjoining to mine, and that I apprehend that he must have overheard me singing. I went to bed in great spirits.

22nd.—Kirby Lonsdale.—We passed through several pleasant villages, one particularly at the foot of that high hill mentioned in the books, and talked of as the highest in England. We entered Yorkshire in that part which is called the Craven, a singular country, rich in pasture, and naked in trees.

23rd.—Skipton.—We went to see the castle, which is a venerable pile, belonging to Lord Thanet and kept by him from decay and dilapidation, capable of habitation, though not in the condition of a house inhabited. The day was dreadfully rainy, and in walking up a severe hill of some miles in length, I got so completely wet as to be obliged the next stage to yield to Burke's solicitations, to take brandy to my boots and breeches, though not to my stomach.

Wentworth.—Here we found Lord G. Cavendish and Lord Frederick with Sinclair and some company from York.

24th.—In the morning I went with great eagerness into the library, and enjoyed there very strongly all that feel, that a library usually excites. A message from Lord Fitzwilliam obliged me soon to leave it, who proposed my accompanying him, Lady Fitzwilliam and Lord George, in a drive round the grounds. I should have been better pleased to stay where I was. I examined in the library with Mr. Burke some passages in Bede, relative to the state of Ireland in his time, which are far, however, from supporting Mr. B.'s opinion to the extent in which he stated it, and consulted Stephens and A. Gellius on the meaning of the word, about which Mr. B.

was wrong. He contended that in the passage of Cicero, '*Gratiosi erant in dando et cedendo loco*,' it was not to be understood in the English sense of the word, but meant that from the magnitude of the favour, they acquired consequence and authority.

25*th*.—Breakfasted at Sheffield. Found myself looking at everything with the eye of a stranger. The town situated upon ground very unequal, dirty, as must be supposed; great marks of opulence, both within and without. At Derby I got some dinner—a large inn on the left hand side, the first time of my being in the town since I was there with Byng and Cholmondeley; much struck with the beauty of the country, for a stage or two before I arrived; town I think very handsome,

26*th*.—I cannot recollect what book I had, but conceive Dalzell's 'Collectanea.' From Atherstone I went to Coventry; stopped at the same inn and looked in to the same room that I was in on my return from Ireland. At Woodstock I accepted the invitation of King, and slept for the night, passing the evening not unpleasantly, though feeling for the first time after a long interval a return of *sensation*. Mention was made of Knight,* and of his proficiency in the study of Greek, though taken up late.

The conversation impressed me deeply with a sense of my own neglect and excited strong resolutions to retrieve them.

27*th*.—Arrived in Oxford to breakfast; called first upon Burgess and Winstanley,† at All Souls'; on Croft, Dr. Stinton, &c.

Thus ended my tour, in the same place from which it began, after an absence of just seven weeks, one day and a few hours.

* Payne Knight, a Greek scholar.

† Dr. Thomas Winstanley, D.D., Camden Professor of Ancient History.

MISCELLANEA ON TOUR.

'Burke's idea of the application of the character of 'Æneas to Augustus, as a person who kept his passion 'for women in subjection to his politics, and was con-'trasted in that respect to Anthony.

'His general criticisms on the book, where Æneas in-'troduces himself to Evander.

'The parallelisms of Virgil: always figurative, his 'verse slow—an idea of a prose style, that might be 'formed from Virgil, of what sort I did not well un-'derstand.

'Johnson and L'Estrange, the extremes of the English 'style.

'Every man has some little corner in his mind which 'he reserves for meanness—a slut's hole.

'Rather be turned out on the India Bill, than on the 'Prince of Wales's business; rather be drowned in the 'Ganges, than be wrecked on the harbourless coast of 'Wales.

'Lord Lovat's remark upon Sir Everet Fawkener, 'when he came to give evidence against him—"both 'their heads in a bad way."

'To some man who was with him when one of the 'rabble called out "to see the old villain,"—"Which of 'us does he mean?"'

October 3rd.—I stayed at Fulham, except for a night or two, till the time of my intended journey into Norfolk. I should do well to recollect how ill I was,or how much at least my illness, such as it was, rendered me incapable of employment, that I may learn to improve with diligence the advantages of health and neglect no reasonable means by which those advantages may be preserved.

Mrs. Siddons to Mr. Windham.

Half-past nine, Monday Night, October 31, 1785.

Dear Sir,—I am shocked and mortified beyond measure at the spiteful accident which has deprived me of the pleasure of seeing you. What have you thought of me; I can't bear the idea. I was out yesterday when your kind letter arrived, and have not been permitted to see it till this moment; the servant put it this instant into my hand, and it is now nine o'clock. He begs ten thousand pardons for having forgotten to deliver it to me before, but, notwithstanding all his humility and penitence, I am obliged to muster all my forbearance to resist scolding him most furiously. The King commands 'Measure for Measure,' next Wednesday, and I am to play 'Mrs. Lovemore'* this week, which will keep me constantly employed till it is over. So that if you will not have the goodness to call on Sunday, if you should happen to stay in town, I shall think myself a very unfortunate woman. If I had not received the letters you were so good as to favour me with, I should not have needed, as you so modestly suppose, to have been reminded of you, and this you know. I thank you for them most sincerely, and should have acknowledged the honour you did me had I known where to address you. If I had imagined you remained in town at this unfashionable season, I should most certainly have made frequent enquiries about your health. I was extremely sorry to hear you had been ill. In the hope that we shall meet before you go (and God knows whether we ever may afterwards on this side the grave),

I remain, dear Sir,
Your most obliged and obedient humble servant,

S. Siddons.

November 25th.—Left London, and arrived at Horsley's, having been put back the night before by the singular fog, which so blinded the road from Whitechapel that no carriages could go faster than a foot's pace; and of those advancing at that rate, most were preceded by lanterns; we could so little keep the road, that in the small distance be-

* In the play of 'The Way to Keep Him,' by Murphy.

tween the end of the stones, and a few yards beyond the turnpike, one of the horses was twice in the ditch, and the carriage near overset. I had drunk tea on my way out of town, with Dr. Scott, and at my return went to Duke Street. Part of our conversation at Dr. Scott's was on the case in which he was concerned, of the smuggler, who being himself on shore, had shot a man in the water. I had settled my own mind on the case, and the principles on which it must be determined, viz. that in reality the fact was committed in no one place, and that it must depend on analogy and construction of other cases, and on expediency, which part of the fact the jurisdiction must follow; this I had settled in my own mind, and I believe rightly, but in talking the matter over with him I argued it most vilely.

December 13*th*.—Returned to Norwich. My thoughts during the drive were employed in settling the question relative to the pressure of fluids.

14*th*.—From Aylsham in the morning; Adey and I rode in most pleasant weather to Holt, this being the day of the annual meeting of the trustees. During the ride home with G. Wyndham,* &c., the fineness of the night and the freshness of the air gave me a feel of youthful spirits not often experienced, even in youthful times.

From this time to the remainder of the month, I continued constantly at Felbrigg; so that here may be concluded the Journal of the year 1785.

* G. Wyndham, of Cromer Hall.

1786.

January 11*th*.—Left Felbrigg, after having been there, with little interruption, since December 3rd. The weather during the greater part of the time severe and bad; the ground deep in snow and the sky often not clear: the cold in the house such as to make me restless and uncomfortable.

Of the manner in which my time was spent there some more particular account should be found than in the preceding journal: upon the whole, it was very diligently employed, and very successfully. As usual, the amount of what was done did not equal what was proposed; but I cannot much charge the deficiency upon any failure of my own pains or powers. The part most omitted was translation. I tried for the interval before my going to Norwich, viz. for about ten days, the disposition of my time by rule, part of which was that I would be in my room by eight, and open the day, excepting in a few cases, with mathematics.

The success, both of my adherence to the rule and of the rule itself, was such as to encourage a repetition of the method. There was a difficulty in the management of the evenings. If I went to the Parsonage after dinner, which was the time least advantageously spent at home, I did not willingly return to tea, which was the time to be spent at home with most advantage. I got into a method at last, to be adopted, I think, on future occasions, particularly in winter, of going to the Parsonage to sleep. Though the pleasure is lost by these means, of that idle reading which may succeed the studies of the day, yet company, perhaps, never comes so seasonably as at the close of an evening, either for the enjoyment it produces, or for its effect on the mind, both before and after.

13*th*.—What happened during my stay at Norwich, don't particularly recollect. I lodged at Mr. Taylor's.

Rainham, 16*th*.—Company at Rainham, besides Miss Montgomery, Paxton, Mr. Perceval * and Mr. Chute. Perceval a young lawyer, and from his quickness and acuteness likely, I should think, to be some time or other a distinguished man.

18*th*.—Set out for Holkham. Drive not unpleasant; feel of great satisfaction on my arrival, which was not rendered less by the circumstance of arriving in the midst of the audit.

During the whole of my stay here I enjoyed myself very much; in this enjoyment the house itself had no small share. Of the modes of existence that vary from day to day, none is to me more pleasing than habitation in a large house. Besides the pleasure it affords from the contemplation of elegance and magnificence, the objects it presents, and the images it gives birth to, there is no other situation in which the enjoyment of company is united with such complete retirement. A cell in a convent is not a place of greater retirement than a remote apartment in such a house as Holkham.

Accordingly, during my stay there, I have read more than I have done in the same number of days in places to which I have retired to read. The easy transition from company to study gained to employment many hours which, by coming in portions too small to admit of any reduction, must in other situations have been thrown aside as useless.

The pond at the back of the house was frozen for two

* Afterwards the Right Hon. Spencer Perceval, who became Prime Minister in 1809, and was shot by Bellingham in 1812.

days so as to bear, and the ice was so clear and the weather so pleasant, that all the pleasures which solitary skating can give existed in great perfection.

21*st.*—Rode after breakfast, and on one of Hoste's horses, to Rainham. Before I set out, went for the first time into the library on the top, which I had heard of when I was last there, and forgot again. The room and the collection answered fully to my expectation, and give a pleasing impression of the use that might be made of it, and the comfort enjoyed in it, by any literary chaplain belonging to the family.

At Rainham, in the room of Mr. Chute and Mr. Perceval, there was a Captain Beauchamp, of Lord Townshend's regiment, a brother of Sir T. Beauchamp and an acquaintance of Symmons.

22*nd.*—Set off before breakfast with Frederick Townshend, who was going, like myself, though on a different footing, to Cambridge. Journey not unpleasant. I read a good deal; among other things, part of Keill's 'Treatise on Trigonometry,' which Townshend was taking with him to Cambridge.

23*rd.*—Spent with Symmons, in Cambridge. Went to see Clare Hall Chapel and Trinity Library: the former newly fitted up, and in wrong taste, in my opinion. Sat a quarter of an hour with the Bishop of Peterborough. In the evening Symmons had to tea with him three gownsmen, one was of Clare Hall, an intelligent man and competitor of Dr. Prettyman, when the latter was junior optimé. I was troubled during the evening with something of fever.

24*th.*—Went to London by the Barkway Road; dined at Ware.

This was the day of Parliament meeting. Doubted between going to the House or to Brookes's; determined, after a little deliberation, both as a commencement of good and a departure from former habits, to spend the evening at home. What my employment was, I don't for certain recollect, but I think it was mathematical; I know, not unsatisfactory.

London, 28*th*.—On the day before, but I think on the 28th, went to Horsley's. This was the time of Horsley's showing me his argument, drawn up in the form of a demonstration, to prove that motion cannot originate in an extended substance. The former part, on which he did not profess to lay much stress, seemed to me completely inconclusive, even in the form of it; the other part, which he seemed to think conclusive, I did not examine with equal attention, but suspect that, like other arguments of the same sort, its cogency would be found, on a close inspection, to amount to very little. An argument introduced in the course of it, against an infinite series, as a thing infinitely impossible, because each succession was impossible, being an effect without a cause, seemed to me completely sophistical: it is sufficient to show its inaccuracy, that it admits the idea of a gradation of impossibility. In all these reasonings, people seem to forget that the demonstration will never be produced by the mere form of the reasoning. If the matter be brass, though you mould it for ever, it will never become gold.

During one of the mornings of my stay, I had a pleasant walk over the encampment.

February.—Of the whole of this month I can give no other account than that it was passed in town, and that it was probably during this period that I said what little I have said this session in the House. The instances of such exertions have been as few in number as the exertions themselves have been inconsiderable. That on the Ordnance was the principal, both in the quantity produced, and still more in what was prepared. Besides that, I don't recollect that I opened my lips, except on three occasions: the seconding Francis's motion; the reply to what Wilberforce said in answer to Burke; and, the other night, on

Major Marsack's evidence on the Ordnance business. When Sheridan made a motion, I said half a dozen words in seconding the motion. This has been the extent of my oratory in this my third session.

March.—The chief event that I recollect of this month is my going to Pytchley. I set off on Sunday, having been the night before to the opera, for the first time this year. The King was there, after a long interval; and the house being uncommonly full, the gaiety of the scene struck me forcibly. I went to sup at the Bellinghams': stayed till late, in good spirits, but distressed rather from not having determined positively to go. The next morning I set off: arrived at Pytchley about eight o'clock.

The company there, Lord Winchelsea, Lord Spencer, Damer, Conyers, and Lord Cathcart, who came down the same day; Isted, Assheton Smith, Harry Churchill, and afterwards Northey. Doughty did not come till the next day. The weather was very delightful, and we hunted the next morning. I rode Doughty's horse, Nobbs, and when we went out in the morning, and for some time afterwards, was foolish enough to entertain doubts of the sufficiency of my horsemanship. We had a day delightful for the weather, and sport sufficient for my powers and wishes. Littleton Powys was in the field, and Hanbury, with whom I renewed my acquaintance.

The next day I went to Lord John Cavendish's, whom I had met the day before. The morning following, I had determined upon returning to town, in order to attend the motion of Dundas for the alteration of the India Bill; on which occasion I had made up my mind to speak. The beauty of the morning, and the distrust of my resolution (should I return) to fulfil what was the purpose of my returning, determined me to accept Lord John's offer and go out a hunting. I continued during every part of the day to think that I had decided rightly, and the event, though it added nothing to the rectitude of the determination, gave me still further reason to be satisfied with myself.

The next day I left him, later perhaps than was necessary and fancied therefore that I could not conveniently get further than St. Albans, where, after some deliberation previous to my arrival, I resolved upon staying for the night. The next morning I rose early, and breakfasting at Barnet, got to town about twelve.

May 1*st*.—Elliot* came in time to partake of my dinner and we set off, after some small delay only, about six o'clock. At Epping Place we drank tea. At Hockrill the people were not gone to bed and we stepped, while the chaise was preparing, into the kitchen. I don't think we began to sleep till towards Chesterford. I felt myself little disposed to sleep at all, partly in consequence of the benefit found from the air, and partly from being amused with the topics we had talked upon: we had a great deal of foreign wars and foreign politics. It was about three or four, I apprehend, when we reached Newmarket; and a good deal after, before we had contrived, by the aid of chaise, cushions, and horsecloths, to make our beds.

2*nd*.—The circumstances of the fight, which was the object of our excursion, need not be recorded. The winner's name was Humphries (Richard, I think); and the butcher's, Sam Martin. The man, by the way, of whom I won my bet, but of whom I probably may not get payment, was Young. The spectacle was upon the whole very interesting, by the qualities, both of mind and body, which it exhibited. Nothing could afford a finer display of character than the conduct and demeanour of Humphries, and the skill discovered far exceeded what I had conceived the art to possess. The mischief done could

* Right Hon. W. Elliot, Chief Secretary for Ireland in 1806.

not have affected the most tender humanity. After the battle we proceeded to the race, and from thence to Cambridge. Symmons spent the evening with us.

May 12*th*.—Went late in the evening with Lawrence to Burke's. By a very foolish determination of mine, stopped to sleep at Uxbridge, though I might have known, and it proved afterwards, that everything was prepared for our reception that night.

14*th*.—Returned to town in order to dine with Cholmondeley, Lord and Lady Harcourt, Lady Anne* and Lady Margaret,† Mrs. Siddons, Stonehewer, and R. Boothby. Went afterwards with Lady Anne and Lady Margaret to Miss Monckton's, where it was expected Mrs. Jordan would have come. Felt, when going home, in a particular good disposition to study.

20*th*.—Dined with Crewe and Mrs. Crewe. Present, Pelham, D. Long, Munday, H. Greville, Lord Edward Fitzgerald.

21*st*.—Went to Mr. Burke's, in order to meet Messrs. Dillon, sons of the Archbishop, Lady Jerningham's uncle. The elder was an ecclesiastic; the other, though not more than twenty-two, had served during the greater part of the American War. The younger spoke English with great facility, and the elder very remarkably for a man who had never been in England before. I went down in my phaeton.

22*nd*.—Went with Pelham and Harrison to the House, where the business was the conclusion of Middleton's evidence. Finding there was no wrangling, and therefore no necessity for staying, came home.

23*rd*.—Stayed at home till I went to the House to attend the Carlisle Committee. Doubts whether I was not

* Lady Anne Lindsay, daughter of the Earl of Balcarras, married to Andrew Barnard, Esq.

† Lady Margaret Lindsay, married to Alexander Fordyce, Esq.

to be nominee. Walked from thence to Sir Joshua's: found Duke of Hamilton and Lady —— together. Walked with Sir Joshua to the Club.

24th.—My employment was some matters in De Moivre.

25th.—Some Irish tunes, from an organ which we had at the door, gave me those sensations of happiness which music sometimes inspires me with, and which I hardly know from anything else.

June 1st.—Day of motion on the Rohilla War. Ordered my servant to meet me at the House of Commons, meaning to proceed from thence to Fulham. Luckily, just before I stepped into the carriage, I considered whether it would not be better to pass the night in town, for the sake of information I might gain at Brookes's on the business of the next day.

I there got from Long the report of the Secret Committee, in which I found great advantage, and settled to come the next morning to Francis to breakfast. I have seldom found myself more clear than during my visit to him, and afterwards, till I went to the House: but somehow, by the time I got there, my mind had got into some disorder, and my spirits into some agitation; and by the time Burke had finished, I found myself in no good state to speak. The same state continued, though with a little amendment, till the time of my rising: yet I contrived somehow to steady and recover myself in the course of speaking, and so far executed what I had prepared, that I conceive it to be fashion to talk of what I did as rather a capital performance. 'Tis a strong proof on what cheap terms reputation for speaking is acquired, or how capricious the world is of its allotment of it to different people. There is not a speech of mine which, in comparison of one of Francis's, would, either for language or matter, bear examination for one moment; yet about my performances in that way a great fuss is made, while of his nobody speaks a word.*

The House adjourned about three o'clock. Burke took me to walk in the Park; not much against my will, though I was more disposed, and it would have been better for me, to have gone home. It was about five when I got to bed.

2nd.—Obliged to go by twelve to a meeting about the wool, at the 'Crown and Anchor.' A good deal affected by the fatigue of the preceding evening. Tempted to speak on an incidental point in the debate, and succeeded so ill, where I think I might have succeeded so well, that any pleasant feeling derived from the preceding evening was completely done away, and a degree of vexation subsisted more than was becoming even for a greater degree of failure than might possibly have been the case: I am afraid that what I said was awkwardly and cumbrously stated. The House did not break up till near seven, and I, having supped at Brookes's and walked afterwards with Fox, did not get home till about ten. Went out with Mrs. Lukin in the phaeton; returned home through Grosvenor Square, where Cholmondeley came to the window, but I would not stop, restrained chiefly by the consideration that it would look like a desire of hearing of my speech: for the same reason I continued at home during the remainder of the evening.

3rd.—I had set out with my head very clear: I found afterwards, from whatever cause, that I was not likely to succeed well in the work I had proposed, viz. Masères, Hutton, &c., and took the opportunity, therefore, of looking over some parts of Voltaire's works, particularly his tract on the 'Civil Wars,' which I read with unusual satisfaction. Dinner was brought early, and after dinner,

* The 'Francis' repeatedly mentioned by Mr. Windham with so much friendship and respect was 'Sir Philip Francis,' to whom the authorship of the 'Letters of Junius' is now confidently ascribed.

possibly from having in some small degree eat too much, I went to sleep. When I waked and was deliberating how to dispose of myself, it occurred to me to ride to Francis's, to whom I meant to have sent before I left town, that is, to have left orders for sending. My feel on arrival was sufficiently pleasant to make me regret that the thought of going there had not occurred sooner. A little persuasion induced me to stay the night.

4th.—Though I dined moderately, I was not able to apply to any other work than the reading Claudian; till, after walking to Kent's, I continued well employed in settling questions relative to the application of the doctrine of chances to cases of suffrage.—*Vide* 'Adv.' p. 49.

7th.—Dined at Sir G. Cornewall's and went to the play. Mrs. Siddons did 'Rosalind' much better than the first time, but not equal to her tragedy: there is a want of hilarity in it; it is just, but not easy. The highest praise that can be given to her comedy is, that it is the perfection of art; but her tragedy is the perfection of nature.

8th.—Dined at home. In the evening went to the Duke of Bolton's and Lady Howe's: did not come home till near four. The light let in at Lady Howe's windows, and the sight of Hyde Park, destroyed all the inebriation of a midnight amusement.

23rd.—Bartlet Gurney had called in the morning about the Bill on Stamps affecting the country bankers. The bill being withdrawn, I was in time to dine with Langton.

24th.—Water-party to Dagenham Reach: Lord and Lady Palmerston, Sir Gilbert Elliot, Mrs. Crewe. Supped at Lord Palmerston's, and came away about one. The whole very pleasant: the first party on the Thames I ever recollect to have been in.

25th.—In my walk from Brookes's I think I was stopped in the street by Peter Bath.

26th.—Went to the House of Commons, where the business was such as very little justified the summons that occasioned my attendance. It was issued, I presume, for the purpose of procuring an audience for Sheridan. After loitering with great impatience in and about the House, went with Fitzpatrick into the court to attend poor Sadler's trial, which he lost by a great preponderance of proof. Whether produced by the merits of the case, or by corrupt practices on the other side, I don't feel quite prepared to say.

27*th.*—Went to De Meinaduc:—Mrs. Crewe, Lady Palmerston; afterwards Miss Crewe, and Mrs. Sheridan, and General Burgoyne. The quackery too gross to need the confirmation of his declining to try it on me.

30*th.*—Did not go out, except to Desenfans' Exhibition, till I set off for Wilberforce's. Present: Sir G. Elliot, Chev. Revel, Mulgrave, and two Cambridge friends of Wilberforce's, — Romilly and Baynes, I think. Very pleasant.

July 1*st.*—Set off in my phaeton for Burke's, whither I was to go by invitation to meet a party. In a few miles overtook General Smith and D. Long.

We arrived all rather too late. Present: Mrs. Crewe, Fox, Sir J. Erskine, Mr. Griffiths, Lord Inchiquin, Adey.

It is very odd that I cannot recollect whether D. Burke, junior, was there; he was the next day I know; but I don't remember him in the discussion on an arithmetical matter started by D. Long.

2*nd.*—At dinner, Sir G. Elliot. Fox gone I returned into my room a short time before dinner, and proceeded with some success in Masères, which I was reading over again; added considerably to the strength of some good resolutions.

3*rd.*—Set off about twelve for Oxford, on horseback. Ride to Tedsworth; spirits gay; thoughts shamefully idle. Dined comfortably at Tedsworth, and should have arrived at Oxford pleasantly enough, if, in riding up Shotover to ease the horses in the carriage, my horse had not taken me by surprise, and turning violently round, and kicking upon being struck with the spur, thrown me off with a good deal of force. Though I was bruised a little, and made very sick, I should not have found myself so uncomfortable as I did, if I had not in some measure charged the fall as my own fault. I certainly fell at last from consenting to fall; yet I am not sure that I did unwisely and think, I am sure enough, that I was not frightened. What, perhaps, made me most uncomfortable was, the feeling that if I had been hurt as much by a blow and fall in boxing,—which was a subject one had been talking of not long before, with the same apprehension, too, of possible serious hurt,—how little inclination at heart I should have felt to continue the combat. I felt that if I had stood up, it would merely have been from fear of shame, and that all the ardour of combat would have left me. I argued, that if such could be the effects of pain so slight and danger so unlikely, what might happen in trials really severe? I hope in this, as in other cases, one should do better than, by inference from smaller things, one should suppose. The impression, however, destroyed the pleasure I should have had in arriving at Oxford. At the Star, I found Knight, who, in a conversation with Burgess, who supped with us, showed a knowledge of Greek literature, chiefly in what related to the antiquities of the language, that reminded me of my own deficiencies. In the course of conversation afterwards, his general powers did not seem to correspond to his particular attainments.

4th.—Called in the morning on Burgess, and spent some time in Corpus Library, the first time of my being there. At twelve we set off, Knight and I, to Woodstock, where we were disappointed in our hopes of meeting King, but passed some time not unpleasantly in seeing the grounds at Blenheim. I supped, at my return, in the common room at University, where was Dr. Croft and one or two young men. Slept at the lodging which I had directed to be taken for me at St. Giles's.

10*th.*—Went into Fisher's rooms. The difference of comfort not to be mistaken. Though I had resisted manfully, during my stay in lodgings, the effect of place not combined with disturbance, yet it soon appeared that such circumstances as a small difference in quiet, an exposure somewhat greater to the sight of moving objects, something less of privacy, and the general character of the objects around, less connected with the ideas of study and comfort, had an effect too important to be overlooked or neglected, both upon the temper of my mind and the disposition of my time.

17*th.*—The morning before last rose earlier than my usual time, after a night not restless but rather wakeful, and all morning felt an unusual flow of spirits and activity of faculties. Yesterday morning I lay later than usual, and, instead of the feeling above mentioned, was troubled with a slight headache. This morning, after a night much like that described above, I rose very early, and, after struggling for three-quarters of an hour with languor and uncomfortableness, suffered myself to lie down again, and slept tolerably comfortably and without much interruption for two hours. Upon my rising I felt certainly more *vegetus* and active, than before, and continue pretty much so at present. These observations are detailed for the purpose of settling, by a collection of such instances, what that management of sleep is, that most suits one's constitution, and is, of consequence, most conducive to health and spirits.

18*th.*—Left Oxford. The last week since my coming into Fisher's rooms was one of the most comfortable I remember to have passed for a long while. When one considers what the effect might have been of a month spent at that rate, it is a satisfaction to think that the experiment was hardly in my power.

Surtees was in college, and Dr. Croft, who had come there to print his 'Bampton Sermons.'

In the morning I breakfasted with Royd, who had come the night before, and joined us in the common room, where I was supping as a sort of leave-taking: in general I had been in the practice of supping in my own room. Before I set out, I bought of Fletcher a little treatise just published by Ludlam, which I read with considerable diligence till my arrival at Caversham a little before dinner. Pen and Miss Riches were out. There were in the house Dr. Loveday and Mr. Bagshaw. Company to dinner, Mr. Powney, whom I had never seen before: he has an odd sort of humour that I was far from displeased with. The effect of time spent in solitary application was perceivable upon this occasion, and I felt in myself considerable difficulty of talking.

20th. — Arrived at Fulham by dinner. Had nearly finished, during the drive, the treatise ascribed to Demetr. Phalereus, of which Burgess had furnished me with a copy newly published in Holland or Germany. Few instances where I have read so long and so attentively. For the last stage, took to the treatise above mentioned of Ludlam. Difficult to repel regret for former waste of time, in which so much might have been done.

21st.—Went in the morning to town, having reason to think that Sir Harbord* had obtained his peerage.

22nd.—From this time I remained constantly at Fulham, excepting two days, as appears by migrations, till the 8th of August. One of the times I dined at Serle's, and the other when I dined at Lord Frederick Cavendish's. At the former dinner were present, Phipps, the Attorney-General, Mr. Atherton, a Mr. Trail, and Woodcock; at the other, Lord Bessborough, Lord G. Cavendish, jun., D. Long and his brother, and Baker.

* Sir Harbord Harbord was created a peer in 1786 by the title of Lord Suffield.

Another day I had been absent, having gone to dine with Sir Joshua at Fulham. This was the Sunday preceding the Eton Speeches, at which, probably, I should have done more wisely to have been present. The days that I particularly remember to have been in town were the 21st and 22nd, as mentioned. The day of my going to the Custom House, viz. the 1st of August, the day on which I was to have dined at Malone's, but went instead to a boxing-match.—N.B. Walked that day a great deal, in weather more than commonly hot, and found in myself, in the evening, unusual clearness of faculties and activity of spirits.

The morning in which I went with Sheldon to town by water, and in my way to the Commons, if I recollect, called in at Elmsley's, and spent some time very satisfactorily in looking into Condorcet, and Bernouilli's comparison, I think, of the reasoning by syllogism and by equation.

August 8th.—Instead of going to town early, as I had proposed, stayed till near three. The lateness of the hour created the necessity of a new road, by going across to Paddington without passing through London. My path led me close to Holland House, and afterwards, by a slight deflection, through Kensington Gardens. The walk afforded much of that pleasure which results from familiar objects seen under new appearances. After a fortnight's absence, one begins again to think of these places with complacency.

9th.—Dined with Sir Joshua. I did not feel disposed to talk much till after tea. Subject started about chance, on which Sir Joshua was teaching his grandmother to suck eggs, by beginning himself with an addled one.

Walked to Burke's, and in the way thought of the question: under the stimulus of a dispute, incited to think with effect of that which, for want of such an incentive, had been presented a thousand times before my thoughts without ever being brought to a decision. Remained to supper, where were only Malone, Courtenay, Boswell, and myself. After I went home, faculties so clear and active, that I did not for some time go to sleep, but continued thinking with considerable power and good effect on the question, Reflection on the advantages of good society. Oh! where is Dr. Johnson?

10*th.*—Sir Joshua, Courtenay, and Malone dined with me. Too much dispute, but pleasant, resulting in some shape, and to some degree, from forbearance of causes which had rendered me less pleasant the day before.

13*th.*—After a morning of much mixed employment of mind and hands, set off reading a book I had just purchased, 'Hartley on Mind.' My destination was Horsley's.

15*th.*—What little I read was in Robins'* 'Treatise on Fluxions.' Read, too, Wilson's 'History of Navigation,' prefixed to 'Robertson's Works,' from which I learnt, among other things that I have forgot, that Willis and Briggs were originally of Cambridge; so that it would seem that Halley was the only eminent mathematician grown from the seed in Oxford. Keill had probably laid the foundation of his mathematics in Scotland.

16*th.*—Drive from Bury to Thetford in the dark: very pleasant. Thought closely and successfully on the principle which Sir Joshua fancies himself to have made out of the beauty of a circle: causes, certain or possible, numerous; that which he supposes he does not understand, and amounts to little when it is understood. After arrival at Thetford, wrote tolerably long letter, and satisfactory one, to Sir W. Jerningham. What an account of myself! How inexplicable to anyone not in the secrets of my mind, that the power of writing such a letter in reasonable time, and with tolerable facility, should be new, and matter to be recorded!

* B. Robins published a discourse concerning the certainty of Sir I. Newton's method of Fluxions and of prime and ultimate Ratios in 1735.

17*th.*—Journey pleasant, though observation employed a good deal on objects about me; faculties clear. After dining at Holt, arrived at Felbrigg about seven, I apprehend, when I found a letter to be answered from Norgate: wrote a few lines to Repton also, which I afterwards burnt. In Gresham Field* I got out of the chaise, and walked the remainder of the way, much pleased with the appearance of objects, and viewing them with the eye of a stranger.

September 1*st.*—Stay at Felbrigg commences.

After some consideration, it appears to me that a period such as the present, in which events are too few to keep a journal constantly going, and what is noted is more matter of reflection than of fact, the account is best kept by entering articles as they occur, without regarding much the order of time. The inconvenience of the contrary method is, that articles cannot be entered as they occur, for fear of others that may remain of a prior date, and claiming of consequence to be entered first. This will oftener happen in proportion as the journal is resumed at longer intervals, and includes facts less distinguished by consideration of their dates. It doesn't appear either, that to the method now recommended much objection will arise from the want of that, which is the principal advantage of the chronological method—the readiness, namely, of finding any fact required, since it is proposed only to follow this way, in periods certainly defined, and not widely extended.

2*nd.*—From half-past eight, when I came into my own room, till twelve, employed (except during the time of breakfast, when I looked into Valla and Voss's 'Etymology') in translation; my attention not quite steady nor my progress great. Dined by myself, and read with much

* The village of Gresham, about three miles from Felbrigg, was the birthplace of Sir Thomas Gresham; and the remains of old Gresham Castle are still to be seen.

satisfaction some extracts in an old Review of '54, I think, from a Life of Sextus Fifth. At five, came into my room, and, though rather tired, wrote a longish letter to Mrs. Byng. Drank tea at Doughtys'. Came home with them. Riding a little in the park by moonlight. Wrote a long letter to Norgate on Custom House business.

9th.—Cromer sittings on Friday; Sherringham on Saturday. At the Aylsham Assembly was Lady Belmore* who had just returned from a long residence at Paris. I am now resuming Masères, after an intermission of, I believe, very near a week. Dined at Lord Suffield's; came straight home.

10th.—From employment and the lightness of the atmosphere, felt languid. Galloped about the park. Interrupted by a messenger from Norwich: formal requisition for my attendance; answer, an indirect refusal, expressed pretty much to my satisfaction. 'Tis curious that those who are thus forward to make use of me are the very persons who, in defiance of their own express assurances, would not advance a sixpence toward the expense of my election, though the object of it was infinitely more theirs than the present one is mine. I think this transaction determines pretty much what I should do about going; and I will go on the morning of the 11th, and not before.

12th.—From eight till nine, closely employed on Masères; from nine to past ten, in like manner with Valla; from that time till now (one) not less closely with Masères. I have not read more than two papers, if so much, of the 'Rambler' since my being down here. Dined at Wolterton on my return: found Kent in the steward's room, and a messenger from Norwich, by whom I was obliged to send a few lines, which cost me too much trouble.

13th.—Had another messenger, my answers by whom, joined to some business in the steward's room, took me

* Harriet, daughter of John Earl of Buckinghamshire; married, first, the Earl of Belmore, and, second, William Marquis of Lothian.

up till near dinner. Letter not unsatisfactory, nor unsatisfactorily written. Great enjoyment of my dinner, and after with Hunt, Hicks, George, and afterwards Adey.

17*th.*—Just returned from Norwich, half-past one. Must return to-morrow in order to be at Sheriff Paterson's dinner and the Assembly. Of the public proceedings of the election, it is not necessary to take any notice. The only observation for this place is, that I did not keep my own thoughts under such control during the time as I might have done, nor preserve sufficient attention to what was proper at every moment to say or do. Had I so done, I should have quitted Norwich sooner by several hours, and by those means have put myself still further from the suspicion of having had any share in the manœuvre of putting up Mr. Buxton.* I do not apprehend, indeed, that anyone will impute it to me.

18*th.*—Since my return from Norwich yesterday, have read in Plutarch the life of Aristides, the only work I have done. I must now (ten o'clock) dress, to set off for Norwich again.

20*th.*—Came from Aylsham, where I had slept. Day uncommonly fine, and spirits uncommonly good. I had a song in my head, which I had heard at the dinner of the day before, descriptive of a fox-chase at some place near Anglesea, as I conceived, and which carried my thoughts into that part of the world, attended with a feel of enjoyment which I seldom know. As these moments of happiness depend often on causes subject to our own direction, it is worth while to enquire what they are, and take such means as may bring them into action. On my arrival at home, I did what was most proper, and sat down to Thuanus, but was interrupted before long, and not unpleasantly, by Lady Buckinghamshire, driving through the park, with whom I rode to Cromer, and con-

* Robert John Buxton, of Shadwell Lodge, Norfolk, created a baronet in 1800.

tinued to attend till half-past three. Well employed till sleep obliged me to go to bed. It occurs to me upon this occasion, that that foolish feel or notion by which one part of a day used to be sacrificed to another, and all power lost of terminating a neglect once begun, has for a long time ceased to operate. I don't recollect that for many times back of my being at Felbrigg, I have ever loitered away a whole evening as I used to do at Hanworth or the Parsonage.

25th.—Visit in the morning from the Bishop, who rode over with Mr. Gooch. Read after they were gone two stories in Boccaccio, with my mind greatly engaged. At twelve o'clock I ordered my horses, to ride to Cromer. Day uncommonly pleasant. Returned about one: sat down to translation. After that, went with Kent to settle things in the park. Just as we were about to return to dinner, saw Legge's chaise coming down Alymerton Common.

26th.—Instances of days, passed like the two last, incline one to look with great admiration at those, who in situations not affording them, to all appearance, a moment to themselves, are able to produce all the works of retirement. Since the arrival of Legge, yesterday till now, past nine in the evening, what opportunity appears to have been lost! yet what step has been taken in study of any kind? I have neither had time to fix in my mind any mathematical question, to sit down to translation, nor to read ten pages of any book I have in hand. Something, however, might yet have been done, and, in fact, has not been altogether omitted, that something which is the cause of the phenomenon above alluded to, which is one of the main desiderata in the management of the mind. It will be well when such advance shall have been made in the discipline of thought, that times, spent as I have described these to be, shall not be lost in improvement. It is some evidence of the good habits in which my life has been passed lately, that an interruption to study such as the present, does not occur without becoming a subject of observation.

27*th.*—After breakfast I went to dress, having been too late to do so before. By the time that was over, I had a summons from Kent to attend the cutting some wood. From thence till dinner was employed in walking and riding with Legge. All the time since has been passed in the library, partly in talk, partly in meditation, neither very instructive, yet not wholly without amusement. I now feel rather impatient of three days wholly lost to any useful pursuit.

28*th.*—Went with Legge to Norwich. We rode by Hanworth, Wolterton, and Blickling; and from Aylsham proceeded in a chaise. Very pleasant. Saw some of the families at each place: at Blickling, Lady Belmore, Lady Caroline,* and Lady Sophia,† dancing.

I am surprised often and shocked at my deficiency in computatory habits. I might console myself, possibly, if I could have before me all the time, employed in any part of my life, in acquiring those habits. I can now believe, what it is my interest to believe, that notwithstanding the attention, which I have always paid indirectly to those subjects, the real time spent in the exercise of them, would make but a poor figure, in comparison of that of any pupil in his third year at an academy.

30*th.*—The time passed at the Bishop's,‡ where I had a bed for the first time, was very pleasant. I read the greater part of one morning in Reid's 'Inquiry,' and acquired several new ideas. His idea of what he calls the 'geometry of visibles' seems to me ingenious, but in some respects requires examination as to the truth, particularly in the supposition that persons having only the sense of

* Lady Caroline Hobart; married William, second Lord Suffield, 1792.

† Lady Sophia Hobart; married Richard, Earl of Mount Edgecumbe, 1789.

‡ The Bishop of Norwich, Lewis Bagot.

seeing could know only two dimensions: that is, stating the question generally, whether reflection alone might not, from the knowledge of surfaces, give the knowledge of solids.

October 1st.—Wednesday, went to Norwich to the Sessions. Heard from Branthwayte, in the court, that there had been talk about the intended camp. Don't know whether to be glad or sorry that the matter was not brought up. I should have made, I think, a good argument for the thing, and a good philippic against the opposers,—but should have said something, perhaps, harsher than I should have thought creditable.

7th.—The Camp. I forgot to get from Hicks a list of the names.

9th.—Blickling Ball. During my ride to Adey's, where I dined with G. Wyndham, Musgrave, Hyde, and Munro, &c., suffered myself to think on idle things, camping, &c., and thought I was the worse for it. While I was dressing, however, added a line or two to the Latin poem I was meditating, and which, by the way, if I do not commit to paper I shall forget. I must not forget, some time before leaving this, to take an exact account of the quantity done since my arrival, and to make some calculations and reflections thereupon.

16th.—Dined at Wolterton, and stayed the night. The Hanworth party dined and supped there. Lord John came about ten o'clock. Particular feel of satisfaction while sitting in the drawing-room.

21st.—Race in the park. The day not good enough for any ladies except Miss Wyndham.*

23rd.—Dined at Cromer. Had G. Wyndham and P. Johnson† to dine with me. Sat late, talking of nothing but hunting: part of the time not unpleasant, as I found my

* Sister of G. Wyndham, of Cromer.

† Rev. Paul Johnson, of Runton.

mind detained with images of happiness, such as they were.

24*th.*—Sat for some time at the Parsonage: Mrs. Lukin very gay and pleasant. Afterwards, continued till past twelve finishing the life of Lysander.

25*th.*—Got ready to go to Norwich. Was obliged to ride fast to Aylsham; ride not so pleasant as the fineness of the day should have made it. The dinner was at William Herring's, the sheriff—twenty present. Lee took me from thence to the Bishop's, where I accepted their offer of a bed. The pleasant feelings I have had for the two times I have been at the Bishop's will, on the simplest principles of association, become a cause of my being pleasant there again. The Bishop told me, upon coming in, of the curious sermon of Prettyman.

26*th.*—I stayed at the Palace till past eleven. Very pleasant. The Bishop and I had some talk about mathematics, on which I found him an advocate for the Newton opinion about the attention due to geometry. He talked of Cotes as a man who had read Newton too hastily; that is, as projecting new things on old principles, without first considering how far those principles should go of themselves. I have borrowed of him Simson's posthumous works, in order to read the treatise 'De Limitibus,' which is a subject I have reverted to of late, and on which I hope to find my ideas clearer and more certain by this treatise.

November 9*th.*—Dined with Sir Robert Laurie. Came home; went on with my thoughts closely applied to Simson's 'De Limitibus.' Alarming account of the Duke of Portland.

14*th.*—Set out for Swaffham meeting. Went to Holt in my chaise, thence in hack to Fakenham, thence on horseback to Rainham. Company at Rainham, only Paxton. Slept in a room at the head of the brown stairs, very comfortable.

15*th.*—Waked by times in the morning, and thought with good effect of that which had employed me during part of the way, and the day before,—the old question of negative quantity. I should have mentioned, that in my pocket, besides the volume of Livy I had been reading, I took with me the collections of Greek epigrams with translations, and began a version with happy success. After breakfast I retired into my room with the second volume of Sanderson, and went through some that I had read before of the Diaphantine problems, fixing in my mind more clearly, I think, than before, the nature of that kind of proposition. I rode out for a short time, and afterwards found myself engaged to a walk with Lord Townshend to one of his plantations.

16*th.*—Went with the ladies—viz. Lady Townshend, Miss Vanneck, and Miss Montgomerie—to Houghton, for the first time since the pictures have been gone.*

17*th.*—Coursing at Westacre. The second time of my attending such a meeting. I cannot recollect in what year the first was, nor assist myself by recollection of the horse I had.

19*th.*—Having settled in the morning to go home, sent forward my horses, and was obliged, therefore, to adhere to my purpose, which the bad weather that came would have disposed me otherwise to change. It was a fall of rain and snow, with a south-east wind, which continued the whole way, and made my ride, both from the cold and uneasiness of the storm against my face, as unpleasant as any I recollect to have had. I continued, notwithstanding, to keep my mind tolerably well abstracted, and concluded a verse or two in some epigrams I was translating and settled a question about the increments of logarithms, from Sanderson, which had rather puzzled me. Arrived at home about four, having set off at a quarter before one.

* The Houghton pictures were sold by George, third Earl of Orford, to the Empress of Russia in 1799, for £40,555.

After changing my things I got some dinner, and, what is remarkable, though I continued by myself during the evening, did not go to sleep.

The evening was spent in a manner particularly satisfactory.

22*nd.*—At three, when I was preparing to go to Wolterton, Lord John and Walpole came, with whom I returned to dinner. Came away in the evening, and supped in Hanworth.

26*th.*—For some time past I have been in the practice of sitting for a considerable time after I have gone into my bedroom, and generally of reading in the 'Recess,' which I have done with unusual satisfaction.

27*th.*—Interrupted at twelve by justice business. Exercised my horse in the riding-ground, and a little cudgelling with young George. Resolved to leave off Plutarch, which I have been reading, sometimes more diligently, at others less so, for nearly the whole time of my being down. I leave off at the end of the life of Lucullus.

28*th.*—'Organum,' for two or three hours. The morning being apparently fine, and George* calling, I agreed to ride out and join him some time after in the wood, where he was going to shoot woodcocks. As I found my inclination not strong to go out, and the comfort considerable where I was, I congratulated myself on an arrangement which gave me near an hour more in my own room, and debated within myself the wisdom of going out at all. I decided at last, perhaps not very improperly, to go, and after walking my horse an hour in the riding-ground, went with the gardener and settled some things proper enough to be considered.

30*th.*—Yesterday the Doughtys dined here, previous to their setting off to-morrow to Northamptonshire. Felt

* George Lukin, second son of the Dean, then about sixteen years old; a great favourite with his uncle, Mr. Windham, from his love of athletic pursuits and excellent personal appearance.

myself in greater spirits than ordinary: I had indeed, in the morning, a special cause of satisfaction—the having made out a problem, not certainly of great moment, but in a manner that was satisfactory to myself.

December 1*st.*—To go on with the effect of riding, or not riding? To-day, between two and three, went out with my brother, and continued chopping and walking till half-past four. Upon the whole, I am of opinion that at this time of the year, and at such times probably in a great degree, the system of staying at home, is, for the day itself much the best; but whether the same proportion of time spent in the house that would be good for a smaller period, would be good also for a longer, is obviously a different question.

5*th.*—Went to Norwich: slept at Taylor's.

7*th.*—Rode home from Aylsham. Day particularly fine. Employed during ride in translating Greek epigrams. Went to Parsonage, and, finding the weather so fine and the horse so much improved, proposed to Mrs. Lukin to ride.

8*th.*—Employed in various things preparatory to departure. A good while spent in the steward's room. Young George came over after dinner, but I was too sleepy to hear him with effect. Spent all the evening at home: employed chiefly in writing out 'Adversaria' and Diatribes on the law, relative to the business of Colby.

9*th.*—Rode over in great haste, and in a vile morning, to Wolterton, fearing to be too late for my appointment—namely, the examination of the man from Colby. Not so possessed of myself, or so handy in drawing up his examination, as I ought to have been, but pretty well.

18*th.*—Returned to town. Finch (Seymour), who is going to the Mediterranean in the 'Pearl,' rode with me as far as the turning to Battersea.

19*th.*—Of the ten days remaining of the year, I can recall but little in addition to what is preserved under migrations. I dined once at Sir Joshua's, and once at Malone's, to meet Lord Sunderlin and Lord Carysfort. On a comparison of the time passed since my return, with time spent at Felbrigg, some striking facts present themselves. In the whole time I have written but about three pages of translation. I have never, that I recollect, sat down two hours together to mathematics. If after this I feel in myself a great diminution of power, if my faculties are perceptibly less active, my comprehension less clear, and the command of my thoughts less certain; if the confidence and alacrity with which I engage in any work are greatly decreased, and a proportionate tendency is felt to relapse into my old distrust of myself, and fear of competition; it may seem unreasonable to charge the alteration to the effects of London air.

I am of opinion that the presence of Mrs. Lukin, however pleasant in many respects, and in some conducive even to the purpose of study, by promoting general spirits, and rendering home more attractive, did, notwithstanding, contribute to retard my progress in different works, and to produce some of the effects above stated: with another person in the room application cannot be quite unbroken: something will perpetually happen to create the necessity of speaking, and still oftener to provoke the desire, which, whether indulged or resisted, will equally operate as interruption. Two consequences will therefore follow: first, that instances of thought, contrived uninterruptedly to a certain extent, will be less frequent, inasmuch as many that would happen will be prevented by the way described; and, secondly, that the prospect of such interruption will both itself operate as a disturbance, and will likewise discourage the prosecution of employment to which continuity is necessary.

HISTORIA LITERARIA.

January.

Books Read.—Dionys. Halic. Rom. Antiq. Dedication of Musurus to Card. Bessarion; prefixed, I think, to Dion Cassius. Several chapters of Dion Cassius; small portions of other Greek authors. (The above when I was at Coke's.) Hesiod. Monthly Rev., Dec. Monthly do., do. Some few pages in Thucydides.

Work Done.—Some work done in Simson. Some small matters in De Moivre, and others of a similar sort, at Rainham. One and a half page of translation.

February.

Books Read.—Philo-Judæus. Narrative of what passed at Alexandria under Avillius Flaccus (Mangey's Philo, vol. ii. p. 517, foll.). Monthly Rev., Jan. Monthly do., do. Orat. of Themistius, viz. 11, 13.

Work Done.—Half a page of translation.

March.

Books Read.—Reviews. Orat. of Themistius, viz. 5, 6. Plutarch (part of). Petavius (part of, in post-chaise).

Work Done.—A little in chapter of Sanderson on Binom. Theory. About this time had finished Quæst. in Simson. Settled some rules and notions for the application of the doctrine of chances to evidence. Four pages of translation.

April.

Books Read.—Reviews. Indian Papers.

Work Done.—Six pages of translation. Martial (in post-chaise).

May.

Books Read.—Abelard and Eloise. Mysterious Mother. Essay on Criticism. Essais de Voltaire. Louis XIV. &c. Plutarch (part of). In this or following month, about 100 pages in the N. Héloïse.

Work Done.—Six pages of translation.

June.

Books Read.—In Nupt. Honorii, &c. (Claud.) De Raptu Proserpinæ (ejusd.) Small part of Diogenes Laert. Reviews. Between this and ———, when I bought the twelfth set of Plutarch, had completed nearly what remained of the first vol., after deducting the five lives read at the close of last year at Felbrigg, amounting to eleven lives: upon recollection, only ten read.

Work Done.—Read over again part of Masères on Logarithms: two pages translation.

July.

Books Read.—H. Tooke's Ἔπεα πτερόεντα—nearly. Progress in the Organum. Treatise περὶ Ἑρμῆν ascribed to D. Phalereus. Some progress in Valla. Novel of Caroline. Several books of Tasso. Book 1 and part of 2nd of Castle of Indolence. Chapter in Abbé Raynal on the Manufactory of China.

Work Done.—Looked over Treatise of Ludlam. Progress in Masères. Articles in Advers., particularly one on Neg. Sign. Translation of seven pages.

August.

Books Read.—Progress in Plutarch. Small portion of Hartley on Mind. Book 21 of Livy. Progress in Theological Tracts, and part of Juvenal.

Work Done.—Progress in Masères; six and a half pages of translation.

September.

Books Read.—Progress in Plutarch. Do. Theological Tracts. Small do. in Organum. Juvenal, in all near half. Occasionally Valla.

Work Done.—Progress in Masères. Ten pages of translation. Euclid with nephew.

October.

Books Read.—Progress in Plutarch. Small do. in Organum.

Work Done.—Progress in Masères. Nineteen pages of translation; and Euclid with nephew. Simson, De Limitibus. Some occasional mathematics.

November.

Books Read.—Completed in Plutarch in all about 400 pages: 379 in present volume. Finished the Recess. Finished all but a page or so of the 22nd book of Livy.

Work Done.—Progress in Simson. Twenty-five pages of translation. A great deal done in all in Adversaria.

December.

Books Read.—Review (Monthly), September. Juliani Misopogon. Markland's Preface to Statius. Began Paley with Mrs. Lukin. Progress in Hartley.

Work Done.—In all, the six books, and part of the seventh of Euclid, with nephew. Simson, De Lim. nearly completed. Chief part of Ludlam. Occasional reading in Wolf. Elem. Part of Preliminary Discourse of Condorcet. Some occasional mathematics in Descartes. Bernouilli. Ars Conjec. Hales, etc.

Memorandums copied from Red Pocket-Book.

Epistolæ Familiares Erasmi ad . . . Basil., lately, 8vo. Much history of the progress of the change of the Latin language to be got from the preface of Dufresne, *i. e.* Ducange. Information of the same thing to be found in the Conspectus Sæculorum of Cave's Historia Literaria. Jonsius, de Historiâ Philosophicâ.

1787.

Velut fidis arcana sodalibus, 1787.

January 17*th*.—Left London for Bath.

19*th*.—It was long a doubt whether I should go to Bath: the inducement of taking in my way a battle that was to be between Ward and Johnson determined me to go, and the event gave no reason to regret my determination. It was not then foreseen that we were to have the company of Cecy.* During the greater part of the way I was employed in some mathematical speculations, in which I met with good success; and from Devizes to Bath, in working out with great pains the recollection of some things read lately in Petrarch. I don't know when I have exercised my mind in a manner to call for greater exertion, or to be attended with more salutary effects: I mean, in the work last mentioned. We got out at the Bear, and proceeded from thence—Mrs. Lukin in a chair, I on foot—to ——. After long difficulty on the part of Mrs. Lukin, I prevailed upon her to remain behind, and came away about ten. There had been a considerable fall of snow and the roads threatened to be very bad, but as we retired from Bath the road became better and the day delightful. I proceeded with great gaiety and in bright daylight to Marlboro', where I dined; and thence, with equal comfort in a clear evening, to Newbury, where I slept.

* Cecilia, daughter of Commodore Forrest, whom he afterwards married, 1796.

My employments during my stay sufficiently satisfactory. I had taken with me Hales's 'Analysis,' and read as much in it as might make these nine days an equal number, taken indifferently from the period of my residence at Felbrigg. Something was also done in Charges against Hastings and something in translation: but of this last, as appears, only three pages. At Bull's Library I called in two days, and read with considerable attention part of Priestley's 'Letters on Mind,' into which I had looked once before, either at Norwich or Cambridge, I don't recollect for certain which. I must confess, that on the great question of the sameness of matter or mind—by whichever name you choose to denominate the common substance, whatever it is,—I feel and I have long felt, very much of his opinion. It seems to me likely to prove one of the greatest discoveries ever made in metaphysics, and to do a great deal in clearing away difficulties upon those subjects. I shall be glad when the course of my pursuits, interrupted and retarded as they are, brings me to the consideration of this question.

29*th.* — London. — The first place I went to was Brookes's; the first time of my going there since my leaving Norfolk. Burke, Francis, Fox, &c.

February.—All my attention was now fixed on the question next to come on—of the Begums. The morning after the first debate, I rode before breakfast to Fulham, and returned, if I recollect, with Disbrowe and Hayes: no opportunity given me for speaking. I continued after that reading pretty diligently the Charges, with a view of making choice of one: by this time attention to these had supplanted nearly all other reading.

18*th.*—I went to Salt Hill, in order to meet Mrs. Lukin, who was to come that evening in the coach from Bath. Much deliberation before I resolved to go and many doubts as to the expediency of it: these were all done away with before I had gone three miles, by the strong feeling I had of the effect constantly experienced from a journey. The day was fine and I felt, during the whole of my absence, an alacrity and vigour of mind clearly distinguishable from anything known since I had passed that way three weeks before. Not many days before, I had gone to the pit to see the 'Count of Narbonne:'* it was one of the pleasantest evenings of the sort I recollect to have passed.

It was some time before this and in this month, that there was the question on the Commercial Treaty,† on which I spoke, and which gave occasion to the dispute I have been involved in with the meeting of the manufacturers of Norwich. Whether they decide or not upon an address, which is the measure they have proposed, in order to do away an impression supposed to have been made by my speech, the conclusion cannot, I think, be to me a cause of any dissatisfaction: I have in my own opinion so defended myself as to stand unconvicted of having done any wrong.

March 29*th*.—The interval from my return from Bath to the date last mentioned, I may add to the present time (29th), has been employed altogether in preparation for questions in the House of Commons, and other incidental business.

Hardly a page of Greek has been read since my leaving Felbrigg: the only exception is, I believe, a short oration of Demosthenes. On mathematics, the work done very little. At my first return from Felbrigg, the same habits continued that I had been cultivating with such success there, and I felt almost to count the days which sus-

* A tragedy by Jephson. It was founded on Horace Walpole's 'Castle of Otranto,' and for that reason was carried through the theatre by Walpole himself.

† The Commercial Treaty between Great Britain and France, negotiated and signed by Mr. Eden in 1786.

pended my intercourse with such subjects. By degrees, however, the feeling wore off; the use of mathematical books discontinued, till the prospect of resuming them faded from the sight, or was followed at last by none of those feelings or purposes which it was accustomed to excite. This was strongly exemplified in the instance of Descartes' 'Geometry,' and of Huygen's 'De Ludis Aleæ' and Condorcet; which I bought soon after my return and for some time felt so eager about as to take them with me occasionally when I went to Fulham. How long have they now stood on the shelf, not distinguished from any of the volumes that rest undisturbed by their side? If one considers generally the length of time, one wonders how so little can have been done; if one considers the several portions as they pass, none seems to be lost.

Among the work done must be reckoned a portion of Paley, read with sufficient care, and of which I felt the immediate benefit in part of the argument on Fyzulla Khan.

I cannot at present recollect any particular facts that have happened; but it seems to me that I have oftener had company to dinner—have been oftener, though not often, to see Mrs. Siddons, and have to a great degree abated the frequency of my visits to Legge's. My calls on Burke have been more frequent, both in mornings and evenings; at Horsley's, I think less. The Club in Essex Street I have never attended, nor have I dined this year with Dr. Scott. At Dover Street I have been very constant. The places at which I can recollect to have dined have been Langton's, Sir Joshua Reynolds's, Malone's, Sheridan's, Boswell's, Burke's, Francis's, Mills', Legge's, Sir G. Cornewall's, Long's, Crewe's, Dover Street, Serle's, Onslow's, Major Grymes's, and Adair's. What a great proportion of dinners must have been at home or at the House of Commons! Balls or parties, except Lady Harcourt's and Miss Adair's, with a Sunday evening or two at Francis's, I have been at none. The Opera, too, I have not yet been at. The period considered three months, bating thirteen days. It would seem that good management and vigorous exertion might in that time have produced more to literature, without deducting anything from amusement or business.

April 4th.—I have a notion that this was the day I moved the Charge. The manner in which my time had been spent for ten days preceding I may well remember. Let me recollect that my reflection constantly was, how much might have been done in every branch of study, how much happier my life might have been, had I exerted in general the same diligence as I now did for this special purpose. The reason I had for this reflection, and the strong conviction I felt of the truth of it, ought to be deeply impressed on my mind. A thousand inabilities which I have admitted to operate against general study, were overruled by the strong necessity under which I then acted.

The experience of the ten days, or more, spent in preparation for that Charge, proved very clearly how much of what one imputes to corporal incapacity, is caused merely by the want of some principle to urge one strongly forward. How often the body is taxed when the mind is in fault! How much of that obstruction which health seems to oppose will shrink away before a resolute determination!

7th.—Our attendance began, if I recollect right, at the India House, on the committee for the impeachment of Hastings. It is observable that the period of my attendance there was a very happy one. The causes which made it so must, one would think, be mental; for during the whole of the time, as for some days before and after, there was a continued decided easterly wind. Notwithstanding this, whether from the advantage of going out often before breakfast, the gaiety of the streets in the City, the novelty of the situation, or the share I took in part of the business, it is certain that my mind was, for the greater part of the time, unusually gay and clear.

8*th.*—For some time past I have proposed to myself to revert to a system, discontinued for a long while, of early rising. The difficulty is not so much in the execution, as in the satisfying myself that it ought to be executed. It has seemed to me that, after a portion of sleep, something more than ordinary, and extending beyond the hour which would be called very early, I rise with more freshness and gaiety, with better spirits and greater alacrity, than at a period such as would be required on the plan above mentioned. The question is whether the observation be true, and then how far the fact depends on causes likely to cease by habit, or removeable by my own effort. To rise without a quantity of sleep such as the constitution requires, will certainly not be good, in the long run, for study any more than for health. But supposing the same quantity of sleep to be taken, will the effects described be connected more with its termination at one time than at another? I rather think not, though the fact may undoubtedly be so; because there are reasons, not depending either on use or effort, that apply to the one and not to the other; such as the state of the air at one period of the morning and at another, the appearance of things, and the consciousness of the relation to which one stands to the business of the day. The experience of to-day and yesterday would determine me to the opinion, that with respect even to the *feel* at rising and for some time after, and independent of other considerations, the earlier hour was to be preferred to the later; for though I felt yesterday, having risen at half-past six, that something of that vigour was wanting which ought to follow sleep, and that a fit of drowsiness overtook me in different parts of the day, yet to-day, when an opposite course was tried and when I did not rise till nine, that languor was perceived, I think in a greater degree, and extended its effects for a longer period. Had this even been otherwise, there is the great consideration of time gained, to which it will not be easy to oppose advantages of any other sort by which its weight can be counterbalanced. I am of opinion, therefore, that, from this day for some time to come, I should rise every morning at seven o'clock, and for that purpose be in bed by twelve. There is a difficulty always in disposing of the time gained by early rising, previously to breakfast, as the hours so obtained are wanted for opposite purposes—for study, to which they are especially fitted, and for exercise, which agrees with me at that time better than at any other. I think the practice, upon the whole, must be nearly such as I have proposed,—that to rides or walks for the sake of health more cannot be allowed than two or three times in a week.

11*th.*—Mrs. Siddons, Sir Joshua, Sir Gilbert, Langton, and Malone supped with me. The evening particularly pleasant.

15*th.*—It was to-day (Sunday), I think, that I went down to Hendon to Mrs. Crewe. The evening preceding was Jephson's play of 'Julia,' to which I went with a party from Boswell's. This is ascertained by the circumstance of my having met Lawrence the next morning at Adam's, where I stayed till near four, employed usefully on Fyzulla Khan. After the play went to Burke's.

16*th.*—At Mrs. Crewe's were present—Sheridan and Mrs. S., Tickell and Mrs. T., Dr. Parr, and Ellis. I arrived just as dinner was going on table. Great enjoyment, and conversation pleasant, till late in the evening, when they involved everything, as usual, in noisy dispute. They so stunned and confounded, with their clamour and altercation, faculties which could not naturally be well turned to reasoning, that after incessant debate, in which I however took no part, they came to a decision, not contradicted but confirmed by their cooler judgment next morning, that it was no consequence; 'that if persons having the clearest conceptions were sometimes the least clear in communicating their conceptions, then the persons the most clear in communicating, would sometimes have the least clear conceptions.' The words taken down were, indeed, 'had not always *the greater* power of communicating;' in which case, as I desired them to note at the time, the conversation did not, in strictness, hold, but that distinction had no share in their objection. Parr was among the fiercest, and brought down all the powers of Aristotle to show, that between those propositions there was no consequence. I applied to them at the beginning the story of the supposed contradiction in the witness who deposed first that the man had one leg shorter than the other, and then that he had one leg longer.

17*th.*—Club-day: present, Sir Joshua, Lord Ossory, Lord Palmerston, Bishop of St. Asaph, Malone, and Dr. Burney. I went away soon, in order to go to Bensley's benefit—Mrs. S. in 'Belvidera.' From Mrs. Crewe's, the day before, I had an unpleasant ride, the wind being still NE., and had the aggravation, on arriving at the India House, of finding, that between uncertainty, whether I should go there or not, and delay in stopping to see a foot-race, I was too late for my purpose, and too soon for my servant to have arrived to take my horse. After dinner I drove to Burke's, where I found Ellis and Dr. King, and should have stayed to supper, but that it was necessary for me to call in Duke Street, in order to settle with Byng about going the next day to see a battle at Barnet between Martin and Mendoza. We agreed to go, for which I was sorry by the time I got home, but did not like to send a message to put it off. In the morning we discovered, fortunately before we set out, that each was going in compliment to the other. Some time, I conceive, in this week—the night I knew of Mrs. Jordan's benefit—I had company at dinner, namely, Adam, Tickell,

Dodwell, Ellis, Cholmondeley, and Courtenay. When we broke up, I went with Courtenay and made a visit to Lord Townshend, who had come lately to town, and has a house in Argyle Street. My visit was well taken, and was agreeable to myself.

21*st*—*Saturday*.—I dined at Crewe's: present, Parr, Tickell, Ellis, Richardson, Mrs. Tickell. Dinner not pleasant, nor such as repaid me, either for the loss of Mrs. Siddons in 'Isabella,' or for a dinner at Adam's with Anstruther and Sir Gilbert Elliot. I had risen very early in the morning in order to read the case of the Salt Ash Petition, of which, if I had known as much as I do now, I should perhaps have undertaken the nomineeship.

23*rd*—*Monday*.—Attended for the last time the meeting on the Wool business; from whence I proceeded to the Committee, and dined upstairs with Francis. From thence I was proceeding straight home, but being induced to go into the House, in order to procure admission for Crome of Norwich, I stayed therefore,—first, from desire to hear Pitt and Sheridan, and then in order to be present when Burke gave some explanation on the paper, thought to be improperly looked into by the Committee.

24*th*—*Tuesday*.—I rode out, after calling on Frederick Montague. Met Lady Buckingham and Lady Emily,* with whom I continued walking till it was time to return straight home. This was the day of the Salt Ash Petition, for which, by the fault of the servants, and partly of my own, I was just too late. The business in the House was Sir Gilbert Elliot's notice, and the Shop Tax.

25*th*.—Burke, Sir G. Elliot, and I dined with Wilberforce; the day sufficiently pleasant, except that we talked more than I could have wished about India, though not in any way that was improper. We came away on foot, and took a turn or two in the Park. I went afterwards to Mrs. Acourt's.

* Emily Anne Hobart: married, 1794, to Robert Marquis of Londonderry.

27th.—I did not wake till near eight, and dressed in a hurry, wishing to breakfast with Kent, but, fearing to be too late, changed my purpose and rode to Burney's, where the event of my visit turned out beyond my hopes. First, found him just going to breakfast, and Porson with him: with them I stayed enjoying myself much, partly from the society, and partly from the pleasantness of the air, till twelve, when I returned home. From one till three I wrote the letter which I had upon my mind, to the Norwich Free Blues,* who had sent me a letter in form from their Society-room, at the Fountain in Clare Market, containing a review of my conduct, and remarkable as an instance of that notion and style and composition which spreads now into ale-houses and cellars.

28th.—This morning I had intended to spend at home, but was forced out about twelve by a note I had received from Burke, mentioning a business of some sort which required me to call upon the Duke of Portland: before I went out, Urquhart called. The business was a report which the Duke had heard, but without believing, that I had been among the persons to advise the Prince on the business now impending. Burke having been at Burlington House, carried me away with him in his carriage, to help to make up a committee at the India House. On the way, he explained to me what had passed in the House the day before relative to the Prince;† on which, as well as on the general state and character of our party, and of some of the persons who composed it, he descanted in a strain of superior wisdom. I made no stay at the India House, but returned on foot, calling at several places and doing several necessary pieces of business by the way.

The walk from the India House to St. Dunstan's, took

* Blue and white are in Norwich the colours of the Whig party.

† With reference to the marriage of the Prince of Wales with Mrs. Fitzherbert.

me, I observed, at a rate somewhat lower perhaps than my ordinary one, twenty minutes. One of my errands was, if I recollect, to order from Nourse the new edition of the 'Tatler,' of which I have since read a volume, and think rather of running through the whole.

This day is to be remarked as having been the foundation, probably, of an Eton Anniversary, never before held, and not unlikely to be continued from this time. Dodwell has, I think, the honour of being the prime mover. The persons present, as far as I can recollect, were as follows: Johnes, Poyntz, Sir Gregory Turner, Sir — Layton, L. Damer, Winnington, Sir G. Thomas, T. Windsor, G. White, Townshend, Neville, Tickell, Cholmondeley, Mundy, Grey, Dodwell, Pulteney, A. Smith. The presence of so many persons, all imparting the ideas of a particular period, and many of them unconnected in one's mind with any other, produced in a considerable degree the effect that one would suppose: it would have done so in a degree still greater if I had not happened to be in a state unfavourable rather to such impressions. As it was, I felt at some periods during the course of the evening sensations of enjoyment, such as one has not often known since life was in the spring, and which contributed in their turn to recall and impress the images by which they were produced. I remained there, rather enjoying one's own feelings than the conversation, which, for its merits as conversation, though not perhaps its effect in recalling past scenes, approached full near that of a party at the 'White Hart,' till near twelve, when I went with Mundy to Mrs. Crewe's.

29th.—Dined at Francis's. Present: Burke's son, Sir G. Elliot, R. Burke, M. A. Taylor. In the evening Mrs. Reid and Miss Adair. No dancing.

30th.—The misdemeanours of Oude having been put off, was enabled to keep my engagement with Mulgrave to meet Lord Longford.

May 1st.—Club, Dover Street. Went from thence to

the Opera, the first time since March twelvemonth. Saw Lady Buckinghamshire there. After the Opera, I continued talking to her till she went, which prevented my arriving at Marlay's, with whom I was to sup, till near twelve. Mrs. Crewe, Mrs. Sheridan, Lady Palmerston, H. Pelham, and Crewe.

2nd.—Met Lady Buckinghamshire and Lady Caroline, and walked with them in Kensington Gardens. Had called in my way on Lady Cornewall, whom I have hardly seen five times this winter. Air very delightful and refreshing. Had intended to think of something to say on the Post-horse Tax, but, for want of time in the morning to turn it in my mind, had pretty much given up the idea. On finding myself alone in the House, sufficiently fresh and clear, resumed my purpose, and offered myself to the Speaker immediately as Pitt sat down. Some one else having been pointed to, and my next offer proving in like manner unsuccessful, I gave up the point for the time, proposing, if I spoke at all, to wait till Pitt, or some one else from the Treasury Bench, should have spoken again; but to this intention an interruption was given by a sally, in the usual manner, from Sir Richard Hill;* in answer to which I hazarded an attempt, not so adventurous as it appeared, because part of what I said had passed through my mind on a former occasion, when Harding † once had made a speech of the same sort, but of which the danger was still sufficient to make me look back to it with terror, and undertook the office of chastising him. The experiment in the present instance seemed to have succeeded to the utmost of my hopes: there is no danger of my being betrayed by its success into a careless and unsafe repetition of it.

* Sir R. Hill was the uncle of Lord Hill, of Peninsular celebrity.

† George Harding was brought up to the bar. He had some reputation as a speaker, but never rose above mediocrity. He finally became a Welsh judge.

3rd.—Went into the Park before breakfast, where two of the regiments of the Guards were exercising, and from thence proceeded and breakfasted with Palmer. Dined at home; and though I ate only some minced veal, some spinach, and eggs, in moderate quantity, felt myself greatly oppressed, so as to afford a strong instance in confirmation of the opinion, that a solitary dinner, for whatever reason, does not so soon pass away as one ate in company. The reason first occurring would be, that for a dinner ate in company some time was taken; but the fact does not seem to correspond; for I have made, if I am not mistaken, as many intervals in dining alone, and have yet found that digestion does not take place so quickly. Besides the effect that company may have on the mind, much, I apprehend, is to be ascribed to the action given to the lungs and stomach by talking. In the evening, about six o'clock, I drove down to Fulham, and drank tea with Liddell, and from thence proceeded to Kent's. On my return to town, proceeded to Burke, who had been peevish and impatient in the morning because I would not stay when he supposed he had something to say to me. With him I had some conversation about the motion to come on the next day relative to the Prince.

4th.—Went out before breakfast, to learn something of the meeting to be held that morning at Carlton House, of which notices had been sent that morning. After the meeting, at which the Prince signified only that the business was likely to be settled amicably, drove with Sir Gilbert Elliot to Mrs. Siddons', to whom we were admitted; then to Gally's, to whom and Mrs. G. I was introduced.

5th.—To Beaconsfield, where I arrived in time for dinner. Drove in my own carriage to Uxbridge: fell asleep by the way, as I recollect to have done in going down last July. Took a long walk at night, notwithstanding the coldness and unpleasantness of the weather. Slept pleasantly, and waked early. Took up a volume of Cudworth and learnt some facts relative to the Atomic philosophers that deserve to be remembered.

6*th.*—Came to town after breakfast. Got upon my horse at Uxbridge, in order to ride some way with the Duke of Portland, who was coming through: journey pleasant. Company at home—Knight, Burney, Porter, Langton, Paradise,* and Lawrence. Of the remaining days of the week no recollection, except that on Monday I went, after dining at home, to Mrs. Siddons' benefit—part, 'Alicia':† sat in Lady Palmerston's box, Mrs. Crewe and Lady Williams.

10*th.*—Dined with Cholmondeley: day memorable for being that on which the ports were opened to French goods and the Impeachment carried up against Hastings.

14*th.*—Having returned home at a little past nine, sat down to Masères on 'Neg. Signs' till past eleven and continued employed on that and some small logarithmic operations, the first mathematics I have read, I should suspect, for full two months. I took to it more readily and with better success than I had reason to apprehend after such long disuse, though still with such sense of deficiency as showed what is sometimes gained by what appeared now to be wanting.

16*th.*—Dined with Sheridan: present, Fox, Parr, Grey, Corry, Lord Robert,‡ Courtenay, Lord Grenville. The same evening went with Lady Palmerston to Vauxhall to masquerade: determined upon going after full debate—not much in mood to go, and very sorry for what I had determined when I found the party: turned out, in the event, perfectly pleasant.

* Paradise was another member of the Johnsonian circle.

† In Rowe's 'Jane Shore.'

‡ Lord Robert (Spencer).

19*th*.—Eton meeting; seventy-four present. Dined with Edwin * for the first time.

20*th*.—Went about eight to Francis's: employed in the useful work of examining bills; to bed in great comfort between one and two. It was my purpose now to get out of town as soon as I could. On Monday, if I recollect right, I was detained at the House waiting to attend Burke, with a message for taking Hastings into custody. It was eight before I came away.

22*nd*.—Did not come home till late, not having finished my dressing when part of the company came to dinner. This consisted of Fox, Adam, Burke, Dr. Scott, Francis, R. Burke, Cholmondeley, J. Lee, Sir G. Elliot. None of them went away till late. 'Twas a very pleasant day.

23*rd*.—I found in the morning the want of a ride and took the opportunity of going to Fulham to see Mrs. Siddons. I did not get to the House of Commons till after the motion was disposed of for printing the report of the Post-office Committee. I returned home again, being to dine with Lord Robert, whose dinner was not likely to be ready till past six. I learnt for the first time, from Sheridan at the House, of the death of poor Canning, the news of which shocked me less in consequence of the account I had heard before—and which shocked me a good deal—that he was past recovery. He was a very friendly, and seemingly a very honourable man, and one so linked with us by political sentiments and by other ties to those whom I am likely frequently to see, that his death makes a void in the prospect of life which will continue to be for some time perceived. The party at Lord Robert's was: Duke of Portland, Lord Hertford, Lord Beauchamp, Lord Palmerston, Fitzpatrick, W. Ellis, Burke, Grey.

24*th*.—Went out, in order to learn from Miss Adair

* Edwin, the celebrated comedian.

whether I was to sup with her or not—or rather to put myself in the way of being asked, having been told by Mrs. Siddons the day before that she was to sup there. Just able to get in time to Malone's, where I was to dine. Went home, if I recollect right, when I quitted his house; that is, after carrying home Burke.

25th.—Felt vexed at my arrival in Stratford Street (Miss Adair's), to find that supper was half over. Erskine there, and Mrs. Erskine, H. Greville, Bentinck. Tired, and rather dull. Took Greville and Bentinck in the carriage, who wanted a conveyance to Lady Gideon's ball. Had an invitation which I should have found, perhaps, more pleasant, but could not have accepted to the exclusion of the other, to meet Lady Harris at Lady Palmerston's.

26th.—Two of the persons I called on were Royd and A. Smith. From Queen Anne Street I went to Duke Street, where, to my great surprise, I found Cecy, just arrived for a stay of two days from Binfield. The meeting her gave me a feel of great satisfaction, and made me hesitate in my own mind whether I should not defer my journey for a day or two. Augusta* was with her: grown in her appearance and size much more womanly, and to my eyes and taste so attractive, that it was with great difficulty I could forbear to mix in my conversation more of softness than would become the relation in which we stand. Miss Rich came in soon after.

28th.—Arrived in Norwich in time to go to the play. The book I read upon the road, which I had bought at Naulder's the day before, collected by H. Stephens from Ctesias, Agatharchides, Memnon, and Appian; of which I read, I think, the whole from Memnon, and the whole or nearly of the 'Annibalica' of Appian. My journey was sufficiently pleasant, but struck me with the difference from that which I made, much about the same time of

* Mrs. Disney, sister to Cecy, afterwards Mrs. Windham.

year, before my going to Ireland, and which, odd as it may seem, considering the anxiety I felt upon that occasion, produced feelings of enjoyment much superior to any known on this.

30*th.*—To Aylsham in a chaise; from thence to Felbrigg on horseback; employed, I think, chiefly in the 'Organum,' which I now resumed till supper. The distribution I have proposed for my time is, to breakfast at nine, to have the boys for their lesson after breakfast, to dine at the Parsonage (which is at three), to return straight home soon after dinner and continue at home till eight; then to ride or walk out, and afterwards, in general, to sup at the Parsonage.

June 1*st.*—Resumed the employment mentioned May 14th (logarithmic operations) for the first time since that date. Query, Whether I have done to-day anything that might not have been done equally well in London? I am better certainly, in no respects, unless it be in health, and the capacity I may feel to employ the remaining hours to greater advantage. To know the full extent of this latter difference, I must take in the probable state, in which I shall rise to-morrow morning. 'Twould not be right to mention, among the advantages of being here (Felbrigg), the impossibility of going out, and the freedom, therefore, from all the distress of choice; that being an advantage founded on a defect in myself, which reason and habit might cure.

3*rd.*—Rose at seven; went to church at half-past nine: a good sermon from Johnson,* which I listened to with great attention. Rode with him to Aldborough, and thence a round by myself till near one o'clock. Read at and after dinner, till finding myself in danger of going to sleep, dressed and walked on bowling green.

4*th.*—Went to Norwich to dine with the sheriff. King's birthday. Slept at Taylor's; he absent.

* Rev. Paul Johnson.

7th.—Brettingham came; though the business on which he came, viz. to assist me in some alterations in the house, and the connection he has with places and times which I reflect on with pleasure, might well occasion some satisfaction in his arrival; yet there was an effect from his company of putting one's mind into a state of cheerfulness and activity, above its ordinary rate at this place, which seems to show that the solitude here is more than is salutary.

9th.—Brettingham went away, and has answered perfectly the purpose of his coming down, having settled what is necessary for the alteration and repair of the drawing-room, and reduced the question of the hall and the library to a state in which it must soon be decided. My present opinion is for opening the flat window again, and lighting the room altogether from the south. The advantages I propose by this are, the obtaining a pleasanter light, more warmth, and better appearance when the curtains are down—and, above all, getting rid of the idea of an end room.

11th.—At home till dinner. I went into the riding-ground, gave a lesson to bay mare. At seven, went out and took airing—Mrs. Lukin going in phaeton, I on horseback—towards Bodham. Struck with the novelty, to me, of the scene.

15th.—I had felt myself particularly strong and clear, but lost some of the advantage by a foolish contest with myself, whether a wish of exercising my horse before dinner, sooner than it should lose a day, should be indulged or not. The disturbance given myself in arguing the question became a reason for deciding it in the affirmative. We drank tea out of doors. When they went away—the party from the Parsonage—which was about nine or past, I came into my room, and continued in my chair, thinking with great intentness on the question in page 261, K. U., till past eleven, when the effect of thought, so long and so earnestly continued brought me into a state different, as it appeared to me, from what I have frequently experienced from the same cause—such as seemed to me a natural precursor of that which, some time or other, will be my end—a paralytic stroke.

16*th.*—From whatever cause, it happened—whether from continuing too long in bed, or from the same as occasioned what is stated above—I felt all this day low in spirits and feeble in mind. I was so drowsy as to be obliged to betake myself to the couch, where I continued fast asleep till I was waked by Mrs. Lukin coming under the window in the phaeton.

18*th.*—Left home for the Guild, Mrs. Lukin, Cecilia and Mary in the chaise, I on horseback. We had settled to sleep at Aylsham in the absence of the Adeys, and in our way to see Blickling. Great pleasure in seeing the house, and afterwards the park. Much occasion to me of reflecting on the influence of place and external objects.

19*th.*—Slept at Taylor's.

20*th.*—Expectation of going to the camp. Great benefit from visit to Norwich. I had felt languid and low before, whether the effect of illness or any mental cause, can't say—a little suspicion of the latter.

22*nd.*—Cromer meeting. Only myself there. Read, in the intervals of business, Q. Curtius, which I brought for the purpose from the Parsonage. Drank tea at home, meaning to continue there all the evening; but Mrs. Lukin tempted me to drive her in the phaeton, which I did, going the gap way to Cromer, and driving a considerable distance below cliff. The pleasantness of the drive atoned for the interruption.

23*rd.*—No progress made in Masères since the 15th. All mathematics cannot, however, be said to have stopped for that time. I must not omit, also, what is continually going forward in teaching George: perhaps, in hearing him his propositions, which have generally taken an hour, and sometimes much more, my faculties are as much exerted and as highly taxed as in any employment I have. I have always accustomed myself a good deal to demonstrate propositions without the scheme before me, but believe the practice to be of great use, not only as an exercise to the mind, but for the truer conception of the proposition. It is not impossible that Pitt's clearness and distinctness of exposition may have been acquired, in some measure, by the habit of going through demonstrations without the assistance from a diagram.

24th.—Went over to Norwich again to dine with the new mayor Harvey, having read about a page and a half of Masères before I set out. The time so short, that I hardly thought it worth while to take up the book, but did it on a principle, which this instance may contribute to confirm, that such kind of transient application, however little it may produce in itself, is of great use for the purpose of connection. A point properly placed will connect objects at any distance at less than the double of that at which they could have connected themselves. It is curious to observe how this principle applies in various subjects, and the use that architects make of it in accommodating to each other the ornaments of the several parts of a building. Brettingham, the other day, while he was contriving alterations for the library, furnished an instance of this.

26th.—Passed the whole of the day at home and alone, except three-quarters of an hour in the evening, when I heard George his Euclid (the same proposition, by the way, in the 12th book, about the section of a pyramid into two pyramids, which was the subject of a dispute so many years ago between me and Cholmondeley), and half an hour in the morning, when I was hearing Robert* his

* Robert Lukin, third son of the Dean, secretary to the Tennis Club, and one of the finest tennis players of the time. He was a most amiable man, and a very respectable scholar.

Horace and Greek grammar. This is the first day passed wholly at home since my coming down. What is the opinion to be formed respecting the passing more days in the same way from the experiment made in this instance? Certainly very favourable. After dinner I was not quite able to keep myself awake, and was very near going over (in despair of working to any effect) to the Parsonage. After tea I grew into spirits more than ordinary, so as to make me dance and sing about the room (effects now very rare), and have continued till now (twelve o'clock) with great clearness and alertness of faculties, which I have employed with grand success in filling the two or three last leaves of the 'Adversaria.' I will now go to bed with no other apprehension than that the activity of mind that I still feel may prevent me from sleeping. The balance between the benefit of hours passed alone and hours passed in company is perpetually changing, as the enjoyment from the latter grows greater continually by their infrequency, and the others by too long continuance may part with much of their advantage.

28*th.*—Norwich. Breakfasted at the Bowling Green. Just time was left to get to Rainham, by what I supposed their dinner. Pleasant ride, and pleasant state of mind at dinner: Lord Townshend, Money, Sir Edmund and Lady Bacon, Dillingham, young Bedingfield and his wife, &c. Settled to go in the evening to Yarmouth, under the guidance of young Suckling, whom I remember a lout at Dereham, but is now a fine officer-looking man. Set off across the marshes; ride very pleasant, when we were relieved from the apprehension of losing our way.

July 3*rd.*—Great folly. After sitting at home till six, suffered myself, without any necessity or any temptation, to be absent till half-past eleven at the Parsonage. What have I gained by this? What I have lost I know.

6*th.*—Received a letter, to my great surprise, from Wilberforce, saying he should be the next day at Norwich, and if he found a letter from me should come on to Felbrigg. As I was going this day to Norwich, it was not necessary to answer his letter. Had the mortification to find that Wilberforce had been gone about half an hour.

7th.—On finding it market-day, wished I had gone home. No room at the Angel to breakfast in. Went to the Maid's Head, to attend the meeting relative to the sending for Mara to sing at the Cathedral. One of my purposes of going there was to meet Sir W. Jerningham, with whom I settled I should go in the evening to Cossey for the purpose of writing my letters.

8th.—Set off on return home, and for the first time came by Cawston and Hevingham. I was employed, I have a notion, for part of the way, in the translation of an epigram, viz. from Greek into Latin, and for part, I remember, in settling anew the question about the advantage of blackening or whitening fruit-walls.

11th.—Went to Norwich for the sessions. Particularly obliged to attend, as it was expected that Barber's cause would come on, and some occasion might be taken by the wisdom of the magistrates to make some observations or propose some resolutions against camping. Slept at Taylor's.

12th.—After dining with the Justices, rode to Cossey, drinking tea by the way at Earlham with Mrs. Gurney, where I stayed some time. Edward Jerningham at Cossey.

13th.—Rode over to Aylsham before breakfast to meet Burney, in order to go to the Blickling Library. While we were waiting in the hall, heard Lady Buckinghamshire's voice in the passage, and could not resist the inclination to speak to her, though the consequence was, what I foresaw, yet did not wish, that I should lose so much time to the inspection of the library. I had not above half an hour with Burney, when a message from Lady B.

obliged us to depart, in a manner sufficiently whimsical in appearance, the reason given being that Lord B. was expected, and the message arriving unfortunately at the moment of a violent rain. It turned out that we departed just in good time, though it might have been the very worst, for in our way to Aylsham we met Lord B. By the greatest good luck, it was in a part of the road which enabled us to escape unseen into Holley's stables, where we remained till he was past. In the library at Blickling, the most remarkable thing that I saw, was a manuscript lexicon of Suicer, in seven volumes and upwards in folio, which appears to have been copied from a printed copy published in 1682, and, by a note at the end, to have been concluded in 1784. It is difficult to conceive, how so large a work could have been written out in the time, as it did not appear clear to me that more than one hand had been employed; and it must have been copied from the printed edition, as the additions were incorporated in the text. If no edition has been published since that in 1682 including the additions of this manuscript, what is here preserved would be a valuable assistance to any future compiler of a Greek lexicon. Suicer was a native of, and a professor, I think, of Zurich, and died, I believe, in the year when this manuscript was finished.

18*th*.—Set off after breakfast to ride to Cossey, in order to proceed from thence to Mr. Ives', at Catton. The day hot, and the fatigue of the latter part of my ride so much that I could maintain no series of thought.

20*th*.—Cossey. Before dinner had some talk with a friar of Calabria, who had come over to collect charity for the rebuilding of his convent, destroyed in the late earthquakes. He spoke no English, so I conversed as well as I could in Italian. The evening, *i. e.* the supper, at Cossey pleasant as before. The whole of my stay at Cossey has been very pleasant. Of the remainder of my stay at Felbrigg I can give but little account, having neglected to make any memorandum till now, a month from the time. The day of dining at Sir Robert Laurie's was the same as that of G. Wyndham's return from Yarmouth by water.

August.—Till the 4th, continued at Norwich or at Cossey; the assizes having commenced on the morning of the 31st ult., and a meeting having been called in consequence of the proclamation. After the meeting, for the debate of which, such as there was reason to apprehend, I found myself less prepared than I ought, I set out for London, going from Thetford to Bury, where I expected to gain intelligence of a man whom I had been applied to, to endeavour to save.

6*th.*—Fell in, fortunately, with a dinner at Malone's. Found much satisfaction in such a restoration to better society, with the health of the country to qualify me to enjoy it. Proceeded to Nepean. Detained between his house and the office till near five o'clock, when I found a set of people going to a battle in Tothill Fields. Got some dinner at the tavern in Palace Yard, and proceeded thence to the scene of action, where, between six and seven, saw very commodiously from a dray, a smart battle between Jack Joseph, a soldier who showed upon his back floggings which he had received to a distinguished amount, and one Hardy, I think, a carpenter. Joseph was bulky, but old and corpulent, and not a match for the other in activity, but he fought most courageously, and after eleven times being either thrown or struck down, gave me a great persuasion that he would win, even if his antagonist had not given out suddenly, in a way very discreditable either to his courage or his honesty. The opinion was, as I heard from Hanger and Ayton afterwards, that he fought booty.

21*st.*—Day of return from Beaconsfield. Had company to dinner; that is to say, Sir Joshua, Malone, Courtenay, who came from Bath, and with him, not unwelcomely, old Mounsey,* at the age of ninety-three. I don't know that he improved the conversation much, but it was not for want of spirits to talk, nor from any cause that might not equally have existed forty years ago. To me his presence was a satisfaction, independent from what he might add or take from the society.

24th.—Dined by appointment at Francis's, to proceed from thence to the play at Richmond.

27th.—Went with Mrs. Legge to Strawberry Hill, and afterwards to dine at Kempton Park. Silent during the greater part of the day, not from want of power to talk, which I felt in an uncommon degree, but from want of inclination, founded on ill-humour. On our return in the evening, I got out at Hammersmith, and had a pleasant walk by moonlight home. I was considering with myself as I came along, whether my walk there was not preferable to such, as I should have been taking probably at the same time at Felbrigg. Nothing entered except migrations and some letters from time to time abovementioned till now, September 7th. I shall set down such particulars as I can remember under the month, and as nearly as I can under the dates to which they belong.

In general my progress in all kind of useful work during my stay in London this time was superior to what it had ever been before, and nearly equal, if not quite, to some of the best times at Felbrigg. My spirits were accordingly gay, and my thoughts pleasant, notwithstanding some periods of languor. I think I may, upon the whole, reckon the month passed this time in London amongst those *cretâ notandos.*

September 10th.—Day of going to St. Paul's; pleasant in all its circumstances.

* Dr. Messenger Mounsey a physician; he was born in Norfolk in 1693, and died at Chelsea College in 1788 at the age of ninety-five. Was noted as a humourist, and numerous anecdotes are recorded which show his great eccentricity.

11*th.*—Determined before I went to sleep that I would stay at home next day; did not go out farther than Steevens' garden. Read Petrarch: much dispute, ending pleasantly.

12*th.*—At Salthill, where I breakfasted. Douglas came in, unluckily not till just before I was going away; he was returning from the circuit and a short tour he had made afterwards. If an unexpected renewal of acquaintance is numbered justly by Dr. Johnson among the pleasing incidents of life, a meeting such as the present, without a prior intermission of acquaintance, may be numbered among the pleasing incidents of a journey. I passed on gaily to Oxford, where I dined.

13*th.*—Set off early. On my way through Cheltenham saw Walsh, Leblanc, Travel, and Lane the counsel. Had been employed chiefly in thinking on some mathematical matters, and continued to be so, particularly on the question agitated between Wallis and Barrow relative to proportion as applied to number or quantity. The discussion—begun now and not ended till during my stay at Gloucester—resulted in a change of my former opinions and a return to the side of Wallis, namely, that proportion is a comparison of parts; *id est*, a comparison of numbers. I arrived at Gloucester in time to hear part of the music, and in consequence to dine with Horsley at the ordinary. The time spent at Gloucester has not much in it to be recorded; it answered very little in the way I intended, any more than visits perhaps to Horsley are in general likely to do. His habits are not of a sort to incline him to talk much; no conversation can arise from the society in which he lives. His studies are remote from the subjects on which I wish to hear him, and his thoughts still more remote, being intent wholly on prospects of Church preferment. All the work I did during my stay was the discussion in my mind of the question before mentioned, the working some questions in Dodson, and the reading what is mentioned in Hist. and Lit. of Plutarch. Though much could probably not have been done, nor much profit made of Horsley's society, the chief failure in the satisfaction of my stay is perhaps to be ascribed to my having been unwell.

19*th.*—Left Gloucester. Had set out with the purpose of dining with the Duke of Norfolk, but finding myself much too late, was glad to arrive just in time for a dinner at Stoke.

20*th.*—Rode with Foley and Lord Wentworth, who had arrived overnight, about the grounds. View grand and beautiful. The whole of my stay at Moccas* uncomfortable from illness.

25*th.*—Went away, proceeding to Knight's at Downton Castle; stayed with Knight; my sore throat getting a great deal better. Read part of the preface to Dufresne's 'Glossary,' and to the 'History of Anna Comnena,' and collected from books and conversation many useful particulars, part of which are probably lost by this time by want of the precaution in making notes. Knight was employed in reading Homer, with a view to the doctrine of the Digamma.

28*th.*—Set off before breakfast; had pleasant journey to Crewe Hall, where I arrived in good time before dinner. In the house Mrs. Greville, Mrs. Sheridan, Miss Lindley, Wilbraham. Charles Greville, Bridgeman, and Sheridan came the next day. Thomas Grenville was there the day of my arrival, but went away to Chatsworth the day after.

October 7*th.*—Went to Capesthorne—Mr. Davenport's; several there, but none whose names I recollect, except two of Mrs. Davenport's brothers. The only lady was, I think, Mrs. D.'s sister.

8*th.*—Came from Congleton on Sheridan's horses, and found my ride pleasant. During the whole of my stay at Crewe I was not so well as I ought to have been,

* Sir G. Cornewall's.

which I ascribe almost entirely to my own mismanagement of myself. I did not suffer my time to pass wholly without profit, having found opportunities of reading, particularly in some mathematical parts of the 'Philosophical Transactions.' On what day we went to Chester I don't recollect; it was before my going to Capesthorne. Our party was Mrs. Crewe, Mrs. Greville, and Mrs. Sheridan; Mrs. Lane must have gone before; Greville and Bridgeman were to join us there. A visit to Chester was one of the things I had looked forward to whenever the time should come of fulfilling my intentions with respect to Crewe Hall. It is sufficient to say of a thing so long expected, that the event did not disappoint me. Both in going and returning I found my faculties particularly clear and my spirits good; and during the evening and the morning—which was all that we passed there—enjoyed as much as I could expect of those reflective satisfactions which I hoped the sight of the place would inspire.

10*th*.—We went to Stafford. I had deliberated whether I should leave Crewe before, in time to go round by London, or leaving it before, should gain so much time in my stay at Felbrigg, or should do, as I finally decided, comply with Sheridan's earnest, though not very authorised wishes, and attend the party to Stafford. The course upon which I decided was, upon the whole, right, both with respect to my own satisfaction, and still more clearly with respect to the difference of satisfaction or discontent occasioned to Sheridan.

16*th*.—Arrived at Felbrigg. My thoughts, for part of the way, were employed drawing up resolutions for a society which Sheridan and I had projected, for the encouragement of ancient games.

Of the particulars of my stay at Felbrigg I can recollect but little, but I know, upon the whole, very satisfactory. Though my professed work (Masères) went on but slowly, the business of explaining to George the doctrine of logarithms has so settled my notions on the fundamentals of that doctrine as to require, I trust, nothing to be corrected or added in future.

November 24th.—As it appears, I left Felbrigg. Of my stay in London little can now be said, except that it was satisfactory, both in respect of the habits in which I lived and the state in which I found myself; I went more into company, and engaged myself more there, and at the same time did more at home than any preceding period of equal extent, except probably the months spent in London at the end of the summer.

December.—Amongst the events of this time I must not forget the speech about Francis, which seemed clearly to have been the best I ever made, and which, by the credit given to it, entitles me to pronounce with greater confidence on the degree of admiration due to public speaking. In the whole of that speech nothing was found that I had not on various occasions said before in company, without exciting any particular observation in those who heard me, or appearing to myself particularly to have observed it. For some time before my leaving town Mrs. Lukin had been with me; she was in town at the time when the speech above mentioned was made, and had suggested, in talking upon the subjects, one of the points which I afterwards made use of, and which was just as good, for aught I know, as any of those with which it was associated. Our journey was delayed a day for the sake of the battle, at Staines, between Ryan and Johnson, which I went to see. Next morning Mrs. Lukin, myself, and Robert set off for Felbrigg.

Neither my time nor my thoughts were employed in this visit to Felbrigg in the same manner as upon other occasions. I had now the business of preparing for Westminster Hall, and my purpose in coming down was to make that my principal employment, keeping other studies in the same subordination as that in which I had usually kept articles of business to other studies. I am afraid to say or to think how little I acted up to that purpose. Let me only set down, that after the excuse of not being furnished with my brief was removed, I did go to work, at first languidly, but, for the last week or so, with sufficient vigour. My regrets might be less if the neglect of one business had made way for a diligent prosecution of another; but, the fact was, I fear, quite the contrary; the time gained by neglect is seldom applied to any useful purpose and relaxation, once admitted, is apt to extend its influence throughout. Of the books I used, or the employment I followed, my recollection is not perfect. De Lolme's work on the 'Constitution' was one which I read through, all but a few chapters, with considerable attention, profit and pleasure; it is surely a work that, by the matter and style of it, as well as by the circumstances in which it was produced, manifests uncommon powers.

1788.

March 23rd.—There is no estimate so fallacious, as that which is made of the duration of neglect. Till the interval was actually noted, could I have conceived, that near three months were elapsed, without the journal of this year having been begun! The neglect, of which this is part, had not its origin even within the year; much of the journal of last year, was not completed till after the commencement of the present and much even yet remains undone.

April.—Let me now go on after an interval of three weeks, added to the neglect before noted, to give such a summary as can be made out, of the part of the year already past; that I may get at length into the regular train of journal, and endeavour, by future diligence, to make up for what has hitherto been omitted. The period of these omissions certainly confirms a remark, which I have often before made, that whatever the connection may be, whichever of the two is cause, or whether both result from some common principles, the punctual continuance of my Journal, and a diligent prosecution of other business, always go together, so that I think I may pronounce safely of any period, in which the one has been neglected, that the other has not been well maintained. I have accordingly been clearly sensible of a relaxation in many parts of study and discipline, during the time above stated, in which I find this blank in my journal. I may likewise, I think, perceive something of a relaxation of power, to be traced directly to the neglect of my Journal, as a cause.

There is perhaps no practice, that keeps so much alive in me the habit of writing, that preserves so much the disposition to take readily to my pen, or improves so much the power of using it with facility. The observation made by Boyle on the use of writing meditations, that the variety of matter, conduces eminently to a promptness of expression on all occasions, may be applied with equal truth to the practice, as I have used it, of journal writing. It is whimsical to recollect the state of my purposes and feelings, compared with their state at present on the business which I am to bring on in Westminster Hall; I was then full of anxiety, full of resolutions of diligence, impressed with the conviction that no time was to be lost; not without a reasonable regret of the neglect already incurred. Three months have now elapsed, being a much longer period than I then foresaw would be allowed me. It is very possible, I fear even probable, that the business will come on in a month, yet I have added no great sum to my preparation and I feel less of all those convictions, than before. My former state was certainly that most consistent with reason and my present composure has more of insensibility, than of rational confidence. I perceive already the beneficial effects of journal writing, when it brings so strongly into my mind, the sense of my folly and the necessity of better conduct in future.

On my arrival in town, conformably to the state of mind above described, I got out, I remember, in Holborn and proceeded in quest of Adam, Douglas and others, who might inform me the course of our business and concert measures for the assistance to be given to my part of it. I had then an idea that the question about Sir Elijah Impey, was to come on the 4th of next month; that question, namely, for which I now think it will be time to prepare myself, in the course of the next three or four days. Douglas was going to Mrs. Legge's, and took me home in his carriage. In the course of our drive, we talked upon Sir Elijah, and I then conceived that idea on the argument about discretion, which I think the true one and with which I hope to clear away, some of the confusion, which has gathered upon that question. The trial itself, however, removed any ill effects, and restored my mind to its full tone. I went down the first day, viz. the 10th, with Sheridan; the weather was fine, the scene unusual and the occasion, among the grandest, that can arise in society; my companion, a man qualified to act in great concerns, everything around carried evidences of the general attention and interest, and contributed to raise the mind above itself, to confer upon it new capacities of enjoyment and new powers of action. Till these impressions had become fainter by repetition and the business in the Hall grew to be less interesting, nothing perhaps was lost of that vigour and alacrity, which I had brought with me to town and which, when afterwards impaired, the commencement of the trial had restored. But, by degrees, fatigue and interruption came to prevail and before the recess took place, employment of all kinds was fallen in arrear, and the balance of the account seemed to be considerably against me.

Felbrigg.—The two days of the journey were far from being better than any of those, that had preceded. Though the air was so genial and the aspect of things so gay, as forced one into something of enjoyment, I had a feeling of impediment upon my mind, more than is now frequent with me.

8*th.*—We arrived at Barton Mills about nine o'clock. I had determined to proceed on another stage to Newmarket, notwithstanding its being the time of the meeting. Luckily, when the horses were actually put to, Mrs. Lukin suggested something, which recalled to my mind what I had myself known, of the difficulty of procuring beds, in the instance when I came down there once with Lord Derby.

9*th.*—The next morning we breakfasted at Newmarket, between which and the chaise being ready, I sat with Fox, while he was dressing and talked about horses and the opinions entertained about them at different times. Fox conceived long ears to be a merit, and was surprised at my telling him the judgment given both by Xenophon and Oppian, in favour of short ones. He did not seem to think either, that the head afforded much ground for judging of the qualities of a horse, although he took notice, that it was generally mentioned as a commendation and instanced the 'Argutum caput' of Virgil, without being satisfied, what the precise meaning was, affixed to that term. I felt to regret at that moment, the neglect one is apt to live in of all one's purposes, which prevented my being able to say, both what the meaning was of *argutum* in that passage and what the result of the judgment was, given by all the ancients on the subject. It was a question I have often thought of satisfying myself upon, and would easily be made out. Upon looking since into Gessner and Heyne, *ad locum*, they seem to consider it as relating wholly to the size. When I returned to the inn we set off, having no purpose of staying for the race; but upon Mrs. Lukin saying, as we went by the course, that she had never seen a race, neither at Newmarket nor anywhere else—there being reason too to think, that the first was over the Beacon course, and would soon take place—we agreed to stop, which I was particularly glad afterwards that we did, the fineness of the day having shown the course to its best advantage, and Mrs. L.'s enjoyment of the whole having been, as great as I could have expected. At Hockerill, where we got some dinner, we found Lord Townshend, who would introduce Mrs. Lukin to Lady T. and Lady

Elizabeth. At Epping Place we joined again and they came in to tea to us. We again came together at Islington, where we drank porter with them, Lord T. having stopped the carriage opposite the public house at the corner. Our stopping at Epping was further distinguished by the circumstance of Mr. O'Brien, the Irish giant, being there, to whom I introduced Mrs. L., in a way to produce upon her the full effect of the wonder.

May 6th.—I have in the first place no complaints to make of myself, on the score of having accepted too many invitations, or of having gone too much to Brookes's. To the Club I have gone every time, I believe, of its having been held. I was at the dinner, also, of the Royal Academy, which I enjoyed to a great degree. Among my dinners at private houses, I must not forget that at Cholmondeley's, the women being Mrs. Lukin and Mrs. Byng, and the men Assheton Smith, Neville (no one else) and Delancey, whom I had never seen before since the time of our being at Eton. Such meetings, when known beforehand, are apt to produce disappointment, by promising a satisfaction which a thousand circumstances may happen to defeat. Being fully aware of the probability of such disappointment, I indulged no expectation, or, rather, had prepared my mind in a way to make the absence of painful reflections a source, to a certain degree, of enjoyment. The dinner—compared with what I had happened to find dinners at Cholmondeley's on former occasions and with what I had expected from this—was rather pleasant.

Ever since my leaving town, that is now near five months, I have been employed slowly and at intervals, on Fyzulla Khan; and latterly, on the Wool business, on which I cannot charge myself to have expended so much time, nor to have sacrificed time to so little purpose. The business on which I have suffered my pains to have been thrown away is that of Sir Elijah Impey. I have looked forward for the period above mentioned, on which, negligent as I have been, I had prepared myself in a way to have appeared, I think, to good advantage and which I have now suffered to pass by, without any use made of it. The debate lasted till half-past seven. In our way from the House we were boyish enough to amuse ourselves with throwing stones at each other during our progress through the Park and oranges when we came in St. James's Street. Since the decision of this question, considering myself released from all further care about the business of the sessions, I have felt my mind more airy and excursive and turned my thoughts with considerable enjoyment to the prospects of literary pursuits.

12*th*.—Dined at Twickenham with Sir Francis Bassett. Fox drove me down in his phaeton, according to an arrangement which I had settled prudently in the morning and which turned out as pleasantly as I could wish. The party at dinner was not so well chosen as it might have been; the only persons whom I should have much wished to meet being Fox, Hare, and Lord Robert, amidst many who had little pleasantness of their own to contribute or could much aid that of others. Captain Morris, who was of the number, was not here in his element and afforded to me a strong proof how much particular performances depend for their effect on circumstances. Captain Morris's obstreporous merriment did not accord well, any more than the persons and manners of many of the guests with the elegance of a Twickenham villa. The beauty of the scene however, the fineness of the weather and the first sight of the country in its spring attire, affected the mind very agreeably and made the party abundantly pleasant. To this enjoyment no interruption was given, when, agreeably to an engagement settled with G. North in the morning, I proceeded to Bushey. Fox set me down, and stayed long enough to get some tea. The next day being 13th I went to Beaconsfield.

14*th*.—We returned to town, Burke taking Elliot and myself in the coach to Bulstrode, which I saw for the first time, and Sir Gilbert joining us afterwards with the horses at the gate.

17*th*.—Eton meeting; the first large and formal one at the Festino. I sat there till ten; very pleasant. The person I had been next at dinner was Sir Peter Burrell.

19*th*.—I was to have dined with Lord Sheffield, where I should have met Gibbon, Lord North, Burke, and Fox; but it was the third reading of the Wool Bill, which it was necessary for me to attend, and on which I purposed, and ought, to have spoken. Enough matter was in my mind, and no particular impediment was felt to prevent my making use of it; but the disposition of the House to terminate the debate furnished a pretence for remaining silent, and before the value of this pretence could be estimated the question was put. I rather regret I did not speak.

20*th*.—In the House the business was Burgess's motion, relative to the expenses of the trial, on which if I had been practised to speaking, as I ought to have been, it would have been right to have said something; but not being so practised, I was right, perhaps, to remain silent. I went to the Club and got some dinner on a side table. There were present Lord Ossory, Sir Joshua, Malone, Lord Spencer, and Steevens. We had a good deal of pleasant conversation. About 9 o'clock I went to the play, where I expected to meet Mrs. Crewe. The play had been 'The Regent;' the farce, which was all I saw, was 'The Romp;' one of the parts of which, 'Miss Tomboy,' I think, was acted by Mrs. Jordan.

21*st*.—I went from Westminster Hall to Hatton Garden; but having met Ives, whom I had called upon, walked with him, talking on Norwich politics, till it was time to turn home.

23*rd*.—Went out in the evening to see Lady Anne and

Lady Margaret before their going to the Duke of York's ball.

24th.—Just time to get ready for our party, with Lady Anne and Lady Margaret, out of town; took things with us, and dined on mount in Richmond Park. Lady Cunliffe, the person who so civilly gave up her place, returned from Richmond to Putney by water; very pleasant. Full ten when we landed.

25th.—Went after dinner to Kensington Gardens, I think rather to my loss. Proceeded to Francis's, thence to Manchester Square again. How fairly may such evenings be called lost when no duty is fulfilled, no improvement made, no enjoyment felt. I had in my mind the question agitated by Priestley, about the impenetrability of matter, but was too much upon the confines of sleep to be able to carry it on.

Mrs. Siddons to Mr. Windham.

Four o'clock, Thursday Morning, May 29, 1788.

My dear Sir,—I take the earliest opportunity to thank you for your very obliging letter, and I should certainly put your kindness to the test were I not obliged to leave town to-morrow morning, not without some regrets at having seen so little of you during my stay. I take my leave of you, my dear Sir, wishing you all the good you deserve, and above all things health of body and mind, for I think the languor of one enfeebles the other. It is lucky for me, however, that I have so pleasant an employment to beguile this tedious night as writing to you. 'Past four o'clock,' says the watch, and I have been unable to close my eyes to shut out the day, or to stop my ears to shut out the noise of my own terrible cough, which has tormented me four nights in the same way. I have this moment taken the resolution of getting all the business of the day done in an hour or two, and then taking a tolerable quantity of laudanum to procure a little sleep, for, though 'Macbeth shall sleep no more,' I fancy a little will be necessary to enable his lady to get through her bloody business to-night. I beg ten thousand pardons for troubling you with this history, but when a lady's in the talking vein, you know ——.

Adieu! my dear Sir. There is nothing of which I am more proud than the honour of being

Your affectionate and obliged humble servant,

S. SIDDONS.

June 9th.—I had been that morning with Fullerton and Palmer to Croydon, to a boxing match, and after dinner went before coffee with Elliot and Cholmondeley to the philosophical fireworks. The boxing match was, in consequence of a purse collected by subscription, under the direction of H. Aston, G. Hanger, &c. The combatants, Fewtrill and Jackson, both of them large; one of them, Jackson, a man of uncommon strength and activity, but neither of them of any skill, or likely, so far as appeared upon that occasion, ever to become distinguished. The fight, which lasted an hour and ten minutes, was wholly uninteresting, it being evident from the beginning which was to prevail, and no powers or qualities being displayed to make the prevalence of one or the other a matter of anxiety. The fight which succeeded this between Crabb, a Jew, and Watson, a butcher from Bristol, under 21, was of a different character; so much skill, activity, and fine make, my experience in these matters has not shown me. After a most active fight of forty minutes the Jew was very fairly beat. There was also another fight, between a butcher and a spring maker, neither of them large, but one of them, the butcher, a muscular man, which though smart enough for the time, ended soon by what seemed a shabby surrender on the part of the spring maker; his plea was having sprained both his thumbs, or, as he called it, but not truly, according to their appearance to me afterwards, put them out.

13th.—Every one of the days, which were four, of Sheridan's speaking, I attended Mrs. Lukin and Miss Loveday, the three first to the great door, the last through the Common Pleas. The third morning, the day on which the business broke off, contained in the parts given none of those brilliant passages which made such impressions on the others. From the time of my feeling assured that there was no likelihood of the charges of Fyzulla Khan being brought on this year, I found my mind much lightened and many inlets of enjoyment opened that had for some time been closed up. Ideas of study began now to repossess my thoughts, and to produce an effect on the disposition of my time. The chief interruption was the having Mrs. Lukin with me, which certainly operates in that way, whatever compensation it may bring in the pleasure of her company. How it is that her presence, so little restraint as it imposes, should be a hindrance to employment, is not discoverable at first sight; nor need perhaps be in fact so, if there was nothing wrong in the habits of my own mind. But as the case is, I have very little doubt of its having that effect. The great desideratum with me is continuity of thought: whatever touches me in that part, is liable to leave a wound that is long in curing; the ethereal substance with me does not soon close, but long divisible. There were several parcels of books which had been waiting unpacked, for a time of leisure to examine them; one was, Euler on 'Sounds,' which I bought in February, and which seems to contain just such a treatise of the elements of music as I have so long wished for. At different times I read with Mrs. Lukin some passages and parts of authors.

I find the same question applying to this period as to many others, with equal difficulty for furnishing an answer. . . . . How it is possible to have passed so many days and weeks with so little visible occupation, and yet to have done so little? I have dined out less often, and still less often have had any company to dinner. I blame myself for this, because I think parties of that sort far from injurious, even to the application of time. The thought necessary to combine such a party, the choice of the persons, uncertainty about the day, the trouble of writing the invitations, and in the present instance, I believe, a circumstance so trifling as the delay of setting my room to rights, are the causes that for a winter together keep me from the enjoyments of conviviality in the society of pleasant friends. Against dining out, the lateness of the hour is with me a principal objection: before five o'clock, if I have stayed at home, I get weary and exhausted and want the relief of dinner; if I have gone out, I am tired in another way, and having done nothing by way of employment during the morning, I am impatient of the prospect of suffering the evening to escape in the same manner. My inclination, I believe, in each instance, is for staying at home, but it is very far from being certain that the inclination in each instance is the rule of happiness upon the whole; and such is often the perverseness of one's will, that one's inclination is for staying at home merely because one is obliged to go abroad. Though it be true, therefore, in general, that both when I do dine at home, I do so by choice, and that when I do not, my wish is notwithstanding to do so, I am still far from certain that more frequent dinners abroad would not be of advantage to me; certainly, in such companies as a little thought and decision would provide. I have omitted, in the enumeration of dinners, one at the Duke of Portland's, where were Burke, Fox, Mr. Ellis, G. North, Lord Stormont, Lord Loughborough, Pelham. It was a very pleasant one. At the Club I never failed when it was in my power. I believe the party with Lady Anne and Lady Margaret to Richmond must have been quite at the beginning of June. We set out about two. Dined in Richmond Park, on the same spot where I had dined once before with Malone and his sisters, and came home from Richmond as far as Fulham by water. It was pleasanter than such parties generally are, or than I expected this to be. One throws always at such play, with a certain advantage on one's side in the circumstances of its being out of town, and conferring all the benefit of fresh air, the effects of which I felt as usual, and must consider, probably, as a principal source of my enjoyment. I must not forget, in the mention of this party, the civility of Lady Cunliffe, who, having been in possession at our arrival of the spot where we were to dine, resigned it with great good humour and courtesy in our favour.

23rd.—Stayed at Cossey. Read in the morning some portion of different French books, among others, for the first time, some of Madame de Sévigné's 'Letters.' The quantity I read was not sufficient to enable me to form any judgment about them, except that they seem to be conversant, chiefly as letters ought, about such little circumstances and occurrences as people object to in the letters of Dr. Johnson. That they do not contain remarks so acute, and reflections so fine, I may venture to conjecture, without having read enough to assert. I will read more when I next go there, that is probably in the course of this week, in order to oppose this instance, if the fact should support me, to the petty and malignant cavils of those who object to the genuine and familiar correspondence of Dr. Johnson; that it does not recite important facts, nor abound in learned disquisitions.

24th.—Set off before breakfast in a chaise, and had a drive, not unpleasant, to Aylsham. There is such a dearth of objects, and poverty of ideas, in the ride from Cossey hither, as makes me always think of it with dissatisfaction, though it has happened generally, in fact, that I have found it tolerably cheerful. It has been the thought of what I was going to, or the impression of what I have left, that has protected me from the mean associations which pightels * and gorse commons, Stratton and Fel-

* The Norfolk name for a small field.

thorpe, naturally draw with them. The parts are, perhaps, not numerous, in which twenty miles could be taken producing so few objects worthy of attention, or so little chance of meeting anything not connected with the spot on which it is found.

Since that time—and it is from then that my residence here (Felbrigg) may be most properly dated—I have dined almost every day at home, and by myself, and have not very often been betrayed afterwards into sleep. The Red Room has been the one inhabited, and some of the hours passed there after dinner, reading either Gibbon, or some accounts of Switzerland, with a view to our tour (these are the books which I have chiefly read at those times), have been nearly as pleasant as those which I recollect to have passed one spring at Fulham—I think that of '85.

July 15*th*.—Went to the Assizes; G. Wyndham took me in his chaise; arrived just in time to be on the Grand Jury. I had a lodging at Sharp's, the back of the inns. Of persons at the assizes, besides those usually there, were Lord Townshend and his son, Lord Charles, Coke, Colhoun, and Galway. Lord Townshend came there for the purpose of establishing his society for the protection of game, in which he has found, I believe, but little encouragement. On Friday we went to the Gardens, and on the way back to Cossey I thought of some matters relative to the construction of logarithms.

25*th*.—By the post yesterday I received a summons from the Duke of Portland to attend the Westminster election, and during a ride afterwards, which I took with Mrs. Lukin, determined to set off immediately. It has so happened that, for the first time possibly in my life, Mrs. Lukin and I have not been separated for, I believe, near six months, and the concern she feels at the prospect of separation now, is such, as does great credit to the goodness of her heart, and claims a strong return of kindness and gratitude from me. I have promised her to-night that my absence will not make me forget her, and certainly if I forget *her*, whom shall I remember? Where shall I ever find one so amiable, so worthy, of understanding so acute, of integrity so confirmed, of disposition so pure, and attached to me from feelings of such genuine affection?

26th.—At my return from the Parsonage last night, I had settled to go this evening to Ipswich, and set off, in consequence, immediately after breakfast. I have since new-cast my journey, partly that I might settle at greater leisure what remains to be done here, partly that I might have the enjoyment of some time spent here with the consciousness of having completed all my business, and partly that I might not leave the country without a visit to Cossey. Something now, if I had time, I should like to say of the character of my stay this time. I must confine myself to the observation made, in part, I believe, before, that though the amount of what I have done, is certainly very small, I cannot complain either of deliberate misapplication of time or defect of power. The summer is perhaps, upon the whole, less favourable to application than the autumn or winter, and at Felbrigg possibly more than at other places, yet this disadvantage has been better repaired in the present than in any preceding summer. On the 26th I took my leave of Felbrigg. I had received a letter announcing the exertions made on the part of the Ministry, and soliciting the attendance of all friends, to support Lord ——* the Thursday preceding, viz. 24th, and had determined in the course of that evening that I must go. The debate with myself continued to the last on the course I should take; I made up my mind therefore to going by Newmarket, and sleeping on the road.

27th.—At my arrival at Newmarket, just as I was

* Lord John Townshend, who was elected for Westminster.

giving orders for something for dinner, and in a state to want some relief from my own thoughts, after an exertion of them continued with little intermission during the journey, I was surprised agreeably with a message from Colhoun and Galway, who were in the house, and at that moment at dinner. Upon comparing notes we found that we were going upon the same errand, and had the same purpose of stopping for the night at Hockerill. We agreed therefore to go on for the remainder of the journey together.

August.—What followed for the next month must be entered very shortly, having been omitted at the proper time, and delayed now to a time, perfectly improper, namely, the morning of my arrival at Calais. During the continuance of the election I sacrificed, far too much time, to the business of canvass, by which I lost hours, which might have been employed to great advantage, and with great comfort, and obtained nothing either in service, credit, or amusement, that compensated me for that loss.

3rd.—The Sunday before the poll closed I dined and slept at Shene, coming up the next morning with Burke and Francis, in Burke's chaise.

5th.—The day following the election, I introduced myself, foolishly, or perhaps rather unluckily, into a party at the Duke of Portland's, having found that Fox was to dine there; the business of which proved to be one in which it was not in my power to have any concern, namely, the settling the application to be made for the payment of the elections.

6th.—I set off on my way to see Hippisley and Mrs. H. at Bristol. I omitted the visit which I had intended, and should, notwithstanding the absence of Penn, have been glad to have made to Caversham.

Bristol.—After a few hours was introduced upstairs to Mrs. Hippisley, from whom I found a reception such I had no right to expect, and has endeared her to me beyond measure. The first and only time my having been that road before was in a journey from Oxford to Bath, with Stanhope, I should think in the year 1780 or '71. H. and I parted at Stoke Church Hill, he going to —— and I straight on to town without stopping, as I had at first proposed at Burke's. The occasion of my hurrying on so much was, that I might write a letter to be inserted in one of the papers, to take off, as far as one could, the effect of the accident at Brighton,* of the death of a man in a boxing match. I finished this, contrary to my usual practice in the execution of anything requiring any degree of thought, the next evening, and the next morning, I think, sent it to the 'Morning Chronicle.'

17*th.*—I went the next morning to Windsor, to see my mother, from whence I proceeded for my first visit to Bulstrode. Burke came in consequence of a note from the Duke, left to be delivered to him in his way from London, where he had been sacrificing himself as usual to the public service, and attending a dinner of Queen Anne's parish.

22*nd.*—I called upon Erskine, at Paddington—the first time of my having seen him there, or seen any of his children, which are now not less than four; it was six years, perhaps near eight, since I have fairly made him a visit. As a habit of preparing for events known beforehand, and requiring measures to be previously taken, is one of those in which I have been all my life dreadfully deficient, but for some time less so than before; it may be as well to note, with respect to that habit, what the character was of the present instance. I think it never happened to me before to be so well prepared and with so little effort, proportionably to the nature of the journey. Notwithstanding the lateness of my going to bed, I was

* A man being killed in a prize-fight at Brighton, in the presence of the Prince of Wales, the Prince declared that he would not in future patronise or be present at any pugilistic contest.

up at five, and was at Douglas's by half-past seven, though for want of meeting a hackney coach I walked all the way, and with some delay, from places that I called at. Adam called just before we set out, which was not till near nine. I felt, as I had done for some time before, that I should have been glad if the journey had not taken place.

Calais, 24*th*.—Strong recollection of the place; same in going after dinner to St. Omer. Went to Comedy; enquired for Paston, jun.; saw old Paston, who expressed a most affecting joy. The uncle, who has spent his life in the French service, came to sup with us; the invitation rather too much of his own seeking.

25*th*.—We dined at Arras. Town well-built, not inferior to St. Omer, but different in some respects, having in the houses a greater mixture of materials. The church which they are building, magnificent work; and the College of Benedictines adjoining, an edifice not unlike the new part of Magdalen College, but upon a much greater scale. As we passed out the town, we saw a vast number of people, well dressed, and with great appearance of gaiety, enjoying themselves on a sort of public walk. The women very remarkable for the neatness of their dress about the legs, and the fineness and clearness of their caps; their caps were all nearly of the same sort, and no woman seemed to be so poor as not to be provided with one. I cannot think that such a collection of well and properly-dressed women, is to be seen among the same class in any part of England.

Cambrai.—Arrived at Cambrai not till late; obliged to wait a considerable time for admittance.

26*th*.—Walked for some time about the town; listened to a man singing upon a stage the history of a malefactor, drawn up in the way of the 'Rake's or Harlot's Progress.'

St. Dizier's.—I first saw the preparation for frogs; Douglas saw afterwards more of the process, beginning with the cutting off half their heads with scissors. They catch them with nets, I understand, and only *fricassée* the hind part; the fore parts are used for soups. Here the road to Nancy and to Langres separate. Near here is a seat of the heir of the Duc de Choiseul. From Châlons we had observed the trees on the side of the road cut down. They have got everywhere much into the use of Lombardy poplars. When grown to a sufficient height, and planted close enough, they have a grand effect in closing the roads as between walls. I never knew before what they were good for.

Nancy.—The wood near Nancy is the most extensive I ever saw anywhere; no trees but elm and poplar and walnut, by the side of the road. Where there were woods there appeared to be oak and beech, but the woods, till we came to Lorraine, were very rare; and until we came to Laon, hardly any at all. Except one oak, that was carrying to Cambrai, I saw no oak of any magnitude, till we reached the forest above Saverne. The commandant had an English groom and English horses, which he very foolishly was riding also in the English manner; his groom had about as much notion of riding, as English grooms commonly have.

31*st.*—Set out by a little past five, or earlier. Did not stop until we reached Saverne, where we viewed the palace, building by the Cardinal de Rohan, a magnificent pile, and I think of very good architecture. The descent to Saverne the most beautiful scene in itself, and presenting the most beautiful view, that we have seen; the grand woods of oak through which you descend, the romantic situation of the town, the richness and beauty of the plain beyond Strasburg steeple, and the view of the Rhine at the end, and the mountains of the Black Forest terminating the whole.

Strasburg, September 1*st.*—Ascended to the highest part of the steeple as before, and though with some anxiety beforehand, with little at the time. I thought myself out of it! The appearance of objects much the same as when we thought ourselves in the balloon quite low.

Schaffhausen.—The true river presented itself to view in all its original greatness. Douglas agrees with me, that it is wider than the Thames at Westminster Bridge, and thinks what we saw first, as wide as the Thames at Richmond. We had hardly set our foot on the other side before we were struck, I at least, with the different appearance of things from any we had seen before. Though the houses were of materials inferior to most of those we had seen, being of wood and plaster instead of stone, and the architecture certainly not more regular, there was nevertheless an air of neatness, in whatever it consisted, that gave to my eye a decided superiority over any buildings of the same rank in France. The country was besides of a sort, that I always think of with pleasure, a rich flat, extending from between high mountains and a great river; everything had a look of comfort, population, and industry. The mixture of great trees and orchards with the houses gave a great resemblance to villages in Herefordshire, but, with the advantage, I think, on the side of these. After Offenburg you begin to enter the hills, the appearance of which has long been as beautiful, as most I have ever seen: they rise with sufficient abruptness, in forms beautifully varied, to a height well entitling them to the appellation of mountains, and everywhere covered with woods or vines. The entry to them is by the river Kinzig, which runs into the Rhine, four leagues to the south of Strasburg, and is taken notice of in the geographical books. A little on this side Offenburg we passed through a village, where there was a fair, and on going into the house, saw the peasants dressed in red jackets, and the women in their common habit, dancing two and two, the sort of dance, which, upon sight of, I recollect to have seen formerly, travelling with Erskine between Lucerne and

Berne, and which consists principally as to figure, in turning round. They have, like the planets, a double motion, each couple turning round half, and the whole in succession moving in a circle. Nothing can be more remote from beauty than the countenances of the women through the whole of the Forêt Noire. We hardly saw one that had the least pretensions to be called pretty; we have observed, indeed, a regular decrease of beauty, from the time of our setting off to the present moment. The women of Flanders were handsomer than those further in France, those in France better than the Strasburgeoises, those better in a greater degree than the Forêt Noire. A woman, in one of the couples I saw dancing as above, was the only one that might be called an exception to these observations.

Donneschingen, 3rd.—The residence of the Prince of Fürstenburg, and further remarkable as being the source of the Danube. Beyond is a village on the summit of a bare and pointed hill, formerly the capital of the principality, and now occasionally the residence of the prince in his excursions of hunting. He is himself about thirty years old, much addicted to music, inclined to reading, and not very fond of field amusements; is married to a princess, described by the host as amiable; he is a man I should conceive, from the appearance of the country and the discourse of the people, well-deserving of his subjects, and from some anecdotes mentioned by our landlord of his civility to English travellers, of great courtesy and hospitality. From the information of our host, that a courier must be sent forward to Schaffhausen in order to secure admission to the gates, Douglas had proposed, that Meyers should go on from the next stage without waiting for our coming. I was of a different opinion, not wishing so long beforehand, to deprive ourselves of an option. After much discussion, part of it not very amicable, and the impertinence of the last postboy, who wished that we might be overturned, it became as much my opinion as it was Douglas's, that we should go forward. It soon appeared that the road was as bad as the people had declared. I walked on, and had rather intended to have walked the whole way, though said to be at least twelve miles; but coming to a hill where the road appeared to be so bad as to make it probable some assistance might be wanted to support the carriage, I sat down waiting its arrival. It was so long in coming that I conceived, notwithstanding the care I had taken, that I must have missed the way, and under that idea set off across the fields, following my ear, and making out my way as well as I could in the dark,* meaning, if possible, to keep in reserve the power of returning in time, supposing the sound I had heard not to be that of the carriage. Luckily this purpose I was able to effect. While I was trying the sound which I had

* This adventure, which Mr. Windham regrets as having occasioned the possible loss of a prospect, was a matter of more serious alarm to the companion of his journey, as appears by the following extract from a little diary kept by Lord Glenbervie during this tour, and kindly communicated by him to Mr. Ellis:—

'Windham walked on before the carriage from the Zoll-haus, from whence the road very soon ascends a steep hill, and passes through the Black Forest. As Mr. Windham walks very fast, I had proceeded a mile or two without seeing him, but without anxiety. When the moon set, I stopped at a cottage to have lamps lighted, by which I was detained near half an hour. I then went on for about another half hour through the woods, when Windham's man, who was following the chaise on horseback, rode up and expressed great anxiety about his master. I had at that moment, under the same impression, called to the postillion to blow his horn; but, by a strange perversity of chance, he was the only postillion since we had left Kehl who was unprovided with a horn. I hallooed as loud as I could, but nobody answered. After proceeding a little farther, I repeated the same experiment, and still without success. There is no made road during this stage, and the track for the first two German miles (or French leagues) is extremely bad. At this place it was so much worse than the rest that the postillion advised me to get out. I did, and then hallooed again, when Windham's voice answered me, from a very considerable distance to the left. Having been misled from the road by a noise and voices, which he took to be ours, he had got into wet and marshy ground at a distance from any habitations, and, as the postillion said, was in the neighbourhood of a lake.'

gone in pursuit of, and doubting whether it could proceed from the carriage, I heard what soon proved to be the sound of Douglas's voice coming from the road which I had left. At a house where we stopped, a little short of the town, we had the satisfaction to hear that our admission need not be doubted. At a little before twelve we arrived at the inn where I had been in the year 1780. Some fruit, a good bottle of Burgundy, made me forget my fatigues.

4th.—The bridge is divided into two arches of very unequal length, not of very regular form, as they make together one arch. Each of these is supported below at each end by about five oblique timbers terminating nearly in the same centre, and the innermost of which does not reach to more than a fifth of the arch to which it belongs. The roof of each arch is supported much in the same manner, except that the oblique pieces do not actually terminate in the same centre, but abut, one after another, on the periphery of the bridge, and that the two interior meet the roof at a distance from each other of less than 3 feet; whether, if produced, they would meet in the same point, I was not able, with such observation as I could give it, to ascertain. Precautions were used at the foot of each, to prevent them from forcing themselves outwards, by pieces of timber, nailed on where they abutted upon the periphery.

The only part of our passage which was not abundantly pleasant, was that which succeeded our leaving Lauffenburg, where the extreme heat of the sun, acting upon us without the intervention even of an umbrella, and at a time, when our stomachs were full, may well be supposed inconsistent with any great enjoyment; notwithstanding, I resisted sleep, and, between reading and looking about, kept my thoughts going pretty well. The short rest we had at Numph, and the fruit and wine I got there, while I lay stretched on the grass in the shade, was in itself a great relief. By what we supposed the ignorance or obstinacy of the boatmen, we were kept an irksome three quarters of an hour waiting at a little door at the east end of the bridge for admittance.

Basle, *6th.*—In the evening, Douglas and I went to see the 'Dance of Death,' thence to the Library, which, though a great object in my imagination when I stopped before at Basle, I had never seen, we now saw very much at length. The professor of theology, the person to show it, was very civil and patient, and we tried both to their full extent. After the cabinet of pictures, in which, besides many excellent and curious pictures of Holbein, there are two portraits, which I saw with much pleasure, of Bernouilli and Euler. We went to the room of manuscripts, where we saw a MS. *in literis uncialibus* of the O. T., the date ascribed to which I don't recollect; another small copy of later date, by which it appears by the private marks, corresponding to those of the printed one, that Erasmus took his edition; and a third, considered by the professors, of the 13th century. It was from this last that we copied the passage at the beginning of St. John's Gospel. There was a curious collection of letters of Erasmus in his own hand, which was a fair and flowing character, such as might be expected from him. Supped at the *table d'hôte* with the two Abbés; curious mixture of ignorance and information about affairs in England, and exhibition of French conversation, which did not render me better affected towards it, though perhaps not worse in itself than what might be met with from persons of the same rank in England.

The natural timber of the country through which I have passed since my leaving Basle, as in the Forêt Noire, as perhaps between Basle and Schaffhausen, seems to be fir, and of the spruce kind. In one place only, and that in the Forêt Noire, I recollect to have seen a silver fir, though I am far from saying that there may not have been a great many. None of them that I have seen, or hardly any, have been of a great size, the reason of which seems to be the want of care and culture, and their being oppressed in consequence by their own numbers. What reason is there to think that in the production of trees nature should just take that course which would produce them separately for the greatest size? Yet this, I remember, was one of the opinions of Mr. Stillingfleet. When I say that I have seen no larger ones, I mean now growing, for of the trees cut down, of the fir kind, I saw some at Schaffhausen, larger than any I remember to have seen, except those at Florence.

7th.—Set off rather before eleven, Douglas in the chaise, for Zurich and Lucerne; I in an open chaise, with Meyers on horseback and Morton in the carriage, for Berne. On the way I met an English carriage, with a person whom, till I came quite near, I took for Fox. The places hitherto in Switzerland, where I have seen the largest and greatest numbers of oaks, was in the great wood, on this side Basle. Before the separation of the road between this and Berne, there was a very large oak on the top of the hill from Soleure. I do not think, however, that I have seen yet any oak tree so large as the oaks at Rainham, Kedleston, or perhaps as one or two at Felbrigg.

9th.—I rose early, and continued in my room, making calculations upon some of the results given in Dutens, till dinner was ready at the *table d'hôte*, where were two friars of Soleure, who spoke nothing but German. I determined, upon a just estimate of probabilities, to proceed straight to Bienne, conceiving that I had in that way the best way of meeting Fox. I supped at the *table d'hôte*, where there were many people, few of them of very decent condition. The man I chose as the person to sit next, was a native of Bienne, whom, from his dress and manner, I should have taken for a rider, and who perhaps might be one, but who had, as he informed me, been an advocate. He wore his hair tied, without powder, had boots, and a large cutlass, which I conceived to be intended for the defence of his property. With the French which he has acquired he seems to have taken in also a proportionate share of French grimace and affectation.

10*th.*—Dined, according to engagement, with Woodruff and Bruce. While we were sitting after dinner, and talking about Eton, received a message that Fox was in the house, and desired to see me.

11*th.*—Almost the whole day spent with Fox, that is, from after breakfast till supper.

12*th, Friday.*—To-morrow will be three weeks since my leaving England, ten days of which will have been passed in Switzerland. For these last two days and a half, I have been living with Fox. We have talked a great deal, but I think not much upon anything but what we have seen, or about to see. We went this evening to the walk over the river, where the fir hedges are, and where I remember to have gone with Erskine, and afterwards took a long drive. In the morning I sat at home till near one; employed, with considerable exertion, nearly the whole time with some matters out of Dodson. When I went to dinner, I felt rather tired and exhausted. I have not been idle; with the help of Dutens' Tables and Dodson I have given myself something in mathematical employment, which I have pursued, perhaps, once or twice, with as much diligence, as at times here most appropriate to such purposes. Among the observations Fox was making, one was the extreme mildness of the government of this canton, and at the same time the great power lodged in an aristocracy, and again, the example given here lately of the greater prudence sometimes, of people in the administration of public money, than in that of their own, so contrary to the position assumed in the discussions, that took place on the India Bill; the Government here having always placed their money in the English funds, while individuals, lured by the temptation of greater interest, risked all theirs in the French.

13*th*.—In the morning, before I went to Colonel Brown, I had seen Lavater, who gave, as Fox informed me afterwards, an opinion of me, which from its peculiarity and agreement with what many have said of me, seemed an extraordinary effort of his art, viz. that I was a man who did not choose to do anything which I was not conscious of doing well; but the whole mystery of this is perhaps done away, by supposing that he took his opinion only from observing that I did not speak French, and yet, judging from my manner in pronouncing a few words, that I could have done it tolerably well had I been willing. We all set off after dinner for Thun, I leaving a letter written in haste, 'but expressing all I wanted for Douglas,' who arrived ten minutes after I was gone. Fox and Mrs. Armitage set off before, Hare and I followed in his carriage, their servants coming in the one I had hired. Slept at inn over the water and above the bridge, not the same I was in the time before. Saw in the morning the old man, whose teeth Erskine had knocked out. Thought to have reminded him of the fact, and have given him some money, but was deterred from the sulkiness of his look; was sorry afterwards that I had been so. Memory of lake hardly so correct as it ought to have been. In passing before, I recollect I had been, for part of the way, calculating in my head, I doubt, whether so actively employed this time. We were four hours in crossing (lake of Thun). Inn the same as before. Went before dinner into the churchyard, and it being Sunday, thought of Dr. Johnson, and for once, happily, did not think in vain. I prayed with some fervour, and feel at this moment the effect of having done so, and of the note, of which

I am now taking of it. Nothing can be more beautiful than the valley, separated rather from the rest, at the end of which Meyringen is.

25*th.*—Quitted Lausanne with Douglas. Everything had been arranged the night before for my setting off by myself by way of Besançon, but upon his coming into my room, and seeming unwilling we should part, I agreed to stay and proceed with him to Geneva. Violent repentance of this, which continued all the next day and the morning following, till Douglas himself, perceiving probably that I was grudging every moment of delay, expressed his opinion that each had better go his own way.

October 1*st.*—It was ten o'clock though I had risen at six, before I set off in a two-wheel French chaise for Paris, by way of the Jura and Dijon. A letter I got in the morning from Mrs. Lukin assisted the effect of a fine day, and made me very gay. I am sorry to say that the pleasantest moments of my tour have been those which I have passed by myself. Something of uncomfortableness hung upon my mind, as it does perhaps still, from apprehension of ridiculous and vexatious distresses, in which I might be involved for want of speaking and understanding sufficiently the language, but that was overpowered by the other sources of satisfaction which I had; the consciousness of having fulfilled my purposes, and the prospect of being speedily in England, and the *feel* of being left at large to the government of my own motions, and the enjoyment of my own thoughts. I travelled on therefore with great gaiety, walking generally before the chaise, the country being perfectly wild and mountainous, till about ten, when I reached at length La Maison Neuve.

4*th.*—We are now at Fontainebleau. We have seen the palace, not quite as I could have wished, the light having failed us, and, in consequence, the time. I have seen it, however, with great satisfaction. The Queen's chamber and dressing room are fitted up in the richest style, with great neatness, as it seems to me, in workmanship, and elegance of taste. The other apartments were magnificent and costly, which I thought less elegant. The whole effect from the outside, from the extent of the building, variety both as to form and parts, and style of architecture, was very grand and princely. I am delighted, too, with the nature of the country, and of its fitness for the purpose for which it is intended. There is art enough to remind one always of the neighbourhood of greatness; but not so much as to destroy the enjoyment of wildness and solitude. The morning was delightful, and gave the prospect of a fine day for entering into Paris; this failed us, however; the air, instead of clearing up, and giving way, as we expected, to a bright sun, continued so thick that nothing could be seen at a distance of half a mile. The Faubourgs, as I was prepared to find, were mean and dirty; but the town itself, even in what I have yet seen of it, surpassed my expectations, and is in various respects superior to London, though in others much inferior to it, and perhaps inferior on the whole: the comparison is very difficult to be made. I have been since to the Italian Comedy, where I found no one that I knew but St. Leger, who had been at the camp at St. Omer. Young Broadhead was also there, and Captain or Colonel Leigh, and two other English, whom I did not know. Leigh's opinion of the French troops was that they were larger men than the English; and the Swiss regiments were the finest he ever saw. He had understood that their war manœuvres were very slow; and, from his own view, he was of opinion that, in respect of their camps, they were very ill-appointed and provided. He mentioned a curious anecdote of one of their colonels, who, in conversation with St. Leger, on the present disputes, expressed his doubts of the troops' acting. From the theatre I came home, and feeling now, 'as I have done ever since my arrival,' much impressed with the idea of being in Paris. Rome certainly was a finer sensation; but this comes next.

6*th*.—En sortant ce matin j'avais l'idée de me rendre chez Haile,* afin de trouver des nouvelles de Burgess.

8*th*.—Went about in the morning with Hare.

9*th*.—Douglas and I went to Versailles; the grandeur of Versailles passing my expectations. Nothing more princely than the great gallery, which is open, I understood, to all persons of decent appearance. We saw the King and the Comte d'Artois. Both Douglas and Mr. Dovrun confirmed strongly my idea of the resemblance of the King to poor Lord Northington. The Queen, unluckily, had not either gone to mass with the King, nor gone to the Comedy. By the aid of Mr. Dovrun, we obtained admission to see the Little Trianon, which I really thought very pretty. This made us so late in returning, that instead of going, as we talked, to the Variétés, which I had not seen, we took a tour only in the gardens of the Palais Royal. Douglas kept me talking till past one. There was a difficulty also about my passport. Particulars of the journey not worth recording. It may be of more consequence to observe of my stay in Paris, that much of the pleasure of it was lost, by careless intemperance and neglect of preserving that degree of high health, which I had enjoyed during the journey. In an evening I was tempted to eat largely of grapes, and to drink proportionately of an agreeable Burgundy, which they sold at two livres a bottle; to this, I believe, is to be ascribed, that, till the last night, when I had not done so, I never had a comfortable night's rest. How much influence this must have had on the pleasures of thought and imagination, may be easily understood on

* There is no evidence to identify this person. Could he have been the Thomas Hales, better known as M. d'Hèle, author of the 'Jugement de Midas,' to whom Mr. Van der Weyer has devoted an interesting passage in his 'Lettres sur les Anglais qui ont écrit en Français'?

reflection, though they were not considered in practice. For my rooms I paid six livres per diem; they consisted of bedroom, sitting-room; ditto, ditto, for servant; they struck me at first as superb, but afterwards as mean, such is the force of comparison. For my carriage I paid fifteen livres per diem, two livres for coachman, lacquais-de-place two livres. Traiteur, for dinner, four livres. Breakfast, coffee and bread, but I think not butter, fourteen sols. For grapes I paid, according to the charge of the lacquais-de-louage, whose name was Thomasin, eight sols per pound. The incidents of my journey I have already agreed not to set down. The quarter of the Prince de Condé's stables, which I counted, contained sixty stalls. The peasants spoke here, as in the neighbourhood of Fontainebleau, with great horror of the mischief done by the stags, boars, and game. One of them, of whom I made the enquiry, was the man who struck me with such a resemblance of the countenance in Hogarth's print of the preparation for war. My arrival at Boulogne was very pleasant, as was my whole journey. It was at some distance from Boulogne, I think, in the stage but one before, that I got the first view of the sea. Pleasure of the same sort as that of the Ten Thousand. The room and reception at Payne's were uncomfortable; a pleasant *feel*, however, at the consciousness of being at home: much struck with the appearance of things the next morning. One of the circumstances most striking, a look of confidence and alacrity in the people, the same as I remember to have remarked the first time of having gone into France and St. Omer. An air of neatness too in everything, which I had in like manner remarked.

November 14*th*.—I went to Sir Joshua Reynolds', and from thence home, where I heard, for the first time, of the death of my late footman, poor James, whose long continuance in my service had enough imprinted him on my memory and whose good qualities enough recommended him to my regards to make the news of his death an occasion of tenderness, which does not fail to return whenever the subject passes through my mind.

How I passed the five days till my leaving London (19th) I don't particularly recollect; but I remember, in general, that little of them was spent at home, not so much from impatience of being there as from habit of vagrancy, and satisfaction more than ordinary, which I found in moving about the streets. The impression of London as a new place was not worn off in those few days, nor the habit lost of fixing my attention on objects around me, and keeping my mind steady while my body was in motion. Of my stay at Felbrigg I must speak in the lump. From the moment of my arrival in England I had left reading French, and from the time of my leaving London had taken to reading Greek.

1789.

February 4th.—If I have again failed of making the commencement of my account coincide with the beginning of the year, I have gained at least on the account of the year preceding. Let me hope that these advantages may be an omen of the superior diligence with which this Journal will be carried on; for I have no reason to alter the judgment, given in the outset of the last volume, that this practice of journal writing leads one insensibly into a habit of composition, strengthens the powers of recollection, and by showing how one's time is actually disposed of, suggests the means and excites the desire, of disposing of it to greater advantage.

It must have been in the preceding month that I spoke upon the Prince's right. All that I have done besides in that way, since the present meeting of Parliament, and previous to the present month, was in that short discussion on the interpretation of the Address to the Prince, in which the only merit I could pretend to, was, that I took the lead, and pointed out first the unfairness of that proceeding. During the whole time of my being in town, as well previous, as subsequent to the commencement of the year, I have stayed more at home, than during any preceding period.

My visitings, however, have been unexpectedly increased by two balls, one at Lady G. Cavendish's, the other at Lady Porchester's. I should have liked both better, if the coat I had on, had not been finer, than I liked.

On Monday last (2*nd*) was the debate on the Phantom,

on which I had prepared myself and conceived I should make a grand argument; * but when the business began, my powers deserted me more, I think, than they have done for a long while back, though not at all in the same way as formerly; and I had given up almost entirely the intention of speaking, when, unexpectedly, an opportunity offered, of which I took advantage. My performance seems to me, to have been as well thought of, as any I have exhibited; and is likely to be better thought of, as a criterion of my powers as a speaker, since it was evidently a speech, which I was not so bent upon delivering, but, that a very slight difference in the circumstances would have put the intention aside.

After the House, having been set down by Lambton at Brookes's, I was tempted to go in to supper and sitting down with Grey and Fitzpatrick, continued there till between twelve and one.

3rd.—I dined at Malone's against my wishes, it being the day of the Club. I suffered myself to go to Beckett's principally with a view to see what had been said by the 'Gazetteer' of my speech the Monday preceding, a curiosity I have seldom felt before and still less often indulged.

The next day was much the same sort. I rose late; was tempted to go out; met Lord Porchester at Burlington House, who gave me such an invitation from Lady P., to go to an assembly which she had in the evening, as could not be declined. I went there accordingly and having been invited to stay to supper, did not get home till between two and three. On Friday, which was the day following, I rather suspect was the day of my dining with Miss Adair, her father and brother, in expectation of

* Before the opening of Parliament 1789, the King being insane, the question arose, by what authority the letters patent for the convocation of Parliament should be issued. The King was described as a phantom and the Parliament itself supplied the temporary deficiency of the executive power.

meeting Mrs. Siddons. What I did on Saturday I don't recollect: on Sunday, I conceive, I dined with Lord Stormont, calling in the evening at Francis's.

It was perhaps the Monday after that I made another little exertion in the House, not on any previous intention, but pretty much at the desire of Burke, who, upon Dundas's getting up, desired me to wait upon him. What I did, answered the purpose sufficiently well. It was immediately an answer to Hawkins Browne; the matter relative to a motion of Lord North's, for appointing by office, instead of by name, certain of the Queen's Council, on which the principle was stated, which directed one or other mode of appointment, and the suspicion to which Parliament would expose itself, by adhering so tenaciously to one of these. Mention was likewise made of the nature of this second office, which Parliament had to perform, and the importance shown to be not less than that of the first. People seemed to think the observations important and well laid down. The recollection of it now produced by these remarks, makes me know, that the observations were not well laid down, and far from powerfully urged.

I think, the day after, went to the battle between Johnson and Ryan at Rickmansworth. The party were Crewe, Fitzpatrick, Grey and George. We had set off in time: the day was fine; the company pleasant. We had an object before us; the country air did its duty by me and I felt all those spirits, which such a concurrence of causes, was likely to produce. The delay that took place afterwards, with the change of weather and vexation at being made too late for the debate, took off all satisfaction and made me well disposed to have gone away without seeing what we came for.

The battle at length took place and was certainly a very grand one. Yet upon the whole I both blame and am sorry for my going. The occasion was one of those on which not to have gone would have been as much matter of remark as the going. And I am not sure that if I had stayed I might not have taken part in the debate.

19*th.*—Went to Windsor. The objects of Eton, seen in company with an Eton boy, produced upon my mind more than their usual impression, and by disengaging my thoughts from present associations gave me for a while a new view of life.* We lodged at the Castle. In the morning, we took before breakfast a short walk on the Terrace, and after breakfast saw the Castle. In our way through Eton, stopped at Mr. Hetherington's (Domine Newman, that was), walked through the school-yard, the cloisters and playing fields, and so to the chaise at the end of the Long Walk.

22*nd.*—Called, I remember, on Lady Howe, and meeting Fitzpatrick near Hay Hill, went back with him to Burlington House to see Fox. Lost time in deliberating whether I should dine at Lord Spencer's or not; determined at last for dining and found in the event, that I had determined very rightly. It was just six when I went there. From the time of my going to that of my returning, was just three hours. What was I likely to have done in those three hours had I remained at home? At dinner, were Sloper, George Conway, Bingham, Charles Greville, Mrs. Howe, old Lord George, and Marchant.

Monday, 23*rd*, was the night of my going to Mrs. Gally. Before supper I came away, not knowing whether the party proposed the Saturday before, was to take place, of going to see masks. About this I received a note from Lady A. Lindsay.

Thursday, 26*th.*—Know not what I did. Upon recollection dined with Mrs. Crewe and went to the play. Mrs. Jordan, in 'Hippolita': † much amused. Play incom-

* Mr. Windham's father died when he was eleven years old. He was sent to Eton at the age of seven, and remained till he was sixteen.

† In the play of 'She Would and She Would not,' by Cibber.

parably well acted throughout; no part, in my opinion, better than Miss Pope's. After the fourth act, went up to Mrs. Crewe in Mrs. Sheridan's box, where were Miss Linley and Miss Tickell, and for awhile, Tickell and Richardson. I don't know when I have seen a play with so much enjoyment.

28th.—Called on Delegates.* Dined with them at Lord Fitzwilliam's, and called afterwards on Lord Townshend —not at home—and at Walpole's, with whom I sat for some time; thence home. Mrs. Lukin uncomfortable at the seeming asperity in my manner. Sat till twelve or past, to take off that impression.

March 1st.—Went out at two to attend a meeting at Burlington House. Dined at Lord Spencer's, with Delegates, Prince, and Duke of York.

Monday, 2nd.—Dined at Adair's. Mrs. Siddons, Burke, R. Adair.†

3rd.—At home all morning, I think. Dined at Club. Numerous meeting; Bishop of Killaloe, Lord Palmerston, Lord Elliot, Sir Joseph Banks, &c. I had felt during the morning, what continued there, something of languor, which made me adopt finally a purpose, before conceived, of going to Mrs. Byng at Drury Lane, where Mrs. Siddons was to appear in 'Coriolanus.' By the delay of the servants and negligence of the waiters, I did not arrive till her part was finished. To accommodate Mrs. B., I stayed part of the farce, 'The Waterman,' so as to take her home.

4th.—Dinner, I think, at home. In the evening, Mrs. Sheridan's, with supper for the Delegates.

5th.—Dinner, I have a notion, in like manner at home. Duchess of Devonshire's ball; stayed till four.

6th.—Employed, I conceive, for part of the morning,

* Meaning the persons to whom the Royal authority was delegated.

† Sir Robert Adair, the intimate friend of Mr. Fox, was born in 1763, and died in 1855, at the great age of 92.

with the business of Sudbury, about which a letter had been brought me, on the Wednesday night, at Sheridan's. Dined at Mill's.

7th.—Employed again about Sudbury. Great self-reproach for having neglected till then, what I had intended so long ago, on my leaving the country in Norwich. Dined at Lord Porchester's; Thomas Grenville, Lord Robert Spencer, Crawford, Sir Gilbert Elliot, Pelham, Lady Almeria Carpenter. Dozing in my own room, till it was time to go to Mrs. Crewe's, to a supper prepared for the Delegates, to which I went with a great deal of reluctance, but where I found myself very comfortable.

8th.—I spent the whole of the morning at home, but was far from being, during the whole of it, profitably employed. The great employment, which should have engaged me from some time back, viz. the preparation of myself for saying something on the King's Message,* I had wholly neglected. Part of the morning was lost in idle talk with Mrs. Lukin and part in deliberation what I should do respecting dinner. One of my visits in the morning had been to the Bishop of St. David's, an invitation to stay and dine there not firmly and skilfully refused, involved me in a sort of promise to go there in the evening. I drank tea, therefore, with him.

10th.—The want of good preparation and the discouragement arising in every quarter to the intention of my saying anything, furnished a pretext for silence, abundantly sufficient for the moment, and that moment once past, nothing was left but to condemn my own want of resolution, and to regret an opportunity which might have been improved greatly to my own credit, and perhaps in some degree to the advantage of the cause.

After the House I went in very bad spirits to dine with Fullarton. About 10 the coach came, and we went to

* The King's Message of this date was to announce his recovery from illness.

see the 'Illuminations;' Lady Margaret and Lady Anne, and Douglas, whom we took up at Lord North's, but from the crowd of coaches we could not get into any of the best streets.

12*th.*—Notice to attend the Delegates at Carlton House, to receive the Prince's answer; went punctually at the time, viz. one o'clock. Journey not unpleasant except to Mrs. Lukin, who was low-spirited and affected with something which I had said beyond what she ought. The drive from Lothian's to Carlton House was the time of Burke's intemperate attack on me, for a difference, which he had forced me to declare, on the affairs of *Baretti.** I must endeavour to obliterate from my mind, the impression, which passion so unreasonable and manners so rude would be apt to leave.

13*th.*—Entry into Sudbury.

16*th.*—After a good deal of business done in Norwich, in the way of calling, came away at half past twelve. From some accounts which I heard, cannot help entertaining doubts of the security of my seat. Will it not be advisable to put the question to people by a species of select canvass? It is very fair to say, that they now know enough of me to be able to make up their minds, and that I may reasonably expect, they should declare their minds, while time is yet left to me to look out for other situations. We arrived at Felbrigg about half past four and went to the Parsonage for some dinner, where we found George Wyndham.

18*th.*—Set out for the purpose of being at Norwich to-night, to be present at the illuminations on the King's recovery; and at Thetford to-morrow to meet Coke, who expects something to be said on the candidates for the county.

19*th.*—After walking about the town the preceding evening, supped at Tuck's Coffee House in the large room

* Baretti stabbed a man in the Haymarket, and was tried for it.

above stairs. The two Crowes, Herring (John), Buckle, Bolton, James Beevor, &c. Felt as gay and happy, as in better company. Slept at Taylor's, who was in London. I had come from Aylsham with G. Wyndham. The thought had occurred to me of going to Wretham, where I found Coke was; but want of timely thought and decision suffered the moments to elapse, till my things were taken to my lodgings, and I thought it too late. It was not too late to have decided upon going, even after my things were removed to my lodgings. The uncomfortableness occasioned by the whole of this, determined me to listen to a request of Alpe's to sup with them at the 'George,' instead of returning to read Simson's 'Algebra,' which I had newly purchased, at my lodgings.

20*th.*—Woke pretty soon and thought earnestly of some matters that had occurred in Simson. Breakfasted at inn (Bell). Day spent as usual on such occasions. The Grand Jury 23 in number. I dined with the judge, Sir Nathaniel Grove. At dinner Hobart was stating the case of a vote objected to at the Colchester committee, to a pauper, but admitted as having never received anything, though he had been excused paying parish rates. Mingay confirmed the decision of the committee in the true spirit of a literal lawyer, because he had never received anything, and the judge seemed disposed to do the same, and so most of the others. But it is plain that, in the spirit of the act, to have a payment remitted is the same as to have a payment made. The only doubt is, as the judge also remarked, whether the principle of construing a disqualification strictly, should not operate in favour of the vote.

22*nd.*—Went away between eleven and twelve and expected to enjoy myself as usual during the drive (to Cossey), but soon found my attention go away without suspecting the cause, which did not discover itself till afterwards to be sickness at the stomach.

24th.—Mrs. Lukin and Mary, who had breakfasted here, returned to dinner; and before dinner was on table George came in from Aylsham fair. We dined in the library. They proposed, between nine and ten, to go home; I rather pressed them to stay, thinking that I was not likely to employ the time to any advantage by myself. But the event showed I was mistaken; for though I was excluded from my own room—the fire being gone out—I remained in the library reading Hume's 'History' with great delight and profit.

25th.—George and Mrs. Lukin dined here, I think, and certainly slept here. I wish I could know at once in what year it was that we used pretty constantly to walk out just before it was dark, taking a circuit through the park and woods and sometimes beyond.

27th.—Day remarkably pleasant. This was an instance of a ride highly beneficial: I was thoroughly languid and jaded before I went out, the justice business having followed on some hours spent in diligent study, and immediately upon getting on horseback felt my spirits revive and rise gradually into a state of enjoyment which continued during the remainder of the day.

30th.—Waked in the morning at five by a messenger from Norwich, informing me of Coke's intention to canvass Norwich the next day. Wrote to Forster my reasons for not coming as soon as I was up. Another express at the same hour. Obliged now to go. Read before I went to bed the account in the papers of the commencement of the settlement of Botany Bay.

April 1st.—Returned to Felbrigg about twelve. Came in the chaise till within about half a mile and thought with great success of questions concerning impossible roots and negative signs, the same as had engaged my thoughts in going from Aylsham.

2nd.—Wrote a long letter to Forster and Unthank, on the subject of the advertisement which had been sent me from the Bury paper, put in by Sir Edward Astley. I had some more letters to write, particularly to the provost of Dublin, which I should have finished during the evening, but did only begin.

3rd.—At three I went to the Parsonage and their dinner being begun, returned and dined in the red room. Very comfortable. I read Hume's 'History.' A week has now passed, for it is just so long since Brettingham came, during which, except about a page or two of translation and some mathematical work carried on in my head, I have hardly had any regular employment, or thought of anything, but cornices, colours, stained glass, &c.

4th.—Instead of betaking myself to any earnest employment, or contriving how to despatch most quickly the attention necessary to be given to what was doing below, I rather abandoned myself to the prospect of interruption and suffered my thoughts to wander, because my time was likely to suffer some slight disturbance. I had hesitated, as the day before, between the red room and the library, but decided differently and dined in the library. I felt so comfortable as to purpose to myself as a memorandum, that one of the ways, 'qua ratione queas, etc.,' was to read English history in the library. It was near eleven before I was settled in my own room. I considered then, not entirely without success, though in a state too near to drowsiness to be proper for such discussions, the question I have had in my mind lately about impossible roots.

6th.—Anniversary dinner. Returned to Aylsham with Adey in the chaise; slept during part of the way and for part, thought of address which is proposed for Fox, in the repeal of the Shop Tax. Though my faculties were not clear, my attention was very connected.

10th.—After walking out for a little while in a mild but hazy morning, I sat down to translation. What is the advantage, for purposes of pursuit, of residence here over residence in London? One consideration is, that every day here is not passed as I am supposing this to be; nor every day there as I have supposed the one stated to be. There is then, to cover all, the great and ruling difference of health, which avails, I am persuaded, more than any other.

12*th*.—Having risen at a little after seven and found the morning very fine, was tempted to order my horse, the first time of my riding out before breakfast since my being here. I went round by Cromer, and called on G. Wyndham, who was just setting off for London. Church was in the afternoon; the congregation fuller than I can remember almost to have seen, even of late, when certainly a change had been made in that respect, and which I cannot help suspecting to have been brought about by the arrangement of Mrs. Lukin, perceiving at different times what my opinions were and particularly, probably upon occasion of my giving to George the living of Runton.

13*th*.—Rose at seven, and the morning being the same as yesterday, followed the same course of riding and have found the same effects. My spirits may be said, in fact, to be over good; for instead of pressing me forward to vigorous application, they have broken out in singing and dancing. Upon the subject of singing, I have discovered a fact which I am not pleased with, that my voice in notes which I used to command, is become harsh and feeble. Whether this is only disuse, or some temporary cause, I cannot tell, but suspect it may be among the number of those changes which years are every day producing, or that it may be the consequence of straining my voice, when speaking this winter in the House of Commons, at the commencement of a hoarseness. The air in which I made the observation was, 'Viene o caro.' From trying again and not finding the effect in the same degree, I rather hope it may be only disuse, a consideration which may recommend the practice occasionally of singing to oneself oftener than one's spirits now prompt one, for the purpose of keeping one's voice in proper style for other uses.

14*th.*—Rose by time and rode out; ride confined to park and woods. This was one of a very few occasions in which dinner seemed to make no break in the day, nor to occupy more than the mere time employed in eating. What a difference it would make in the quantity of one's time and in the degree of one's enjoyment, if this was always to be so! and is there not very good reason to believe that it depends on oneself only to have it always so? Surely this is worth the experiment.

15*th.*—Rode to Hanworth. Dined, as I had purposed, at Parsonage. Mrs. Lukin, after dinner, produced some letters of mine, some of which she had shown me the night before, from dates as early as —63. Of later dates she has a great many, which I am to see. Those which I have seen hitherto show no powers of any sort, yet they have more regularity than I should have expected from my letters of those periods and have occasionally, I think, something in the structure of sentences resembling my present writing.

16*th.*—Spent the chief of the morning in the library, in a kind of desultory mathematical reading; and when the time came for riding out, supposing that a ride was to be taken before dinner, found myself so much distracted and exhausted, as to stand very much in need of that relief.

17*th.*—Justice meeting at Cromer. The weather having been rendered by the rain uncommonly pleasant, took a ride round by Runton, calling, in my way, at Johnson's. I had decided to return home before I went to the Parsonage and I continued employed with great success, from seven to half-past nine, in stating at length the nature of the argument used by Simpson (Thomas) in assigning the sum and of the series 1^2, 2^2, 3^2, &c.

18*th.*—Rode out with Mrs. L. before dinner, confining our ride, from the lateness of its commencement, to the park. I had to settle the place of some fir-trees, to be added to those at the S. E. corner of the house. We dined in the red room. The supper in the library appeared to me more domestic and convivial than I had ever probably found it before.

19*th.*—Uncomfortable from the same causes that had made me so before. I had not dispatched my business as I ought, nor felt the power to do so now. The feel was increased by some irritation, more than was wise, at the folly of George bringing his boy John to breakfast, to be stuffed with chocolate, &c., at the expense of our conversation. After various delays I set off with George in the chaise, not till it was so late as to leave little hopes of reaching Ipswich before eleven. In setting off, it occurred to me that I had done wrong not to ride to Aylsham. I accordingly ran back for my horse and thus had the satisfaction of again taking leave of Mrs. Lukin, though my riding back so unexpectedly occasioned a momentary alarm.

20*th.*—Left Ipswich not till near twelve. Saw Humphries there and was entertained for the first time with some sparring: felt much amused with the whole of the business. During the whole of the way I was employed in thinking—first, on a proposition; then, on some questions about combinations, particularly about the affinity between an increase of a rectangle, the nearer the parts get to equality, and the increase of the combinations, the nearer the numbers being complements to each other, and which may be taken an equal number of times out of the proposed number, get to equality. There must be something of a principle common to these two processes. We dined at Witham; drank tea at Ingatestone, where we were detained some time for want of horses.

May.—It is now more than three weeks since I

arrived in town. My departure from England last summer is the point, perhaps, at which I may state myself to have made, in this progressive improvement, the greatest step. It deserves to be remembered that, according to this statement, the greatest improvement seems to have been made at times when least opportunity was afforded to solitary study. Let me recall, as far as I can, in what manner my time has been passed, that some opinion may be formed as to the causes of this effect and some inference as to the most advantageous application of time in future. I had company to dinner, I think the 10th, when Byng, Palmer, Courtenay and Malone dined with me. They stayed a short time and I walked afterwards about the streets, meditating on some business—the Censure, I think, on Burke and the Managers, which was to come on the next day. I have spoke in the House this time oftener than usual—once on the Censure—that is, one day; for I spoke in the course of the day three times, on the Repeal of the Test, &c., Acts, on the Hawkers and Pedlars, viz. 18th.

To-day (20th) a few words on the bringing up of a Bill to prevent the robbery of gardens. Of these speeches, what the estimation was, I don't know. That on the Censure, appeared to me to contain a statement of part of the question, sufficiently obvious, but which had by some means been overlooked and which I thought more forcible than any that had been urged. Pigott was of the same opinion. I don't recollect, however, that from others I heard much commendation of it. Let me recollect, by the way, that there must have been another opinion of my speaking on the same question, since part of what I said now, was, in answer to remarks made on what I had said before. What I said the other day, on the Hawkers and Pedlars, seemed to me to have more the air and character of a speech, and to be treated in a way, more calculated to take with the hearers, than anything

I had ever done. Some things, too, which have been said to me since, might favour that opinion; yet, whether it is that the thinness of the House and smallness of the occasion made less notice to be taken of it, or that all praise is relative to previous expectation, and that where more is expected more must be done to gain the same praise, I have heard less of this (though certainly as much as it deserved) than I have heard on former occasions. It certainly seems to me very odd and is a proof how much the notion of a speech raises in people's imagination the value of what it consists, that anything I have ever said in the House should have been thought of a second time. Much of the praise given on these occasions, certainly depends on the circumstances and estimation of the speaker.

Let any one remember the reception and examine the language and matter of any of Francis's speeches and then say what the proportion is, on matters of this sort, between praise and merit. Francis's speeches are regular compositions, exhibiting in many parts great force of thought and conceived, throughout, in language peculiarly elegant and energetic. I know not any one whose speeches, in respect of clearness and force of diction, can stand in competition with Francis's. What I have said at any time must come infinitely short, since I should despair very much, even, of writing such language. What I have said can, in fact, rise to no higher character, than that of a few loose points, acutely argued and sometimes forcibly expressed. So much for that.

I do not recollect when I have felt so gay and possessed my faculties in such good state. Yet I do not from hence infer that this latter condition is the consequence of those preceding it. These spirits and this good state are rather the consequences of causes quite opposite, which give the greatest proof of their efficacy, by having produced an effect capable of resisting the operation of present habits and possibly of being even improved by them. It has been by different habits of life that I have succeeded so well in the present ones. I am inclined to place them, as well as everything else that is good, principally to the operation of causes more remote and of which the seat is in the mind. It is exceedingly difficult to ascertain the true point. It is exceedingly difficult, to put one's wishes and purposes respecting sleep, in such a state, that the effort to wake shall just have force enough to overcome sleep, when sleep is the effect of vicious indulgence and not when it is wanted for the repair of weariness. I think I am now in danger of extending it too far, and it must always be remembered, that the error on that side is the most hurtful, as it involves in it, not only the abatement of the use of time, but the absolute and total loss of it. When I first came to town I went on with what had been my employment at Felbrigg, changing only the immediate object, and resumed the question in Jones about the circulating figures. Though my first attempt was not quite satisfactory, I seemed afterwards to be making some progress, when the interruptions of other concerns obliged, or at least occasioned, my laying it aside. From that time I can only say that I have hardly done anything in mathematics, except a cursory solution of one question in Dodson, and the completion of a proposition in Stuart, on the day I went to Salt Hill (April 17th). It is remarkable that the getting into the country air seemed to restore at once all my inclinations and all my powers. Probably situation, such, namely, as exempted one from interruption and association, had their share in this, as well as the influence of air and motion.

All mathematical studies have, therefore, been suspended, or as nearly as I have stated, since 20th April to now, 30th May. A great difference this from what I had looked forward to. In the midst of so much interruption as business and engagements must give at this time of year, it may be questioned whether mathematical studies had not better be wholly laid aside, than prosecuted so imperfectly as they must be in such a state. Another class of studies wholly laid aside have been classical studies. Since the year 1785, in which I conceive it was that I went to Scotland, I have not passed so long a time as I have, measuring back from the present, without looking into a Greek author. I have not read a line of Greek since I came to town. The same may be said of my stay at Felbrigg and even of the whole of my time since my return from abroad. The last Greek I read, or rather meddled with, was in the chaise with Douglas. The last I read professedly was in my journey to Bristol, just before that. Of Latin, I have read none for a much longer period. Indeed I hardly know when I have read any, studiously or professedly, at any time.

25*th.*—Dinner at Sir Horace Mann's.

26*th.*—Boodle's ball.

27*th.*—Westminster Hall.

30*th.*—Out in the morning, viz. meeting at Burke's, Norfolk Club. Hippisley's afterwards, where detained in dispute about Slave Trade with an old gentleman, who proved to be Judge Gould's brother.

June 1*st.*—Dinner at Douglas's. Went with Sneyd to Lord North's.

2*nd.*—In my way out of town, called upon Lord and Lady Lucan, with whom I sat for a quarter of an hour. It was eleven when I got to Bocking, where I stopped the night. The country was in its highest beauty and co-operating with the mildness and freshness of the air, inspired considerable feelings of vernal delight. I had stopped for a few minutes at Repton's.

5*th.*—Arrived at Felbrigg between twelve and one. Got to the Hall and into my room about two. My stay at Felbrigg, which lasted only two days, had nothing remarkable, except its having been the time of my beginning Smith's 'Harmonics,' and acquiring whatever knowledge I have of the subject, beyond the inspection of the first pages of the same book, when I bought it; and a similar inspection of the introductory discourse of Euler. I arrived at Felbrigg on a Friday morning and on Sunday, while I was sitting at dinner at the Parsonage, received a letter which made it necessary for me to return immediately. The occasion was the vacancy of the Speaker's chair, by the advancement of Grenville to be Secretary of State. I set off in about two hours after I received the letter, taking Mrs. Lukin in the chaise to Hanworth, where we drank tea, and from whence I set off on horseback, following the chaise. My journey, which continued all night, was not unpleasant; and if I had executed what I had intended and intended in such a way that I thought the execution safe, I should look back to it with pleasure; but, the vexation I feel at having suffered myself (I know not why) to be restrained from speaking upon the occasion, makes me impatient to drive from my memory the whole of that period. The consequences of such omissions are probably much greater than one is apt to reckon them. The way to estimate them would be to consider, what portion such a day would have made, of all the political fame and consequence, that one has. This, in number, would not be inconsiderable; but, if it be taken, as it ought to be, according to its proportion in value, the difference will be such, computing it at so much per cent., as would make up the interval between cheap and dear, good and bad, in a bargain or in a fortune. However low one may estimate such kind of fame—and certainly no one can care less about it than I do—one cannot but regret the loss of an advantage comparatively so considerable, and that might have been secured at so cheap a rate. I am quite sure that if the occasion were to occur at this instant, without borrowing anything from what was said by others, I could make a speech, which, at the rate of fame allowed to such exertions and enforced by the particularity of the subject, would have been remarked very generally throughout the country, and have been remembered by many several years hence. Nothing now remains, but to convert my regrets to the purposes of reformation and to learn by what I have done amiss, to avoid similar misconduct in future.

12*th.*—Mundy's: Elliot, Cholmondeley, Legge, Harris, *i. e.* Lord Malmesbury, Sir G. Cornewall, Lady Middleton —then said to be unwell, now, alas! dead. We all gay, and going to the masquerade at Mrs. Strutt's. This was an instance of a masquerade, not exciting any high hopes, yet producing much pleasure. I don't know when I have felt stronger satisfaction, or found my mind in better state.

14*th.*—At two, set off to go with Lady Palmerston to Sir Joshua Reynolds', at Richmond. Went in the carriage with her and Sir H. Englefield. Present: Lord Palmerston, Lord Carysfort, Lord Darnley, Lord Malmesbury and Lady M. and Ellis. Supped at Mrs. Crewe's: Lord Macartney, Lady Duncannon, Sheridan and Miss Draper.

16*th.*—My stay at Felbrigg, which continued for twelve days, had nothing remarkable, except that, in proportion to the enjoyment I had lately had in London, I felt more the want of such enjoyments where I was. I missed the satisfactions I had left, and experienced that effect, which I must always to a degree lay my account with, and which in the general conduct of life I have never enough considered, that as opportunities of study are multiplied, the incentives to it are often in the same proportion withdrawn. I found certainly, according to Dr. Johnson's expression, a very great and sudden refrigeration of application. I forget how much of my time was employed in business, which I cannot without inconsistency condemn, since I have long condemned the omission of it, namely, in reading letters and papers, transmitted to me from my father and which for the greater part I have suffered to remain unread for now near twenty years, that I have had access to them. It is a singular fact that in all that time I should never have found a fortnight, to know whether they were interesting or uninteresting, important or unimportant. What life has mine been, that has afforded time for neither business, pleasure, nor study!

29*th*.—The family from the Parsonage had supped and lay at Felbrigg, as they had done the evening before that. The excesses in my banker's account had forced upon me this time an attention to my affairs, which I had never practised in equal degree before, but which I hope from this time not to discontinue. I am quite persuaded that the habit of attending, as much as was necessary, to practical concerns, so far from diminishing the time given to other pursuits, would be found to enlarge it and certainly to increase the progress made in them.

30*th*.—On my arrival in town, went to Burke's and found that, as I had expected, they had had a brilliant day in Westminster Hall. I fell in with Adair, Fitzpatrick and Lord John Townshend, who were going to Brookes's, and by a degree of weakness not to be thought of with patience, suffered them to drag me with them.

July 6*th*.—Boxing match at Wimbledon: Darch and Gainer, James and Tucker, Hooper and Tyne; the three first victors. I came away before the last battle was over, in order to be in time for the Committee. Dined, I have a notion, upstairs and spoke, I think, a few words upon proposal of sending some corn to the relief of France. Did not state my meaning satisfactorily, nor obviate, as I might have done, the complaints of Wilberforce.

7*th*.—'Albo lapide notandum.' Spoke a few words for the first time in Westminster Hall. I am quite sure that the effect of this, inconsiderable as the event seems naturally to be, will be felt through the whole summer, as its consequences may run on for a much longer period. I acquitted myself in a way not so good as might have been, but enough so to make me think myself well off. I dined at the Club; Lord Macartney, Dr. Fordyce, Sir Joshua Reynolds, Malone, Lord Elliot.

8th.—Trial ended for this year. I went to Lincoln's Inn afterwards, taking a boat from Westminster Bridge.

9th.—Was to have been the day of Sheridan's motion about the million, but, forty members not having been in the House by four o'clock, it was put off.

10th.—Motion came on. I went away to dine with D. North. Came away before the division with Villiers.

11th.—Party to Chertsey. Southgate Farm and Lord Portman's; Francis's family, Mr. and Mrs. Culveden, Goring and his daughters. Very pleasant; much struck with the beauty of the place; felt the country perfectly new and strange; surprised that there should be so much near London of which I knew so little. Reflections on the little acquaintance I have had with such modes of pleasure and such scenes of life.

13th.—Stayed at home till between four and five, when I went to the House, in order to attend Francis on the Indian Budget. Dined upstairs with General Burgoyne. Drank tea with Sir Joshua.

15th.—When I left the House, hardly forty members remained. A long debate took place afterwards and lasted till past eleven, Fox having come down to make a sort of protest against the Tobacco Bill.

16th.—Went to the House to attend business of Scott (Major), and came away with Burke, Sir Gilbert Elliot and Courtenay, to dine by appointment with Sir Joshua Reynolds. When we came away, I walked some time with Burke and Lawrence, in St. James's Square, talking on general subjects.

19th.—Am vexed that, before leaving Windsor, I did not contrive to give some more reproof to the insolence of the innkeeper. Saw part of the Castle at Windsor, and called on Robert at Eton.

21*st.*—Dined at Club as a point of duty and at the expense of a party from which I expected satisfaction, at Francis's. Only Courtenay and Sir Joshua, Malone having (not very fairly) stayed away.

22*nd.*—From the kind memorial furnished me from Norwich, of which mention will be made below, this was, I find, a day by no means to be forgotten, being that on which I made the motion, or rather, I am sorry to say, proposed the motion, for receiving the inquiry about the exportation of corn.* It is curious to observe how differently proceedings in Parliament appear, according as they are viewed in their causes or their consequences, in the talents necessary to conduct them and the effects they produce, or the impression they make out of doors. This motion about the grain is an event almost in the history of the times. It has not only occasioned a good deal of talk here, but has engaged even the attention of a neighbouring nation. Yet to the production of this so little thought went, that the merest trifle would have turned the purpose aside, and in the support of it nothing more was said than the most cursory consideration suggested. The measure, which may have made an impression on the mind of a great nation, was adopted with as little consideration and dismissed with as little execution of mind, as could be given to any opinion thrown out in a private company.

* Towards the end of this session Mr. Windham called the attention of Government to a requisition from France, which was then suffering the greatest distress from a scarcity of grain. The object of this requisition was, to be supplied with 20,000 sacks of flour from this country. So small a boon ought to be granted, he thought, from motives of humanity and might be safely granted; but a committee of the House of Commons having decided against it, the Ministers, though they professed themselves disposed to afford the relief sought for, would not, after such a decision, undertake to grant it upon their own responsibility. The leading part which Mr. Windham took in favour of this requisition occasioned amongst some of his constituents at Norwich a considerable clamour. He allayed the storm by a printed letter, addressed, 'To those of the citizens of Norwich who are most likely to be affected by an increase in the price of provisions.'—*Vide* Amyot's *Life of Mr. Windham*, vol. i. p. 20.

23rd.—Dined at Mr. Culveden's for the first time of my having been there; great many persons played at trap-ball. Went home with the Francis's after supper.

August 4th.—To-day I received the letter from Norwich enclosing the handbill relative to what I had said about the exportation of corn. The necessity of thinking of something to be said in answer to this, added to what else I had to do, occasioned my staying at home till dinner, when I had, as I mentioned, company.

5th.—At work all the morning and till the post went out in writing and copying what I was to send to Norwich in answer to the handbill; well-satisfied with my punctuality and dispatch and not dissatisfied with my performance. By taking the form of a letter to the common, which was likewise the properest, there was less necessity for being solicitous about the writing. It was good enough not to be ashamed of, and was very well calculated to answer its purpose.

11th.—*Brighthelmstone.*—The morning after my arrival I saw Fox, and had a very pleasant hour with him before his going to St. Ann's. Till last night I have been in his house, an advantage of comfort and retirement which I have not made the most of. On Friday, the day after our coming, I dined with the Prince and had the satisfaction of seeing in the morning and again in the evening, a fencing match with the great St. George; when every one was retired in the morning, I took up a foil with Roland one of the fencers, and was shocked to find how much I had lost, not only in skill, but of strength and activity. I think I was considerably below what I was some four or five years ago at Oxford. The mode of life is as new, almost, as that of another country, and though, hitherto, not such precisely as I should wish to continue long together, yet I am far from thinking that a month or two here might not be spent with equal profit and pleasure, and that if it had not been a slackness in me, in the pursuit of satisfaction, that I have never been here before with a mixture of company, with leisure and good air, must give great advantages to this over the solitude and languor of Felbrigg.

12*th.*—The regular day of the packet was yesterday, but I had given up the thought of going on account of the business of to-day, namely, the celebration of the Prince's birthday. Accounts are said to have come from London discouraging any English from visiting or staying at Paris; but I cannot prevail upon myself to lay any stress upon them. Except the danger of accidental mischief to which every one may in some measure be exposed, who comes within reach of a tumult or of dangers from robbers, which these times may certainly increase, but against which prudence may guard, I cannot conceive that anything more is to be apprehended than in travelling in France at any time.

13*th.*—The entrance to Rouen was magnificent beyond my expectations, though the evening had began to close in, so as to take off something of the view. The post before, we had seen a notification which prepared us for some difficulty likely to occur, on account of their having suffered us to go from Dieppe without a passport. The Garde Bourgeoise thought themselves obliged to carry us to the Hôtel de Ville, while our chaise remained at the gate, and much ceremony took place, attended, however, with great civility throughout. Before it could be settled, that we should proceed to our hotel, upon the strength of my letters which I mentioned to Messrs. Quesnel, without them or the testimony of some person of the place, we should have been obliged, they seemed to think, to go back to Dieppe.

September 8th.—All the time I had for employment at Paris was occupied in reading and writing French for study. The advantages gained in the acquisition of language or in the efforts made for that purpose, would have redeemed the time from suspicion of having been ill employed. But it is by no means necessary to have recourse to that consideration; much pleasure was felt and many impressions received. The advantages received consequently cannot be doubted. The day spent in the National Assembly, the walk to Chaillot, the dinner with Dillon, are all instances of that opinion. The day of Jephson's and my leaving Paris was, it appears, the 6th. Gardener, Digby, and Throgmorton called the morning of my going, and sat till near the time of our departure. Nothing could be more gay and pleasant than the whole of our first day's journey. The magnificence of the Castle of Gallion,* and the views in the first stage from Mantes and still more the view in the approach to Rouen, will be thought by many superior to anything, which the island can show. In the last instance and in certain respects I am inclined to that opinion myself.

9th.—Arrived at Brighthelmstone. About an hour before our arrival I came upon deck and was well enough to enjoy the prospect, literal and figurative, that was before me. I wish I could think that, by better management in contriving to come in for the close of the Prince of Wales's dinner, I had enabled myself to enjoy equally the retrospect. There never was anything so stupid as my not going (notwithstanding the lateness of the hour before I was enabled to dress) to see, at least, whether I might not have gone in.

10th.—Another folly, that, before I set out and quitted a dinner so pleasant as was offered me, I did not think of inquiring whether Lord North had not left Tunbridge. The whole of my dinner was poisoned by the reflection of my former folly. Before our arrival, too, it was dark and the weather cold and gloomy. When I arrived and

* The Château de Gaillon, near Vernon-sur-Seine, was built by the Cardinal D'Amboise in 1515. It was demolished at the Revolution, with the exception of the portal. A gateway from the château was removed to the École des Beaux Arts, in Paris.

found Lord North was gone, the measure of my uncomfortableness was full.

11*th*.—The only thing well done at Tunbridge was the rising in the morning (agreeably to what I had purposed overnight) so early as to be ready a little after six o'clock. The day promised nothing but incessant rain and the appearance of things was much less gay than I had been accustomed to. We went into London, however, tolerably cheerful and arrived there between two and three. Having got out at the end of Parliament Street, I went to Lord Palmerston's, whom I did not find at home, and to Mrs. Guise, whom I did. From her I heard for the first time the story of her daughter's marriage and of the unhappiness she was likely to meet with. It had evidently preyed much upon Mrs. Guise's spirits, nor does it appear too much relief is to be hoped. The advice I gave them, of securing a good understanding with the parents, is, I am persuaded, the best. I have seen them again since. I had dined, as we had settled, at Malone's, where were Courtenay and Jephson; and in the evening Sir Joshua, whom I had called upon in my way and found in as melancholy a way, with respect to his eyes, as the newspapers had represented him. The six days I passed in London had nothing in them remarkable, particularly after the time passed there in nearly similar circumstances last year. The degree of enjoyment in both cases nearly the same, that is, in both very considerable and proceeding in both from much the same causes. I walked the streets with a mixed sensation of strangeness and acquaintance, looking at it as at a new place, yet enjoying the comfortable reflection all the while that I was at home.

12*th*.—I should have done more to my satisfaction if I had dined with Lord Palmerston and a large party at Shene. The cause preventing my going was, that I could not afford the expense of taking a chaise on purpose. This to me is nothing new, but would seem very odd to those who judged of one's means of expense by one's nominal income. Having given up the party to Shene, I went after dinner to Kingston House, to Lady Anne and Lady Margaret: there I stayed till between ten and eleven.

16*th*.—I don't recollect for certain but, I think, went to a fencing match and sat for a good while with Ramsden, the first time since my acquaintance with him in the year 1772. I decided rather hastily upon sending a number of books back to Felbrigg, particularly my set of Commentators, which, though proper enough to be kept at Felbrigg, are perhaps too valuable and in too good preservation to be trusted to the risk and accidents of a passage by sea.

17*th*.—I set off, it appears, on the 17th. The purpose of going by Thetford, and of meeting Lord Robert, though not Fox, I accomplished. The occasion is to be remembered from its having put me upon thinking with more care of the puzzle which I heard of once before in the same society, of the expediency or act of a person meaning to go to a certain point, changing his place, unless he knows beforehand of the relation and distance to the point sought, of that to which he is required to change. They state the question something differently, but that above contains the substance. Lord Robert, who was the person that started the question, showed, as might be supposed, that he knew nothing of the doctrine to which it belonged. I said at the time what was an answer to his objections, but did not understand the full extent of the difficulty, nor make out the true solution till I thought of it in my post-chaise the next day. I must make an entry of the solution in the 'Adversaria,' as the reasoning is of a sort not quite obvious.

18*th*.—I arrived at Norwich early, having risen between five and six and traversed the town, not without some little anxiety and more I think than I ought to have felt, for the reception I was to meet with. My anxiety perhaps was more properly mortification at finding, or seeming to find, that my publication had not been well thought of. Yet, I don't know why I should be much moved by that, for the publication certainly contained nothing that was absurd nor ill calculated for its purpose, and more than that, it did not pretend to. I stayed the evening and had a supper, neither unprofitable nor unpleasant, at Taylor's.

October 4th.—Felbrigg.—My mother went away.

12*th.*—After the Sessions, the next thing seems to have been the Camp, which took place to-day. The particulars need not be set down, both because they are unimportant and because they are well remembered.

19*th.*—I went with Mrs. Lukin to Coke's. Party there: Fox, Dutton, E. Fawkener and Boothby. There were others whom I had not known of before; Captain Roberts, a relation of Coke's, who had served a great deal in America; and afterwards Rishton, &c. My stay, which continued till the Saturday following, was sufficiently pleasant, would have been much more so, if the pain in my face had not at all times given me a certain degree of annoyance and occasionally been such, as to destroy all thought and comfort. I contrived, however, notwithstanding all impediments, to do something, particularly to go on for several more propositions in the treatise 'De Arte Conjectandi,' which I had judiciously brought with me. I read likewise several useful papers. One paper, an investigation by Dodson, in the year 1754, of some questions of survivorship, which presented a fair mark to the exercise of one's thoughts and on which they have been employed till this time.

24*th.*—At my return home on Saturday, I found Dodwell, who, not having received my letter, had been arrived since the Thursday. The sight of him at Felbrigg excited very pleasing emotions; he is a man for whose character I feel great respect, in whose company I have much pleasure, and to whom, from early acquaintance and sense of his regard for me, I feel much attached. I hardly know any one whose esteem I should feel more pain to forfeit, and whom I would go greater lengths to serve.

30*th.*—I had gone to Fakenham. That night was memorable for an event long to be remembered by the calamity it has occasioned; a storm which, from its suddenness as well as its violence, has produced a greater destruction among the shipping on the coast, than any that has been remembered for a long while. The traces of it are seen everywhere, some less shocking, as vessels stranded, the crews and cargoes of which have been saved and others more melancholy, as the wreck of those which have perished altogether and the carcases of the unfortunate crews.

November 5*th.*—Lady Buckingham's ball, which was to have been on the 3rd, was put off on account of the death of poor George Byng, to the 6th. I did not go, partly because I did not like it, but more because Mrs. Lukin did not go. I felt a little dissatisfied at her not being asked, but was less influenced in staying away by that dissatisfaction, than by a desire of qualifying any disappointment which Mrs. Lukin might have felt.

7*th.*—Palmer and I and Lord Frederick went to Rainham; Lord Frederick slept here the night before; Palmer and he went in the chaise, I on horseback. The poor Marquis is so broken that possibly he may never return from Bath; it is hardly possible that he should live long; the prospect of leaving life seems to soften his mind and renders him sensible to attentions. I am happy in having shown all that was in my power in this instance.

9*th.*—On our return we rode as far as Holt. I thought that from the common near Chads we saw what was Felbrigg woods; Query, if it is so?

12*th.*—Palmer left me and the same day I set off to Holkham to meet Lady A. Lindsay. The day was very bad, and I had hesitated so long about going or not, as to add to the uncomfortableness of the uneasy feel of being too late. I went on, however, very well, thinking with sufficient earnestness of the paper in the transactions mentioned above of Dodson's; and at Holt, while the horses were baiting, had the satisfaction of hitting off a mode of reasoning, which the result showed to be right. It is not easily to be conceived how much effect this has had on the course of my thoughts ever since, how much all my enjoyments have been improved by it and what new animation it has given birth to. I should not have had, I am persuaded, so much pleasure in the fox-chase this morning, if I had not hit upon this solution of the case contained in that paper. What encouragement this to proceed, even, now? What cause of regret, that in years and years, I should have proceeded so little, hitherto! Why might not I, at this moment, have been among first-rate mathematicians?

22*nd.*—The effect, however, of these reflections seems to have ended very much with the making them; for I cannot cite the ten days that have elapsed since then as among the times when the prosecution of particular pursuits has been most diligent or most happy. I sat down about nine o'clock to other employments, particularly the resumption of the proposition left unfinished in Theodosius,* and found my faculties in a state of activity and clearness such as can hardly be matched but by instances far removed from this, or from each other. I felt at this time that there was no question so troublesome or difficult that I was or need be afraid to encounter; nor did this *feel* leave me till myself chose to dismiss it, thinking that a continuance of execution so late at night, would prevent my going to sleep readily and leave something of weakness next morning. The expectation in both parts seemed not to be without foundation. It was past

* The Σφαιρικά, or Spherics, of Theodosius, a profound and accurate work, on what we should now call Spherical Geometry.

eight before I rose, and to dissipate what I thought was amiss in myself, ordered my horse and took a short ride. From that time till church, which was in the afternoon, I did little but read the French papers; neither resuming translation, which stood first in order, nor completing what I had begun overnight in Theodosius, nor engaging in a work hardly less necessary—the writing another letter for the papers, on the same subject as Mill's. At ten o'clock I determined, after some consideration, to go over and sleep at the Parsonage, and the event abundantly confirmed the propriety of the decision, for I felt instantly relieved and animated.

23*rd.*—About three went out to exercise my horse, and give some directions about planting. At four rode over with George to Hanworth; Doughty just returned from a good chase with Coke's hounds near Holt. In the evening found I could do nothing but read Cook's Voyage, which I did till twelve o'clock.

24*th.*—From about ten till near two, with little intervals, have been looking into some books of my father's, which stand upon my table.

29*th.*—*London.*—Dined at Malone's, where was a meetting relative to Dr. Johnson's monument. Present, Sir Joshua, Sir Joseph Banks, Metcalfe, Boswell, Courtenay and R. Burke.

December 1*st.*—Dined at Lord Lucan's with a large party of French. There were a Madame de Boufflers, Duc and Duch. de Luxembourg, French ambassador, and the daughter of Madame de Boufflers. Of English: Sir Ralph and Lady Payne, Lord Macartney, and in the evening, Mr. Walpole.

4*th.*—Set off for Norwich. Drank tea at Newmarket. Between Chesterford and Newmarket I had thought with great success of Proposition 13-2 of Theodosius, which had been left incomplete, when I came away from the country. Journey as usual very pleasant.

1790.

April 2nd.—My Journal has been neglected, it must be confessed; but in return my neglects in other articles have been less than at any former period. It is in some respects consolatory and in others grievous, to consider how different my life has been this time from what it ever was before. I have now began to discover, for the first time, that as much may be done in London as at any other place. To what is this change owing? Is it a fact that has always been true and only now discovered; or is it, that some change, not depending on myself, has really made the difference? I suspect that there is a concurrence of causes, but that the principal is in my own determination. Let us say in what this change consists. Internally and substantially, I make a greater progress in all sorts of employment. I possess my faculties in greater perfection and enjoy throughout the day, in every situation, either of solitude or company, a higher degree of happiness. The places at which I can recollect to have dined are Coke's, Sir G. Cornewall's, Lord Palmerston's, Lord Malmesbury's, North's, Francis's, Mr. Culveden's, Burke's, my mother's, Tierney's, &c. Of these, the only place besides Thomas's at which I have dined frequently, has been my mother's. Since my coming to town this time, I have perceived the first instances in her of a decay of faculties. It consists principally in a continual forgetfulness and misapplication of names. From the moment this has been perceived, whatever impatience used formerly to be felt, has been lost in the general wish to alleviate the sense of such a misfortune, should it chance to be felt and to render what may remain of life as happy as possible. The consequence has been, that I have dined with my mother, as often as I have been disengaged, and have sought by every means to contribute to her satisfaction, whatever was in my power.

Previous to my departure from Felbrigg to London and from the beginning of the year, my chief employment was Theodosius and translation. For some time before I went, the time spent by myself and in hard and vigorous application, came to be more considerable. I felt accordingly my powers of application increase and my faculties strengthen. Many, however, both during that period and still more before, were the omissions with which I had to reproach myself. Little care was taken to regulate the course of thought, when it was not regulated of itself, in virtue of some express and positive employment.

My journey into Norfolk on the 6th instant was not intended as an excursion of pleasure, nor made in circumstances likely to answer that purpose. I should have liked to have gone down, when first the business requiring one's attention was at end, and when I should have had before me the prospect of staying at Felbrigg for some weeks. My journey both in going and coming was less fatiguing or disagreeable, than I had been inclined to expect; so much less so, that if it were not for some objection in point of decorum, I should be tempted every now and then to obtain by those means a week or two in Norfolk, when it may not be convenient to lay out 20*l.* in a journey thither in a postchaise.

16*th*.—Day of the Tobacco business.—I spoke more from the consideration of the use, which a speech could be of in its effects at Norwich, than from any hope of my speaking in a way to gain credit. In this, however, as in other instances, the event bettered my expectation, so cheaply is reputation in this way obtained, or so much has my manner a power of setting off, what in point of matter had certainly nothing extraordinary. I believe it rather the former. The only points that in my own opinion had any merit, I either forgot, or had not an opportunity of introducing. Some time after this, I think on the ——, came on the Duke of Atholl's business, on which I executed more completely what I had intended and felt during the time more master of what I was about. In the judgment of others therefore, this had more of the performance of a practised speaker than any other speech I have made. I soon after spoke a little in opposition to the Silk Bill proposed by Wilmot. As I am upon the subject of speaking, it may be as well to add here, though by a slight prolepsis, that I have spoken this year twice in Westminster Hall; the former time more at length, though less to my satisfaction, as I only repeated matter, which, though my own, had been stated by others, either of themselves, or at my suggestion; the last time more shortly, but more satisfactorily, as I succeeded, in my own opinion, in clearing a question of misconception, and placing it upon its true footing, when the endeavours of the Court and other Managers had failed.

May 8th.—At home all morning, employed in preparation. Dined at Club: only Lord Spencer, Lord Palmerston and Lord Ossory. Went afterwards to Burlington House, principally for the purpose of procuring admission to the Hospital. Found there Lord and Lady Walpole, Lord John, &c. Doubtful whether or no I should go the next morning without hearing Fox.

Monday, 10th. — In consequence of notice in the papers and an answer given to me, as the result of an inquiry, which I had directed to be made at Carlton House, I dressed and went thither in a chair: had then the mortification to find that there was no *levée*. This was to have been the day of Burke's motion for the resolutions respecting the trial. I went afterwards to dine at Brookes's in order to talk over the motions to be made by Grey on the Wednesday following. When I came home I found William was arrived.

11*th*.—Spoke, in Westminster Hall; Burke's motion, which must have been put off the day before. I may remember the fact, by the circumstance of its having been the subject of enquiry when I came into the Club, where I could only get a hasty and imperfect dinner before it was necessary to go to the meeting at Burlington House.

12*th*.—Employed the greatest part of the morning in walking about with William, so as to have little time to consider what I should say upon Grey's motion. Spoke, however, and sufficiently well; a little more consideration would have enabled me, certainly, to have spoken better, both by furnishing me with passages ready prepared and better, therefore, than those I could frame at the instant, and by leaving my thoughts more at liberty to go in quest of others. The ludicrous instance of Lord Burleigh, I took from Sheridan, who, as he could not use it himself, wished it to be employed by some one else. If I had recollected it at the time I would have introduced it in a way, to allot to Sheridan the merit of his own thoughts; for, besides my general rule of forbearing in any instance to appropriate to myself the reasonings or remarks of others, I would not countenance, by any seeming return, what Sheridan does, with so little scruple, with respect to others, and to me among the rest.

13*th*.—Employed again during the morning in walking about with William. In the House Francis's motion for an account of the appointments and salaries of ambassadors to Spain.

14*th*.—Went out to pay some necessary visits in the morning and meeting Lord Macartney, accompanied him to Mrs. Bouverie's and afterwards to Macklin's Exhibition in Pall Mall. I dined at Lord Radnor's, where were Sir Edward Littleton, Sir Matthew Ridley, the Solicitor-General, Bouverie and Lady Bridget, Annesley and Adams. At nine I walked away and calling upon Mrs. Crewe, sat with her, talking over many curious particulars of the set in which she lives.

15*th.*—Though it is now past four, I have sat entirely at home; I have done nothing but meditate a speech, on the old subject of evidence.* From four till it was full time to dress for dinner, I was employed in a letter to the Library Committee at Norwich, who had transmitted to me a petition to the Duke of Norfolk, praying that they might have the use of the Roman Catholic chapel for their books. As I had formerly applied for this on behalf of the Roman Catholics themselves, it was necessary to explain to the Committee, why I could do no more for their petition than present it. Dinner at W. Stanhope's. A University party; sat there talking, for the best part of our subject on matters of law, till about ten and walking away with Sir W. Scott, went for an hour or more to Lord North's, from thence home, where I found from Mrs. Crewe a book with verses by Lord Holland, which I continued reading till twelve. The verses seem to show a fertile and formed mind and a very amiable disposition; their exact merit can only be estimated by knowing the age of the writer, and comparing his productions with what has been done by others, at the same time of life.

16*th.*—Rose at nine remarkably fresh and active. Employed for the greater part of the time on Bernouilli, till I was surprised at finding that it was near four.—Dressed in haste, much satisfied with my morning's work,

* The late Lord Chief Justice Denman, upon being asked by his son-in-law, the Rev. J. Beresford, to name the best speech he had heard during his life, and that which he thought the most worthy of study, answered, without hesitation, 'Windham's Speech on the Law of Evidence.'

and went to my mother's. At about seven or before went to Mrs. Siddons', who was not well enough to admit me. Returned home, drinking tea and reading Shakespeare till nine.

17*th*.—Went at six to dine with Coke. I sat next to Burke, with Fox next to him, and had a tolerable share of conversation, the principal subjects of which were Bruce; the conduct of the judges on the Impeachment; Dunning; farming; architecture and painting. Fox was stating, as a test of the merit of Blackstone's 'Commentaries,' that if a man had all that ready in his mind, he would be a better lawyer, possibly, than any man in the country. He was giving an opinion too against Baron Eyre, compared with Wilson, or even with Buller. Others were inclined to rate Buller above Wilson. Burke was speaking in terms of high commendation of a design in the Exhibition, given by one Bond, for a new House of Parliament.

18*th*.—Trial. Spoke a little. Dissatisfied with myself that I had not spoken more. An opportunity had been given to introduce that which I have so long meditated and certainly, if I am to judge by former instances, would have been considered as good.

20*th*.—The next morning I felt not remarkably fresh, but was, as usual, brought into a better state by the trial. Spoke again more at length. Elliot (not Sir Gilbert) told me that he thought I, more than any of them, 'hit the nail on the head.' It is the praise in such cases most to be aspired to, but I am not quite sure that I deserved it. I am afraid, too, this will be my opinion when I come to see the report of the writer of shorthand. In the House of Commons afterwards, I spoke on Francis's motion relative to the appointment of ambassadors and salaries of ambassadors to Spain. What I said was delivered readily and with good possession of myself; I should suppose without much impression, for it was the effect of very little previous thought and merely uttered that I might practise myself in getting up, and might do what I thought would be gratifying to Francis. I had engaged myself to dine with Thomlinson, to meet Lord Buckingham and Charles Townshend; but being made too late for his dinner, recurred to an invitation, which I had before declined, from the Duke of Portland, where was a large and pleasant party. Present: Fox, Burke, Sheridan, Erskine, Lee, Mansfield, Lord Loughborough, Grey, Orde, Mr. Ellis, G. North.

21*st.*—Went in the morning to meet Burgoyne at Burke's, relative to the motion to come on in the House. Little time to think of the business, namely, motion for censure of Scott.

22*nd.*—Dined at Knight's. Went afterwards to Lady Payne's. There were present: Lord and Lady Jersey (the latter of whom I then saw, I believe, for the first time), Lord Carlisle, Monsieur Barthélemy, Del Campo, and one or two other foreigners.

23*rd.*—Dined at Sir Henry Englefield's: Stanley, Miss Stanley, Miss Berrys and Miss Seton. Engagement made in the morning very pleasant. An Hungarian or Austrian engineer, called in the evening, who had lost an eye by excessive watching, five days, as was said, at the siege of Belgrade.

25*th.*—Stayed at home employed, as I have been for a day or two past, on the question started last year, at Francis's, in consequence of a discussion of it, by Lord Kaimes, relative to the claim of the owners in case of jetsom. At five went to Club, where the question was to be put, of filling up the number to forty. Present: Lord Ossory, Lord Macartney, Lord Lucan, Sir Joshua Reynolds. The death of Thomas Warton, the news of which had arrived a day or two before, changed the question of enlarging into that which was the real object of it, a ballot proposed by Sir Joshua for the election of Lord Carlisle.

26th.—At a little past four set out to the House in order to attend a business about the Wool Bill. Stayed there to hear a little discussion about the alteration of the Tontine: it was near six when I came away. Tierney, who brought me home, prevailed upon me to come into the house to dine with him; but I decided finally upon coming away and dining, for the first time, almost, since my coming to town, alone. At about seven, or a little past, walking, not so much thinking where I should go to, as impelled to go somewhere. The place of most attraction was Duke Street, from the hope of seeing Cecy. I there found Byng and Col. Bertie, who had come that day from a tour into Sussex.

27th.—Though I meant to take a part in the business that was to come on in the House, viz. the adjourned debate on Major Scott, I could not bring myself to settle well to thinking on the question, but rambled into speeches in Westminster Hall and what was still more remote, the question which has employed me lately respecting jetsom. When I set out to walk to the House, the fineness of the day and the gaiety of my thoughts, rendered me still less capable of meditating on what I might say, which inability was again increased, by the length of the walk and the company of Courtenay. With all this, when I spoke afterwards I seem to have done as well as at most other times and to have gained, perhaps, something of new credit, by my resistance to a hot attack from Pitt.

28th.—Called at Fox's to know whether attendance at the House was necessary. I was detained by the case of the poor man who was vomiting blood in St. James's Street and with Mr. Ferguson, of the House of Commons, who took his full share in the act, continued occupied in finding means of relief, till we determined finally in sending him to his home in Bishopsgate Street. When this was done, instead of going to the House, where Scott was to receive his reprimand, I proceeded to the Club at the Globe.

29*th.*—Called on Lady Cornewall before going to Revely's. The drawings are of views and antiquities, made during travels into Greece and the countries of the Levant, in company with Sir Richard Worsley. I had great satisfaction in seeing them. It was a whimsical circumstance that the first person who presented himself to my view, and with whom I was placed cheek by jole, was Mr. Hastings. The conversation, too, or rather the exposition, by Revely, of some of the particulars of the state of Athens, was of a singular character, considering the auditors, being an account of the violences and misconduct of the governors. Mr. Hastings did not stay long—not in consequence of that conversation, though probably in consequence of the company with which he found himself joined. Some of the particulars learnt upon this occasion, not of the greatest consequence, but convenient to be remembered, are:—

That Alexandria is now a very inconsiderable place, being entirely confined to the isthmus between the two harbours. That all around towards the land, is desert, into which no one goes,—not entirely because there is no temptation, but because it is full of Arabs, who plunder all that they lay hold of, though, if resistance is not made, they are not disposed to offer farther violence. The horses throughout all these parts, he describes, and has represented in his drawings, as full of that sort of action, which is usually ascribed to them. He described particularly the practice of all the Turks, who alone for the most part, are either indulged in, or can afford the use of horses, of putting their horses on full speed and stopping them as suddenly, and that this stopping was, as it ought to be, on the haunches.

30*th.*—Dined at Lord Spencer's. After dinner went with the rest for an hour to Brookes's, principally with a view to see Grey and settle about going the next day to the launch. Continued talking there pleasantly till near eleven. The conversation was likely to appear to me pleasant, as part of it consisted in flattery to me of what I had done the Thursday before in the House. Let me recollect, however, on all occasions of this sort, the remark I whispered to Pelham, and have often repeated to myself, that ——, while he acted with a party, often heard compliments of the same sort.

31*st.*—Wrote to Mrs. Lukin in the morning, and, with that and other notes, did not get to Grey till twelve o'clock. Called on Vandeput and went down by water: perfectly pleasant. We were there in good time; but did not manage well, not to go first on shore and see more of the nature of the operation, as well as ascertain more satisfactorily what would be the best situation to take in the effect. When I parted from Grey and his brother, I went to Smith's at Lincoln's Inn; but after waiting for three-quarters of an hour, slumbering over 'Gilbert on Evidence' and which seems to me, as it has done before, to be written in a legal, antiphilosophical style, was obliged to go away without seeing him.

June 1*st.*—Dinner in Dover Street. Ballot for Lord Carlisle, who was rejected: present, Sir Ch. Bunbury, Sir Joshua, Lord Lucan, Dr. Fordyce, Dr. Warren, Malone, Courtenay, Steevens, Dr. Burney and Fox.

2*nd.*—Trial;—nothing remarkable. Discussion afterwards between Fox, &c., about Tontine. We were obliged likewise to wait in expectation of motion from Scott. Walked to Mrs. Crewe's. After supper, Sheridan came in, who has put a case to me, about Tontine, which may have the effect of making me apply a little to that subject.

4*th.*—At a little before six walked to Crewe's, where I went to dine. Afterwards of company—Mrs. Sheridan, Miss Linley, Tom Sheridan, young Crewe, Charles Greville. The first time of seeing young Crewe since his return from abroad. He looks something between a German count and an Italian singer.

7th.—First day of Fox's summing up. By delay in staying to settle things previous to prospect of leaving town, I did not get to Westminster Hall till after Managers were gone in. Business not begun till the attention of the audience was wearied. Day upon the whole, not brilliant. Dined by engagement at Sir Joshua Reynolds'.

9th.—Straight to Westminster Hall, where I came, not till after Fox had begun; performance very brilliant; glad that I had come. From thence I went home and continued employed, I conceive, in preparations for going till near seven. By staying so long before I went to Malone's, I wearied myself considerably and was too late for his dinner.

Suppose I had stayed only half the time and left undone the things, whatever they were, that occupied the remaining half, should I have been worse, except in imagination? Would not all the things which I disposed in their places, have been just as safe and remained just as quietly, though I had left them where they were at first? They would so certainly, and often much of the anxiety which one gives oneself upon such occasions might well have been spared. But I believe it may generally be said, that the trouble taken at such times, is at least the means of saving trouble at some future time, and often such, as would not at any future time be equally effectual. One does, what must some time or other be done, and must be done with greater effort or with less effect, if not done then. Such is almost constantly the case with letters: such is very much the case with things suffered to get into disorder.

10th.—Breakfasting at Newmarket, arrived at Norwich about seven in the evening.

What took place afterwards it is not necessary to detail;

as much of it will be remembered as is worth remembering. The whole business, on my part, was conducted in a manner perfectly satisfactory to myself, except in the single instance, of my yielding to the persuasion of others, and consenting to let Wilkes go to town.

15*th.*—The Tuesday, at night, I had gone over to Felbrigg; the occasion too memorable to be forgotten—Mrs. Lukin's illness.

18*th.*—Day of election.

19*th.*—Slept at Taverham.—Coke there. In great spirits and great possession of myself during the whole time of the election.

July 7*th.*—Promised Lady Buckinghamshire to ride over to Blickling.

8*th.*—After walking about very pleasantly and drinking tea, I accompanied Lady Buckinghamshire and Lady Caroline in their chaise, till I set off for home by the Barningham Road.

Now for a little criticism on what I have done. I have found an amazing drop or fall, in mathematical studies, meaning by that word, in the present instance, my liking and appetite, rather than my power. The thought of any mathematical book no longer excites the same longing to be employed about it, nor the same impatience of any thing that holds me from such studies. The times which residence here is likely to afford me are no longer employed by imagination in great advances to be made in that region of knowledge. It is strange that in so short a time—not more than six weeks—and with so little abatement of power, so great a change should be made in what may be called feeling. I suspect that during the whole of the time since my return to Felbrigg I have not been quite well.

19*th.*—Now is certainly the time to make a vigorous and steady effort to place myself in some situation in those studies, from which I may hope, at the end of the race, not wholly to be left behind. So much remains to be done, that unless great increase of powers comes with employment, life will not suffice for my completing but a very small part of it. Some increase of powers is felt almost every day—a great one, certainly, within this year or two. A fair trial, by application to such studies, continued from day to day through a long period and made what it ought to be and what it might, in each instance, has never yet been given. To apply for a certain number of hours each day and for a certain number of days,—neither one number nor the other, being such as to call for any extraordinary exertion and to preserve, during the times of such application, a degree of attention as has at all times probably been in my power, but is now become perfectly easy, will, I am sure, place me in a situation, with respect to those studies, altogether new and leading to consequences in all ways the most desirable and important. What infatuation, bordering upon madness, that in the number of years that have now rolled over my head, such a trial should never have been made!

I borrowed from the library at Norwich, Capparonier, or Vauvillier's edition of Sophocles, which, so far as I have used, promises well.

The plan settled in my mind at present, though far from settled irrevocably, is, that after Sophocles, I should read some Pindar, then a book or two of Thucydides, then a large portion of Homer, taking Plutarch perhaps at the same time; either then too, or after, I must take a good many plays of Aristophanes. The incidents by which the uniformity of life may be varied are of course not numerous. On Sunday, the 18th, George Wyndham dined here.

The evening of our going to Cromer was very fine and the party altogether very pleasant. We went, for the first time for me, to the New Inn, which promises to be a great accession to our comfort. Poor Alsop has spared me all difficulty and delicacy with respect to him, by finding it necessary to abscond. Such a reduction at the close of life is very melancholy. The scene on the beach was enlivened by an object, quite new to me, and new, perhaps, to the place—the unloading of a foreign vessel. She was a Norway brig from Christiansand. The captain spoke tolerable English and was a well-behaved man, more so probably than the average of such men with us.

August.—Just previously to my setting off for the Assizes and almost, I may say, on the very evening Saturday, 24th July), I felt that strong sense of the unhappiness of my own celibacy—that lively conception of pleasure I had lost—that gloomy apprehension of the conviction which I should feel of this hereafter, clouding all my prospects, relaxing all my motives and in an especial manner destroying all enjoyment, that I might ever have in residence here, that unless I could resolve manfully to fight against such images, and force my mind from the contemplation of evils, admitting no remedy, the most fatal mischief must ensue, both to my happiness and to my powers. Of this resolution the necessity was not at first foreseen, nor the resolution of consequence fully taken. These images, accordingly, continued to pursue me during the time of my absence at the Assizes. It is, indeed, sufficiently plain, that wisdom must condemn the thinking on uneasiness, which thinking cannot mend. The hint or symbol for enforcing that truth may be the reflection on the broken teacup in 'Rasselas.' The precept will not come with less weight for coming from Doctor Johnson, nor will it be unsatisfactory to me to owe to him, what may alleviate some of the sorrows of life.

September 1st.—In riding from Wrexham, I settled some matters about the distribution and construction of Quadratic Equations, and again more lately, viz. when I was last at Holkham, that I repeated the demonstration of the proposition learnt from Condorcet: that when the majority of votes is given (neither more nor less), the probability of each vote being supposed always given, the probability of a right decision is always the same whatever be the number of votes.

2nd.—I went over to Mrs. Lukin with the horses and we rode to Cromer—the ride not being uncomfortable—and I repeating to her with great fluency, a part, additional to what she had already heard, of 'Theodore and Honoria.'

5th.—Many causes occurred to render this visit a period of great note—some, indeed, to distinguish it only as an interesting passage in the journals of the year, others as making it a marked epoch in my life, the most fatal, it may be, that I have ever known. The meeting at Rainham—a party of persons connected with, and newly arrived from Ireland—could not fail to revive, strongly, the recollection of a period which I never think of without very particular emotions; but, when these persons were of the number of those I had formerly known there and were now seen in a place, having, in itself, always a considerable tendency to put me upon reflections on past times and distant situations, the effect would naturally be greater. It must be greatest of all, where one of the persons was Mrs. Beresford, who made early so strong an impression, with whom I have continued since upon such a footing of friendship and whom I see only at such long intervals, the last having extended from the year of my going with Mr. Burke into Scotland, a period of five years.*

The conversation, too, which we had, was more than at any other time calculated to increase the impression, above alluded to. The two days passed there were, accordingly, quite of a distinct character from any that preceded or have followed them, and sufficiently marked

*** In 1783 Mr. Windham was made Chief Secretary to the Earl of Northington, Lord-Lieutenant of Ireland, under the Coalition Ministry. He resigned this appointment in August of the same year.**

by the impression they made, though not by the consequences they produced, to become one of the smaller epochs of life; but the great fact which distinguished this period, is that above pointed at, and which I must now proceed to state. Let me state it at once and without further circumlocution, for it is a subject too painful to be dwelt upon.

It has happened to me more than once within, perhaps, these three or four years—for the instances preceding this time have not excited sufficient attention to be correctly remembered—to be seized with sudden suspensions of the power of recollection, which have made me [suppose], with little serious apprehension, that I thought my memory was not so good as it had been. The first time when this happened—so as to occasion a real alarm, or to make an impression that did not immediately wear off—was on Saturday, the 4th inst., the day preceding my going to Rainham. In going to Hanworth with Mrs. Lukin I found myself unable to recollect the name of Maria Cosway,* a name sufficiently familiar to me to come, I should have thought, into my mind the moment it was wanted; that is, to have followed instantly the image on description. It was not, however, as I recollect, till after several minutes, that the name was recovered; and the suspicion excited by this failure having put me upon trying my powers in other instances, the defect seemed so considerable as to leave little doubt of a change either permanent or temporary, and to fill me, in consequence, with the most alarming apprehensions. The impression of these was too strong not to remain upon my mind the next morning, and to put me upon a continuance of the same trials. The result, so far as related to the recollection of names, seemed every where the same; I even fancied that the impression of the objects themselves, and of many

* Maria Cosway, wife of the English artist of that name, and artist herself.

scenes, both of an earlier and later date, seemed to be more faint than they naturally should, and than they used to be. It may not be amiss to set down some examples of each ; a better judgment may be formed of these apprehensions, and something of a foundation laid for ascertaining the truth of new ones that may arise in future. I had one day—I think on the Sunday of my going to Rainham—a considerable difficulty of recollecting the titles of Lord Ashburnham, Lord Bulkeley, Lord Belgrave, Lord Deerhurst, and Lord Jersey. The name of Lord Fitzwilliam's huntsman I have likewise been unable to recover. These were the principal instances and many of them sufficiently strong. There were various others, particularly of those which, though of a sort to come into my mind upon the first call, did not present themselves till after a sensible pause and interval.

It is not to be conceived that one should submit readily to the belief of a fact so fatal, as that which the above instances gave reason to apprehend, or that one should not try every means of accounting for the appearances in question in a manner less painful. One reason to apprehend that there was a real change, and to prove that the name forgot was such as one ought to recollect, *i. e.* belonged to an object known with that degree of familiarity that the name should naturally follow, was that the failure of the recollection came as a disappointment and frustrated an intention which one had been proceeding to execute as matter of course. One's only mode of explaining this, was by the effect of a sort of latent prospect of failure, operating like what would be called baulking, in the case of any bodily feat; like that inability which seems to take place upon having attempted once or twice, without success, some difficult leap. In every other respect, so little reason had I to apprehend any decay of faculties, that I had been remarking sometime, that with respect at least to the effect, whether from increase of natural power, or what was indeed more likely, from improved habit, my powers seemed to be advancing.

14*th.*—I rode out with Metcalfe and Mrs. Lukin, round by Cromer and afterwards had Astley, Mrs. Astley, and Lady Stanhope to see the house; I made my excuse against dining with them at Cromer.

19*th.*—Went with Mrs. Lukin to dine at Wolterton. Lord Frederick had just arrived from D. North's. We came back in the evening. At dinner I felt myself in brilliant spirits.

27*th.*—Dined at Hanworth; out of humour, when I came back; and led of consequence through a succession of causes into taking an uncomfortable ride about the park, in a beautiful moonlight night, and retiring early to bed tired and dissatisfied.

28*th.*—It was on the 23rd, I think, that John and James Gurney, Mr. Barclay and Mr. Robert Herring dined with me. The manufacturer and the merchant showed a superiority over the country gentleman, and we had a pleasanter day, than I have here often experienced.

October 11*th.*—A day uncommonly fine. So well employed, as to make me late in getting ready for the Camp. By the time I was dressed, Doughty and Isted came, who went round the grounds, while I was settling some justice business, &c. We afterwards rode together to the ground: perfectly pleasant, as was the whole day.

15*th.*—Cromer meeting; day remarkably fine; Lady Buckinghamshire had called and left some violet roots. It was so late before I got down, and such in other respects was the course of circumstances, that though I arrived at Cromer before Lady B. was gone and found her and Lady Caroline, on the steps leading from Terry's, I had little opportunity of staying to talk with them. Was not at the Parsonage to-day nor saw Mrs. Lukin. Unusual this, as it is plain from the fact being so long remembered.

17th.—Rode in the morning, after church, after exercising my horse among the fields near Runton. Day so fine, that I could not do otherwise than enjoy my ride, though I contributed little to it by my own efforts. When I came back employed with Kitty;* Mrs. L. went home about ten. I had been for some days, viz. since Thursday, out of humour with her, in consequence of her neglect of herself.

20th.—On the Tuesday, Monday, or Saturday preceding, I don't for certain recollect which, my morning was very much taken up by a visit from Mr. Elwyn, with a brother of his, who lives near London. He (the brother) has a good deal of knowledge of pictures, and told me, that the little picture under the large one in the bow-window room was by Sallart, and the 'Finding of Achilles' in the middle room by Vanharp.

22nd.—Some passages of Aristotle examined, and the morning before, a passage in D'Alembert's preface to the 'Encyclopædia.' I believe this morning I examined more carefully, than I had ever done before, the arrangement of the collection which is here, of the 'Philosophical Transactions.' I still cannot find any account of a paper of Dr. Clark's, referred to in the manuscript paper, inserted in old Barnes's hand, in the copy that was here of Saunderson.

25th.—Till Nicholls went, engaged with him. Mrs. L. and Mary breakfasted here. Rode as far as Marble Hill with him.

26th.—Day of Blickling Ball. In our way to Blickling tried my memory as to 'Theodore and Honoria,' and found that I had not lost it; for the remainder of the way talked with Mary about music.

29th.—Was preparing to go to Cromer upon hearing that Lord Charles Townshend and Colonel Barré, were there, when the whole party from Wolterton came,—Lady

* Kitty Lukin, second daughter of the Dean of Wells.

Walpole, Lady Wodehouse, Mrs. Townshend, Mrs. Hussey, &c. Morning spent at Cromer.

Mr. Windham to Mrs. Crewe.

I have behaved very ill in point of correspondence, and very undeserving of all the merits you have shown towards me. The cause has been, not as before, any uncomfortableness of mind that disinclined one to exertion, but good genuine dilatoriness, such as makes one often defer things that are upon the whole pleasant, as well as those that are unpleasant. It is so long since I received your letter, that I hardly remember distinctly the points in it that I ought to answer. The time fixed for your going to Welbeck was the 18th, I think. I was not without thoughts of joining you; but finding upon enquiry, that it was a hundred and eighty miles from here, my heart failed me and I resolved upon grubbing on quietly where I was. You must know that in one respect the longer I stay here, the longer I feel disposed to do so: for though after a length of solitude company becomes more pleasant, there is both in long continuance in one place something that incapacitates one for moving; and to me here, an occupation in various pursuits, which the more time I have to engage in them the more hold they take of my mind, and the more unwilling I am to quit them. In London these things have never time to attach; but here they have nothing to weaken and dissipate their effect, and, as they were my first love, recover all their original empire. It would have been better for me, perhaps, that I had never meddled with anything else; or, meddling with other things, that I had begun to do so sooner. From some cause or other I am now a little of two characters, and good in neither: a politician among scholars, and a scholar among politicians. As Dr. Johnson said from Pope, of Lord Chesterfield, 'a wit among lords, and a lord among wits.'

Under the present half of this divided empire, I am very sorry that Parliament is to meet before Christmas; and look with great concern to the termination that is to be put in three weeks' time to various schemes which I fancy now, if time was given me, I could pursue to some effect. Of the business that we are to meet upon I am as ignorant as need be, and don't at all know what the right judgment is about Pitt's proceedings, or what the points on which principally he is to be attacked. I have in fact, for some time past, nearly forgot that I had anything to do with it: though a late great politician, who has been unexpectedly thrown upon this coast like a whale, has within these few days a little awakened my political ardour. The little fishing town that is within two miles of me has contained no less a man than Colonel Barré. The history of his coming here is not a writ of outlawry nor any warrant issued against him for treasonable practices, but his having been on a visit to Lord Townshend, and been tempted to proceed thus far, on occasion of some of the children having been sent hither to bathe. To you who don't know the seclusion of this corner of the world, but who live in all the resort of the Palatinate, there may appear in this event nothing wonderful: but you cannot conceive to us what the appearance is of any one besides the natives, or, as we should describe it, of one out of the shires. As I could not prevail upon him to take up his abode with me, I must go down, I think, and see him again to-day.

One of the circumstances to render me less inclined to remove to London at this time, one at least of the motives wanting, is, I conclude, that we must not look for you there. I fear I shall hardly be able in the interval between the breaking up and the meeting of Parliament, again to get as far as Cheshire. I had an invitation the other day from Lord John, to renew my hunting in Northamptonshire, and I made during the winter a half promise to Lady Spencer to go at Christmas to Althorpe. But all this is dark and doubtful; and nothing certain but death and taxes, and that Pitt will come out with new lustre from all the present measures, and heap new confusion on us oppositionists. Farewell! I must live upon hope, with the aid of a letter now and then. Remember me, pray, to Crewe, and to all that are obliging enough to think of me; my thanks to Mrs. Lane and Miss Rover, and believe me, &c. &c. &c.

W. WINDHAM.

Felbrigg, Oct. 30th, 1790.

30*th*.—Dined with Colonel Barré and Lord Charles at Cromer. A considerable regale.

November 7th.—On Thursday I conceive it was, that a material incident happened—the arrival of Mr. Burke's pamphlet.* Never was there, I suppose, a work so valuable in its kind, or that displayed powers of so extraordinary a nature. It is a work that may seem capable of overturning the National Assembly, and turning the stream of opinion throughout Europe. One would think, that the author of such a work, would be called to the government of his country, by the combined voice of every man in it. What shall be said of the state of things when it is remembered that the writer is a man decried, persecuted and proscribed; not being much valued, even by his own party, and by half the nation considered as little better than an ingenious madman!

8th, 9th, and *10th*.—Nothing particular that I recollect, except one of the days I did not see Mrs. Lukin; Mary had called in just before dinner and sat with me at dinner and for some time afterwards; I read with her part of a satire in Boileau and a chapter or two out of Harris's 'Hermes.'

13th.—Day uncommonly fine. The night was so clear and mild, and a ride appeared likely to be so beneficial, I preferred coming from Wolterton with George on horseback, to a ride with Mrs. Lukin in the chaise. It was a great doubt with me whether I should not go with them to the Parsonage, thinking that little could be made of the remainder of the evening, but here was an example how ill many things are judged of, till they are tried. I had not been in my own room five minutes before I congratulated myself upon having come, and passed the time till my going to bed both in useful employment and a satisfactory frame of mind.

16th.—Set off with Mary for Norwich. Meeting about a new Bill respecting Wool. Dined at young Forster's: comfortable from memory of the election. Ball in the evening sufficiently pleasant; Lady Buckinghamshire, &c. there. Mary and I sat up afterwards at the Angel.

* Mr. Burke's 'Considerations on the French Revolution.'

17*th.*—Did my business, and came in time to dinner at Aylsham. Something of fatigue in coming back, which disqualified me from thinking of anything very earnestly; talked with Mary therefore about music.

20*th.*—A day or two before our setting out for London, Edward Coke came over to Hanworth, where I met him at dinner, I think on a Monday, and on the day but one after, he dined at Felbrigg, when we made the bet about the woodcock.

27*th.*—Upon the whole, however, I must say that the account of the whole period, amounting to a good four months' delay, even from my being settled at Felbrigg, fell miserably short, both as to the work done and the effect produced, of what I had expected. The conviction of this, coming as it has done progressively, and being a general truth, composed of several successive ones, has not failed at various times to make a deep impression on my spirits. All that I have done will be seen in 'Hist. Liter.' and small indeed is the amount. No other reflections need be made on this. It may be as well to pass on to the month that has elapsed since my return to London. The journey is set forth as much as need be in the migrations.

28*th.*—Having arrived at Kimberley not till four o'clock and despairing of being able from Thetford to reach London the next night, we agreed to stay and so make three days upon the journey.

30*th.*—It was three o'clock, I conceive, or rather earlier, when we arrived in Hill Street. George and William were there to receive us. They returned to dinner, I have a notion, after accompanying me part of the way to the House. As I was too late to take my seat, I was obliged to sit under the gallery and here, either from the heat or the effect of a good deal of mathematical thinking as I came along, or else from causes which I dread to think of, I found a return of failure of memory, having for a long while been unable to recollect the name of 'Brown,' member for Dorsetshire; the title of Lord Muncaster, and, what is the most serious, the name of Sir Adam Ferguson. This last is a very alarming instance.

December 1*st.*—In general, excepting one dinner at Burlington House, where were Burke, Fox, Grey, Tom Grenville, Hare, &c., I cannot recollect to have dined once at a private house for the first three weeks of my being in town.

4*th.*—I must add to the above, a dinner the Saturday after my coming to town, at Sir Joshua's, where were Burke, Lord Palmerston, Boswell. I went afterwards in the evening to Lord Guildford's.

5*th.*—Went to Francis's with young Richard and Elliot. Elliot and I returned in the evening. Mem.—I had to pay the whole of the chaise, which I am sorry to say is an expense not too small for me to be obliged to consider. It was proposed that Francis and I should have had a conversation about Burke's book, but the presence of young Richard of course prevented that design.

19*th.*—I went again to Francis's, with Burke and Sir Gilbert, in Burke's coach, and returned with Pelham and Lord Palmerston in Lord Palmerston's chariot.

20*th.*—Was the first debate, I conceive, on the continuance of the Impeachment; the day therefore on which Bastard made his motion, seconded by Colonel Macleod.

22*nd.*—The second day of the same debate. I went home about eleven, before the end of Pitt's speech. We had sat that day on the Committee, in order that we might finish the Counsel, till five o'clock. Douglas singularly unfortunate, so as to seem, from weariness or dissatisfaction of himself, to have lost all taste and judgment.

23*rd.*—Made our report. I stated what I had to say satisfactorily to myself at the time, but upon reflection, not so clearly and forcibly as I might, with a cause so clear. I ought to have made it impossible for any man of common fairness or judgment to have refused his vote on the side for which I was contending. Yet that was clearly not the case; nor had Coke and Gally been less decided, should I have been able possibly to carry a majority. It is singular that to the last Milles had a very imperfect understanding of the question. After the Committee broke up, I came home to dinner and was tempted to stay afterwards, not thinking that any very good speaker would rise so early, till I was too late to hear a speech of Burke's, which is confessed by all, to have been in his happiest manner, and in that manner, in which I should most of all, have liked to hear him—I mean of wit and pleasantry.

27*th.*—I called with Elliot on Masères, and received the portion, which he has lent me, of the work of his, which is printing.

28*th.*—At the Club; past ten when we broke up. I was tempted to go with Boswell and Langton, after calling on Courtenay, who was gone to bed, to Boswell's lodgings, where, with his daughters and sons and young Langton, I sat disputing with Langton, on the American war, Keppel, &c., with more heat than I liked, till between one and two.

31*st.*—Not out during any part of this day and the preceding. What is this change, that should enable me now to pass two days continually in the house without any perceptible inconvenience? It is probably no change but in my opinion of my being able to do it. 'Possunt, quia posse videntur.' What a pity that this discovery was not made sooner!

1791.

January 10*th.*—The account itself opens with an event the most unpromising and distressful. Yesterday, the 9th, was the day of Mrs. Lukin's being seized with the fit, which exhibited her to me for a moment or two as actually breathing her last, and which for a much longer time left one in suspense what was to be the consequences of it. Of the remoter consequences the apprehension must still remain; but all immediate danger I trust, is removed; and future danger will, I hope, be prevented by that caution which will have been taught by the present attack.

12*th.*—It is to be regretted that I have not, by a more regular observance of the practice of journal writing, ascertained the extent to which this habit has been carried. It is more to be regretted that a habit, known at all times to be so salutary, and now found to be so easily practicable, should not have been begun years and years ago. What a difference it would have made at the time! what a difference it would have made in my present condition, and in all the future fortune of my life! It is not too much to say, that, to this single circumstance, considering the way in which habits propagate each other, the whole difference may be ascribed of my being something or nothing. But such reflections it is vain to pursue further. I have certainly never enjoyed in London such perfect capacity for application, nor have been in such good spirits; it has likewise seldom or never happened, notwithstanding the quantity of time spent with Mrs. L., that I have made so much progress; I must state the whole as a golden period.

17*th.*—The battle at Wretham, which I went to see, and which made up the whole a very pleasant and interesting day, must have been on this date.

29*th.*—A dinner at Fox's, with Grey, St. John and General Burgoyne.

30*th.*—Set off with Mrs. Lukin and Mary for Bath. I had not decided on the journey till the day before, partly from uncertainty about my own wishes, and partly from a doubt whether there might not be in the House something to make attendance necessary. Mrs. Lukin did not know of my intention till after my return from dinner at Fox's. We arrived at Caversham, where Mrs. Lukin was expected, between seven and five; the first time of my being there since Mr. Loveday's death.

31*st.*—We proceeded to Marlborough with all possible satisfaction. The very memory indeed of this, as of all other parts of our journey, will always be to me a source of great pleasure.

February 1*st.*—My stay different from any preceding time, as all places have in fact come now to be viewed with different sensations. The great change began during my residence at Felbrigg last summer.

6*th.*—The day after my return: dined at a large dinner at Fox's.

7*th.*—After the House, dined at Brookes's: Hare, Fox, Grey. Dispute about question of Chance (Sir J. St. Clair).

8*th.*—A consideration for some days of the question started at Brookes's relative to the advantage which a person has by a right of leaving off play at his option.

18*th.*—Within this time Kitty had come, but on what day, I don't recollect. The change which her coming has made in my habits has been something, though not very considerable. For some time, while the 'Anabasis continued, the attractions of that work used to prolong my stay below after breakfast and lead me often into her room when I came home. The same was in some measure the case while she was going through Theophrastus.

March.—My habits as to dining at home, or reading with Kitty, have been much the same as the latter end of the last month. She has been reading for some time Plutarch's 'Apophthegms,' in a small edition which I bought lately, by Stephens. At breakfast or at dinner I have generally made her read some to me, and either from her reading having become more distinct, or my ear more practised, I find that I understand better. About this time, in consequence of correspondence with Masères, began to get again into Mathematics.

21*st.*—The Lauder Committee began, which has given me so much vexation, from the reflection, that if I had stood by my own opinion, I might have prevented at least the vote of vexations. It ended on the 23rd.

26*th.*—Dined with Lord Fitzwilliam: company, Sir Thomas Dundas, Lauderdale, Lord Stormont, Lord Porchester, T. Grenville, Mr. White (the Counsel), Sir William Cunningham, Lord North, Major Maitland, Grey. From dinner we all went to the Opera House in the Haymarket, where for the first time they performed for money; the singers, to avoid the Act, coming in their own dresses and confining themselves to the airs. It will be seen whether this restriction will be considered sufficient.

27*th.*—Dined with Coke: present, Fox, Burke, Duke of Portland, Lord Fitzwilliam, Grey, Fawkener, Mr. Anson, D. North, Lord Tichfield, Lord Petre. Went with Fox and Fawkener to Mortimer Street, to Sir James St. Clair's; thence in Fox's carriage to Lady Webster's; from thence walked home.

28*th.*—Dined at home, previous to going to House to hear King's Message; was to have dined with Sir Joshua, but sent excuse, in order to go to see Mrs. Siddons, in 'Desdemona;' got a place in Mrs. Erskine's box. Foresee great plague from Miss A——.* Great enjoyment of the entertainment. From thence to Burlington House: found my faculties there clear.

29*th.*—Went to the House, prepared to speak if necessary; found myself in particularly good state for speaking, though without anything very material to say. Vandeput had called in the morning and taken up a good deal of time, which I was obliged to submit to—the purpose of his visit having been to serve me in respect to William. When Pitt had spoke, I rose to answer him, and never, surely, was a better mark presented to such an intention. I am as well satisfied, however, that Burke's rising at the same time gave me an opportunity to remain silent. It was not twelve when I came home, but finding Simcoe's book, which Major Grymes had sent me, I continued reading that till near one. An instance here occurred of failure of recollection; I could not, I believe, till next morning, recall the name of 'Lawrence,' the person taken prisoner during the American war and President of the Congress.

30*th.*—I rose late and was hurried during the morning with continued notes and messages. I spent a good deal of time, too, in hearing Greek from Kitty. At three Fox called to go with me to Wilberforce's. When we went to the House, at a little before five, it was up. I went into the Lords, in hopes of having an opportunity of speaking to Lord Grenville, about the Wool Bill, but found them debating about the production of the Treaty with Russia. After staying there as long as I could, I proceeded to the Eumelian's, where I found a large company.

31*st.*—Before I went out Tierney called and had a

* Miss Adair.

long conversation with me about his business, which was to come on that day. I did not go out till it was so late, that I had only time, previous to my going to the House, to leave a card at Sir Henry Hunlocke's. In the House there was a discussion about the right of the sitting members to separate their interests, in which I took part, but, as usual, did not state satisfactorily my own ideas.

April 1st.—Went to the House to attend the Catholics' Bill.

2nd.—Went in the morning, according to engagement made the night before, to see the optical deception in Bond Street. Dined at Lord North's. Instead of joining the party to the Opera I came home and employed myself reading the absurd work of Dr. Cooper in answer to Priestley. Such a compound of dulness and self-sufficiency I could not have expected even from him.

3rd.—Dined with the Speaker. After dinner Sir Gilbert, supported by the Speaker, got into a puzzle, about the going of a horse, conceiving that there was such a thing as stepping with one leg shorter than with the other. Sir Gilbert was more confident than he ought to have been, in a matter where he was so wrong.

4th.—Read till breakfast with great diligence in Apoll. Rhodius. My reading this, is another instance of books read in consequence of being bought. The copy is a very pleasant book of Stephens's printing and has the recommendation, which made me prefer it to a better copy of the same edition, of having the name of 'Barrow' posted in it.

5th.—I had been employed probably during the morning in thinking of Grey's motion which was expected next day; I was not very well and accordingly not comfortable. In the evening went to a meeting at Burlington House.

6th.—Went to the House, and most foolishly was too late for the ballot, though the night before Fox had given notice that endeavours were likely to be made by the other side to prevent our attendance.

8th.—Committee met at eleven. Went down between six and seven expecting to find the Quaker Bill, but found the Catholic Bill, on which I said a little relative to advowsons.

9th.—From the Committee walked with Sir Gilbert Elliot and continued so, hearing much political information, till half-past four. Mrs. Crewe had asked me to go to the 'Siege of Belgrade,' but I sat at home, not doing quite well, yet not very ill, having made some progress in settling a question revived by what occurred on the Committee, relative to the estimate of the probability of the truth of a decision, according as the question is divided or not, or otherwise varied. According to the result of what I was trying last night, supposing no error in the operation, the probability that a decision, determined by three out of five questions on each of which the probability of right decision was $\frac{2}{3}$, was right, would be $\frac{38}{243}$, the remaining cases being not merely those of wrong decision, but of no decision at all. I must enter this however more particularly in 'Adversaria.'

12th.—Day of Grey's motion. I made more than one attempt to speak, but without any great wish of succeeding, though I found myself in very good state as to bodily *feel* for the purpose. It was not more than two, I think, when we got home. Numbers 173 to 253. Pitt could not be called up; and Fox accordingly did not speak; Sheridan most brilliantly.*

13th.—At about ten o'clock or past, went with Burke and his son to the door of the Duchess of Leinster's, where they sat me down. Rooms intolerably hot and so crowded that I could not get away till for so long, that it was twelve before I got home.

* Mr. Sheridan's brilliant speech on the 12th April, 1791, was delivered upon Mr. Grey's motion respecting the preparations for a war with Russia.

14*th*.—Dined at Burke's.

15*th*.—Dined at home. Day, I think, of Burke's motion, on which I spoke. Speech, I believe, compared with others of my own, thought to be good.

16*th*.—Committee as usual. Dined with Wilbraham.

17*th*.—Committee. Went with Mrs. Crewe to Hampstead; dined with Hippisley; pleasant walk back over Primrose Hill, where I found by the way a man of superior condition, to his auditory at least, declaiming against the Russian war and the Ministry. *Q.* Whether this might not be only a way of declaiming against all government, *i. e.* of exciting general distrust and discontent?

18*th*.—Committee. What became of me afterwards I don't recollect. I ought to have been employed, thinking of the question of the Slave Trade that was to come on the next day; but I suspect I was not—certainly not to any purpose.

19*th*.—Day of Club, but I was not there, though I forgot to send any excuse. This was the day of the question, so long expected, of the Slave Trade, on which, after all, found myself unprepared to speak. However blameable, I was for not having been better prepared, I don't know that in the state in which I was, I need feel much regret at not having spoke.

22*nd*.—Committee. Dined at Lord Malmesbury's. Lady Margaret, Lady Anne, Lady Payne, and Sir Ralph; the General Conway that served in America, &c. In the course of the evening I had a good deal of conversation with Sir Gilbert, on the discussion intended to be introduced by Burke, relative to the Canada Bill; on which subject we agreed so little and Sir Gilbert did in my opinion show so much asperity, that we parted, I am afraid, not quite in charity with each other. Burke was there, but I was glad to avail myself of the conversation in which I had been engaged in the corner of the room, so as to go away without speaking to him.

25*th.*—Committee. Called in my way home on Lord Monboddo. My habits of thought are not quite what they ought to be, but I tremble lest my powers of thought are not what they ought to be. I certainly have continually most alarming instances to confirm the fears first conceived during the course of the preceding summer.

26*th.*—Committee. Went with Bishop of Clonfert, Lady Claremont, and Elliot, to dine with Mrs. Crewe at Hampstead. Elliot and I walked after dinner to Hippisley's; much conversation by the way on Burke's intention, which stands for Friday next, of discussing the French Revolution.

27*th.*—Committee. Eumelian; sat next to Lord Monboddo; the Polish and Prussian Envoys there.

28*th.*—Committee. At nine we drove to the Lyceum, meaning, if it had proved the night, to have taken so much of Dibdin's foolish performance, as I presume it is, of 'Ways and Oddities.'

30*th.*—Committee. Dinner at Royal Academy; the second time, I think, of my dining there. Very pleasant. Sat with Marley and a French gentleman, a Mons. de la Tour du Pin, whom I liked so well that I have proposed to call upon him. The account of this month is far from being favourable. Little has been done and I have felt for a great part very much out of spirits. Both circumstances are perhaps to be accounted for in some measure from the same cause, viz. this most wearisome Committee, which business occupying so much of one's time and exhausting the mine of one's strength and spirits, has not brought the usual compensation of increase of knowledge and good exercise of faculties; but has, on the contrary, left one's faculties for a great part of the time in a state of repose; or, so far as it has employed, has not exhibited them to myself in a state of advantage. Whether it is want of habit, want of exertion, or want of power, I do not find in myself a capacity of exercising well, at the same time, both memory and judgment, or of collecting and digesting on a sudden, a multitude of small particulars. The suspicion that this deficiency may have some connection with the change lately suspected in myself and serve as a new proof of its existence (a proof, I fear, not necessary), has contributed very much to depress my spirits.

May 2nd.—Marley, Courtenay and his son, and Boswell dined with me. The first dinner of the sort which I have had this year; liked it very much. When they went away, which was about ten or past, continued below stairs and had Kitty to read Theocritus. Glad to find my memory of it so good.

4th.—After dinner, made Kitty read Milton to me till I found it necessary to go to sleep; afterwards came up into my room and during coffee and for some time after read Theocritus with her.

6th.—Committee. Fatal day of rupture with Burke!* I had gone down earlier in consequence of note from Wilberforce and did not return home from the Committee, but got some soup with Francis, at the Spring Garden Coffee House. It was latish before the House broke up.

7th.—Committee. Dined at Lord Stormont's. I came away with Lord North, who set me down at home.

8th.—Dinner at Sir G. Cornewall's: went from there to consultation at Sir Gilbert's about his motion on the Test Act as affecting Scotland: present, Erskine first, afterwards, Fox.

12th.—Committee. Did not return till near five,

* On the 6th May, 1791, the Quebec Bill was re-committed and Mr. Burke made the speech which led to the termination of his friendship with Mr. Fox. See Lord Russell's *Life and Times of Charles James Fox*, vol. ii. p. 253.

having had long conversation at Burlington House with the Duke, Lord Fitzwilliam and Lord Robert Spencer.

13*th*.—At nine or before, went to the Star and Garter. Present: Fox, Sheridan, Grey, Lord Robert, Grenville, Tarleton. Very pleasant. Came away at eleven with *feel* of enjoyment, or rather, perhaps, capacity of enjoyment, rarely felt.

14*th*.—Fretted by necessity of writing to Bath and uncertainty of dining at home or with Miss Adair, with whom I was to go to see Mrs. Siddons in 'Zara,' who acted for the Fund.

15*th*.—Breakfasted below with Mary and Kitty, reading St. Simon. After that, went out to call on young Richard Burke, whom I was glad not to find at home. Called in my way back and sat some time with Mr. Siddons, Mrs. S. being from home. I had sent a note to Lord Petre, to excuse myself from dining with him from the expectation of meeting Mr. Burke, and otherwise from wishing rather to dine at home. By an answer from him, however, I find that Mr. Burke has excused himself, so I must still go. The company at Lord Petre's were Coke and Mrs. Coke, &c.

16*th*.—Conclusion of the Quebec business. The House being up I went into the Lords and lounged there with little enjoyment or benefit, in consequence of the effect of the heat, till, I believe, ten or past. The business was the continuance of the Impeachment. The House very full both within and without the bar; and the whole scene such as, but for the heat and my coming so newly from dinner would have afforded me much enjoyment. The only circumstance that did give me satisfaction was some overtures of reconciliation from Burke.

17*th*.—Committee. Day of decision; there having been two questions, each of two votes, on which the rest of the Committee were equally divided: my voice has certainly determined the election. I hope that on both, my decision has been right, but on neither, certainly, was I very confident. On the last, however, which was a question of law, considerably more than on the first, I should have had no difficulty on the question of the four votes mooted by Lord Radnor on the second day, and substituted for the eight that had voted on the first.

19th.—Employed chiefly in reading part of Erskine's speech upon Libels and thinking over that question which Fox was to move the next day.

20th.—Went to the House by about half-past four; the business did not come on till past six. Continued in the House and attentive during Fox's speech and the greater part of Erskine's. Then went into the Court of Requests, endeavouring to settle my ideas into some form, such as might admit of my speaking; afterwards sat some time with party of Grey, Sheridan, Grenville and Anstruther at coffee-house. Found grand schemes for the masquerade at Miss Pulteney's (the public one was at Ranelagh) and regretted that I had sent back my ticket. Came home doubting whether one would not be sent me in consequence of message, which I directed Mary to give to Lady Buckinghamshire. Just as I was going to bed, Lady Anne and Lady Margaret called, with whom in about an hour afterwards I went, and with whom I stayed till between three and four.

23rd.—First day, I think, of the trial. Found the good effect, as I had been accustomed to once before, particularly last year.

26th.—Trial. Dined at Sir Godfrey Webster's (very pleasant), and went afterwards to Sheridan's box to hear the first part of 'No Song, no Supper.'

28th.—Went to play. Mrs. Jordan in 'Rosalind.' I am still of opinion, there is more in her person and natural manners than in her acting. Her merit lies out of her part. The words set down by the author she does not repeat with greater propriety of tone, emphasis, or gesture, than others. But she has of these, certain peculiarities, which indicate dispositions, such as take strong hold of the affections, at least of the male part of her audience; and therefore, when the part is of a sort to admit a large portion of these, she produces a great effect. The true acting of the part may, in many instances, not require what she throws into it, but it may admit it; and if the expression so thrown in is of the sort described, the effect of the whole will be improved, though the part is thereby neither better nor worse acted.

30*th*.—Trial. Recollect nothing more. Yes, it was the day of Sir James Erskine's summing-up. I had walked, I have a notion, with Fox in the Park.

31*st*.—Something in the House that prevented my dining at Club; possibly conclusion of business on Libels; on which, by not speaking, I lost an opportunity of stating what I may now say with confidence would have been creditable, because Fox has said in part, previously, precisely what I had intended and not having stated it so distinctly as I know I could have done, all the House appeared struck with the truth of the statement, and disposed to give to the person who made it, great credit for his ingenuity. It is very vexatious that I would not produce these ideas when I actually had them and thus have made an impression, which I know would have been strong at the time and not speedily forgotten. The proper occasion for doing what I am thus regretting would have been at the opening of the business, viz. on the 20th.

June 2*nd*.—At the House. Grey's motion. Spoke. The House broke up by about half-past eleven. I in good spirits, probably from having spoke. Having been dressed, I had nothing to do but get my domino and proceed to the Duke of Bolton's, where I enjoyed myself more than at any masquerade for a long while.

3*rd*.—Went home, I have a notion, to get some dinner

with Francis. Don't recollect what became of me, but I conceive nothing good.

7th.—Dinner at Lord Radnor's. University people. After dinner went to Lord Townshend's, in order to speak about Courtenay's business. I walked to the opera at the Pantheon; there, had a conversation with Lady Jersey for the first time.

10th.—During the journey to Bath I don't think I felt quite the same as on other similar occasions. The air seemed as usual to refresh me, but I doubt if I felt the same enjoyment of the country.

12th.—Went to Abbey church. Walked after church with Wilberforce who had arrived the night before and whom I had called upon as he was at supper; our conversation on religious subjects. He adopts, as I understand, the Trinitarian doctrine, but not in any absurd way. I had settled with Mrs. Lukin to go to Marlborough in the evening, but having in the meanwhile met with Elliot, he prevailed upon me to stay that evening, to which, indeed, I was further inclined by having received intelligence of a boxing match that was to take place on the Tuesday and to which I proposed to go with him. Went in the evening by agreement with him to the Duke of Devonshire's, where I settled to dine with the Duke the next day and to meet Lord Charlemont.

13th.—I could not persuade Elliot to go to the boxing match which I had heard of, and was of consequence not very eager about it myself.

14th.—Set out not till near eleven; had little prospect of being in time for the combat, nor felt much expectation that it would be both at the place or hour that would enable me to see it. To my surprise, however, I found it just where I thought to expect it and luckily for me, not yet begun. Nothing could be more unlike a meeting for such a purpose in the neighbourhood of London. No great crowd, no traffic of people hurrying along the road nothing that could be called tumult; it was, as I observed in my letter to Elliot, more like a congregation of Puritans assembled to hear one of Cromwell's preachers. The name of the victor was Jones; of the other, Lawrence.

15*th.*—*Caversham.*—Miss Riches dined there. In the evening Captain Manley called, the sea officer who had been in one of the voyages with Cook, a man of remarkably pleasant countenance and manners. I think he and Pelham are the instances of persons with whom I recollect to have been most struck.

16*th.*—Went to play; the 'Clandestine Marriage' and 'Midas.'

18*th.*—*London.*—In the morning, I think, in my way to Burlington House, whither I was going as for some days before, met the Duke's note with account of French King's escape.

24*th.*—Mary went in the evening with the Misses Malone to Ranelagh. It was the day before that we had the terrible fracas about her neglect of providing William's things.

29*th.*—Nothing done during the whole of this month in way of literary labour and very dissipated habits contracted. With the practice of literary pursuits the inclination too lost and new sentiments and new feelings superinduced. I may date a great alteration since Mary's coming, which appears to have been May 12th. All these causes have, of course, been greatly increased since the arrival of Mrs. Lukin, viz. since the 18th.

July.—The progress of this month hitherto has been much the same as the time described above. I can recollect but little of what I have done, nor is there anything useful to be recollected. Something, however, has been effected. I have, though late, and after an interval for which latterly no excuse can be made, resumed in some degree mathematics. The accident of some correspondence with Masères has been the means of this reform.

It is dreadful to find how much I have lost during this intermission, or perhaps from an earlier period; not perhaps of the power, but of the ardour of inclination for such studies; I may say, indeed, during the last year the ardour or zeal for all studies. Something must be done to oppose this evil, 'crescenti et in dies serpenti.' I fear a dreadful change in my mind in all ways; the prospect is very dreadful, considering all circumstances and begins already to affect my spirits, though not to any great degree.

Let us pass from this to the manner of late in which I have managed my time and to the state of my mind in other respects. I have certainly for a long while, perhaps for a twelvemonth, remitted greatly that exertion and vigilance which I used to employ in the government of my own thoughts. I have lost likewise much of my ardour for study and, since Christmas at least, of my diligence in the prosecution of it. The relaxation in the government of my thoughts is the more inexcusable, as the exertion of the power would have been more easy, and the effect more complete; though it is perhaps from this very cause, that so little exertion has been made. While my mind was in that strange state, that nothing but continued endeavours would preserve any thought at all, something was necessarily done and the necessity of that something, like the defects of northern climates in the production of the finer fruits, led to exertions that did more than supply the deficiency to which they were called. When without any exertion at all, I could be in a state of tolerable comfort, I acquiesced in what I had, and not being below mediocrity, never rose above it. But little pains has been taken to strengthen my memory, by the recitation of passages formerly known or purposely committed to it; no pains hardly taken to confine my thoughts to any prescribed course, or to restrain them from idle and unprofitable subjects; no exertions made on subjects of an opposite character; little in short done, except at times of stated business, to carry on the great work of mental improvement. It is with a view, therefore, perhaps to what might have been (certain things being admitted as actually possessed), rather than to comparison of what is with what has been, that I complain of the deficiencies of my present state. I am not what the same habits that I now possess would have made me a little while ago. Let us endeavour to find other causes for this besides that most unwelcome one of a commencing decline in my own faculties. To ascertain these let the facts be first stated. My readiness of application at least, if not my ardour, had suffered no decrease during the time that I was employed in drawing out an explanation of the principles of common arithmetic for George and Mary and in writing those papers for the newspaper, on the subject of Pugilism. The latter of these employments must have begun a little more than a fortnight before my going down to Bath. My eagerness for a return to literary employment subsisted likewise, I remember, when that journey took place, for one of my reasons against deciding for it, was my ideas of the manner in which I could employ the ten days or a fortnight likely to intervene, before the business of Parliament should begin. It is a pity that an opportunity of realising these ideas was not given, and that I did not decide against the journey. It would have been well if I had noted the progress of it from day to day, so as to have had in one view the manner in which they were severally passed, and the causes by which either time had been occupied or thought disturbed. A few only of these can now be called to mind. One morning, not long since, was spent very well in seeing Mrs. Harte (Lady Hamilton that is to be) and the display of those powers which seem really to form an epoch in the history and study of antique grace. This must have been the 13th, for it was on the day following, I think, that I dined with Knight and that day was the 14th. The company at Knight's were, Crachrode, Johnes, junr., and Charles Greville; besides, I mean, Sir William Hamilton and Mrs. Harte.

19*th.*—In the evening I went to Colman's first; Mrs. Byng there, with whom for part of the time I sat in Colman's box. The play was 'Inkle and Yarico;' the farce was a translation.

25*th.*—About seven o'clock or past, I went out, taking Robert with me, who had come fresh from Eton (which he had left now finally). Called at Paradise's, where I found Count Zenobio.

27*th.*—Day without a breath of air and very oppressive. Dined at Lord Loughborough's. About ten went to Paradise's, where I was engaged and where, after some time and by means of Boswell, whom I met and brought in with me, got some tea: present, Woronzow, Matsante, Zenobio, Knox, whom I had formerly introduced to Fox.

31*st.*—Stayed at Aubert's till nine or thereabouts; Marsden there, whom I remarked as a man of something more than common.

August 3*rd.*—Dined, I think, with Malone. I could not for the life of me make Malone comprehend that, till the game of draughts is brought to a certainty, no man can complain that it does not afford him an opportunity of showing the extent of his skill.

August 5*th.*—Francis called in the morning, the first time of my having seen him since his return from Paris.

7*th.*—Dinner at Sir Joshua's. After dinner, Sir H. Englefield and Beattie, whom I saw for the first time. Though I was desirous to see more of Beattie, I felt when I went up to tea at eight o'clock so desirous of a little air abroad, particularly of that on the terrace of Somerset House, that I suffered myself insensibly to be drawn that way.

12*th.*—I had called at Burke's in the morning and had

accepted an invitation to dine at the Gray's Inn Coffee House, with O'Hara. On the same day I had gone with Burke and Sir Joshua to see the Duke of Grafton. The dinner at O'Hara's was far from unpleasant; there was a medley of odd people; one of whom, however, was very curious, a Mr. English, an Irishman, who writes the historical part of the 'Annual Register.' When we parted, I came home with Burke and Sir Joshua and afterwards to Burke's to receive the Greek translation of 'Wolsey's Speech,' by Young, Dr. Brocklesby's nephew, who is said to be not more than eighteen.

15*th*.—I went with Sibille, having dined between two and three, to see a rowing match between two men for a private wager; the names of the men were Cooke and Holmes, both of Hungerford.

21*st*.—During the morning of which I went out and saw Sir William Hamilton and Mrs. Harte. I walked afterwards with Charles Greville, whom I met in the streets.

23*rd*.—Mary went to Somerset House. I had at dinner Burney and Porson. When they went away, I walked with Porson as far as Somerset House.

27*th*.—*Canterbury*.—After seeing the Cathedral the first time since my being there in the year 1780, I remember within a word or two, the lines which I had noted in the epitaph of Prude.* As to the place of the tomb, I was not

* In the Warriors' Chapel, Canterbury Cathedral:—

'Sacred to the memory of William Prude, Esq., Lieut.-Colonel in the Belgick wars; slain at the siege of Maestricht, July 12th, 1632.

'Stand, soldiers! ere you march (by way of charge),
Take an example here, that may enlarge
Your minds to noble actions. Here in peace
Rests one whose life was war, whose rich increase
Of fame and honour from his valour grew,
Unbeg'd, unbought; for what he won he drew
By just desert: having in service been
A soldier, till near sixty, from sixteen

quite right, but nearly. At Dover, dined with Walpole; found Mr. and Lady M. Churchill there; amused ourselves in walking upon the pier.

29th.—Sailed in the morning for Calais; passage four hours and a half.

September 1*st.*—Dans la seconde poste après Amiens, il m'est arrivé un accident qui aurait bien pu me coûter la vie ou au moins un œil, et qui me laissera peut-être des marques très-difficiles à effacer. Ce qui me consola pour le petit mal que j'avais éprouvé c'est que je restai si entièrement maître de moi-même dans une crise où pour quelques moments je ne pouvais m'attendre à rien que d'être écrasé.

J'étais occupé à tenir le cheval par la bride, tandis que le postillon ôtait ses bottes pour détacher les pieds du cheval de la limonière; et dans l'instant il me donna un coup de son pied sur le nez, sans cependant rien blesser que la peau, me renversa sous son ventre, et pendant que j'y étais, continua de piétiner avec toute sa force. C'est un miracle que je sois échappé, et sans avoir reçu le moindre mal excepté ce coup sur le nez. Quoiqu'il n'y ait eu point de Providence particulière en tout cela, je n'en dois pas moins en être reconnaissant à Celui qui prend soin à tout ce qui se passe dans l'univers.

3rd.—J'ai cessé de me faire force en tâchant d'éveiller dans mon âme des sentiments qui peuvent paraître convenir à de certaines circonstances. Je ne laissai pourtant de sentir quelque chose de particulier en entrant dans Paris, soit que je le considère tel qu'il est en lui-même, soit par rapport aux autres fois que je m'y suis trouvé.

Years of his active life; continually
Fearless of death, yet still prepared to die
In his religious thoughts; for midst all harms
He bore as much of piety as arms.
Now, soldiers, on, and fear not to intrude
The gates of death, by example of this *Prude.*'

4th.—Il nous vient milord Palmerston, qui est dans la même maison, et qui pense même d'y rester encore quelques jours. J'ai eu occasion aussi de voir, pour la première fois, milord Thanet, qui avait été sur la route en même temps que moi, et qui m'a prévenu infiniment en sa faveur.

6th.—En allant ce matin à l'hôtel pour accompagner Payne aux Tuileries, j'ai fait connaissance avec Monsr. le Vict. de Noailles. Aux Tuileries j'ai vu pour la première fois la Reine. Nous les avons attendus, pour les voir (le Roi et la Reine) en allant à la messe.

9th.—C'est peut-être ce jour-ci que milord Palmerston est passé chez moi, pour me conduire à voir les tableaux dans la Galerie, où tous les deux ans on en fait l'exposition. C'était par la faveur d'une dame qu'il avait la liberté d'y entrer. Il y avait cette dame, une jeune demoiselle assez belle, et Monsgr. l'Évêque d'Autun.* Il paraît être l'amant de madame, et justifie par là le rapport qu'on en a entendu faire.

Mr. Windham to Mrs. Crewe.

I don't like to let another post go without a line, though I have not time enough to make a letter suited by its contents to be sent such a distance. 'Tis something, however, to know that your letter is received, Rue des Petits Augustins, at Paris. The most important information, however, in its consequences to me is, that a letter to find me here should be sent to Mons. Perregaux, banquier. I hope I shall not be long without profiting by the communication. To earn my hopes by the readiest way that the time will allow, let me tell you that on my arrival I found at the Hôtel de l'Université, J. Payne, General Dalrymple, Lord Palmerston, Lord Hardwicke and W. Wyndham, Lord Egremont's second brother. The two last had come over, leaving their wives at Spa and are now both gone back. To replace them are arrived Sir William and late Mrs.

* Afterwards so well known as M. de Talleyrand.

Harte, now Lady Hamilton. They came the day before yesterday and I am going this morning to see them; but, however I may fear being too late, I will not miss the opportunity of sending this. There is another lady also expected here whose presence could not fail to make Paris very interesting to *me*; but as she was to come with Lady R. Douglas, and Lady R. is said to be prevented by a miscarriage or some increase of ill-health, we shall probably lose the pleasure of her company. This is all that I know of company about which you will be much interested, not having yet seen your son or knowing for certain whether he is here. I might have mentioned indeed Lord Thanet, who arrived the same day as myself, with a Hungarian lady, whom as a brilliant achievement he carried off from her husband at Vienna and who, as well as himself, is now suffering for their sins, by the most complete weariness (as I should suppose) of one another. Crauford (James) is likewise here, and in the same hotel with myself. Hare has likewise been here for some time. Having begun, like a good Englishman, with an account of the English company, I may now just mention the little event that took place yesterday of the King's acceptance of the constitution. By the extreme friendly activity of Noailles (ci-devant vicomte) I got a place in the Assembly and was present at the whole ceremony. There was great respect and great applause, but the nature of the proceeding was necessarily humiliating and some circumstances in the conduct of it rendered it still more so. Before the King appeared, two very splendid chairs were placed, one of which I was surprised to see occupied by the president, who pronounced from thence—he and the King being for some time the only persons sitting—a long lecture, in which, besides the objection on account of its length, there was somewhat too much of 'la nation,' and somewhat too little of 'le roi.' I hope that we shall be the people to keep up a little of the 'vieille cour' in our manners, while we lose nothing of the solid advantages and privileges that the new system can promise. But I get nervous and illegible by writing in a hurry, so I will finish with begging my remembrances to all that are so good as to think of me, and professing myself with great truth, &c. &c.

W. WINDHAM.

Paris: Sept. 15, 1791.

11*th*.—Ce fut dimanche, et je dînai chez l'Ambassadeur.* Il y avait beaucoup de monde.

17*th*.—Chez l'Ambassadeur. Après y être resté jusqu'à huit heures passées, je retournai au logis.

19*th*.—Mitford, qui est arrivé depuis deux jours, me vient faire visite. Dîner chez Beauvillier avec Douglas etc. Après dîner, les Italiens, où l'on joua, pour la première fois depuis la Révolution, 'Richard Cœur de Lion.'

20*th*.—Je sortis avec Douglas, qui était arrivé depuis dimanche. Nous allâmes voir si nous pourrions entrer dans l'Assemblée Nationale. Heureusement nous rencontrâmes De Noailles, qui, selon son ordinaire, nous y conduisit tous deux. Après, à l'Opéra, où étaient le Roi et la Reine, pour la première fois. Après, chez Madame de Flahaut, à laquelle j'ai présenté Douglas.

23*rd*.—C'est, je crois, le jour que je fus à l'Assemblée Nationale quand il s'agissait de l'affaire des colonies. M. Barnave ouvrit la discussion par un long discours. Douglas et moi nous sortîmes ensemble.

24*th*.—Je sortis avec milord Holland et Hare avec l'idée d'aller après chez Madame de Flahaut. Un jour, je ne me souviens pas la date, je suis allé avec M. et Madame de Flahaut, et Lady Anne Douglas, voir les Gobelins. Un jour avant j'étais allé voir le Jardin Botanique du Roi.

October 2*nd*.—Souper chez Madame Ghiberti.

6*th*.—Rinci (maison de chasse du Duc d'Orléans), avec Madame de Flahaut etc.; journée très-agréable.

15*th*.—Partie à Belle Vue, maison bâtie par Madame de Pompadour au bord de la Seine. Après être resté chez Madame de Flahaut, causant beaucoup avec l'Évêque d'Autun, et tirant du discours assez de profit, je suis rentré au logis. Un peu avant dix heures je retourne chez Madame

* Earl Gower.

de Flahaut, où au lieu de sentir cette facilité de parler que j'avais éprouvée pendant la journée, et qui m'avait attiré les éloges de l'Évêque d'Autun et de quelques autres, je trouve que je ne pus dire mot.

November 1*st.*—Nothing entered for a fortnight. I dined at Lord Gower's, several times with Lady Anne, at the Palais Royal and with Crauford. Of other events the arrival of Francis is one.

The day before I had breakfasted at Jerningham's and met the Count of Albany.

6*th.*—Morning, walked out with Francis and called on Christie. In the evening at Lord Gower's, having dined with Digby and Mills and his brother at Beauvillier's. At Lord Gower's many persons, Miss Berrys, Mrs. Cosen, &c. I stayed till near eight and should have stayed longer but for the Abbé Roger, whom at last, by his impatience and absurdity, I missed, as on a former occasion.

8*th.*—Went to the Petites Maisons with Madame de Flahaut and Stuart. Dinner at Lord Sunderlin's. I should have stayed longer but for the desire of meeting Roger, which I don't think paid me for my pains.

9*th.*—It was, I think, to-day that I went with Madame de Flahaut to the convent at Chaillot, where the *religieuse* lived, Mrs. Trent, under whom she was bred. It was to me an interesting visit. Mrs. Trent had quitted the convent where she had spent the greatest part of her life, in consequence of the melancholy she felt on the death of a friend whom she lived with, I think, thirty years. She said that her family, and I think she herself, were of Kent; she had left England so young, that, with the long interruptions which she had had since in speaking it, her command of the language was hardly that of a native, though her accent was, except that she had a little tincture of the Irish.

11*th.*—Went in the morning to the College Royal to meet Cournaud and Mercier, and proceed from thence to the Abbé Auger. In Cournaud's room there was Stephens' edition of Plutarch, which he said he read currently. *Non constat* that it was so.

12*th*.—The evening was occupied in preparing for my departure the next day. I don't know how to regret it at present, but it might seem hardly wise to come away at such a moment as the King's refusal of the decree, or to have come away from the Louvre at the moment when the Évêque d'Autun and Simolin and Mr. Sautfois, &c., seem disposed to enter into an account of what had passed in the day.

17*th*.—It was five when we arrived at Calais. The room the same as that which I had slept in, in 1788, or at least the next to it. The room I had slept in the night before the same as I had had, I think, in the year 1778 or 1777, namely, the first time of my ever being in France. In the evening having heard that the Duke and Duchess of York were here and having a note to St. Leger, he called, and carried me to them. I was much pleased with the Duchess both as to manners and physiognomy and was tempted in consequence to stay some moments longer perhaps than was quite regular.

19*th*.—During part of the journey that was in France, I had been occupied with the question which has before employed me, relative to the argument urged by Boscovich,* Priestley, &c., against the existence of matter. The result of my reasonings then was, that the argument was not conclusive, but would equally go against the existence of space. For about a week or something more after my arrival at Paris, read over again the first half or more of Keill's 'Lectio Physica' and thought a great deal of the prop.: after that nothing but study of French. It was only once, I think, that I even looked into the volume which I had brought with me of Dodson. I should have

* A learned Jesuit, born at Ragusa, 1741, died 1787.

observed indeed, that during the first fortnight I not only read what I mentioned in Keill, but went on with the subject which I had in my head at leaving England, viz. the doctrine of necessary proposition. It has not been till since my return that I have got to the true explanation of that. On the journey I read in D'Alembert's 'Mélanges,' &c., and employed myself in the consideration of the question about the impenetrability of matter.

1792.

January 19*th.*—Went to Wolterton; large party at dinner and we too late. Found there, from Kent, that Fox was at Holkham and that Coke wished me to come.

21*st.*—All the way as I went to Holkham, occupied most earnestly about problem. Thought and settled question about the difference of the velocity of shot or bullet when fired upwards. Head sufficiently clear.

25*th.*—Parsonage, I think; dined here and supped here; such has, I think, been in general the practice, I mean as to dining. They have generally dined with me, or I with them.

30*th.*—Dined at my mother's; in the evening at Paradise's, where I met Madame de Genlis, thence to Lord Guildford's. Something of the *feel* of London.

31*st.*—At home all the morning, and employed in writing letter to Madame de Flahaut, having heard that Bishop of Autun was in London and fearing to meet him till I could reflect that my letter to Madame de Flahaut was sent. Called in my way on the Bishop and M. Truguet,* who was come with him.

February 2*nd.*—Dined at Douglas's, Évêque d'Autun and M. Truguet, Lord Loughborough, Pelham, and Lord North.

* 'Truguet (Ministre de la Marine) était un homme loyal et à grands moyens, mais n'ayant pas pour les personnes les ménagemens nécessaires à la tête d'une grande administration.'—*Thiers.*

4th.—Dined at my mother's. Theatre, Mrs. Crewe's box; Mrs. Siddons in the 'Gamester.'

5th.—Dined at Lord Buckinghamshire's. Afterwards to Mrs. Siddons', where were Mrs. Twiss and Mrs. O'Neil.

6th.—Fox's motion on Libels; no opposition.

7th.—Went to the House to attend Indian Committee. Dined at Hippisley's by particular desire, to meet Duchess of Bolton; present besides, Lady Margaret and Lord Kinnoul. Went as soon as cloth was moved to play, to see Mrs. S. in 'Queen Elizabeth.'

8th.—Dined at Mr. Shee's; dinner intolerably late (full seven o'clock), and by no means pleasant, except that the badness of it and the difficulty of getting anything, made it to me very moderate. I scarce got away in time for a meeting of a few people at Burlington House, in relation to the motion by Maitland for papers.

9th.—Called at Sir Joshua's, where I found Sir George Baker. No hopes! yet I have urged Miss Palmer to what I ought to have urged sooner—a consultation.

Debate soon terminated by compliance on the part of Ministry; felt not indisposed to take part if occasion had offered; walked away with Francis and called at Burke's to suggest what had been the subject of conversation with Miss Palmer. Shown into a room with a whole company who had dined there, on occasion of Richard's birthday. Came home and continued employed writing and reading part of a letter from Mr. Burke to Sir Hercules Langrishe. Went to Mrs. Crewe's, with whom I sat tête-à-tête till twelve.

10th.—Dined at the Globe: Masères, Maskelyne, Count Bruhl, Lally Tolendal, Horsley, &c.; thence to Mrs. Crewe's, where sat very pleasantly, though rather drowsily, with Canning and Lord Macartney till near one.

11th.—Dinner at Burlington House: present, Lord Guildford, Lord Carlisle, Lord Loughborough, Lord North, Mr. Ellis, Fox, Lord Stormont, Grenville, Grey

Pelham and Lord Rochester. The consideration of the company, which I liked, made me stay till it was too late to go to the play-house even for the entertainment.

12*th*.—Dined at Francis's.

13*th*.—To-day I went out and walked as far as the Serpentine river with Mrs. Armitage and Fox, from thence all about the Marylebone part of the town, making various visits.

14*th*.—Malone and I went to the play. I had got a place with Mrs. Crewe for M. Truguet. I stayed for the farce, and brought M. Truguet home.

15*th*.—Eumelian's; sat till ten and then went to Lady Lucan's. It was the day, I think, when Carr would have made me believe that all the undergraduates at Christ Church, read the 'Principia.'

18*th*.—Got to the play, not till Mrs. Siddons' part was nearly over; there was only the scene of walking in her sleep. Truguet was there, whom I brought home. The dinner at Sir Peter Burrell's was so pleasant that I was very unwilling to go. I had left a note for Truguet in my way at the Margravine's.

20*th*.—It was to-day that Grey moved for papers and that I spoke. It was the day when Pitt was speaking as I came in and that I spoke in answer to him, particularly on the proceedings of the year '84. Went in the evening to Lady Salisbury's.

21*st*.—Trial, I apprehend, in the morning, but don't know; must get an account of the days of trial. Cholmondeley's dinner, I have a notion. Edmund and, I think, Henry Phipps and Lord Winchelsea; I have a notion, too, Pelham. Stayed late and with great satisfaction. Got with Cholmondeley on the subject of reckoning by so much per cent., which gave occasion to a paper which I drew up the next morning, having thought upon it at night.

23*rd*.—Trial. Dinner afterwards with Mr. and Mrs.

Gally and going in the evening to Cumberland House, where I stayed to supper. It was the first time of my having been in company since my return, with the Duchess of York.

24*th.*—Dined at York House; dinner very pleasant.

25*th.*—Called at Burke's, who was not at home and thence to Malone's, where I sat till near about eleven, waiting for Malone's return, who was with the other executors of Sir Joshua, who must have died the day before.

28*th.*—Called upon Fox about one o'clock, and had a pleasant walk with him, on a delightful day, previous to our dressing to go to the Duchess of York's drawing-room.

29*th.*—Business of the Russian Armament, &c.; spoke later and when I had no reason, from my *feel* to expect that I should speak well. I did, in fact, forget much of what I had intended, and of what had been made perfectly familiar to me; and of that which I did produce all the colouring had sunk in. Such as it was, however, it was thought by some, the best of what I have ever done and even gained great credit. So easy is credit gained, with us at least, by public speaking. One of the topics which I had meant to work, I mentioned the next day to Fox, who adopted it, and used it with very happy success.

March 3rd.—Day memorable as funeral of poor Sir Joshua.

5*th.*—Some time spent in Debret's shop reading Burgoyne's 'Narrative,' by which I was a good deal struck. Burgoyne certainly is not without powers of writing; he has a noble and amiable character, which he has learnt the art of exhibiting in composition. Went to my mother's, who looked ill and was low-spirited, so as to make me glad that I had gone thither. Came home and changed my dress and went to Lady Salisbury's, where was the Duchess of York.

6th.—Am to call this morning on Duchesse de Pienne; day fine. Went to the House, where was to have been the ballot for the Bedford election. No house. Not being engaged to dine, went with Fox, Lord Robert, Francis and Burgoyne, to Whig Club. I had called on Fox when I first went out, and walked with him and Thomas Grenville through the Green Park to the House. Lord Robert and I went to the play; Mrs. Siddons in 'Cordelia.' Sat in Mrs. Bouverie's box. Went after play to my mother's, who continues ill.

8th.—Morning very cold, though clear. Among other visits, saw Lord Orford, *i. e.* Horace Walpole.

10th.—Stayed at home till past four, when I went to dine with my mother; afterwards at the play, whither I went—Mrs. Siddons in 'Portia.' I had been invited to dine with Fox, but thinking that the invitation came rather in circumstances where it might have been more matter of necessity than of choice, did not go. After the play went, I have a notion, to my mother's (alas! now no more), and then home.

11th.—Dined at Lord Lucan's, thence to Lady Hampden's; thence (the last time!) to my mother's. She was going to bed and described herself as having been tolerably free from what seemed her only complaint—attacks of coughing in the night. I took a kind leave of her, little thinking then that it was the last I should ever take.

12th.—Was to have dined at Lord Palmerston's. Came home, doubting whether I should remain there or join Burgoyne after dinner at Lambton's. How strange and how unfortunate that the thought should never have crossed me to take the opportunity of going to my mother's; but that having sent to inquire, I should conceive that I had done enough! 'Tis true that I had no suspicion of danger, but danger ought never to have been supposed away with any ailment at eighty; and had my mind then been rightly prepared, the very pleasure which I should have given would have been motive enough. Alas! these ideas come too late.

The fatal day which took from me a mother who, with all her faults, loved me certainly with uncommon tenderness; whose joy latterly centered in me; whose happiness I might have completed by sacrifices so slight as hardly to be known under that character. What a bitter reflection that this was not done! How bitter are those regrets which spring from the consciousness of omissions towards persons whom death has taken from us; to whom no compensation can be made; whom no sentiments f kindness can reach; who cannot even have the satisfaction of knowing the pain which that reflection excites in us! How different would my state of mind be at present, had I acted for some years past under impressions similar to those which I now feel and such as I should have acted under had my mother's life been extended a few years longer! 'Tis dreadful to think how much happiness has been lost to a person whose happiness I was bound by so many ties to promote, merely for want of such attentions as it would have cost me nothing to pay and such as in a short time I should have paid with great pleasure. That these things were not done at an earlier period may be accounted for in a way that will leave me not without excuse. I must not wholly dissemble the faults of my mother, which checked affection on my part; nor condemn as wholly unfounded the reason I had for questioning the extent and nature of the affection on hers. Latterly those faults were either worn away or lost in consideration of her infirmities. Her affections became less liable to suspicion and less mixed with causes, that disguised or perverted them, and all that I forbore then to do, short of a studious attention to her happiness, stands as a direct charge against myself and a source of lasting reproach which time can never wholly efface. My only consolation must be, that latterly the difference between what was done and what ought to have been done, was less than at any former period, and was every day decreasing, so as to make, I am sure, a great difference in my mother's happiness—perhaps so as to make her feel, reflecting on what was past and anticipating what was to come, that her wishes were nearly satisfied. I do know, however, how much more a little reflection even would have made me do then, and how much more would have come of itself, had her life been a little prolonged. That this additional period was not granted, and, still more, that that reflection was not made, must be a subject of very painful regret. In the picture of my mother now impressed on my mind, nothing is seen but what inspires tenderness and kindness; her faults disappear, and her merits only remain.

14*th.*—After staying in the House overnight for some time and dwelling on the image of my mother as she lay in her bed, in which state, as appeared afterwards, she had wished me to see her, I came home and in an hour or two afterwards went to bed.

17*th.*—Examination of will and papers.

19*th.*—Began now, or perhaps the day before, to recover the ordinary tone of my thoughts, which before that had been altogether destroyed. I don't pretend to say that I was in any state so violent, or that by an effort I could not have attended to, perhaps have interested myself in, any business in which I should naturally be interested; but certain it is that all other interests were for the time suspended, and gave way to a strong feeling of regret, unmixed with any sentiments of satisfaction, of which I have at different times been jealous, at the advantages accruing to me in point of fortune.

21*st.*—Day on which the body was removed. A new question had arisen within this day or two, whether it would be proper for me to go down; my own opinion was at that time against it, conformably to the opinion of Lord and Lady Walpole.

25th.—Day of funeral. I did not find myself much affected; the same thoughts as for some time past occupied my mind, but they had lost much of their effect. Should some thoughts which passed in my mind during the period spent in church, be the happy foundation of a system of belief, less liable to doubt and uncertainty than any that I have hitherto formed, I shall have reason to number this occasion among the happiest of my life, and to add this to what I already owe my mother for early habits of piety and devotion.

26th.—This evening I walked out after dinner, and found the walk less unpleasant than walks after dinner have generally been. But going to Kitty, she produced me two passages in Thucydides, which, though at last I did make them out, tasked my attention in a way that I know not to be good after dinner.

28th.—Read over again in Keill, the part relating to the precession of the equinoxes, about which my brother had got some foolish notion, which he had supposed himself to have learnt from Mitford's 'History of Greece.'

29th.—During an hour that I spent afterwards in my bedroom, instead of thinking on the question of the Slave Trade, which was to come on in four days, I went over the words marked at the end of one of the volumes of Schmid's 'Lucian.' I could not have thought of the other with any effect—the party from the Parsonage having stayed to supper. We were pleasant, from a letter from William.

30th.—Wanting a walk, went over to the Parsonage before breakfast; back by ten; read papers, and did a little, very little, on subject of Slave Trade. Went then into library, and occupied myself in tumbling over books —Cluverius, Aristotle, Demosthenes.

April 1st.—Arrived in London between eight and nine

occupied on question of Slave Trade almost all the way, with tolerable success for a post-chaise, which for such subjects does to me answer well; found at times my thoughts getting fixed.

2nd.—I went to the House at five; no prospect of beginning for some time; did not begin till considerably past six. Wilberforce spoke three hours or more. Thinking that when he had done Tarleton would get up, I went out a little before and got some tea. Mind not in a good state, little mobility of thoughts. Hearing that a Mr. Baillie, a West Indian, was speaking, did not go in. 'Hinc prima mali labes.' I should have answered him, taking for my cue the opening that I had at first prepared. That I did not do so, has been to me certainly a considerable loss; since, however ill-disposed I might have found myself at the moment, so much was the matter prepared in my mind, and such is always the tension given to my mind by the effort of speaking, that I am quite sure I should have spoken in a manner to raise the opinion of my powers, I know not in how great a proportion. When it is considered how rarely such another opportunity is likely to recur; how impossible almost, taking in the curiosity and anxiety felt about it by the nation; the particularly good effects, also, that a speech on this occasion would have had with respect to me in balancing what I shall be obliged to say whenever the question of Parliamentary Reform is brought on, I cannot but feel a good deal vexed that the opportunity was suffered to pass away. The thought, too, what I might have said, and of the impression I might have made, so rush into my mind at this instant, that I must quit the subject, and turn my mind to other things to get rid of the vexation. Let me think, then, how I may employ the ten days that I am come to stay here (Felbrigg), for the advancement of things for which, after all, I am much more eager than for any fame or excellence to be attained in public speaking.

6th.—Arrived at Norwich by eleven. Went to see poor William Crowe,* who lies, I fear, on his last bed. Arrived at Felbrigg about ten.

7th.—Morning being delightful, went out to prepare for what I have so long talked of, the measuring a base from the single tree to the church, thence to mark some trees which I had neglected the last time of my being down.

8th.—Read to myself a little before supper in Sophocles. Afterwards to Mrs. Lukin a little of Swift. We supped in the library.

9th.—Miscellaneous reading all the morning, principally continuation of the 'Vespæ,' which I had left unfinished when I was here in January. Dined at Parsonage. Mrs. Lukin having been to see her old nurse at Thurgaton, where she is lying in her last illness, we did not dine till near five. I passed the intermediate time with Kitty, who had some passages to be made out in Thucydides.

10th.—Up by twenty minutes before seven. Went on with Aristophanes. When I was here last, viz. at the end of last month, brought up into my bedroom an old deal desk which I had remarked below, the comfort of which is more than I could have conceived. It is astonishing upon what little things one's comforts and habits, and even the application of one's time to things important, depends. The use of a desk in London has, I am persuaded, made the whole difference of London being or not a place of study. It has determined my making my bedroom my place of study, and that circumstance draws after it every other. The putting a desk in my bedroom here produces similar, though not wholly equal effects; in the work of translation its influence will be prodigious. My having a place at which I can write

* W. Crowe, his servant.

with ease, where the book will lie ready to my hand, unmixed with a multitude of other things, where it will be presented to my eye the moment that I quit my bed, and where I can take to it without interruption to my dressing, both then and in the middle of the day, will be the means, I am persuaded, of the work's going forward with a degree of facility hitherto unknown. Such being the virtue of desks, I shall take care to have another for the sitting-room: I have an idea, also, of making the sitting my bedroom, and vice versâ. I must see first, however, the effect of its being fitted up, and the change which in this respect also may be made by a desk, by enabling me to write with my back to the light. The difference of sitting with my face opposite to that large and high window, I have discovered lately to have been the cause of great annoyance. 'Tis half-past one, and I have done nothing as yet but read Aristophanes, and a tract of three leaves in Philo-Judæus.

12*th*.—Recollect nothing particular. I had begun a day or two before, what I had so long talked of—a measurement of the distance from the single tree on the east side of the park to the church tower, in order to form a base for the measurement of the other distances of other objects within view. By making the several stakes upright, by means of a plumb-line, and measuring from one to the other on a level taken by the instrument, I got the distance with sufficient ease and competent exactness. The foot of the single tree is about level with the top of the great window in the church.

13*th*.—Meeting at Cromer. I did not go down till late, having been well employed with Simpson's 'Treatise of Porisms,' which I took down by chance, as I had done once before, and found myself engaged by it, as I did then, in a manner to make it very desirable that I should not soon lay it by. This promises to be another instance where studies, springing up of themselves, flourish better, and make more vigorous shoots, than those regularly planted. I rode as far as the white gate with Girdlestone, and doubted whether I should not ask him to come home; perhaps I might as well, though I have a notion that after I came from the Parsonage, where I drank tea, I continued pretty well employed till bedtime. We drank tea, for the first time for me, at the new house called the Hotel at Cromer. I felt amazingly the benefit of the party.

15*th.*—Read in the evening 'Clarissa.' N.B. We have almost always, this time of being here, sat in the bow-window room. Employed well on 'Porisms.'

16*th.*—Sat some time with Mrs. Lukin, talking principally about Kitty, whose conduct does provoke me very much.

17*th.*—Mrs. Lukin and Mary slept at the Hall, the night before our departure, *i. e.* the 20th; after they had left the library, I read a little in Philostratus, 'De Vitâ Sophist.' I cannot now recollect either the part or the use of a word which I met with there for the first time.

20*th.*—We arrived in London in good time. I went immediately to Brookes's, where I found every one full of the business of the Association.*

April 23*rd.*—The particulars that have happened in this period, such as are either remarkable in themselves, and calculated to assist recollection, may be stated to be my speaking in the House on the Slave Trade, April 26th; on Grey's Motion; on Proclamation; on Police Bill.

There were three confidential meetings at Burlington House. One the day or two preceding Grey's notice; the other about the Proclamation; and the third about

* The *Association* was 'the Society of the Friends of the People,' which was formed about this time to agitate the question of Parliamentary Reform. It was denounced by the Government as Jacobinical, and, on the 21st May, a Royal Proclamation was issued for the suppression of seditious correspondence and publications.

the Address. There was a meeting also at Fox's the night before the debate on the Proclamation.

The great consumers of time have been, after the House of Commons, Westminster Hall, and dinners. By these and other interruptions it has happened that I have worked less in any way of literature than during any period almost of equal extent. My mind has likewise been proportionably inactive; free indeed from those disturbances by which it used to be harassed, when not intent on some stated employment, but without being occupied by better thoughts, and what was worse, in some respects, without impatience of not being so. What a prodigious deal might be done if, with the advantages which I have at length attained, I retained my ardour and activity.

May.—Of this month, as of the latter end of the last, no account whatever has been kept; much however has been done in it in respect to public business, and of such events as might make part of a journal. The same cause will account for there having been little of that which should occupy a place in the 'Hist. Liter.' It is indeed to be noted as a period in which there has been less of that lost than in any period of equal extent. It is still more to be noted as a period in which the want of that has been also less felt. The change that has taken place in myself in that respect is striking, and by no means comfortable. The facility with which I yield now to engagement; the little desire of avoiding or contracting it; the composure with which I submit to interruption; in a word, the little account which I take of time, or regret which I feel at the loss of it, are circumstances altogether new and alarming. I experience now a change of mind, such as general experience teaches, I believe, to expect, but of which I had no trace till within about this year. A great abatement has taken place in the ardour of pursuit. It is but very lately that I could not have withdrawn for ever so short a time, in a way ever so pleasing, from the pursuits that usually engaged me, without feeling a strong impatience at the interruption, and earnest desire to return to my accustomed task; I may say, I think truly, that I never quitted home for any purpose with the prospect of being absent for several hours, without feeling at the moment that my inclination was rather to stay than to go. The moment too of my return, if my state was not such as to preclude my hopes of useful application, and indeed even when it was, was always attended with pleasure; I quitted home with reluctance, and I was impatient to return. When I add to this the constant reckoning which I kept of the times of my absence, the estimate I made of the loss thus sustained in the prosecution of certain purposes, the constant reference of time to objects; few states can be more unlike one another than that in which I lived till very lately, an that of which I have been conscious since that time. It is, in one word, that I have lost the ardour of pursuit. The consideration must be, whether this can by any means be restored. The task is undoubtedly arduous, and little countenanced for its success by general experience; yet I do not think it hopeless. In the first place, this change is not of long standing; in the next place, it seems capable of being accounted for by causes which it is in my own power to remove. The intermission of all pursuit, which is the sure way to destroy the ardour of it, need never be of long continuance, and except by my own fault, need rarely occur in the same degree. I know by invariable experience how certainly, in the case of employment, the will returns with the act; and how much of the act has lately been suspended for reasons created altogether by myself. To ascertain as nearly as possible in what degree this has happened, let me make out the best account I can of the manner in which my time has passed.

June 11*th*.—Dined at Lord R. Spencer's: present, Fox, Stanhope, Lauderdale, M. Chauvelin,* Évêque d'Autun, Fitzpatrick, Sir S. Stepney, Lord Cholmondeley.

13*th*.—Dined for the first time at Lord Ossory's. Th. Grenville, Charles Greville, Mr. Morris, Lord Holland's companion.

14*th*.—Dinner at Hampstead;† Mary and Canning, Pelham, there.

15*th*.—Dinner at the Globe: present, Masères, Hutton, Maskelyne, Noel, Dr. Pierce; talked on subject of prayer; strange stiffness and slowness of understanding in mathematical men on other subjects. In the morning before I went to dinner, I had a sitting with Nollekens.‡

16*th*.—Went after dinner to Burlington House, I think, for the first time, since the Duke's conversation; if so, Fox and Lord Malmesbury§ came in, in consequence of which I soon came away and called at Mrs. Crewe's.

17*th*.—Called on returning from Greenwich, at the Duke of Portland's, to know whether anything further had passed; stayed but a short time, Lawrence being there; nor was there otherwise anything in fact to communicate. What an example this is, of change in the administration happening, or being liable to happen, from causes impossible to be foreseen, and by a sort of dccay, like that which every day terminates the existence of our bodies, without any distinct cause of failure.

20*th*.—Arrived at Felbrigg. I have since been wholly occupied with the 'Loci Plani,' which I mean to read through, at least the greater part of them, with all expedition. Great part of the benefit which I propose from this, will consist in the use which I propose to make, and

* M. Chauvelin, the French Ambassador.

† Mrs. Crewe's.

‡ Nollekens executed several busts of Mr. Windham during his life, and one from a cast taken after death, which was placed on the monument erected to him in Felbrigg Church, where he lies interred.

§ *Vide* Lord Malmesbury's 'Diary,' vol. ii. p. 461.

which I have made hitherto, of my new case of mathematical instruments. I have frequently thought that the practice of delineating the propositions which one went through, particularly in the case of a work of this sort, would be very good, and I am sure I have to regret that I did not take it up years ago.

For several mornings together I rode out before breakfast, commonly to Cromer, and back again, taking Mary with me, on a pony belonging to Hicks.

July 1*st.*—Went over to Norwich, to attend the meeting on the Address.

3*rd.*—Rode to Gunton, to make a visit to Mr. Harbord and Lady Caroline; went round by Hanworth. Coke dined here, the first time as it happened of his ever having been at Felbrigg when I have been here; he went away to Holkham early in the evening.

10*th.*—During the whole of the time of my being here, or at least during the greater part of it, it must be noted that I have not been quite well; the cause of which I take to be no more than some little mismanagement in point of regimen, with something possibly produced by the circumstance of sleeping in an east bedroom. This satisfaction, however, remains, and is generally attached, I think, to residences at Felbrigg, that the latter part of the time is better than the former, and that as my stay is prolonged my diligence increases. I certainly feel that this will continue to be so. I feel well satisfied at having abandoned a party, an excursion, namely, with Sir William Scott,* to Paris, which in other respects promised many advantages.

24*th.*—We had our camp at Sheringham.

August 2*nd.*—Came from the Assizes with Lord Loughborough. A great deal of conversation as we came, about state of political negotiations; he sounded me, as I rather

* Afterwards Lord Stowell.

understood it, about going to India. Day pleasant; Erskine at dinner.

4th.—During my stay at Norwich for the Assizes, had received a letter from Sir William Scott, proposing an excursion to France or the Netherlands, in consequence of which, from the time of my return till about the 16th, I remained in constant expectation of being called away, and with my things prepared for departure. My opinion about the advantages of this tour fluctuated very much, at some times presenting, as was natural, the satisfaction it would produce, and the benefits that would result from it. At others, being more busy in showing the use that was to be made of residence here, and the prejudice which that might sustain by such an interruption. The inclination of my judgment was, upon the whole, against the tour, and this sentiment continued, which does not always happen, even after the decision was taken. I was once so near setting off as to have packed up all my things, and to have the horses waiting only for my orders to come to the door; this I think must have been on the 15th. I luckily resolved, after long deliberation, to wait at last for one more letter from Sir W. Scott; and it was fortunate that I did so, as that letter showed me that had I gone to town, our tour would hardly have taken place, and that if it had, it would have been much against his wishes. From that time to the 22nd I continued at Felbrigg, feeling in the very intention of going part of the benefit which such an excursion might be supposed to give, when upon notice of Sir Joseph Banks being at Holkham, and a message from Coke, I went over there with Mrs. Lukin and Mary.

20th.—In the morning went as far as Holt on horseback; from Holt I went on in a chaise, thinking, as I had been before, on the question respecting the paces of a horse, and in general the motion of four-footed animals.

The meeting at Walsingham much like others, except that Coke, by some things said, by all possible kindness, but without perhaps an equal degree of prudence, put me under the necessity of making what is called a speech. It may be supposed that I did not let it be very long.

22nd.—Went after dinner to Holkham.

23rd.—At Holkham; rode in the morning, Coke lending me a young horse of his, 'Caractacus,' the hardness of whose mouth and disposition to break away made a degree of attention, as well as exertion, necessary in riding him, that took off something of the pleasure of the ride; it was however, on the whole, not unpleasant. At my return I read, partly Lord Bolingbroke's letter on 'Patriotism,' partly Dionysius Halicarnassus. I had left a paper in this book from the time of my being at Holkham, two years, I believe, before.

24th.—Returned to Felbrigg. I do not recollect what I thought of during the drive back; I was employed on something pretty diligently; I am not sure whether it was not part of the disquisition in Bernouilli on the 'Principles of Evidence.'*

September 5th.—Sir William Jerningham and his son came. In the morning I had walked out on the bowling green, when Mary came to me and stayed for a few minutes. Employed in thinking of the proposition which is in page 172 of 'Adversaria.'

7th.—Rode out in the morning with Sir W. and Mrs. Lukin. I was so exhausted, that I was fain to lie down and sleep, and was unable to do that without many of those convulsive shocks with which I have for some time past, and particularly I think during this summer, been so much annoyed, and which I fear are the forerunners of a paralytic stroke. A night now not very often passes without my experiencing some of these seizures, in a way

* On 'Ars Conjectandi.'

to make me apprehend that the event is actually taking place.

10*th.*—Up as usual in good time and with *feel* of health. Read on in 'Loci Plani,' in my sitting-room till nine, when, with a view to spending some time in the steward's room, breakfasted there with the boys, several of whom are obliged now to sleep here, on account of the numbers at the Parsonage. After dinner rode out with Robert round the race-ground; from thence went with him riding on the heath.

12*th.*—Good deal of talk, not otherwise interesting, than as it was about the late dreadful accounts from Paris. Remained in the drawing-room reading the 'Political Catechism,' left here by Sir William Jerningham, and bearing the name of the Abbé Auger.

14*th.*—Kitty, I have a notion, dined here and stayed the evening. Read with her Diodorus Siculus and Aristot. vol. i., till after tea.

19*th.*—Tempted to walk round the wood with Kitty.

22*nd.*—Went out on foot, and did a great deal in marking trees, and laying out walks—a work much wanted.

26*th.*—Rose well. Seeing G. Wyndham with all the horses, felt it a gay scene.

27*th.*—Breakfasted in the steward's room. Went up afterwards, and continued well employed: first, settling the questions about the motions of a horse in walking; and then the question about necessary propositions, which, I think, I have for some time past settled pretty satisfactory. I have a letter from Mad^e. de Flahaut.*

29*th.*—Set off with Ives for Norwich, in way to London. Slept part of the way; for the rest employed on proposition—viz. one of those which are at the end of Horsley's 'Apollonius.' No tea to be had at Attleborough. Fox being expected every moment from Elden,† where he

* Mother to the present Count de Flahaut. † Elden (Hall).

had been dining with the Duke of York, I waited for him till near one, amusing myself with a French novel which I found there.

30*th*.—In the morning I breakfasted with Fox, and sat there, partly from the natural motive of wishing to have all I could of his company, and partly from uncertainty about the course I should take—viz. whether to go round with him to Bury, and so visit Madame de Genlis, or whether I should proceed straight on my journey.

October 3*rd*.—Rose early. Despatched what was necessary, and set off in good time to Bulstrode. Arrived before the Delegation. Found there Lord Stormont, Mr. Ellis, Lord Malmesbury, Sir W. Scott, Lawrence, Burke, Dean of Christ Church, Bishop of Oxford. Very sorry that I had not come sooner. Dinner and whole business very pleasant, though not so much so, I am persuaded, as if I had come sooner. Employed in coming down on problem.

6*th*.—*Oxford*.—Called on Stinton. Spent short time with Malone, in the Bodleian. Read letters of Pope and Dryden. Went into coffee-house at Mitre, in hopes of finding some later papers, but did not succeed. Crisis very anxious. Great doubt which way things are to turn, whether the French affairs to be overturned, or the combined armies to retire, confessing their inability. If so, farewell, for a long time to come, to all good government throughout Europe. All establishments at least will be overset and everything changed, down to the minutest article of manners. I cannot help having great apprehensions.

7*th*.—Rose a little before eight, and before breakfast did little but dress and read my letters, with a little Sophocles: at breakfast Winstanley came in, afterwards Robert; and, before I went out, Mr. Osborn, who is here, employing himself in some enquiries in his own way in the Bodley. At a little past one, I went to Malone's, meaning to walk with him to Langton's, at Headington, but the weather was such as to prevent us. I sat, therefore, some time with him, reading letters of Hobbes, Halley, Sir I. Newton, Hook, Lock, and others, of no consequence in themselves, but affording at least specimens of their hand-writing: they were written upon various occasions, to Aubrey, whose life and history Malone is now employed about. We walked out, calling upon Robert; and, lastly, going into the library at the University. I can never enter there without particular sensations, partly pleasant and partly painful. Having sent some letters off, I had thought of allotting the remainder of the evening to a diligent reading of Sophocles; but the problem came across me, and having once got possession of my thoughts has carried me on, though without success, till now, eleven o'clock.

Though there is in this something unfavourable to satisfaction, I have a *feel* of enjoyment, such as I should hardly enjoy were I now in my mansion of Felbrigg, master of a large house, in the midst of an ample property, surrounded by those who look up to me as in the highest situation of splendour and happiness to which their ideas reach. I am, instead, in the worst inn's worst room; in an ordinary room, at least, in an inferior inn, with nothing superior in my situation in point of comfort and distinction, from that of every ordinary traveller. That this should be the happier situation, proceeds from causes, in part common to many others, and founded on natural principles, in part peculiar to myself, and the result of circumstances.

12*th*.—University College: large party; partly invited by Dr. Simpson, and part, by young Wetherall. In a morning I have generally sat pretty free from interruption till twelve or one o'clock, and have during that time been principally employed in attempts at the solution of the problem. That I have carried on this in my head entirely without any aid from writing or consignment to writing of steps occasionally made, has been a disadvantage, retarding perhaps both the progress of the work and abating the diligence with which it has been pursued.

The time that I have been from home has been in a morning employed generally in part in the Bodley. That more has not been so employed has been owing to the inconvenience felt there in consequence of the cold.

13*th*.—Dined at Malone's: only he. After sitting some time, during which I finished manuscript 'Life of Milton,' that I had begun before dinner, and had a good deal of not unpleasant talk, we walked out, and drank tea at coffee-house at the Angel, where I met Newnham. Thence, after another walk, more productive of pleasant images than a walk in Felbrigg woods, to my new lodgings at Kettle Hall. During the whole of my time of being here, I have felt strongly the share which place may have in determining the course and character of one's thoughts: all that it has done here has been for the better. My mind has been more gay; my thoughts more satisfactory; stronger impressions have been made; more of that has been felt which advances us, as Dr. Johnson says, in the order of thinking beings. The whole of this effect, however, must not be ascribed to the change of place or habits. I cannot but suspect that the sickness which I had on the 9th, was the crisis of a degree of illness which I have had for the greater part of the summer. It is a great question with me this morning and last night, whether I should not leave Oxford to-morrow, and some time was lost in the consideration. I determined at last to make trial of a lodging, if it were only that I might make trial of the difference. The result is, for any time longer than a few days, there must be no hesitation about taking a lodging. My situation at the inn (the Cross) was for the time I stayed by no means uncomfortable. I could sit there in an evening or a morning, and think with as much effect as anywhere else. The bustle of it, too, was not more, than after such a residence at Felbrigg, was pleasant rather than otherwise; but there was always an idea of exposure or interruption in it, and an impossibility of engaging in anything requiring the use of books or papers. Besides the fear of intrusion, there appeared something incongruous in the appearance of an inn room thrown into the state of a study; so that, in fact, during the whole of my being there, I never did employ myself in any way but such as was merely mental or required only the aid of a book, to be put away without difficulty on anybody coming in. My enjoyment in my lodging continued during the whole of my stay, equal to what I had reason to hope on my first entrance. Its situation in the town, the distribution of the rooms, and the collegiate air which it still retained (its title also remains Kettle Hall), all made it a place of pleasant abode, and mark it out to be chosen in case of any future visit.

14*th.*—Dined with Malone.

15*th.*—We dined, I think, with Vivian. The morning had been bad, and I had sat at home all the time reading till past two, the 'Œdip. Col.' I meant to have finished it, and have joined Malone in Corpus Library, but Sir William Young coming in detained me. I came home, and employed the time before our going to sup in University Common Room, in sending to the Duke of Portland an account of what I had heard from Sir William Young in the morning.

16*th.*—Dined with the Dean of Christ Church, Dr. Stinton, and Mr. Horne, who had read with Lord Holland, a Mr. Kitner, who was tutor to Lord Waterford, Jackson, the Dean's brother.

18*th.*—Had Robert in the evening, and played at draughts with him, as I had done before. Glad to find that I recovered my play, which from some games played when I was at Felbrigg, I was afraid I had lost, not from want of practice, but from loss of the quickness of youth.

Debate with myself about going the next day, which ended in determination to go.

19*th*.—Set off at time proposed. Intent all the way on problem, or on one derived from it; journey therefore not marked by any particular temper of mind. Arrived at Hippisley's just before dinner. The only company there Miss Caroline Vernon. Children humoured, and, at table, disagreeable.

20*th*.—Went away before breakfast. Breakfasted at Egham. Still problem.

22*nd*.—*London*.—Dined with Tierney at Thomas's. Had a note announcing the arrival of Mad[e] de Flahaut. Went to her, parting with Tierney.

23*rd*.—At one of the dinners at Cholmondeley's we had Frederick North and Legge; and, in the evening, M. de Narbonne, who was minister a year or two ago, and now obliged to fly.

I let myself foolishly be drawn by Boswell to explore, as he called it, Wapping, instead of going when everything was prepared, to see the battle between Ward and Stanyard, which turned out a very good one, and which would have served as a very good introduction to Boswell.

November 4th.—During the whole of this period the distribution of my time, and the use made of it, has not been what it ought to be, though it has passed not uncomfortably. The time has passed pleasantly though not profitably, the reasons of which, besides those which may operate always, have been—first, the prosecution of this problem which has engrossed my mind when I have not intended it, and then left me in a state in which I have been indisposed to or incapable of other employment: secondly, the obligation, to which I have been sensible, of putting together my ideas on the great questions about to come on, and the inability to set myself earnestly about the work. This has had the effect which such a state of mind always has had with me. I have just thought of what I ought to do, sufficiently and no more to make me neglect everything else. For want of plan or want of adherence to such as had been formed, a fortnight or more has slipped away, not unpleasantly nor wholly unprofitably, but without effect or exertions adequate to the time and opportunities.

6*th.*—Dined at the Whig Club. Morning occupied almost entirely by conversation with Fox and Grenville.

8*th.*—Called on Grattan and De Noailles. Drank tea at Cholmondeley's. Walked thence to Brookes's, where I stayed till half-past eleven, talking on State affairs with Stanhope, Boothby, Lord William Russell, Charles Wyndham, &c. All those right.

9*th.*—Called on Malone, who had gone to Blair's, and as I did not choose to follow him knowing that political conversation could not be avoided, and that in the present state and in that quarter, it could produce to me nothing but mortification, I dined therefore at the hotel in Conduit Street.

10*th.*—Dined, I think, with Malone: present Boswell and Courtenay. Long discussion about passage in Parnell: amazing noise and want of clearness. Malone's interpretation right, however.

11*th.*—Went in the morning to breakfast with Burke. When I came away from there, called on Mad^e. de Flahaut and found Lord Lansdowne: the first time of my speaking to him since I called on him in the year '81 or '82.

12*th.*—Breakfast with Burke: continued there almost the whole morning. In returning from there saw Williamson, who is just returned from Sir Lionel Copley's, and is a furious Jacobin: one of his reasons, that merit meets with no reward; and one of his proofs, that he has met with none.

Time and thought from this period occupied almost

entirely with the great business of the time. For a long whi e there has been a suspension of all my usual literary pursuits. I have neither read nor thought of anything but what had reference to public concerns. My day, too, has been for the greater part spent in promoting the measures necessary at this time to be pursued. Conversation at Burlington House with Fox, Grenville, and Duke of Devonshire.

25*th.*—Called in the morning in consequence of a note from Lord Loughborough. Adair had called upon me before, and walked with me the greater portion of the way. Heard the result of his communication with P., being a refusal of the seals: his letter very good. It was the day before that I had been with Mr. Pitt.* I went early to Lord Mulgrave's, who imparted to me the measure, in which I have since concurred, and which I hope now to extend with effect to this country. From him I went to Mad[e]. de Flahaut's, thence to Burlington House.

* The following extract from the 'Diary' of Lord Malmesbury throws additional light on the relations of the different sections of the Whig Part with Mr. Pitt and with one another at this time:—

'Lord Loughborough called on me; he was greatly hurt at the Duke of Portland's inaction, and Fox's violence. He adverted to our conference on the evening of the 12th; said it was one of wrangle—that Lord Derby was there to report to Brookes's all that passed. He urged the necessity of his talking to the Duke, and also that of forcing him, by taking the sense of the party, and going to him in a body to compel him to declare himself either decidedly for, or decidedly against, Fox. We all agreed it was absolutely necessary for the Duke of Portland to declare his sentiments and ours to the House of Lords. I was to go to him first, and afterwards Windham. This we did, and he engaged to say the next day, when Lord Grenville was to bring in a Bill relative to the power of the Crown over aliens, that he was disposed to support it, and in general, as long as the circumstances or the crisis lasted, to support the Government of the country. Lord Fitzwilliam left London from difficulty how to act, and distress of mind relative to Fox. Windham, also, came to me; his opinions entirely coincide with ours; he was for an amicable separation, not a rupture with Fox.'—*Lord Malmesbury's Diary*, vol. ii. p. 478.

1793.

Monday, January 14th.—Dined with Mrs. Cholmondeley and Mrs. Pitt.

Tuesday, 15th.—Dined at the Club: present, Duke of Leeds, Dr. Wharton, Dr. Fordyce, Dr. Warren, Malone, Dr. Burney, Steevens, Sir Charles Bunbury.

16th.—Arrived at Norwich in time for the Sessions.

19th.—Upon coming into the court at Norwich, I was assailed by Sir Berney Brograve, who, in consequence of what had been said by some one respecting the being joined with him in a commission about the sea breaches, wanted to draw from me, as he had done from others, a declaration, that in similar circumstances no such objection would have been made on my part. Luckily, the singular character of the man put me upon considering the question before I gave an answer; and that consideration showed me that no answer ought to be given at all. The refusal, which greatly astonished him, put him upon talking in a way during dinner which it was necessary to check, but which should have been checked with a lighter hand than that which I found myself using, and which had more an air of quarrelling than I liked to wear or than the occasion required.

March 13th.—I reached London in good time, and getting out of my chaise in Oxford Road went previously to any other place to Lady Payne's. There I saw for the first time since his appointment the new Chancellor, who desired me to call upon him the next day. All the period since then is chaos, a confusion, containing events more important than usually find a place in this Journal, but not remembered with sufficient distinctness, nor so ascertained in their relations to each other, as to be capable of being referred to their several dates. The times of my having spoke in the House were, I think, as follows:—On the Alien Bill, on Fox's* motion on the War, on Sheridan's motion for a Committee to enquire into Seditious Practices, on Powys's motion respecting Canals; that is, these are the occasions, down to the present (24th March). To distinguish what happened in January, what in February, and what in the present month, is, for the most part, beyond my power.

Among events which answer the description above given, viz. as being more important than those usually asserted in this account, are the two meetings which we have had in this house, and the measure of taking our names from the Whig Club; the dates of them, however, I don't know.

In other respects, my mind has for now, a period of years, almost been so totally free from those disturbances which used to affect it, and company and interruption produce an effect upon it so much less injurious, that it is provoking to think that more should not be done. What would have been the enjoyment which I should have felt some years ago with a possession of myself such as is now habitual!

20th.—Dined at Eumelian's. In my way home on foot, for I could not stay for the carriage, called on Mrs. Crewe, and found there Grenville and Hare. The latter rather flippant. Sorry that I did not put myself upon answering him; which if I had done, the means, I think, would have occurred.

21st.—Went down, I think, between two and three to

* **Mr. Windham spoke on the 1st February, in answer to Fox on his debate on War with France.**

the House, in order to have a conversation by appointment with the Attorney-General * respecting clause in what is called Treason Bill.

24*th*.—I was engaged to Bastard to meet Sir H. Clinton and some one lately arrived from Simcoe, in Canada, a party which I should have been glad to meet, but which I cannot after the benefit I have found, or suppose myself to have found, from staying at home; particularly as I could not have gone there, without the necessity of going afterwards to Lord Buckinghamshire's music and spending the whole evening, of consequence, abroad.

25*th*.—Stayed at home all the morning and dined at home, expecting business in the House. Mr. Townshend, and afterwards Burke and Sir Gilbert Elliot, had called in the morning to announce the late, and I hope conclusive, successes of the Austrians against Dumourier. The last and principal action took place on the 18th inst.

26*th*.—Not out in the morning, nor till I went to the House. Employed usefully in entering an article in 'Adversaria.' Dinner at home. Went with Malone to Mrs. Crewe's, where were Major Crewe and Sir R. Payne. Thence to Byng's, where talked for a little while with Byng and Cecy.

27*th*.—Went to House early on private business; back by dinner, at home, having refused both Lord Lucan, where Burke was to be, and Sir G. Cornewall, where I should have met Lord Malmesbury and Sir Gilbert Elliot. Sat at home till a little before eleven, then went to Half-Moon Street, where I found M. de Talleyrand, M. St. Croix, and an Italian secretary, I think, to the Venetian ambassador: stayed till near four.

29*th*.—By five got to Chesterford, where, before my dinner was brought, was found by Sir Charles Bunbury, in whose room I dined. We then proceeded together to

* Sir John Scott, afterwards Lord Eldon.

Newmarket. Books with me: a volume of Hume's 'History,' *i. e.* Smollett's continuation; a small edition, lately bought, of 'Conciones et Orationes,' printed by Elzevir; volume of 'Mélanges de Littérature, &c.' by D'Alembert; volume of Dryden. 'Hume' and the 'Conciones' the only ones used, except so far as to refresh my memory on the question which I have been considering for some time past in the 'Mélanges, &c.'

30*th.*—At Swaffham by twenty minutes before twelve; away at twelve, having called on Russell and Mrs. R., from the latter of whom found so hearty a welcome as well compensated for the delay. Finding that the chaise would want greasing at Fakenham and recollecting that it was market-day at Holt, got some dinner at Fakenham. At home by a little after six, or rather at the Parsonage by that time, after walking from the Aylmerton Gate, which I found locked, and going upstairs at the Hall.

31*st.*—Employed a considerable time in endeavours to improve my hand, by trial of different methods of holding my pen; by one, in particular, apparently very little promising, but which I saw lately used by Nepean. I cannot yet much boast of my success, yet the attempt must not be relinquished. After what I have remarked myself, confirmed by the remark which I once heard made by Burke, I am convinced that a good hand is not wholly without connection with a good style. I can make out, in a manner sufficiently satisfactory, what the connection may be. Faculties clear and good, such as to show the effect of the journey and country air. Had taken down Beveridge's 'Chronology,' in order to recall the rules respecting the Dominical Letter.

April 1*st.*—Up before eight. Read part of an ode of Pindar; wrote some translations; shaved before breakfast. Suffered myself to fall into reveries about military service. Finished first 'Pythiad,' which I find I had read formerly, and which remained very fresh in my mind.

3rd.—At three or a little before went down to Cromer, the day being very fine, and a motive being furnished by the arrival there of a company of the Leicestershire Militia. The first time of my being on horseback since my being down. Ships on the beach. Ride on the whole very delightful.

4th.—Up by half-past six. Doubt about going, but resolved that I would put myself in a state to have the decision in my power; prepared everything, therefore, and was at the Parsonage with the chaise by more than a quarter before eight. Then fairly determined against going; and, though I see disadvantages, from the possibility of having lost an opportunity of distinction, and from appearing, perhaps, to desert those who may be willing to look to me, yet such is the chance that these things may not happen, and such the satisfactions and benefits which I shall find from a few more days here, that I cannot as yet think that I have decided wrong. From time of coming home till dinner employed in writing letter to Sir G. Young about troops quartered in Cromer.

6th.—After finishing part that remained of the papers, read in Maclaurin the account of the theory of the tides. Went on then with house accounts. At two went out walking with Mary, round by Joshua Denny's, then by Aylmerton village, through the Savannah, and home by the Lodge. Found, on coming in, that I had walked too much. After dinner, Mary and Mrs. Lukin going to sleep, Kitty brought down a volume of the 'Scriptores Græc.' of Stephens, and read part of an idyl of Theocritus, but I got to sleep before it was ended.

8th.—Up by the same time as morning before. Huntingdonshire Militia marched out of town: good-looking corps. Went out before breakfast to see them. Dined at Epping. Arrived in town between five and six; journey all the way pleasant, and thoughts pretty well employed. Got out of the carriage in Holborn, and stopping for a moment in Craig's Court, where I found Kent, Hicks, and Pearce, though it was not with that hope that I stopped, went on to the House of Commons, being taken up by Sir Gilbert Elliot by the way, from whom I heard of the meeting at Burlington House, and other things that had passed in my absence. Debate not to come on till next day. Having gone out therefore during a division, and drank some tea, proceeded afterwards with Sir Gilbert to Burke's, where I stayed preparing for the question that was to come on till about ten.

9*th.*—At home all the morning, preparing, or pretending to prepare, for the debate.* Preparation ill managed. Instead of securing the reasoning that I had been collecting on the main question, lost my time in framing exordiums and transitions, or rather lost my time by not preparing them with assiduity and exertion. From the manner in which the debate came on, no opportunity was given for speaking, but by rising immediately after Fox. This being suffered to pass, partly by design, partly from accident, and no other given, the debate concluded without my saying anything; though I had a great deal that would, I apprehend, have been said with considerable effect, and that certainly on every account ought to have been brought forward. The regret I have felt for this, and the effect it has had, on the general course of my thoughts since, ought to be a lesson not to trust the feel of the moment, nor to decide in any instance but on the consideration of what one shall be glad or sorry for afterwards.

11*th.*—Read part of an ode of Pindar; wrote some translations; shaved before breakfast.

The imperfect estimate often made of time, and the different apparent distance of events equally distant in reality, is very remarkable at this moment. I was not

* On the Traitorous Correspondence Bill.

at all aware that it was near three weeks, eighteen days, since my return to town.

29th.—No application next day, nor for a day or two afterwards, to what ought, for a long while past, to have engaged my attention, viz. the motion about Parliamentary Reform announced so long ago by Grey.* Despair of rallying my thoughts well upon that subject, and unwillingness to abandon it altogether, put me in the state most fatal for any useful application of time, and from which I may think myself fortunate in having escaped before it was too late.

May 2nd.—Set out with Mrs. Lukin to Clapham. The benefits of the country were very sensibly felt. I took a long walk, and found my thoughts move with a degree of activity to which I had long been a stranger, except perhaps during the drive to Gravesend on the 24th. It was during this walk that I first got my thoughts in order, and prepared in part, that scheme and arrangement, which I afterwards followed in my discourse.

3rd.—Went to town by about four, being to dine at Parsloe's, with the persons, whom it was agreed we should endeavour occasionally to get together. Our company at dinner was, Sir Gilbert Elliot, Mr. Burke, Lord Beauchamp, Lord Malmesbury and Lord Porchester.

6th.—Morning fine. Stayed at home. Chose the method, very fortunately, of making a general preparation in my mind, without attempting to bring each part to the state of being committed to paper. Resolved to speak, and succeeded fortunately in some parts beyond what I had reason to expect.

7th.—Walked about in the morning, to recover the fatigue of overnight.† and to enjoy a *feel* so different from

* Afterwards Charles, 2nd Earl Grey.

† On the 6th May, 1793, the debate on Mr. Grey's motion for Reform in Parliament began. Mr. Windham spoke on that day. The same debate was continued on the following day, May 7th.

that which attended me after the debate on the Traitorous Bill, where, with matter nearly as good in my head, I suffered the debate to pass off without saying anything Late in the debate, I had occasion to say a few words in reply or explanation, which I should have done well enough, if the House had not been so intolerably clamorous, that every word one uttered seemed the last, that would be heard.

9th.—Dined with the Duke of Portland: present, Mr. Burke, W. ditto, R. ditto, Lawrence, Sir Gilbert Elliot, Mr. Montague, Lord Inchiquin, Lord Titchfield.

11th.—Dined at Lord Fitzwilliam's.

12th.—Drove down, I think, after dinner to Clapham, and came back by Battersea; when I went to the Bishop of St. David's, to talk over some things respecting mean time, &c. Found on this, as on many other occasions, that the Bishop often lays down with great confidence, what turns out afterwards to be wrong. Had settled before, in my own mind, the true conception of the thing, that I was enquiring about.

14th.—Walked out in the morning directly after breakfast, in order to be at Count Brühl's,* where there was to be a meeting of the sub-committee. I left the carriage for Mrs. and Miss Lukin, conceiving that the treasure of the register ship† was to be brought in, in triumph. Went down to the House of Commons to announce the good report of the workmen, on the merits of the invention.

15th.—Canning called for me, to go to the Eumelian. Went with him afterwards to the play.

16th.—Dined at Lord Spencer's: present, Lord Mansfield, Lord Malmesbury, Lord Frederick Cavendish, Duke

* Count Brühl, a Saxon nobleman, married, in 1767, Alleine Marie, widow of the Earl of Egremont.

† The Spanish register ship, 'San Iago,' was captured in April 1793, having on board a large quantity of silver, gold, and jewels, valued at £1,200,000.

of Portland, T. Grenville, Duke of Devonshire, Lord Bessborough (late Duncannon).

20*th.*—At six, saw Ramsden, who came full of trouble about the report, which is not, in point of expression, quite what I could wish it. Spent part of an hour with Malone, who showed me some letters of Dryden, and Vanbrugh to Lintot. From thence home, where, instead of going upstairs, I sat eating a little supper, and hearing Mary on pianoforte. Cholmondeley has just made her a present of a new one.

21*st.*—Went out before twelve, in order to see the Chancellor,* and communicate to him the substance of a conversation which I had with Mr. Townshend, relative to the reported appointment of Lord Auckland.

25*th.*—Was set down at Lord Townshend's, where was Mrs. Beresford, who was going the next morning. Something not quite pleasant in respect of our parting. I had shown myself, during the last moments of her stay, too intent on talking with Loftus on the subject of the last news. Walked home rather in a melancholy mood.

26*th.*—Was to dine at Hampstead. Canning and Elliot went in my carriage: no other persons were of the party, except possibly Mr. Wallace. Miss Hayman was with Mrs. Crewe, and her brother came in after dinner, on his way from Wales to join one of the battalions of the Essex Militia, in which he had taken a commission. He was a very gentle, pleasant man, with a happy mixture of modesty and manliness, and having been in the Army and served for nine years in America, including the war, conveyed to me so much the idea of Lieut. Gauntlet in 'Peregrine Pickle,' as to make his company to me very agreeable. Miss H. too has, this year, hit my fancy very much.

28*th.*—Was to have dined at the Club, but kept so long at the House waiting for Wilberforce's business, that I was obliged to dine upstairs.

* Lord Loughborough.

29*th*.—A wish had come upon me to see the bowmen at Blackheath, and if Miss Hayman, &c. had not been gone before my note arrived, I should have been tempted to have quitted my employment and have got a place in their carriage. A long conversation with Mrs. Crewe, with a view of learning something which the occasion required, brought me so late, that by the time I reached Whitehall, I gave up the intention. My dinner was hardly done before Mudge came, and with him and afterwards with Graham, I continued employed till near twelve o'clock. After they went, I continued for some time thinking of the great question newly submitted to me.

June 13*th*.—A month now nearly elapsed with nothing entered in Journal, and certainly nothing done in the way of literary employment. Everything indeed of that sort so long neglected, that the very idea of it almost lost. What a change of life has taken place since my quitting Oxford, about the end, I think, of last October! The only return to former habits was during the week spent at Felbrigg, from 30th March to 7th April. Has the change been for the better, and has it been necessary? I may venture to say to the last, that it has not been necessary quite to the extent to which it has been carried; and with respect to the first, that so far as it has not been necessary, it has not been advantageous. I may say, in general, that my time has been less happily spent, than it would in other occupations. Political events, not a little important, have taken place during the same period: it is not the least proof, how much my habits have been irregular, that even these have been unable to recall me to the use of my Journal.

14*th*.—The day of my receiving the first note from Pitt, just as I was setting out to Wycombe. It was the next day, Saturday, that I must have gone there.

16*th*.—Dined with the Foreign Ministers, at the Duke of Portland's.

17*th*.—Saw Pitt; finished Mudge; and made speech (a singularly bad one) on Fox's motion.* Went home, and supped with Burke.

18*th*.—Cannot recollect precisely, but Lord Spencer, I think, called in the morning, and declared against acceptance. Certainly felt it as a great load off my mind. My *feel*, both before and after, a sufficient proof of the state of my mind with respect to real liking of the object. Lord Spencer went out of town in the evening.

19*th*.—Interview with Pitt to give my answer: not wholly satisfied with my own statements, they were at least much inferior to his.

27*th*.—Nothing particular that I can recollect, except that to-day I went with a water party to Greenwich. Being told of an old pensioner of the age of 103, we sent for him, and found him a man of extraordinary strength and possession of faculties for an age so advanced. His hearing seemed as quick as any of the company, nor was there any appearance of defect of eyesight; his memory was of course not entire, but such as to enable him to speak positively to many facts of his life; and he seemed not at all inclined to speak positively of facts, of which he was not certain His name was John Harrison, the son of an English father and Scotch mother, and born at Inverness. By sea and by land he had served sixty-seven years.

30*th*.—For some days past, from the time of public business ceasing, all my employment had been the preparation of going from London, and all the occupation of my thoughts in the intermediate times, the journey that was to succeed my return from Oxford. As there may arise in this, situations altogether new, and not a little important, it is necessary 'omnia præcipere atque animo ante peragere.'

* Mr. Fox's motion was for the re-establisment of peace with France.

July.—The whole time passed at Oxford was pleasant and interesting. Let me impress deeply upon my mind the reception, that I met with there, that it may prove an incentive to persist in conduct, which may ensure such a reception at all future times. That conduct is eminently before me.

5th.—From this time till my departure I was employed very assiduously in preparing what was necessary, particularly in settling my will, a draft of which I had had for a long time lying by me.

9th.—At a very little after the time appointed was at Kent's, ready to set off and with a few things left undone. There I found the Duke of Manchester, who, as Fullarton had told me before, was to be of our party. During the time that I was waiting there, Fullarton not being ready, I wrote a letter to Madame d'Albany,* in answer to the one, which I had received from her a good while since, on the subject of her affairs.

10th.—Stayed at Dover. Found there Jenkinson, with the Prince and Princesse de Léon, and Madame de Belzunce. Walked in the morning with Jenkinson to the Castle, where we were assailed with my old torment, the warder or gunner, but luckily a sergeant of the Devon came to our rescue, like the animal that attacks the Roc, in the 'Arabian Nights:' during their conflict we escaped.

The arrival of Spalding, and the care of his friend and countryman F. to settle him as one of the party, increased the difficulty considerably of our going in the same vessel as the Princesse de Léon, &c. After much doubt, which continued till the last moment, and was the cause of some succeeding inconveniences, we went in the boat, that had been secured for us and in which our horses were. The wind was contrary, as much as it was possible to be, but the water was smooth.

* Louisa de Stolberg, married Charles Edward Stuart, grandson of James II.

The captain's name was Hall, an old smuggler, who had lived in that capacity at Cromer, where, as he stated, he had often seen me.

12*th*.—After running along the coast for some hours, within view of Dunkirk, Furnes, and Nieuport, we arrived at Ostend, the sea having begun then to be rough, but not so much so as to prevent me from getting upon deck and enjoying, in a very great degree, the sensations and reflections incident to the scene before me.

13*th*.—After seeing Gen. Ainslie and Sir Charles Ross and others, we set off for Valenciennes, by the way of Courtray and Tournay, which we were told was the route constantly taken. Nothing could be to me pleasanter than the journey. The country, the occasion, the incidents that occurred, the health that I enjoyed, all concurred to give me a sensation of pleasure greater than most in degree, and certainly different in kind, from any, that I had ever experienced before: the effect was that of realising a situation such as had before existed only in imagination; and putting my mind in a state, in which it is to be lamented, that it was not put years ago.

14*th*.—About four o'clock in the morning we were called up by the arrival of the Duke of Manchester and Spalding. In the journey of to-day, between Courtray and Tournay, we overtook some troops whose language nobody could understand, but I know now must be part of O'Donnel's corps. At Tournay, the Duke of Manchester and Spalding had ordered dinner, which I wanted to have been at the *table d'hôte*, but it is lucky that it was not, as with all the advantage of dining half an hour earlier, the delays of our setting off (which Fullarton is a bad hand at lessening) retarded our arrival at Condé till the hands of the sentinels were actually upon the chain of the drawbridge. This part of the drive was amongst the pleasantest that we had had; the way was through part of the Bois de St. Arnaud. We heard, or we supposed to hear, some of the firing at Valenciennes,* and as we approached Condé, evidences were everywhere seen of the effects of military operations. On our arrival great difficulty was found in procuring a place to put ourselves in; we at length got beds in a private house, and had a supper prepared at the inn. Our horses had nothing to eat, or next to nothing, and no place to lie down. *Note by Mr. Windham.*—The number of shot, &c., thrown from the 18th June to the 26th July, without counting the batteries from Brignet and Mount Augin, were shells, 45,000; cannon shot, 76,000; of all sorts, 146,000; making of shells about 1,250 per diem.

15*th.*—We set off as soon as we could get away and arrived in camp about two o'clock. As this was the hour of dinner at head-quarters, we did not go there directly, but dining with the mess of Hulse's battalion, left our names for the Duke in the evening. In our way from Condé, we met two carriages, containing, in appearance, persons of eminence, one of whom we heard afterwards was Prince Charles, the Emperor's brother.

16*th.*—It was this morning, if I recollect right, that I had made the engagement to go with Hulse to the trenches. I had risen early in the morning and written a letter to Mrs. Lukin, enclosed in one to Cholmondeley. Just before we set out, news was brought of a flag of truce having been sent in. Everybody was in expectation of its being a preliminary to a surrender; but it turned out to be only an application from Custine for permission to a Madame de Sillery to quit the town and withdraw to Paris. The permission was given to quit the town, but the *terminus ad quem* restrained to Mons, Condé, or some other imperial town. The scene that took place in consequence of this truce was the most interesting that can be conceived. We

* Valenciennes was besieged from May 23rd to July 14th, 1793, when the French garrison surrendered to the Allies under the Duke of York. It was retaken by the French in August, 1794.

descended on both sides and held an amicable conference in a space, which, the moment before, it would have been death to either party to enter, and of which, the moment after, the possession was to be disputed with equal obstinacy. It recalled to my mind the lines, which I cannot recollect in terms, in the second Æneid, where a description is given of what took place, at the supposed departure of the Grecians.

> Juvat ire, et Dorica castra,
> Desertosque videre locos, litusque relictum.

One of the persons whom I talked to was of the name of Petit, of the 29th, or regiment *ci-devant* Dauphin, had served on board the Brilliante (French frigate), in the East Indies and spoke English; in which language he made no difficulty of confessing to me his disinclination to the cause, and his wish that the town might surrender. He desired particularly that it might be signified to the Hanoverian officers, that two of their corps, Messrs. Kilmansegge and Scheiter, who had been taken prisoners, were well, and in his keeping. After talking together in this way for a quarter of an hour, or twenty minutes, and drinking to each other's good health, notice was given to retire; which was not so effected, however, in some parts, but that many were wounded and some killed, on both sides, before it was known that the truce was expired. The Duke of York said, that his orders had been, that five minutes should be allowed after sounding the trumpet.

17*th*.—Though I had thus seen the plan of the trenches, and the manner of their formation, more effectually than I could in any other way, yet I had not seen, or rather had not experienced, what was most the object of my curiosity, the situation of persons employed in doing duty there. I therefore accepted readily the offer of Major Crawford* to accompany me thither the next morn-

* Afterwards Sir Robert Crawford, killed at Ciudad Rodrigo.

ing. It was not without anxiety that I ventured into a situation so new and untried, as that in which I was about to enter. It was impossible to tell the effect of circumstances, which have been found occasionally to operate so strangely on minds not distinguishable beforehand from the rest of the world. How could I be certain, that the same might not happen to me, as happened to certain persons, that one knows of? I did all that could be done in such a case, 'omnia præcepi atque animo mecum ante peregi.' How far I had succeeded could be known only by trial. The result of the trial answered, I am happy to say, to my most sanguine expectations. I think, with confidence, that during any part of the time, I could have multiplied, if necessary, a sum in my head. We continued walking about the trenches for two hours. The officers that I recollect to have seen there were George Fitzroy, Archer, poor Tollemache, who has since been killed, and some of the 53rd or 14th. Of my employment during the following days I have no regular account; they were employed chiefly in riding about the country, viewing the different posts and hearing the particulars of the principal actions. By these means, I have got an idea of military operations, more precise and distinct, than ever I had before. The profit of these rides, as well as the pleasure, would have been greater had I not found myself oppressed with heat and fatigue.

19*th.*—This was the day of our seeing the French camp from the little mound with a pole upon it. To St. Arnaud, the Abbey, the Vicoque, and Bonne Espérance, and back by Augin. This was the day following the preceding, and that on which they fired some cannon shot at us, by one of which Phipps' horse was wounded. I shall never fail to regret my foolish dilatoriness, and want of consideration, in not having decided then to take my leave. Had I gone then I had stayed a blessed time! By suffering myself to stay on beyond that, I have outstayed my interest, and left myself with a doubt upon my mind, for which, before, there could not have been a pretence, whether something more should not have been done. I had seen the trenches the day of the truce; and when there was no danger, I had then gone down twice besides, once by daylight and once by night; at the former of which time there was a good deal of fire of cannon and shells, and at the latter of musketry. It was at the latter of those times that a sergeant of the 14th had his head shot off. I had rode about everywhere, and, as it happened, had run some risk. I had done enough to satisfy myself and to show to others, what, if it is very necessary to be conscious of oneself, it is pleasant also to have known. By not going to the storm of the covered way, though I forbore only, what everyone would have said it was absurd to do, except at least a few people, whose opinions perhaps are not worth much, yet I felt something below what some might have expected. One way of putting it may be, Was it a thing, which would have been more praised or blamed, had it been done? Would it, considering all circumstances, have raised the character of the actor or have depressed it? It is the hope, that it might have had with some good judges even the latter effect, that can alone reconcile me to the not having done it. The decision taken of avoiding any intermediate course, if I was not wholly to engage, was, I think, right. I observed at least a distinct line, that of keeping throughout with the Duke of York. It is most fortunate for my own satisfaction that the Duke went into the trenches and not amiss, that there was, during the time, a pretty smart fire. The head of an Austrian was knocked off, who was walking a few paces before the Duke, and a guardsman was knocked down while we were standing near the battery. This was, I think, the 25th. Why did I not go away on the 23rd? The two days following the 25th, as well as all the time since, has lost its enjoyment in consequence of the regrets above stated.

29*th.* — Lord Elgin and I set off for Brussels. Had Fullarton and the Duke of Manchester stayed a day longer, I should have been tempted to have gone with them. It was not till after dinner that we set off. My regret was not, and is not, at all done away. One should learn from this, what must be the effect of doing anything wrong, when the suspicion only of not acting to the outside of right is sufficient to make such work with one's comfort. Had I gone away before this question had arisen, I should have walked upon down; had I achieved the adventure, I should have trod the air.

30*th.*—By seven o'clock we were set out and arrived at Brussels at ten. I found that my recollection of the town from passing through it in the year '80 was not very distinct. The course of the day had nothing to be observed, but my seeing Mad[lle.] Duplessis and the Princesse de Léon (Mad[e.] de Belzunce was not at home), and my meeting James Crawford, whom I had not seen since our parting at Paris, in the year '90. My attention was occupied during the greater part of the day in determining, whether I should go back with Lord Elgin, or proceed to England from hence. After much consideration, and at a late hour, I determined upon going back with Lord Elgin. Nothing that I now do can afford its natural satisfaction. Names of persons, chiefly foreigners, whom I saw during my stay with the army: Prince de Saxe Cobourg, General Ferraris, Prince Reuss (he was a small black and ill-looking man, in the style of ——; he came on one of the wet days after the capitulation, in a brown cloak); Major Frone, Orlandini, Diedrichstein, General Dalton, General Erbach, Count Merfeld, Prince Lichtenstein, Mr. Swinbourne, Marquis de Bouillé, General Jarnac.

August 1*st.*—Up at six in order to be present at the

grand ceremony of the troops marching out, and laying down their arms. Few scenes in life can be conceived of equal magnificence. Such a union of troops drawn from countries the most remote, and considered as of the first character at this time in Europe; such a display of officers, of the highest rank, and most distinguished reputation, such splendour of appearance, such variety of character, such a combination of strong interests, can hardly be imagined to have been found on any one occasion. In the midst of the general feeling excited by such a scene, it was a fine thing to have had as parts of it, corps of the British troops who had either had their share of honours in the preceding duties, or were calculated to do credit to the country, by their appearance and equipment.

The day which at first was cloudy, turned out afterwards, to be as brilliant, as could be wished. Nothing was wanting to me, to the *feel* of enjoyment of the occasion, but that I should have been party to the service which immediately produced it, or should at least not have been in a situation in which I could have been party to it.

It was late before I got into the town, and I was then so uncomfortable with heat and fatigue, that I readily yielded to the consideration of my being too late, to give up the great dinner, that was to be at the Duke of York's. In this also the same feeling operated, that had governed me ever since that fatal night of the storm. I cannot help viewing myself in the character of a man, who has fallen in some measure below, what was expected from him. Though that is, I hope and trust, a false impression; yet, even if nothing has been lost, it is difficult not to regret, what might have been gained.

2*nd.*—As soon as the Duke was returned from the *feu de joie* and breakfast was over, I set off, and after an hour or two spent in Valenciennes, where I was conducted round the works by Fitzroy and Thornton, Mr.

Lambert lending me a horse, proceeded on my journey, and got into Tournay, time enough to have reached Courtray, as soon as would have been necessary. I got a good bed, the same as belonged to Lord Herbert, by the interest of Noble, who was then in Lord Herbert's service, having formerly lived at Holkham.

3rd.—Notwithstanding my efforts it was half-past five before I got away. At Courtray I breakfasted, and completed what was wanting to my dress, part having been gone through before I set out. The country inspired me with the same sensations as it had done in going; it suggested the ideas of perfect retirement, without seeming to remove one out of reach of the world. I got to Ostend about four o'clock, just as the journey began to be tiresome, and the want to be felt of some refreshment.

Ostend, which appeared to me in coming to be a very considerable place, seemed now a vile stinking hole, from which one could not be too soon released. The same happened to me each time of my seeing it before, viz. in the years 1780 and 1781.

After dining not uncomfortably, except from the company of Mr. ——, who upon the strength of having seen me in Norfolk, chose to sit with me, while at dinner, till he became as bad as the nightmare. A man more dull and vulgar, more vacant of all thought, and destitute of all refinement, will not easily be found even in a regiment of dragoons. To him succeeded Sir John Peters, whom I mention from the circumstance of his having detained me, during histories of his own meritorious services, till he hardly left me time to answer a letter, which I had just received from Hippisley.

4th.—In sailing through the Downs we had the view of a fine fleet of West Indiamen, just arrived. I was wishing to have found the 'Minerva,' who probably was among them.

5th.—The delay of the arrival of the packet, which is

only just come in, and the still greater delay of the Custom House, which, by an abominable abuse, does not open till half-past nine, will make it impossible for me to get to London this evening. If Payne should happen to be at Chatham, of which I fear there is but little chance, I shall think the delay no loss; at all events, Rochester is a place at which I can stay without much impatience.

6*th*.—Set out by eight o'clock, and seeing what the number of ships were going up the river, conceived the idea, which I might as well have had before, of calling at Gravesend, and taking my chance of either finding the Minerva there, or knowing when she might be expected. The first answer that I received, gave me reason to think, that I had missed the time by a moment only, and that it even then was not too late to recover it. I accordingly got a boat and was going in pursuit of the vessel, that was pointed out, when we met a man, who gave me complete information by saying, that he had parted with William the day before, and that he was at that time in London.

15*th*.—This was the day of a considerable dinner at Sir R. Payne's, to which I had been invited, and where, as I found afterwards, Pitt dined. I did not think it very well that Sir Ralph had not informed me of that circumstance; for though it is possible, that might have made no difference, he was certainly not at liberty to presume that it would not.

16*th*.—The prospect of my going to Hartingfordbury was continued from morning to evening, as well as from the day following. One day, when probably I might have gone, I was stopped by the news of the action at Lincelles; my anxiety about which, and the fate of the officers, made me agree readily to go with Boswell, to get intelligence at the orderly room.

A more favourable time for pursuing in London any pursuits, which one had in hand, or making London a place of study, could hardly be found, the town being so completely empty; yet it did not seem to answer.

24th.—A fine autumnal evening; bright, but rather cold. Thoughts not unpleasant, principally recollections of past times, mixed with late scenes, and present condition. Waked at Dunstable and thought of occasions on which I had known that inn; the same at which I had stopped, on coming from Ireland.

25th.—Pleasant drive next day to Althorpe where I arrived in good time. Read a good deal in Hamilton's 'Conic Sections,' in which I was beginning to read again.

At Althorpe the only company that I found, was the Comte de Coigny, a man of some note; so well thought of as an officer, that he had been chosen to conduct the emigrant army in their retreat at the end of last year. During my stay at Althorpe, pleasant enough, except that I found a considerable deal of that symptom, which is altogether new, and not a little alarming, of a relaxation of the organs of speech, so as perceptibly to affect my pronunciation. The first of this, I think, was felt after some times of great fatigue during my being at the camp.

September 2nd.—I think it was to-day that I was surprised, agreeably, by a visit from young ——, attended by his late pupil, one of the sons of Richard Gurney. After talking with them some time below, I went up to dress, having engaged them to stay to dinner. By this token, I recollect that Mrs. Coke, &c. called to say they would dine here the next day. Mrs. Lukin was the only person from the Parsonage that dined here; conversation very pleasant; few such visitors to be found here. I felt, however, how much less interesting such a guest was, than he would have been formerly. Increase of knowledge, and contraction of the period, to which hope can extend, are both enemies to that sort of interest.

3rd.—Some days afterwards, I don't recollect when, Ives and Mrs. Ives, Miss Day, Mr. Wright, John Harvey and John Gurney dined here. The day was far from unpleasant. I had been at Cromer some days before to call upon Harvey and Gurney.

10th.—Went to Cossey; in my way I called at Marsham's, and in consequence did not reach Cossey till near eight; it was dark, and I had taken the wrong road.

The Townshends dined at Cossey. Both mornings were pretty well employed in writing letters. I felt for the greater part of the time a considerable tendency of former *feel*; proceeding in part perhaps from indisposition, but more probably from the effect of a state, which has always been most injurious, and to which it has always been my misfortune or my fault very much to expose myself, that of being in company, in which I was not amused. The fatal hours spent in that way during one period of my life, were the cause, I believe, of a great part of the mental maladies under which I have always laboured, as were the hours to which I was condemned by Norbury, in his pupil room, at a still earlier period.

27th.—My chief and almost my entire work has been, a continuation of the 'Organum,' not so much by advancing into the work, though that has been in part done, as by examining points, that have been before under discussion. I am afraid that even in this less has been done, than might have been expected. I have certainly not the power of working quickly, though in that probably, as in other habits, by the time I am ready to leave life, I may have made some proficiency.

To-day went to Holt, to annual dinner. William and I went in chaise. Day fine. I had been employed till going and had my thoughts still employed, on question about necessary propositions, on which I probably have now, got all the knowledge, that I am likely to get. It will be very difficult to show that in 'Bocardo,' O being necessary, the conclusion shall not be necessary, on any principle that shall not be altogether arbitrary. If the major is necessarily denied of some of the middle, and these some are also part of the minor, what can be wanting to the proof, that the major is denied necessarily of some of the minor, I do not see. In my way back I came in the carriage with Coke.

28th.—Day of camp.

29th.—Fenced before dinner with William.

October 1st.—Review. The regiments—the Leicestershire, East York, and Middlesex. Called afterwards on Sir John Dalling, having first been to see the French prisoners. Dined with Lord Townshend and the officers.

2nd.—Called on Lord Townshend: met there Captain Berkeley, and settled with him to go on board the 'Assurance.' Long delay in consequence of this intention, and of idea started, of his taking William up at Cromer. At North Walsham I was obliged, rather reluctantly, to take horse; the ride, however, was less unpleasant and less fatiguing, than I might have expected. My thoughts were tolerably well taken 'out o' th' ignorant present time!' I got in about eleven to the Parsonage, where they were all gone to bed; the house was raised, however, and we stayed and supped there, instead of doing what might have been better, viz. removing all to the Hall.

3rd.—From the prospect of this vessel coming, I went to Cromer, and in that way lost the greatest part of the morning.

From Mr. Windham to Mrs. Crewe.

Felbrigg: Oct. 5th, 1793.

My hostility to Jacobinism and all its works, and all its supporters, weak or wicked, is more steady and strong than ever. If Pitt is the man by whom this must be opposed, Pitt is the man whom I shall stand by. If I do not act with them in office, it is only because I think I can be of more use as I am. Sir Gilbert's acceptance of the appointment offered him, has my perfect concurrence. Farewell! I will write when I have anything that I think you will like to hear. By the way, your friend and admirer, Mr. Malone, is going somewhere into your neighbourhood, and would be very glad, I am persuaded, of any encouragement to make you a visit. Will you authorise me to give him such, or, what would be still more gracious, write him a line yourself? I wish I were able to accompany him. Your most faithful and obedient, &c.,

W. W.

Lord Spencer is in Norfolk, and will spend a day, I hope, before long with me; Powys is also here. You have made Mary very happy by your wish of hearing from her.

6*th.*—*Felbrigg.*—Lord Spencer came; he and Powys* dined here.

7*th.*—Lord Spencer a-shooting. I rode out to Gresham, as an act of attention to poor Mallet, who is dying. Met Powys, and having led him to ride with me, thought myself obliged in return to go part of the way with him, as he was to dine at home, at Hanworth, in order to receive Sir George and Lady Robinson; Assheton Smith, Doughty, and the rest of the party having promised to dine with me. Both this evening and before, Lord Spencer and I, after the company were gone, had a good deal of conversation on what was a principal object of our meeting.

9*th.*—Set off in a beautiful morning and in good time. About seven miles short of Norwich Lord Walpole overtook us: at his desire, which seemed to be earnest, I got out and went on with him. Dinner at the Swan. Ball in the evening. Dinner like other sessions' dinners; but ball distinguished by the presence of Mrs. Siddons, whom I have not seen, for more than a twelvemonth; the ball,

* Powys, afterwards Lord Lilford, and brother to Mrs. Doughty of Hanworth.

too, was very full and good, and contained many people not always seen there—Powys, Mr. and Mrs. Wyndham of Earlham; company with them, viz. Mr. Bowdler, and, what was more interesting, a very fine sister of Welham. Her looks, her manners, the circumstances under which we met, all gave me a degree of interest which was well calculated to lay the foundation of great attachment. Lady Jerningham, too, was there; Coke and Mrs. Coke.

10*th.*—I dined at the Bishop's.* A party of, I suppose, fifty, chiefly clergy. I felt the same enjoyment that I frequently do at large dinners; they afford, in general, what never fails to be pleasant, solitude in a crowd. My satisfaction, however, was much clouded by finding that I had acquiesced in calling in my own mind 'Randall'—'Marshall.' It is in vain, I fear, to entertain a doubt, that the event, which excited so much horror, when I first suspected it two years ago, has really taken place, and that memory gives signs of decay.

In the evening Colonel Money's ball. Stayed till past one. Not at all tired nor impatient of the time passed there.

11*th.*—Stayed at home for the greater part of the morning. One of my employments sending letter, which I had before written to Pitt, with Hippisley's papers. Day remarkably fine. Dined with sheriffs at King's Head. Robinson the late sheriff was there, and much as he may be below his own opinion of himself, he is more to talk to, than the generality of those, who are found on those occasions. I could not help reflecting on the very low state of talents or understanding, in those, who compose the whole nearly of the society of Norwich. The French are surely a more generally enlightened, and polished people.

12*th.*—I had gone in the evening to Catton, having first drank tea with Unthank, and called at Mr. Harvey's

* Charles Manners Sutton.

at Catton, where Mrs. Siddons was finishing the reading of 'Jane Shore.' Biggs was with Ives and made a great accession to the society.

25*th.*—This was the day when there was confusion about the papers, and on which, therefore, the news of the murder of the Queen of France must have come. What have I been about? It is certain that I have known, since I have been down here this time, feels of ill-health not experienced or not observed before, and which are perhaps of the most alarming kind, as arguing a general decay, and decay in that quarter which seems conclusive of all the rest, I mean of the powers of digestion and appetite. Care may, I believe, correct much of this; and some, I am inclined to think, has been the consequence as well as the cause of my not having engaged so earnestly in a regular course of study. It is certain that latterly I have fallen into a great neglect and oblivion, of all, that I have had to do, either of study or business. Such a state, particularly at this place where there is nothing else to do, is always unfavourable to spirits, and through them to health.

I went to Norwich to-day to dine with the Mayor. I drove there, stopping only at Aylsham, to give the horses a little hay and water. My thoughts on the way moved gaily, though they were employed on no useful subject, but that of idle fancies on impossible things. From dinner I went, agreeably to my original intention, to Cossey; I went with Sir W. Jerningham and his son in their chaise.

26*th.*—Dined with the Chevalier, who was at Cossey, with Mr. Townshend, and met there Lady Guildford, and Lady Anne and Lady Charlotte North. The former had been the subject of my speculations in my way to Norwich. Day very pleasant.

27*th.*—Stayed this day also at Cossey; my whole stay this time being very pleasant; and it was a very interesting period for news, the accounts having arrived at this time of the raising of the siege of Maubeuge, and great doubts being reasonably entertained for the safety of Flanders, and even of that army.

November 1*st.*—About this time Mary and Kitty began the business of putting the library to rights. They have performed a task which was very necessary, and which had been so long neglected that it is difficult to say to what period it might have been deferred. The comfort of having the books in the state to which they are already brought, I feel very sensitively. Let me use the consideration as a notice for completing what remains to be done.

15*th.*—In a morning I have generally gone out, and have taken up the employment (not a bad one), and very necessary for its own purposes, of directing what should be done for the woods: part of these directions have related to the larger trees and part to those planted in my time in the Oval. The employment has kept me in the air and without fatigue; the occupation, too, is as good as most that is likely to fall in the course of a ride. If I exclude any useful trains of thought, it keeps the mind fitted at least, and in motion, and prevents either stagnation or emptiness. There is a sense also that what one is doing is not without its use, though the consideration of that cannot be much indulged, for fear of generating unpleasant ideas.

19*th.*—*Norwich.*—Persons at dinner with Barnard—Ives, Rigby, Taylor jun., Martineau. Little politics but what they forced on. The fear of appearing too polemic made me hold back, I think, more than was desirable. The subject would easily have enabled me to give them a *squeeze*, which I think should have been given.

27*th.*—Adey came to keep courts. Something in the meeting which gave me the idea of old times; one cause of its doing so was obvious, that it was a court chiefly heard of in the Feudal institutions, but another local and accidental reason had, I am persuaded, its share, the view of this place on the side of Aylmerton being rather less familiar to my sight and thoughts; the impressions which I received there were of a more general nature, and extending of consequence more freely into antiquity than those which, being more frequent, were more bound down by recent associations.

28*th.*—I had sent a note in the evening purposing that the party should dine with me. I was very pleasant in my own room, when Adey and my brother came, proposing me to join them in Aylmerton Field a-coursing. Weather at first so pleasant that I was glad to have gone, but sorry afterwards. A rule this for like cases in future. The event of questions relative to liking are best told perhaps in this way, knowledge of what one likes very empirical. In the evening when the post came, found that I had better resolve at once to go to town; cause, immediately determining, letter from Edmund Phipps and Lord Mulgrave.

29*th.*—It was decided just before I set off, that Anne should go with me. Dark and unpleasant drive to Cossey; we should hardly have got there but for the kind and hearty assistance of a man, of the name of Christmas, who lives at St. Faith's.

30*th.*—Set off with the intention of calling at Bodney. Found at Watton that it would be attended with great difficulty and certainty of being in the dark, on a bad road and wild country with a postboy who did not know the way.

December 5*th.*—London.—Dined at Blair's, to meet Mr. Erskine.

7*th.*—Went in the morning with Burke to have conference with Pitt. Dined, by appointment, with Lord Loughborough, Burke (R. Burke, I think), Anstruther, Gibbon, Pelham, and Pitt. The first time of my dining with Pitt since my being a member of the Club of Grosvenor Street in '82 or '83. Great disposition in Pitt to be agreeable. Conversation certainly far from deficient in liveliness or pleasantry (but its pleasantry, I think, rather artificial than spontaneous—rather the produce of art and culture than the natural growth of the soil). The day upon the whole not disagreeable. Instead of going home with Burke which I avoided from mere habitual dread of consequences, I walked with Elliot to Gally's, whom we found with Mrs. G. at home and with whom we sat some time. It would have been better this time to have gone with Burke.

8*th.*—Went to Sheen by engagement, and dined with Francis: nobody there but family. My coming away at night which was unexpected, prevented probably our having any political conversation. I did not shun the subject, but rather, I think, encouraged it, but not much so, not being in a talking humour.

14*th.*—Dined with Douglas; told him of de Sérent's wish that I should undertake the embassy to the Princess. He seemed greatly to concur in it, and almost brought me over to that side.

16*th.*—Dined with Edmund Phipps* at St. James's Coffee-house. It was his first Guards' dinner. I upon this occasion felt again what had ceased for a long while past, some regret at not having gone on the storming party. My health better since I have been in town, the consequence perhaps of the last prescription of Fordyce, viz. the steel drops, which I had been taking for some time, and which appeared to agree with me.

18*th.*—Went to Cossey in time for tea; found there an emigrant Abbé of the name of Couture, who had found a reception with Suffield. Quarrelled with Lady J. about him.

* General the Hon. Edmund Phipps, born April, 1760; died 1837.

19*th.*—My stay in London was upon the whole not unpleasant or unprofitable. I recollect only of dinners, Malone's and Mulgrave's twice, once the day after my arrival and once towards the end of my stay, with Graham and a Captain Hope who had left Toulon on the 13th, just before Sir Gilbert Elliot's arrival. From my return to Felbrigg my time has been passed much better than during any period of the three months passed there before. How very vexatious that what has been done now, should not have been done during the whole or the greater part at least of that previous time! One cause of this was no doubt the difference of the season; more time was naturally spent at home in the winter, than when the pleasantness of the weather, and the length of the days afford more temptation, as well as opportunity, for going abroad. Other causes, depending more on myself, were, that I had become more sensible of the value of time as the quantity that remained was less; and again, that I had weaned myself more from the supposed necessity to health of riding. Many more days were spent this time entirely in the house; and when I did go out it was only for a short walk. I ought to keep some account of the symptoms that I experience with respect to the complaint that may reasonably give me most alarm. For some short time past those convulsive catches at my first going to sleep have been, I think, less frequent.

From Mr. Windham to Mrs. Crewe.

Felbrigg: Dec. 26th, 1793.

I am waiting with great impatience for the papers. Things in Flanders seem to have got round again; and Weisemberg opens the prospect, I hope, to great consequences. For Toulon, too, I hope no fears need be entertained. The Queen, the fate of the poor Queen, for whom now I begin to justify all Mr. Burke's enthusiasm, saddens even our prospects of success, so much I wish that she might have lived to enjoy them. The Bon——e school do not think her, I hope, excluded from all compassion and respect, though she should be suspected of one or two intrigues which, I believe, was the extent.

What others' intentions may be I know not; but my determination is open steady war against the whole Jacobin faction, and junction for that purpose with whomsoever it may be necessary to join. That it will be necessary to join anybody in office I do not mean to say. You need not fear my doing it alone; first, because I do not think it will be advantageous to the general cause to do it in that way; and next, because whenever the time comes, that that question shall arise, there will be others, I hope, disposed to do it with me. These are my ideas upon the subject, and which there is no necessity to make any secret of. The sum of the opinion is, that I am a determined foe to the new system, and that I shall oppose that, either in or out of office, according as circumstances shall show that one or other mode is most effectual.

Your correspondent from Burton, as well as the other who talks about Lord Howe, both provoke me; but I think the last the most, as he is perfectly foolish, while the other may only be wicked; and folly, though less odious, is more provoking than wickedness. These clamours against the Duke of York are for the most part utterly without foundation and in all very nearly so.

They originate in the mere licentiousness of the officer part of the army. The Duke of York is, I believe, a most respectable character; his conduct is, I am sure, in many respects perfectly exemplary. Nothing material in the campaign has suffered from him, if anything at all has; and all the latter part has been of a sort to do him the highest honour. Both the court of Vienna and the Austrian army are full of his praises. The charges against Lord Howe are so perfectly senseless, that one wonders, how rational creatures can be found to utter them. I wish your correspondent, who thinks that Lord Howe is so careful of himself, was bound to stand by Lord Howe in all the danger to which he would be willing to expose himself. If I were to guess at your correspondent from his language on this occasion I should set him down as some Tory clergyman, who had learnt to abuse the Houses because they did not conquer America. Pray let me know if I am right.

Farewell! till we meet. The hour of attack approaches; and I am beginning to throw off my weeds of peace and furbish up my armour. I am luckily too, at present, in much better health than I have been through the greatest part of the summer. Your faithful and loyal Chevalier,

W. W.

1794.

Ille velut fidis arcana sodalibus olim.

January.—I must not omit the practice of noting, as the first fact of my Journal, the time at which it began to be kept, however reproachful the confession may be in this instance. It is with a view to the pain that such a memorial may occasionally create, that such a practice is in part established. One should not escape the memory of one's own neglect. It is now the 22nd March. This has been therefore a delay exceeding, I believe, any of which we have an example in any other year. The effects, too, have perhaps kept pace with the increase of the cause. I have latterly fallen very much into those habits which the practice of journal writing is intended to correct. As it is a painful thing to dwell on the estimate of one's own losses, I shall leave the amount to be collected from such particulars as I can now recall.

9*th.*—Day of Parliament meeting. Before this my time had been taken up very much by various consultations and communications ending in the D. of P. taking the station that he has, and which relieved me from a state of considerable doubt and anxiety. The effect of this measure was felt, I think, immediately in the alterations made for the better in the King's speech, and has since that had, perhaps, its influence on the counsels of the State in some material articles. My speech on the first day of the session fell considerably below my own expectations and I suspect below that of others; yet I cannot think, upon a review, that it was not better than many of those (I mean of my own) which gained better credit; so true it is that the estimate of speeches is formed less on their own merits than on their relation to certain preconceived opinions and expectations of the audience. The first great interruption was the business of M. de la Robrie, the date of which, I mean of its commencement, I wish I knew precisely. From the time when this began, it became necessary to open my doors to all Frenchmen, and the number soon increased to such a degree as hardly to leave them shut for whole mornings together. My evenings were likewise frequently occupied in the same manner, as well as much of my time both morning and evening taken up by communications, written and verbal, with Nepean and other incidental matters.

February 1st.—At the same period, perhaps this month, I engaged, at the suggestion of Brocklesby, in a course of chemical lectures carried on by Higgins, and attended by a select society, of which Marshal Conway is at the head, and of which Pelham is a member. I do not regret, however, my having engaged (though at the price of five guineas), as it has already brought me to a degree of acquaintance with some of the elementary notions of chemistry which I should not otherwise have had, and put me upon enquiries, which may lead on to some enlargement of knowledge on that side.

March.—My speakings in the House have been only four in number, except perhaps a few words said upon the St. Albans Canal Bill. These times were—the first day of the session, the motion respecting the Hessian Troops; the motion of Adam, about Muir and Palmer; and latterly, which may better be set down under its proper month, the motion respecting Subscriptions. On all these, excepting the last, I have been thought not to be perhaps in my best manner. I know not, however, very well, what the judgment has been. In my own opinion, the speech on the first day, though delivered with less effect, had really more thinking in it than any one of the others. The talk of speaking leads to the mention of a fact connected indeed with that very intimately, but connected also with consequences affecting the whole condition of life, and finally life itself. That affection in the organs of speech which I experienced for the first time when I was abroad last summer, has increased to such a degree, as to become a considerable inconvenience, besides the apprehensions which it may naturally excite, of proceeding to a still greater length. It was an impediment to me when I was speaking on the first day of the sessions. It is an impediment at all times, at least, whenever the thought occurs, or is recalled by the fact, by the distrust which it produces, and the disinclination which it causes to talk. I have intended from time to time to take some medical advice and have in fact already consulted Fordyce; but I fear that there is little to be done. There can hardly be any local application, and, with respect to general strengthening of the habit, I think I am at this time better than my ordinary state of health. I attribute this very much to better management of myself. I have left off tea, and breakfasted for a long while on chocolate; I ascribe something also to the virtues of porter, which has a narcotic property, favourable possibly to a habit too much subject to irritation particularly in the nerves of the stomach. I have for a long while, too, very much avoided late hours. Considering how much in weak frames not only enjoyment of what is to be enjoyed, but the use of faculties, depends on health, it is folly to neglect any means, which mere attention and forbearance can furnish for preserving it.

The Right Hon. William Windham to Captain Lukin.

Hill Street: March 22, 1794.

Dear William,—A letter from you to your mother, which I have just received, might remind me, if I had otherwise forgot it, that I ought to have answered a letter of yours sent long since to myself. I should, I believe, at any rate, have written to you by this post. It is not that I have anything very particular to say; but your former letter, with an account of what you observed on the coast of France, deserved an acknowledgment; and I foresaw, as the event in the present instance proves, that without being encouraged by such an acknowledgment, you would perhaps not send me another. The papers yesterday had announced your return to the Downs, with some Danish vessels, arrested in consequence of the late orders. I hope it may turn out that they may be made prizes; in which case, this Danish corn, I suppose, may come in pretty well to replace the profits derived heretofore from the transport of St. Vincent's sugars. The conduct of these Swedes and Danes is so perfectly rascally that I have no sort of compassion for them; and none, I dare say, will be felt by those who will find such good account in this kind of neutral war. The only danger is that they may be driven at last to join themselves openly to those to whom they are now giving every kind of clandestine assistance. Though they will find their own destruction in this, they may, in the meantime, embarrass considerably our operations. No great stroke has yet been struck by any of the armies on the Continent. Our campaign here too, in the Houses of Parliament, is pretty quiet. If it was not for the trial of Mr. Hastings, and the delay created by his friends, by insisting on the presence of the Judges, and adjourning the proceedings in consequence till after the circuit, we might be at liberty in a few weeks, and I should then be tempted to make an excursion towards the coast, and to meet you probably either at the Downs or at Portsmouth.

There is another business, indeed, that may call me towards Norfolk. With a view to the possibility of a descent, troops of different sorts are proposed to be raised in aid of the militia, one class of which are to be volunteer cavalry, composed of persons who are in a state to furnish their own horses, and till they are called out of the country, which is to be only in the case of actual invasion, are to receive no pay, nor anything from Government but their saddles and arms. What think you of the possibility of my raising a troop of fifty such persons, including such as part of those concerned may be willing to hire or bring with them in addition to themselves?

Mr. Courtenay, the member who dined with me yesterday, was showing me a letter which he had got from a Mr. Hayes, one of the lieutenants, I conceive, on board the 'Boston,' in which a particular and interesting account is given of some of the principal circumstances of the action. It appears by his account that the 'Boston' had only two hundred hands, not above thirty of whom had ever before been on board a square rigged vessel, while the 'Ambuscade' had four hundred and fifty. This difference, I suppose, must have told considerably; much more than the difference of four guns, which the French frigate had beyond ours. The conduct of one of the lieutenants, Mr. Kerr, seems to have been singularly gallant, who stayed on deck after he had received a canister shot through his shoulder, and till a splinter, striking him on the face, altogether blinded him. The first lieutenant too, a Mr. Edwards, though wounded badly in the hand, came up again after the Captain's death, to take the command of the ship. In a former account it was said, I think, that he had fainted from loss of blood. It is said in this letter that there was a French fleet in sight at the time when the 'Boston' bore up.

Let us know when you have got anything to tell, and believe me,

Your affectionate Uncle,
W. Windham.

April 7th.—In addition to the times mentioned in which I happened to say anything in the House, I must mention now the day of Adair's motion for legalising what had been done about subscription. It was on the 7th, I think, when the motion having been expected respecting the Emigrant Corps, I had been less attentive to the motion that actually came on and was therefore not well prepared when M. Ang. chose to bring up the business of my speech at Norfolk in 1778.* What I said in answer to that was not satisfactory to myself nor so advantageous certainly as it might have been, though I was glad to find lately that Mr. Townshend thought it was pretty well. But the want of finding something to throw at Grey, after the lofty and impertinent manner in which he chose to take me to task, sat very heavy upon my mind and upon my stomach, and continued till the late business of Norwich forced my thoughts to another object.

8th.—Sheridan attacked me again. I was prepared to make better fight, though still, I think, not quite in good heart, when, without any fault or want of endeavour of mine, the opportunity of speaking was withheld till it would clearly have been unadvisable.

9th.—I met Hamilton, who told me of the death of Big Ben who had died the night before, and, with a magnanimity worthy of his conduct on other occasions, was anxious that he should be opened after death for the benefit of the brethren of the art; his death being the consequence of a hurt which he got so long ago as his battle with Tring. I felt considerable anxiety about the conduct of the Norwich business, and was apprehensive that on this, as on almost every other occasion, I should find myself at last unprepared.

10th.—I left my own house between twelve and one, but not so soon as to be in time for the appointment that I had made at Mr. Smith's with the purchasers of the estates at Sudbury.

12th.—The proceedings of this day, viz. that for which the county meeting was called, are too numerous to be

* His first speech, at a meeting at Norwich, which pointed him out to be a man of marked ability, was occasioned by a call made on the country for carrying on the war with our American colonies in 1778.

One of the canons of the cathedral and a great supporter of the American war, said (although a churchman), 'D—n him, I could cut his tongue out.'

The part which Mr. W. took was in opposition to the subscription and to the war itself.

recorded in their detail, and the principal events may be trusted with sufficient safety to memory. Though we were in court near five hours, if not full that time, though the heat and crowd were very oppressive, and though for one complete hour I was talking continually at the stretch of my voice, and though both before and after that, my voice had been in a great state of exertion, yet my fatigue with all this was so little, that I could with ease, as it seemed, have continued the debate as long again, nor did I find myself immediately after or during any part of the remainder of the day, in any degree oppressed or overcome. The first and obvious way of accounting for this is, from the effect of a journey, from country air, but I am persuaded that a part is to be ascribed, perhaps the largest part, from the circumstance of having had my mind well at work, and above all, to its having worked satisfactorily to myself, principally as to the mode of its operation and then as to the effect produced. The constant irritation resulting from disappointment in consequence of exertions not producing their intended effect, without including the effect of general uneasiness, is, I am persuaded, that which consumes the animal spirits much more rapidly than the exertion itself, of which it might not be difficult to find instances, both of cases, where a small endeavour, when unsuccessful, produces great lassitude and languor, and, on the contrary, where great and continued exertions do not produce that, provided they are throughout followed by success.

16*th*.—Walk with Hicks and George, looking over plantations and led on by vernal delight and joy, the weather being delicious. It was near three by the time I returned. Continued then till it was time to dress the volume of Plato which I had taken up, and in which I was reading the second book of the 'Republic.' Dined at Parsonage. Mrs. L. had put into my hands Mary's

'Petite Histoire;' and Kitty afterwards showed me, which I must look further at, her Greek extracts and compositions with a dedication to me.

25*th*.—Fair-day at Holt. Stayed some time for George to overtake us, he having agreed to follow on horse 'Madame,' which I was to lend him. Gay scene. Soldiers firing a *feu de joie*. Arrived at Holkham about two. Found Coke and Anson. Walked before dinner, which was not to be till six, into the kitchen-garden. I was sorry that I had not spent that time in tumbling over the books. When I came in, took down my own copy of Dionys. Halicarn. and read on from the paper.

May 1*st*.—*London*.—There has been the trial, and latterly, *i. e.* I think, from about the 13th or 14th, the Committee of Secrecy. This last has been a considerable occupation, as we have met at an average at about half-past eleven o'clock and not separated at an average till five. One circumstance that may have contributed to render me less settled and has occupied no doubt a part of my time, is a matter certainly of no trifling importance, the forming a general political arrangement. This was first mentioned to me on the day when I dined at Burke's, and met for the first time Mr. Wylde. Dundas had called at my house and not finding me, had sent a note desiring me to call in the evening, if I could, at Somerset House. The professed object of the conference was the progress made by the seditious clubs and the necessity of taking some steps to counteract them. But as I was going away, the other subject was resumed, and as I stated that I could no longer answer separately, it was requested that I would learn the sentiments of the Duke of P.

We had a meeting on the following Sunday which I conceived to have been the 11th, though it was perhaps the 4th; whenever it was, it was the day on which the discovery had been made, or the proceedings at least began, about Jackson, Stone, &c.

Such were the days of the 16th and 17th when the question was debated of the suspension of the Habeas Corpus. The second of these was the day on which I spoke, and there was a great deal of angry work between Grey and me, and Fox and Pitt, &c. The night before was the time, I conceive, of their persisting so foolishly in dividing the House.

The Right Hon. William Windham to Captain Lukin.

May 12, 1794.

Dear William,—The two cutters, which I mentioned to you, the 'Earl of Chatham' and the 'Phœnix,' are at this time at Plymouth. After a thousand vexatious delays they were chased in last week—at least, obliged to put back—by some frigates detached from a French fleet of twenty-five sail, which they fell in with off Ushant.

If they should be still at Plymouth and you should have an opportunity, I wish you would go on board of them and learn what you can of their proceedings. The expedition is a secret (though perhaps not very well kept), for it is to carry some emigrants to the coast of France. The captain of the 'Earl of Chatham' is of the name of McDougal, a sort of half smuggler and half king's officer, who has executed other services of this sort well enough, but does not seem to have done quite so well in this. The principal French gentleman now on board is M. de la Robrie; but he, unluckily, does not speak any English. I am not sure, however, whether his companion does not; and at any rate you will find some means of communicating with him. He is a very good sort of young man, and will be very glad to see anyone connected with me. McDougal also will talk to you freely, if you tell him that you come from me. If I have time to-day I will mention in my letter to M. de la Robrie, that you may possibly visit him and that he may talk to you without reserve. Keep only in mind that, in talking before any other people, the object of the expedition should be as little known as possible. M. de la Robrie is aide-de-camp to one of the chiefs of the Royalists, and was, till he was despatched hither, in all their service.

Another gentleman whom I have known here for these two years past and was of their party, is just on his way back to London.

I am sorry for the misfortune of your Admiral, which I had heard of before I got your letter. Farewell! Let me hear of you when anything occurs.

Great anxiety here to know the event of an attack, which may be expected to have happened by this time.

Yours, &c.,

W. WINDHAM.

18*th.*—I dined by engagement with Mrs. Crewe at Hampstead. Burke had fetched me out in the morning and in my way back I called at Grenville's, where I found the Duke of Devonshire. At Mrs. Crewe's we had Malone, Mary (who went with me), Erskine and Mrs. Erskine, Sheridan and Richardson and were very near having Grey. The day passed very pleasantly; the charm of Sheridan's conversation and memory of past times, made me regret the differences that now separated us. Besides the above, I should have mentioned Lady Anne North, Frederick, I think, and Elliot.

19*th.*—Committee as usual. Whether this was the night of my going to Sadlers Wells to meet the Ellis's and Lady Malmesbury, I don't recollect.

20*th.*—I dined, I think, at Sir R. Payne's, and met Lady Clermont, Banks and Mrs. Banks, Mrs. Howe, and Lady Clive. I had before dined at Sir Ralph's and met Mr. and Mrs. Ellis, Mr. Stuart McKenzie, and Grenville. Some day before I had dined, at the instance of Grenville, at Lord Lucan's, where I met Beresford, Sir John Parnell, and other company, that I did not expect; I had gone with the idea of only Lord Spencer. This, if so, was the night of the Queen's ball.

21*st.*—Dined with Mulgrave to meet Sir W. Meadows.

June 1*st.*—Dined at Douglas's, in consequence of an

engagement made long before, and enforced by strong instances the evening preceding: the party, Lord Mansfield, Sir J. Skinner, and Archbishop of York, with Mrs. Markham and Miss M. The first time of my having been in company with the Archbishop of York (Markham). I would have avoided it now but for the remonstrances of Douglas. The Duchess of Portland not so well to-day.

3rd.—The accounts of the Duchess still favourable. From the Hall and the Committee I was prevailed upon with Grenville to go to dinner at Lord Clermont's, whither I had before sent an excuse. Lord Spencer, Lord and Lady Auckland, Lord Lucan, &c. At nine we were to have gone to a private meeting at Burlington House, so prosperous was the Duchess's situation thought to be. But, alas! a great change for the worse happened and word was left at the door that the Duke could not see anyone. I got this message before I came away having stayed after Lord Spencer and Lord Grenville, whom I proceeded in consequence to join at Grenville's. We sat there talking of what would have been the subject of our meeting at Burlington House and not much alarmed at the change that had occasioned the meeting being put off, conceiving that it might be something of no great consequence. Whatever it might be, as no effect could be produced upon it by my enquiry, I suspended my anxiety, and instead of accompanying Lord Spencer, who said he should call there in the way home, went home myself. I am rather sorry that I did, as I think I should have been better satisfied to have received there the news of the fatal event, which had then recently happened, than as I did at the committee next morning.

4th.—Birthday. Dined with Dundas: present, as nearly as I can recollect, Duke of Buccleugh, Powys, Lord Dalkeith, Lord Apsley, Stanley, Beaufoy, Lord Douglas.

10*th.*—Accounts had been received that day and the day before, making it highly probable that some action had taken place between the fleets.* The probability was so great that it would have been well worth while to have gone to the Opera on the chance of what might have been heard there during the course of the evening; I went, however, straight home and by that means missed the grand scene which ensued, when the news of Lord Howe's victory was announced, on the authority of a letter received by Lady Chatham. I continued in ignorance till between eleven and twelve, when, having strolled in at Legge's, I found, as might be expected, the whole company full of it. Lord Mansfield was one of those present; soon after Douglas, who had been down at Nepean's, in order to get the particulars to be sent to Ireland.

11*th.*—Went to the House and on my way back with Sir W. Scott called at Dundas's in order to recommend illumination. Continued walking with Wilde and conversing pleasantly.

12*th.*—Illuminations continued. Dined at Nepean's: present, Lord Mornington, Douglas. Went from thence to Lord Spencer's who had come to town in consequence of letter. Sat with him and Grenville till near twelve.

13*th.*—Wrote in the morning to Nepean urging that the illuminations should not be suffered to continue. Found in the evening that they were continued, though not so generally.

19*th.*—Dined with the Chancellor, and met Pitt, Lord Grenville, the Master of the Rolls, the Speaker, Dundas, with Lady Grenville, Lady Haddington, and Lady Arden. There had been business in the House, in consequence of which I had gone down at four; but this being put off for want of forty members, I was left for two hours, not knowing well what to do with myself, and afterwards, viz.

* Lord Howe's victory over the French fleet in the Bay of Biscay, June 1, 1794.

from six o'clock, when I went to the Chancellor's, was obliged to wait for dinner till near half-past seven.

20*th*.—This was the day of thanks to the Managers and thanks to Lord Hood. I stayed for the former and spoke a little.

21*st*.—Wrote in the morning to Lord Mulgrave, proposing journey to Portsmouth. Met Grenville who led me away and delayed me, partly by the delay that is occasioned by people walking together and partly by carrying me to Lady Melbourne's, whom I called on for the first time this year. I got off, however, by seven, and went on pleasantly enough to Guildford, where I arrived about twelve, stopping at the same inn at which I had been so many years ago and in company that should make the recollection of it strongly impressed upon my mind.

22*nd*.—I arrived at Portsmouth about two and soon found Payne and Pakenham and the rest of those whom I looked for. We went immediately to look at the French ships and continued so employed till a late dinner at Pakenham's. Before our going there, Payne went with me to Lord Howe.

23*rd*.—After dinner went in Payne's barge rowing about at Spithead.

24*th*.—Great enjoyment of prospect in parts between Lippock and Guildford, though could not help remarking the difference of the impression now, compared with what would have been made by the scene formerly, when my mind was much more susceptible of that species of enjoyment. When I got back was to have dined with Paradise's to meet Mr. Jay, the new American Minister, but felt for some reason no great inclination to go, and accordingly dined at the Club.

July 2*nd*.—The continuance of the negotiation occupied a good deal of my time and thoughts and prevented my engaging in any regular employment. All idea, indeed, of such employment seems to have been laid aside for a long while past.

4th.—Was the day, I conceive, on which the Duke of Portland called upon me in the morning with the proposal of my taking the place which I at present hold,* and on which there was the meeting in the evening, from which I was detained by the conversation with Cholmondeley.

5th.—Went in the morning, before breakfast, to Grenville and afterwards to Burke's, and afterwards to Burlington House, where I relinquished the objection made in my letter of the night before and contented myself with apprising the Duke with what I conceived to be the misunderstanding. Engaged to dine with Mr. Ellis at Twickenham. Fell in with Lord Spencer on the road and proceeded in his carriage. At this time all seemed likely to be at an end, it being found that what I had apprehended had completely taken place.

6th.—I found a message from the Duke and the conference that succeeded was of the most important nature. It continued till two in the morning and ended in a way that left me full of regret and dissatisfaction. Grenville and Lord Fitzwilliam, from whom I parted at the top of Berkeley Square, went on together without my feeling any wish to continue of their party.

7th.—Rose early and went to Burke's and then to Lord Spencer's; with him to Burlington House. When the Duke went to Downing Street, Lord Spencer and I came away, he to Lord Lucan's and I home, where I expected M. de la Robrie and La Vieuville. Upon recollection, I believe it was M. Cerderon who was with me when Lord Spencer called. This made us so late when we got back, especially as I stayed to write a long note to Cholmondeley, that the D. of P. was returned and the other persons met. We then found that

* Mr. Windham was sworn in Secretary at War on the 11th July, 1794, in Mr. Pitt's administration, which he continued to hold till 1801.

the whole was concluded and not long after Pitt came in to sign and seal. The history of the canvass or of the election need not be given; except so far as to say, that I never was engaged in one that proceeded so satisfactorily as to the manner in which it was conducted; every circumstance being managed as I could have wished, except that one of my not having determined, notwithstanding the remonstrances of a portion of my friends, to be chaired the same night. The folly of that decision or acquiescence is such as I cannot forgive myself or account for. The only way in which I can explain it is, that I was driven out of a right opinion by the badness of the reason by which it was supported.

August 27th.—The general character of the time has been wholly unlike that of any preceding period and has by no means differed as being more satisfactory. Its first difference has been that all improvement of the understanding has appeared to be at a stand. It may have happened that some habits have been acquired of great practical utility and which might be applied with advantage to pursuits of whatever kind; but no accession of knowledge has been acquired, nor any improvement made in the exercise of particular faculties.

It often happened that when I was going to Fulham, the impatience of London had grown so strong as to make a night in the country an object of great desire, and it seemed a necessary relief. It would have been more advantageous and sometimes more pleasant, had I found the House empty.

Such an intermission of the use of books I have never known, and reflection, I am sorry to find, has very much gone with them. The times not engaged by business I have considered as exempt from all necessity of exertion and as yielding enough if they afforded that enjoyment which arises from mere cessation of toil. It has been a mere animal kind of existence, having neither prospect nor retrospect, but confined wholly to the pains and pleasures of the moment.

30*th.*—It was towards the end of this time, the day I don't precisely recollect, that the proposition was made of my going with the resolution of the Cabinet to the Duke of York. The affair continued in suspense or preparation till to-day, when it appears I left London. Before six passed the Horse Guards. I had sat up working very late and I was dreadfully tired. After getting some dinner, and writing a letter at Deal, went aboard the 'Pomona' to sleep. The naval business appeared more interesting than it will do now, after seeing the more important operations of armies.

September 2*nd.*—Landed at Helvoet. Got up before we came in and very much enjoyed the scene. Went on to Rotterdam. Found out by the Duke de Sérent; carried with him to the Comte d'Artois.

3*rd.*—Late in arrival at Bois le Duc. Pleasant drive over the heath, though not without the opinion that it was possible that we might be within reach of patroles, as it turned out afterwards that we were. Found the Duke was at supper in the town, with a large party, particularly Lord and Lady Palmerston, Lord Grandison, Lady Gertrude Villiers — a beautiful and most pleasing young woman — Lord Mountmorris, W. Payne, Monson, Murray, Miss Carter, General and Mrs. Harcourt, P. William.

5*th.*—Went over and took up our quarters at Berlikom. Dined while I was there with Hulse, General Harcourt, General Fox, and Prince William. The day of dining with Prince William was the day of visiting the post at Oudenrode, where I saw General Hammerstock and the day of receiving the account of the forcing of the post at Boxtel. I had been so tired with my ride in the morning, that when this account came after dinner, the slight agitation which it occasioned (and so slight it was that I could say with truth it would in itself have been wholly unknown to me) threw me into the state which I have known of late on many occasions, of being almost paralytic. My muscles were moving in various parts of my body without my having any control over them.

We soon after set out for camp, I riding one of Craig's horses which was ready sooner and seemed to me to be better, than Major Murray's. It was so dark before we got to camp that we could hardly see our way. The night was spent at General Stuart's quarters, close by the Windmill (Heswick): we got some supper there; and some beds were made and a cot hung in an adjoining barn. It was a grand and (to me) a new situation; I am angry with myself that I did not seek to impress my mind with a fuller sense of the magnificence of it. The army of the enemy, of which we had heard so much, were advancing upon us. The action was going on in the close country in front. An attack, it was likely, would be made upon us in the morning. The fate of the British army and with that of the whole cause, probably, depended upon the event. What a situation for the imagination of Burke or Dr. Johnson! I am afraid I must say that I felt this hardly more than a grenadier; I hope only that I felt as much as a grenadier, at least, that if I felt it but little in one way I felt it but little also in another. At an early hour a report was brought, first by a drum boy, who had fled on a wounded horse, afterwards by Colonel Churchill, that the 12th regiment were taken prisoners, and, as the latter had got it, that the reserve and General Abercromby were cut off. Then, indeed, the prospect was bad. The line was ordered out and the Duke of York rode along it. I kept chiefly with Craig and was glad to see that the men turned out with alacrity, with no appearance anywhere of perturbation and in some parts with indications of confidence. I wish I had been more particular in my observations; but with so many things to attend to it was hardly possible. I took what occasions

I could to say something animating to the soldiers; but as that kind of eloquence has much of chance in it, I did not always succeed. The Duke of York, in an attempt or two that he made, failed most miserably. It is one of the talents in which he is defective. It was soon known that the reports which we had heard were not true; and after a certain time, there was reason to think that the enemy would not attack us that day. It was then a question only how soon should we retreat, of which the first idea was, that the order should be given for moving at dark; the second, for a time so much earlier as that the movement should actually take place by dark; the third and rational one, that the army should get in motion as soon as it well could, that is, by four o'clock.

A wish had early occurred to me of going away with the reserve; but the fear of appearing ostentatious and seeming to grasp at a show of doing something, where what was done was really nothing, had very nearly made me abandon the design and resign a purpose which now I see would have proved, if neglected, a perpetual subject of regret. Luckily, therefore, after riding at first to the head of the line with Sir W. Erskine, I came back and joined General Abercromby at the mill, enjoying myself very much till it was time to go, or rather till General Abercromby went; for from that time till about ten, when the cavalry who remained there were to begin their march, I lay down and got some sleep. It appeared to me that our situation there was not quite safe, if a body of the enemy had been willing to push forward and make a spirited attempt to surprise some that stayed behind; but the opinion seemed to be overruled and I did not think either my belief of the risk, or the state of my wishes, which really inclined to go with General Abercromby, of weight sufficient to the apprehension of appearing over-scrupulous about my own safety. The corps that stayed were Irving's, some light horse under Churchill and a number of Darmstadters. The march was conducted in silence and had something very fine and striking. The same may be said of all the remainder; but fatigue destroyed the greatest part of the enjoyment; for the greatest part of the time I found it hardly possible to keep myself awake.

16*th.*—In the morning I arrived at Grave: the arrival there in the morning would have been full of delight had I either been less fatigued, or had the occasion been more satisfactory. How much better pleased, however, I was, I am sure, at coming in with the reserve, than if I had come in with the other party. My fatigue during the morning was not so strong as to take from me my satisfaction. In the evening I attempted to write, but found it altogether in vain: the thought that I had a troublesome letter to write was among the causes probably that diminished my satisfaction.

17*th.*—We went in the evening to the new quarters, the place of which was Wichem. The chateau here of the Duke's was very comfortable; my quarters not so much so, the bed being uncomfortable, the room on the ground-floor and the house full of bad smells. We continued here for four days, during which the Comte d'Artois arrived, whom I saw both at the Duke of York's and at his chateau, on the road to Nimeguen. The Duke de Castries also came over, and had a long conversation with me. In general there was a considerable resort here of foreigners of different descriptions. Of the French were, besides those already named, M. Archambaud Perigord and his brother, the Baron Rolle (a quasi French), the Prince de Léon, the Comte de la Fare, who came from the Duke de Laval, at Cologne, about his depôt and wanted to go on to Lord St. Helens'; the Comte de Bétisy, M. Puysegur, attendant upon the Comte d'Artois; the Duc de Sérent. Of others a very illustrious one was Prince Frederick of Orange; with him was a Colonel Bentinck; and the

I could to say something animating to th
... has much of ch
... The Duke of York. i
... failed most miserably.
... is defective. It was s
... which we had heard were not
... there was reason to think
... It was then
... we retreat, of which th
... should be given for movin
... a time so much earlier as tha
... take place by dark; the th
... army should get in motion a
... four o'clock.

A wish ... occurred to me of
... but the fear of appearing
... at a show of doing s
what was ... was really nothing, had
... the design and resign a p
... would have proved, if neglected, a
of ... Luckily, therefore, after ri
head of the line with Sir W. Erskine
joined General Abercromby at the m
very much till it was time to go, or
Abercromby went; for from that time
the cavalry who remained there were
I lay down and got some sleep. It
our situation there was not quite
enemy had been willing to push
spirited attempt to surprise some
the opinion seemed to be
either my belief of the
which really inclined
weight sufficient to
scrupulous about
were Irving's,

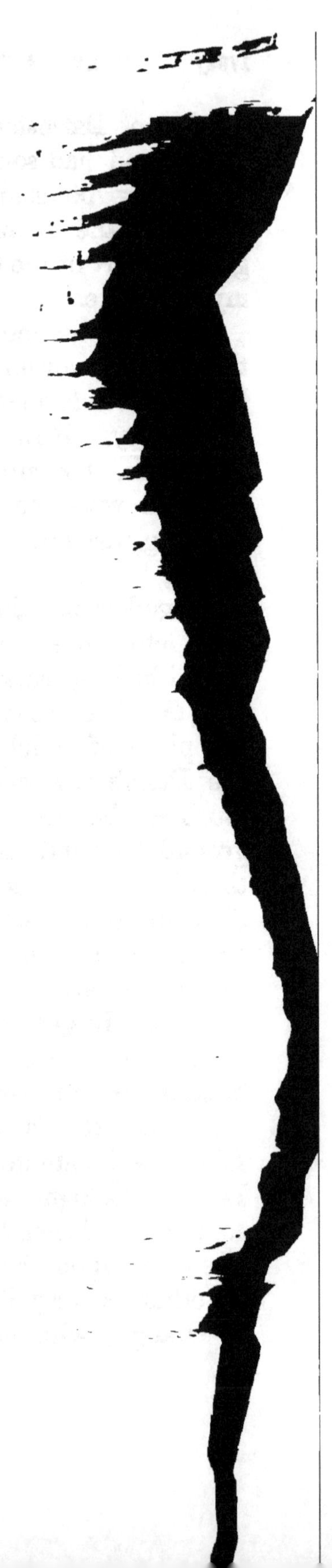

[illegible] enviable [illegible] not think [illegible] in this [illegible] liament. [illegible] country [illegible] despair. [illegible] strongly [illegible] our poor [illegible] if things [illegible] d. I am [illegible] leeply for [illegible] the general [illegible] orm, is the [illegible] am, the man [illegible]

[illegible] chiefly con- [illegible] have strong [illegible] I was clearly [illegible] e have for the [illegible] same evening I saw for the first and only time General Walmoden.

December 10*th*.—*London*.—Levee. Dined with Pitt: besides Cabinet, Douglas, Grenville. Had done no business with the King, as he was to go to the play.

12*th*.—Dined with Dundas and the Cabinet to meet the Duke of York.

16*th*.—Dined at Francis's: large party.

17*th*.—Did not get to St. James's till Lord Thurlow was with the King. When I came to dinner found the company to consist of the Irish colonels, with the addition only of Lord Spencer, Lord Hawkesbury and Grenville, to which must be added Lord Chatham. Dinner to me singularly pleasant.

18*th*.—By delays and interruptions of various kinds, kept till late, though I had early ordered the horses and meant to have gone to the office betimes. A sad state of hesitation and uncertainty then succeeded, which lost me at least an hour and ended in my neither going to the office nor sending in time to say I should not go. As the only refuge from my own uncomfortableness, I rode desperately down to Fulham, with a determination, which I have pretty well kept, that I would not suffer indolence and indulgence so to creep upon me after dinner as to lose the employment of the evening.

22*nd*.—Came up to a council at Lord Grenville's; the subject, the accounts received from Lord St. Helens of the Deputies sent to the Convention.

23*rd*.—Went to the War Office at twelve, thence to a meeting of the Council at the Duke of York's, and from thence to Burlington House, to determine with the Attorney and Solicitor Generals, whether the indictment should be pursued against Martin.

The Right Hon. Edmund Burke to the Right Hon. William Windham.

October 16, 1794.

My dear Sir,—My state of mind was not the most enviable before the present unhappy misunderstanding. I cannot think without horror on the effects of a breach in the Ministry in this state of our affairs, and just before the meeting of Parliament. It will complete our ruin! Every honest man in every country in Europe will by this event be cast into dismay and despair. It looks as if the hand of God was in this, as it is strongly marked in all the rest. However, we must still use our poor human prudence, and our feeble human efforts, as if things were not, what I greatly fear they are, predetermined. I am out of action, but not out of anxiety. I feel deeply for yourself—I feel for my other friends—I feel for the general cause. Ireland, the country in which I was born, is the immediate subject of the dispute: Lord Fitzwilliam, the man in the world I am most obliged to, is the party chiefly concerned in it. To Mr. Pitt—the other party—I have strong and recent obligations. Before I had any such, I was clearly of opinion that his power, and all the chance we have for the rescue of Europe, were inseparably connected. You know that, though I had no part in the actual formation of the present system of a coalesced Ministry, that no pains were wanting on my part to produce the dispositions which led to it. You, of all men, therefore, are the best judge how much I am in earnest that this horrible breach should not be made. How to prevent it I know not; I cannot advise. I can only make statements, which I submit entirely to your judgment. I do not write to anyone else, because you alone have desired to hear my sentiments on this subject. I will trouble you with no other view of the matter than as it concerns the interest, the stability, perhaps the existence, of Mr. Pitt's power. I was one of those who were of opinion that he could have stood merely on his own basis; but this was my private speculation, and hardly justified, I fear, by the experience of mankind in cases any way similar. But to have gone on without this new connection, and to bear the loss of it, are two very different things. The accession of a great mass of reputation taken out of a state of very perilous and critical neutrality, and brought to the decided support of the Crown, and an actual participation in the responsibility of measures rendered questionable by very great misfortunes, were the advantages which Mr. Pitt derived from a coalition with you and your friends. I say nothing just now of your weight in the country, and the abilities which, in your several ways, you possess. I rest only on your character and reputation for integrity, independence, and dignity of mind. This is everything at a moment, when opinion (never without its effect) has obtained a greater dominion over human affairs than ever it possessed; and which must grow just in proportion as the implicit reverence for old institutions is found to decline. They who will say that the very name which you and the Duke of Portland and Lord Fitzwilliam, and Lord Spencer, have, as men of unblemished honour and great public spirit, is of no use to the Crown at this time, talk like flatterers who despise the understandings of those whose favour they court. It is as much Mr. Pitt's interest, as a faithful and zealous servant of the Crown (as I am sure he is), to hold high your honour and estimation with the public, as it is your own. Can it be preserved, if Lord Fitzwilliam continues in office after all that has happened, consistently with the reputation he has obtained; and which, as a sacred trust for the King and country, he is bound to keep, as well as for his own inward satisfaction? I will not say that Lord Fitzwilliam has not, in some respects, acted with a degree of indiscretion. The question is, whether Mr. Pitt can or ought to take advantage of it to his own material prejudice? You are better acquainted than I am with the terms, actual or understood, upon which the Duke of Portland, acting for himself and others, has accepted office. I know nothing of them, but by a single conversation with him. From thence I learned that (whether authorised or not) he considered without a doubt that the administration of Ireland was left wholly to him, and without any other reserves than what are supposed in every wise and sober servant of the Crown. Lord Fitzwilliam, I know, conceived things exactly in that manner, and proceeded as if there was no controversy whatever on the subject. He hesitated a long time whether he should take the station; but when he agreed to it, he thought he had obliged the Ministry, and done what was pleasant to the King, in going into an office of great difficulty and heavy responsibility. He foresaw no other obstacles than what were found in his own inclinations, the nature of the employment, and the circumstances in which Ireland stands. He, therefore, invited several persons to converse with him in all the confidence with which men ought to open themselves to a person of honour, who, though not actually, was virtually in office. Whether the Duke of Portland and Lord Fitzwilliam had reason for this entire security, you are better able to judge than I am. I am sure they conceived things in the light I state them, though I really think that they never can reconcile it to the rigid rules of prudence with regard to their own safety, or to an entire decorum with regard to the other Cabinet Ministers, to go so far into detail as has been done until all the circumstances of the appointment were settled in a more distinct and specific manner than they had been. But I am sure they thought that a very large discretion was committed to them; and I am equally sure that their general places (so far as I know them) were perfectly upright and perfectly well understood for the King's service and the good of his empire. I admit, and lament, the error into which they have fallen. It must be very great, as it seems Mr. Pitt had no thought at all of a change in the Irish Government; or, if he had, it was dependent on Lord Westmoreland's sense of the fitness of some other office to accommodate him on his resignation of the great place which, for five or six years, he has held. This puts off the business *sine die.* These are some of the mischiefs which arise from a want of clear explanation on the first digestion of any political system.

If an agreement is wished, criminations and recriminations, charges and defences, are not the way to it. If the communication hitherto has not been as full and as confidential as it ought to have been, let it be so now. Let it be such as becomes men engaged in the same cause, with the interest and with the same sense of the arduous trust which, in the most critical of all times, has been delivered over to them by their King and country. In this dreadful situation of things, is it not clearly Mr. Pitt's interest, without considering whether he has a case as against his colleagues or not, to keep up the reputation of those who came to his aid under circumstances liable to misconstruction; liable to the exaggerated imputations of men, able, dexterous, and eloquent; and who came to him when the whole of the affairs under his administration bore the worst aspect that can be imagined? I am well aware that there is a sort of politicians who would tell Mr. Pitt that this disgracing his colleagues would be to him a signal triumph, and that it would be to the public a splendid mark of his power and superiority. But alas! it would be a triumph over his own force. His paramount power is well understood. His power is an object rather of envy and terror, than of contempt. I am no great dealer in general maxims. I am sensible how much the best of them are controlled by circumstances. But I am satisfied, that where the most real and solid power exists, there it is the most necessary, every now and then, to yield, not only from the real advantages of practicability, but from the advantages which attend the very appearance of it. What is given up by power, is a mark of moderation; what is given up because it cannot be kept, is a mark of servility and meanness. What coffee-house politician is so grossly ignorant as not to know that the real seat of power is in Mr. Pitt, and in none of you who by the courtesy of England are called Ministers. Whatever *he* gives up will be manifestly for the King's service; whatever *they* yield will be thought to flow from a mean desire of office, to be held without respect or consideration. If he yields any point he will be sure to put out his concessions, to be repaid to him with usury. All this unfortunate notion of triumph, on the one part and the other, arises from the idea, that Ministry is not *one* thing, but composed of separate and independent parties—a ruinous idea, which I have done everything in my power to discourage, and with a growing success. I can say almost with assurance, that if Mr. Pitt can contrive (and it is worth his while to contrive it) to keep his new acquisition of friends in good humour for six months more, he will find them as much of his party, and in my opinion, more surely to be depended upon, than any which he has hitherto considered as his own. It is of infinite importance to him to have it *thought* that he is well connected with others besides those who are believed to *depend* on him.

If it is once laid down, that it is true policy in Mr. Pitt to uphold the credit of his colleagues in administration, even under some difference in opinion, the question will be, Whether the present is not a case of too much importance to be included in that general policy, and that Lord Fitzwilliam may very well give up the lieutenancy, and yet hold his office, without any disgrace? On that, I think, there can be little difference in opinion. He must, to be sure, resign; and resign with every sentiment of displeasure and discontent. This I have not advised him to do; for, most certainly, I have had no conversation with him on the subject; and I am very glad I have not had any such discourse. But the thing speaks for itself. He has consulted with many people from Ireland, of all descriptions, as if he were virtually Lord-Lieutenant. The Duke of Portland has acted upon that supposition as a fundamental part of his arrangement. Lord Fitzwilliam cannot shrink into his shell again, without being thought a light man, in whom no person can place any confidence. If, on the other hand, he takes the sword, not only without power, but with a direct negative put upon his power, he is a Lord-Lieutenant disgraced and degraded. With infinite sorrow I say it—with sorrow inexpressible—he must resign. If he does, the Duke of Portland must resign too. In fact, they will both consider themselves as turned out; and I know it will be represented to them, because I know it has been predicted to them, that their being brought into office was no more than a stratagem, to make them break with their friends and original natural connections, to make them lose all credit with the independent part of the country, and then to turn them out as objects of universal scorn and derision without party or adherents to resort to! I believe Lord Fitzwilliam has in his bureau one letter to this effect—I well recollect that he was much affected by it, and indeed doubtful of accepting—perhaps more than one. I am certain, that whether they stay in under a state of degradation, or are turned out, their situation will be terrible; and such as will be apt to fill men with rage and desperate resolutions. Both their coming in and their going out will be reviled; and they will be ridiculed and insulted on both by the Opposition. They will affect to pity them. They will even offer to pardon them. Amongst Mr. Pitt's old adherents, as perhaps you know as well as I do, there were many who liked your coming in as little as Mr. Fox or Mr. Sheridan could do. They considered Mr. Pitt's enlarging his bottom as an interloping on their monopoly. They will join the halloo of the others. If they can persuade Mr. Pitt that this is a triumph, he will have it. But may God in His goodness avert the consequences from him and all of us!

'But why,' will some say, 'should not Lord Fitzwilliam take the Lord-Lieutenancy, and let the Chancellor remain where he is? He will be good-humoured and subservient, and let the Lord-Lieutenant do as he pleases.' But, after what has passed, the true question is, which of these two is to govern Ireland? I think I know what a Lord-Lieutenant of Ireland is, or I know nothing. Without a hearty and effectual support of the Minister here, he is much worse than a mere pageant. A man in the pillory is in a post of honour in comparison of such a Lord-Lieutenant. 'But Lord Westmoreland goes on very quietly.' He does so. He has no discussions with the junto who have annihilated English government. Be his abilities and his spirit what they may, he has no desire of governing. He is a Basha of Egypt, who is content to let the Beys act as they think proper. Lord Fitzwilliam is a high-minded man, a man of very great parts, and a man of very quick feelings. He cannot be the instrument of the junto, with the name of the King's representative, if he would. If Lord Fitzwilliam was to be sent to Ireland, to be exactly as Lord Westmoreland is, I undertake to affirm, that a worst choice for that purpose could not be made. If he has nothing to do but what Lord Westmoreland does, neither ought Lord Westmoreland to be removed, nor the Chancellor, no, nor the Chancellor's Train-bearer. Lord Fitzwilliam has no business there at all. He has fortune enough. He has rank enough. Here he is infinitely more at his ease, and he is of infinitely more use here than he can be there, where his desire of really doing business, and his desire of being the real representative of the Crown, would only cause to him infinite trouble and distress. For it is not to know Ireland to say, that what is called opposition is what will give trouble to a real Viceroy. His embarrassments are upon the part of those who ought to be the supports of English government; but who have formed themselves into a cabal to destroy the King's authority, and to divide the country as a spoil amongst one another. '*Non regnum sed magnum latrocinium*:' the motto which ought to be put under the harp. This is not talk. I can put my hand on the instances, and not a doubt would remain on your mind of the fact. His Majesty has the patronage to the Pashalic, as the Grand Seignior has to that of Egypt, and that is all. Such is the state of things. I think matters recoverable in some degree; but the attempt is to be made.

If Ireland be well enough, and safe enough, as it is; if the Chancellor and the Government of the junto is good for the King, the country, and the empire, God forbid that a stone in that edifice should be picked out to gratify Lord Fitzwilliam, or anybody else. But if that kingdom, by the meditated and systematic corruption (private, personal, not politic corruption) of some, and the headlong violence and tyrannical spirit of others, totally destitute of wisdom, and the more incurably so, as not being destitute of some flashy parts, is brought into a very perilous situation, then I say, at a time like this, there is no making questions about it mere discussions between one branch and the other of administration, either in England or Ireland. The state of Ireland is not like a thing without intrinsic merits, and on which it may be safe to make a trial of skill, or a trial of strength. It is no longer an obscure dependency of this kingdom. What is done there vitally affects the whole system of Europe. Whether you regard it offensively or defensively, Ireland is known in France. Communications have been opened, and more will be opened. Ireland will be a strong digue to keep out Jacobinism, or a broken bank to let it in. The junto have weathered the old European system of government there, and brought it into utter discredit. I look in this affair to Ireland, and in Ireland to Great Britain, and in Great Britain to Europe. The little cliques there are to me as nothing. They have never done me a favour nor an injury. But that kingdom is of great importance indeed. I regard, in this point, all descriptions of men with great comparative indifference. I love Lord Fitzwilliam very well; but so convinced am I, on the maturest reflection, of the perilous state into which the present junto have brought that kingdom (on which, in reality, this kingdom, at this juncture, is dependent), that if he were to go with a resolution to support it, I would, on my knees, entreat him not to have a share in the ruin of his country under the poor pretence of governing a part of it. Oh! my dear friend, I write with a sick heart, and a wearied hand. If you can, pluck Ireland out of the unwise and corrupt hands that are destroying us! If they say, they will mend their manners, I tell you, they cannot mend them; and if they could, this mode of doing and undoing, saying and unsaying, inflaming the people with voluntary violence, and appeasing them with forced concession; their keeping the 'word of promise to their ear and breaking it to their hope;' their wanton expenses, and their fraudulent economy;—all these, and ten times more than these, but all of the same sort, are the very things which have brought government in that country to the state of contempt and incurable distrust under which it labours. It cannot have its very distemper for its cure. You know me, I think, enough to be quite sure, that in giving you an opinion concerning Mr. Pitt's interest and honour, I have not an oblique regard, at his expense, to the honour and interest of others. No! I always thought advice the most sacred of all things, and that it always ought to be given for the benefit of the advised. I am now endeavouring to make up my accounts with my Creator. I am, almost literally, a dying man. I speak with all the freedom, and with all the clearness of that situation. I speak as a man under a strong sense of obligation to Mr. Pitt, when I assure him, under the solemn sanction of that awful situation, that my firm opinion is, that by getting rid of the new accessions to his strength, and especially upon the ground of protection to certain Irish politicians (at what distance of time I cannot say), but he is preparing his certain ruin, with all the consequences of that ruin, which I tremble to think on. God bless you all, and direct you for the best!

Ever, ever, your affectionate and unhappy friend,

EDMUND BURKE.

The Right Hon. Edmund Burke to the Right Hon. William Windham.

Beaconsfield: October 16, 1794.

MY DEAR SIR,—What I enclose to you with this is to yourself principally; but if you enter into my ideas, it is ostensible to

Mr. Pitt and Mr. Dundas; and, if you will, to the Chancellor. This I don't desire, because, in case of our agreement the arguments will come with far more authority from yourself. But if you think that my opinions would tend in any way to strengthen yours, you have my permission to show them to any of the three upon whom you conceive they are the most likely to make an impression. Mr. Pitt is surprised that your friends should think of breaking the Ministry at such a time as this; sure it is equally surprising that he should do so by putting them out of their offices, for it is plain they cannot stay in them under the present circumstances. It is he who is chiefly responsible (almost, indeed, wholly so) for carrying on the public business in this dreadful season. It is his system and his power that are to be supported; and I never knew a minister that would not do a thousand things to gain, and to keep, men convenient, at least, to the support of his power and reputation, especially when the greatest interests ever stated were depending. When he will do no one earthly thing to keep them, they must think, and the world must think, he wants to get rid of them. I wish you to speak fully to Dundas on this business. I conceive all others ought to be postponed to it. I don't know what part he has in the intrigue. But if he is clear of that, he is open to reason, and is not without influence. You mistook me about Grattan. I did not wish Mr. Pitt to reason him into a dereliction of opposition to Lord Westmoreland, for I well knew that a dread of that opposition would be a principal inducement to Mr. Pitt to be reconciled to your friends; I wished you to get the Duke of Portland and Lord Fitzwilliam, with whom he was in confidence, and to whom he came over in order to destroy the system of the junto, and to pledge himself to support them in opposition to it; to consult with him what it was best for that purpose to do, whether to resign or not, or what other course to take. I should have made a great scruple of conscience to do anything whatever for the support, directly or indirectly, of a set of men in Ireland, who, that conscience well informed tells me, by their innumerable corruptions, frauds, oppressions, and follies, are opening a back door for Jacobinism, to rush in expenses, and to take us in the rear. As surely as you and I exist, so surely this will be the consequence of their persisting in their system. As to yourself, you have my most ardent prayers that

God would direct you, through your reason, to the best course. I am glad that neither the Duke of Portland, nor Lord Fitzwilliam, nor you, have called on me for my opinion on your conduct. Whatever you do will be well intended and well advised. You will then smile, and ask me, why I am so free in my advice to Mr. Pitt through you, who has asked it as little as the rest? Why, because the whole depends on him. If he mistakes, so as to let this Ministry go to pieces, we shall, along with him, be all undone. The Lieutenancy of Ireland is an arrangement subservient to the reformation, or to the continuance, of the abuses reigning in the country, and he who is the real minister can alone support or destroy them. I ought to have sent my packet earlier. But I have been oppressed with such sinkings and dejection of spirits, that in adding, after the coming of your messenger, to what I wrote the night before, I have been obliged to go into the open air from time to time, to refresh myself, and thus the time went away. This is dreadful! dreadful! beyond the loss of a general battle. I now despair completely. I begin to think that God, who most surely regards the least of His creatures as well as the greatest, took what was dearest to me to Himself in a good time. Adieu!

Your ever faithful and obliged friend, and humble servant,

EDMUND BURKE.

The Right Hon. Edmund Burke to the Right Hon. William Windham.

Beaconsfield: October 20, 1794.

MY DEAR SIR,—I had your letter. Everything is undone, if the matter is put upon private and personal ground. If it be a question of men and of favour, it is quite clear what men and what favour must prevail; and, as to the public opinion, it will be clamorously against those who come in and go out lightly in the most critical seasons. I have thought this matter over and over. I have looked back at our former experience: and I have considered the genius of the new times. I have considered the character of the men you are come to act with, and your own character; as well as the character of the Opposition and the bystanders. I have compared all these with the situation of England, and of Poland, and of Europe. I never gave anything in my life so thorough a sifting. The result is, that I am clearly and decidedly of opinion that the Duke of Portland, nor Lord Fitzwilliam, nor yourself, ought to resign; but to wait—for what I foresee will be the case of some of you—to be turned out. You are in a post of strength, if you know how to defend yourselves. Whereas nothing but obloquy, unpopularity, disfavours above and below, and complete impotence, will follow you, if you are once out; and never can you come in again but on the ruins of your country. But when I say the resignations ought not now to be thought of, I do not say that the matters for which you contend ought to be abandoned; but the very reverse. You are where you are, only to act with rectitude, firmness, and disinterestedness, and particularly to resist, *ad internecionem*, the corrupt system of Ireland, which goes directly to the ruin of the whole empire. I seemed to think, in my last letter, of the resignation of the Duke of Portland and Lord Fitzwilliam as inevitable. That letter was the result of my second thought. You know that in my first, to which I am now come back, I stated this position to you as a thing between the two alternatives. In substance, perhaps, my opinions are the same: go out they must. I believe it is a thing that does not depend on them to avoid—the question is on the manner of it. Clearly, the most reputable thing in every point of view is, that they should not commit suicide; but be slain on their post in a battle against this Irish corruption, which is another thing than the misapplication of so much money. If, indeed, my opinion was wholly changed on reflection, why should I be ashamed of it in one of the most difficult questions that ever was? Whatever is done, I am against all squab proceedings, such as seem rather the effect of temper than principle. They are very ill-used—very ill indeed; but their own conduct has been such that they have put themselves in the wrong; and it is not by base yielding, or by a stubborn perverseness, they can get right, but by producing such a body of principle as *really* actuates them, and which will make their mode of proceeding, however irregular, a thing of very subordinate importance. The closet must be resorted to, with all sort of gentleness and attention; the matter stated the substance given in, in writing; opinion and direction rather asked than resolution declared on their part; lamentation rather than blame. Honour and principle are never the worse for being conducted with address. Two things—not to resign, not to abandon the ground of dispute. With good conduct the whole may yet be gained—points, office, all. But then, the temper to be used, in my mind, ought not to extend to the Irish job system. You can only defend yourselves by open, avowed unappearable war, against that, as long as no temperaments of any kind are held out; when they are, their value will be considered. I shall write, I think, a note to this purpose to Lord Fitzwilliam and the Duke of Portland. I wrote, last night, a *threnodia* to the Chancellor; but I did not enter into any particular whatever: it would have been quite useless. He is a very able, good-humoured, friendly man; and for himself, truly, no great jobber, but where a job of patronage occurs, '*quanquam ipsâ in morte tenetur.*' For in the article of death, he would cry, 'Bring the job!' Good God! to think of jobs in such a moment as this! Why, it is not vice any longer: it is corruption run mad. Thank you for the account of the few saved at Bois le Duc—Pichegru has more humanity than we have. Why are any of these people put into garrison places? It is premeditated and treacherous murder. If an emigrant governor was, indeed, appointed, a better thing could not be done. Then we should hear of a defence: it would, indeed, be a novelty; and one would think, for that reason, would be recommended. But cowardice and treachery seem qualifications; and punishment is amongst the *artes perditæ* in the old governments. I am very miserable—tossed by public upon private grief, and by private upon public. Oh! have pity on yourselves! and may the God, whose counsels are so mysterious in the moral world (even more than in the natural), guide you through all these labyrinths. Do not despair! if you do work in despair. Feel as little and think as much as you can: correct your natural constitutions, but don't attempt to force them.

Adieu, adieu!

Yours ever,

Monday evening. EDMUND BURKE.

The Right Hon. Edmund Burke to the Right Hon. William Windham.

October 28, 1794.

My dear Sir,—I am in a state of mind as near complete despair as a man can be in; yet whilst there remains the faintest possibility of doing good, I think you whose duty it is to act, and who have vigour of body and mind sufficient to that duty, ought to omit no rational means of removing the evil which presses the most nearly, and is the most within your reach. A mediator is wanted in this business. I doubt whether you are exactly in that situation. I think the Chancellor is. I feared he might be too much influenced by the jobbery of his Irish connections, particularly that of Douglas. But I rather think I wronged him. I have heard from him, and by the strain he writes in, I am sure he wishes this rupture to be made up in some proper way, as you and I do. Now I apprehend he may be a little crippled in this business of a useful go-between, if there be not some confidence shown to him by our friends. I just throw out this hint, not being able to say much more than what I have already troubled you with at great length. How comes it that I have heard nothing of Dundas in this business, no more than if no such thing existed? and yet he must certainly tell for a great deal in it. I know this affair can never come to any sort of amicable conclusion whilst they treat the matter in dispute exactly in the spirit and upon the principles of ministers of adverse courts (and very adverse courts too), debating on a matter in negotiation and not as members of the same Cabinet Council and servants of the same King. The order of the questions, and all this fencing, tends to keep alive the hostility. There is something of the worst tendency imaginable in the whole mode of their carrying on business.

God bless you!

Ever yours,

Edmund Burke.

To the Right Honourable W. Windham.

1795.

February 14*th.* — Council for reading instructions to officers who were going to Cape.* Blanket already at Portsmouth, waiting for nothing but his instructions.

In walking down to Council took the opportunity of stealing to see a battle of which I had just had notice, between Ward (Jos.) and a man of the name of Starling; the same, I have a notion, whom I had seen, I know not how many years before, fight as a boy with a groom whose horses stood at Fozard's.

18*th.*—Attended a Council in which the embargo on shipping was laid. Dined at Lord Grenville's. Cabinet dinner. Stayed till near twelve o'clock discussing the question of making further endeavours to obtain co-operation of the King of Prussia, that is, further endeavours with respect to those used last year; and also on the important and delicate crisis formed by the last letters of Lord Fitzwilliam, which the Duke of Portland had showed to me at St. James's. Heads of the budget also opened. No conclusion come to, either on the Prussian or the Irish business.

19*th.*—Letter from Puisaye, stating that Nepean had no money to advance for articles which he had applied for, and that the order had not yet come for the money, which he has been so long wanting, and for which Mr. Pitt told me yesterday, that he had given an order. Wrote

* Cape of Good Hope.

to Lord Cornwallis about a small quantity of arms, supposed to be kept back. Walsh called on matters connected with the same business.

March 13*th.* — At home till near five. Saw M. de Caraman and the Comte de Bouillé, both from the army, M. de Vauban, Mr. Lewis. Dined at Sir George Cornewall's: only Cholmondeley and M. de Caraman.

24*th.*—Went to the House; Fox's motion on the state of the nation.

April 6*th.*—News arrived of victory in the Mediterranean.

8*th.*—Day of marriage.* Came to Mr. Dundas's at twelve to meet the Duke of York. Council at two.

9*th.*—Meeting again with the Duke of York.

10*th.*—Council at two, on conclusion of business of King of Prussia. Home; thence to House of Commons, where congratulations of marriage; thanks to Admiral Hotham,† &c.; charge against Sir B. Hammet.

11*th.*—Council at two: Prince of Wales's debts. Office till past five. Went home to meet the Marquis de Tinténiac and Madame de Marconnaye—*jolie on ne peut plus.*

13*th.*—Militia Bill—Committee on.

15*th.*—Went to levee with Prince de Rohan; missed presentation; went afterwards to the King. Dined at Lord Mansfield's.

16*th.* — Drawing-room, first after Prince's marriage, with Prince de Rohan.

18*th.*—Saw Mr. Pitt about order for allowance of meat.

29*th.*—Drank tea at Francis's. Francis with leeches for his arm.

* Prince of Wales with Caroline Amelia, daughter of the Duke of Brunswick.

† Admiral Hotham received the thanks of Parliament for his victory over the French fleet, gained on March 14, 1795.

30*th.*—Admiralty to get order for passage of MM. d'Allègre and Boisberthelot.

Mr. Windham to Mrs. Crewe.

December 7, 1795.

All the gentleman-like spirit of the country being fled, it seems to me that a descent into Jacobinism, easy and gradual perhaps, but perfectly certain, is at this moment commenced. Were I twenty years younger, I would pack up my books, and retire to some corner of the world where I might hope to enjoy the use of them unmolested and leave the world to settle its affairs in its own way. There seems to me to be but two modes of life to be followed with any satisfaction, military and literary. The management of civil affairs, depending, as they do, on the consent of others, is liable to be thwarted at every step by their sordidness and folly, is the most thankless employment of all. I am sick of the world and dissatisfied, though not for anything that I have done in the way of public conduct. Farewell!

Yours faithfully,

W. W.

Mr. Windham to Mrs. Crewe.

December 27, 1795.

The world is undone by shabbiness, at least in this country, and by this sacrifice of the right expedient. To a certain degree, it must be made, and it may be the fault of Mr. Burke that he does not make it enough; but I am sure that, by a habit of erring on the other side, as great mischiefs are done, though more gradual and silent, and that the counsels and character of a country become insensibly debased and impoverished, as is eminently the case of ours at present. By this continual yielding, the higher nature becomes at last subjected wholly to the lower, and we are accordingly not governed by Mr. Pitt and others, that we naturally should be, but by Mr. Wilberforce and Mr. This-and-t'other that I could name, and who have not only low and narrow notions of things, but their own little private interest to serve. There are one or two of our friends that have minds of a more plebeian cast than I had been willing to hope. I am not in this number including Pelham, whose views of the war are, according to my conception, perfectly just. I must now go down to some Frenchmen that I have waiting for me in different apartments, and by means of whom I hope to improve the temporary gleam of comfort that has lately come across me.

Yours faithfully,

W. W.

Mrs. Siddons to the Right Hon. W. Windham.

Manchester: May 24, 1796.

My dear Sir,—Your kindness to Mrs. Temple has reached me here, and hurried as I am (for I play every night), I will not suffer the coldness of delay to hang upon my thanks for your kind disposition in her favour; but with a grateful sense of your goodness I seize the first moment of time to tell you that I am, your infinitely obliged and very humble servant,

S. Siddons.

1796.

April 18*th.*—Came to town late. Loan business. New attack by Sheridan about Sombreuil's letters.

23*rd.*—Received fatal news of death of both the De Sérents.

24*th.*—Saw Mr. Pitt; obtained authority to pay Frotté his arrears, and to engage for continuance of the £1,000 per month; letter to that effect to P. de Bouillon by Fruglaye, who set off that night. Letter also written some days before to Gen. Gordon. Saw Lord Spencer: had long conversation about the Royalists.

26*th.*—Wrote to poor M. de la Vieuville's brother confirming the news of his death; surprised by arrival of William, who had come from Corsica in twenty-three days; from Leghorn to Cuxhaven in thirteen.

27*th.*—*Beaconsfield.*—The Comte de la Tour du Pin the only visitor.

May 2*nd.*—Rode in the Park after office. Battle in the ring. Lent horse at my return to William.

7*th.*—Saw Sir Ed. Pellew at the War Office, who confirmed completely all my ideas about Quiberon as a naval station, independent even of view to the Royalists.

9*th.*—Rode in the Park with the Duke of Portland, talking, among other things, of affairs in Corsica.

11*th.*—Letter from Fruglaye mentioning his return with two Frenchmen, one of them the Abbé Raimond, the friend of Charette, the other M. de la Roche St. André.

27*th.*—Finished address in time for press. Dined at Aylsham calling in way at Stratton. Mr. Marsham far in eighty-ninth year; Mrs. Lucy, eighty-six. Walked to

Blickling and drank tea with Mr. Harbord and Lady Caroline.

28*th.*—Came to Felbrigg with George in time for dinner. Walked down to see dragging of ponds.

June 11*th.*—To Beaconsfield by dinner with Mr. Cazales; in the evening to the school with a new party of boys, among whom was Fruglaye's nephew. The Marquis de Rocquefeuille was at Beaconsfield having come down to see his children, one of whom had had the small-pox.

16*th.*—Had been to Drawing-room: introduced to Princess.

23*rd.*—Called on Duke of Portland about Thellusson's business: busied with problem in Maclaurin.

25*th.*—Conversation with Canning* at Foreign Office.

30*th.*—Dinner at Lord Spencer's: present, Lord and Lady Grenville, Lord Pembroke, T. Grenville, Lady Horatia Seymour. Saw M. de Frotté, *le jeune*, and gave him back draft in favour of Comte Williamson: heard his narrative of his meeting his brother.

July 2*nd.*—Called on Mr. Pitt who was gone to Lord Liverpool's, and from thence was to go to Wimbledon. Wrote to Huskisson.

3*rd.*—Letters from P. de Bouillon of 29th, announcing notice of invasion, and mentioning that money (I suppose the 6,000 in specie) not received. News of capture of St. Lucia.

4*th.*—Saw M. de Frotté, M. Mandat, his adjutant-general. M. Mandat had been with the Austrian army and twice gained the medal. Paper from Duc d'Harcourt, with M. de Boterel's memoir circulated by Lord Grenville. Wrote to M. de Frotté (*alias* Couterne) that his arrival was known. Spoke to Mr. P. about M. Thellusson's business†

* Mr. Canning was at this time Under-Secretary at the Foreign Office.

† Captain Lukin married, in 1801, Anne, daughter of Peter Thellusson and sister to the first Lord Rendlesham, which explains Mr. Windham's interest in this business.

at Cabinet; business of Boterel's memorial. Order for departure of Guards recalled.

10*th*.—Saw again M. de Chatillon: received from him picture of Charette.*

18*th*.—Arrived at Beaconsfield; Mrs. Crewe and Lawrence there. Did not leave Beaconsfield, *i. e.* Mr. Burke's, till ten or past. Mr. B. far from well.

19*th*.—Council at Lord Grenville's: question of Duc d'Angoulême; received letters from Puisaye brought by the Abbé Guillo.

20*th*.—Dinner (Cabinet) at Duke of Portland's; business renewed of the Duc d'Angoulême.

21*st*.—Received from Long 3,000*l*., part of what is to be given to Frotté.

22*nd*.—Saw Baron de Rolle: first time since his return from Verona.

24*th*.—Dinner at Lord Liverpool's: present, Duc de Bourbon and M. de Vitry, Lord Macartney, Lord Lewisham, Lord Hawkesbury, Lord Hervey.

28*th*.—Resolution about the King of Prussia, unanimous: reflections belonging thereto.

September 1*st*.—Gave letter of Monsieur to l'Abbé Guillo; second conversation with M. d'Almeida;† despatches from Hammond after interview with King of Prussia.

2*nd*.—News of Lord Mansfield's death.

3*rd*.—Dined with Mary *tête-à-tête*; went upstairs soon after; remained at home all evening, principally employed in reading communications from Duc d'Harcourt, that were sent in circulation. Saw Sir Charles Grey who was just come to town.

4*th*.—Agreeably surprised by meeting Mr. Tryon with letters from Puisaye of the 15th ult.

* Charette, a Vendean chief, executed at Nantes, April 28, 1796.

† M. d'Almeida, Portuguese Minister at London.

th.—Council, where decision respecting Naples confirmed; statement of means of defence; promise of sum for French driven from Jersey. Letters from P. de Bouillon mentioning denunciation of Cointre and landing of Abbé Guillo; close search of Puisaye.

17*th.*—Account of Crawfurd's being killed.

19*th.*—Account from Crawfurd's brother of the 29th August: Crawfurd only wounded. Answer from Naples to French message, saying if France entered the Pope's territories they would likewise. Language from Austria full of magnanimity. Agreed with Long that the money with Sir Edw. Pellew should be appropriated for Dutheil; that he should signify to the same that the 7,000*l.* was ready.

20*th.*—Concluded letter to Duke of York. Proposition from Empress; 300,000*l.* for outfit; 125,000*l.* per month; 300,000*l.* for return. Woronzow to be seen the next day. Mr. Dundas conceived there had been a misunderstanding of our business.

21*st.*—Further defeats of Jourdan's army.

25*th.*—Received letter from Dutheil saying, that money was not paid: wrote in consequence to Lord Grenville and Long. Saw Tryon.

29*th.*—Council again on Russian business: decision that nothing further could be done with respect to assurances to Nelson of keeping the fleet in the Mediterranean.

Mr. Windham to Mrs. Crewe.

Fulham: Sept. 30, 1796.

Where can Pelham have got the notions which you describe, and which are at once so false and contrary to what I conceived him to have entertained? There can be no doubt about the matter. Peace made and the Republic established, there is an end of the power, independence, government, morals, of this country, as well as of every other throughout Europe. It is another Roman Republic that is coming into existence, equally fatal to the independence of other nations and infinitely more so to their virtue and happiness. Yet this is the consummation—a consummation from which nothing but new wars can save us—what the booby politicians in this country are all wishing for and holding out as the only means by which our ruin is to be averted. It is really such a state of stupid infatuation and desperate baseness, as destroys all interest in the country, and puts one, for one's relief and as the only means of escaping from the pain of one's own reflections, upon the fatal expedient of locking oneself up in insensibility and seeking one's satisfactions only from private and personal gratifications.

One fact let me set you right in. There has been nothing amiss in the appointment of Lord Chatham to the presidency. Mr. P. would have been perfectly willing and desirous to give it to the Duke of Devonshire, nor has the D. of D. refused it, I believe, from any opinion that it was not fitting and becoming of him to accept it.

Who is right upon the subject of Irish politics I am not competent to say. Mr. B. is wrong, by excess and exaggeration, I dare say; but whether he is so in the main, I should much doubt.

The Austrian victories stand, at present, as favourably as at any period and are a strong proof of what is to be done by magnanimity and perseverance. We must not holloa, however, even in that quarter, before we are out of the wood.

Farewell! and count upon me as your Redde-crosse Knight to the end of the adventure.

For knights in knightly deed should persevere,
And still continue what at first they were;
Continue and persist in honour's fair career.

W. W.

October 1*st.*—Saw Captain Reedsdale who had been taken in the Corunna packet. Asked Cazales' opinion about the *Agens du Roi:* he did not know much of them, *but* did not seem to have much opinion of them. Had not heard of M. Brottier. Thought them *des gens timides*, and who might be doubted in every respect. Application from Tryon about Morin and his brother: has got his 1,000*l*.

3rd.—Money to Dutheil not yet paid but promised for to-morrow. Saw Hammond, who showed me a letter from Harderberg, relative to prospect of things in France; he deprecates peace till after the ensuing elections.

5th.—Dinner at Mr. Pitt's before cockpit. Drove back to Fulham after cockpit was over. Found that passport was come from the Directory.

7th.—Dinner at Woodford's with Mr. Burke. Reading 'Regicide Peace.' Wrote to P. de Bouillon on subject of following Puisaye's wishes relative to agents.

8th.—Went to Somerset House to know if anything could be done about William. Conversation with Cazales who was setting out for Edinburgh. Mentioned to him fact about the Duc de la Vauguyon and consulted with about *les Agens du Roi*. Agreed that it was best that no movement should be made at present in the interior. Wrote to Duke of Portland about situation of those forced from Jersey and who were not *aux secours*.

16th.—Sunday. Breakfasted in drawing-room. Set off for Beaconsfield. Day delicious. Indulged in musing.

18th.—Day in the House about additions to militia, &c. when I expected to be obliged to speak. Motion about increase of defensive force.

19th.—Cabinet dinner at Lord Spencer's. Decided on not evacuating Corsica and on despatch to Empress.

26th.—Went in to King. Cabinet at Lord Liverpool's. I mentioned the business of parole to prisoners and General Pitt's* letter, and the idea of school for soldiers' children. Mr. Dundas and Chatham not there.

30th.—Letters from Sir M. Eden,† of the 8th, I think, and from Wickham about same date. Account in latter of M. Pellet, sent by King of Prussia to raise the Swiss regiments formerly in pay of Holland. Directory oppose the measure. Haugwitz co-operates with them

* Brother to Mr. Pitt.

† Sir Morton Eden, Ambassador at the Court of Vienna.

against Bischopswerder. Dissatisfaction supposed to be felt by Directory of contrariety and opposition in Prussian counsels.

Mr. Windham to Mrs. Crewe.

October 31, 1796.

Your letter is so good, such a genuine effusion of pure, virtuous feeling and native sense, that after taking away the last page in which there is something about Irish politics, which in the intolerance of Beaconsfield might not pass, I shall send thither the remainder, as the most gratifying praise that Mr. B. can receive.

Do not imagine that in such a state of things I shall be induced to take a new lease of my connection with the Ministry, or do more than drag on in my present situation till I see what turn things take. If I could have been sure that Lord Malmesbury's despicable embassy would succeed and that peace must be the immediate consequence, I should have been out long since. It does not appear to me at present, though in that one must be regulated by circumstances, that I shall ever outlive, ministerially, the arrival of a French ambassador in London. It is enough to outlive the knowledge of an English minister in Paris. But that alone, though conclusive as to honour, is not quite so as to ruin. When the other event takes place, from that moment we go sinking, lower and lower, into Jacobinism; Mr. Pitt, however, remaining astride of the country, unless,

> —— by some *good* chance
> The strong rebuff of a tempestuous cloud,
> Instinct with fire and nitre, hurries us,

either aloft or sideways, as it may happen, but with some violent concussion that may throw Mr. Pitt out of his seat and substitute Mr. Fox in his place, to be succeeded by Sheridan, by Horne Took, and so on through the long dynasty of murderous democrats and proconsuls of France.

My mind gets so soured by all that passes and that has long passed, that I can image to myself no pleasure but in the prospect of the vengeance that will be taken on all those who, by their baseness, their selfishness, their wickedness, or their folly, have contributed to bring on the ruin that awaits us. We abuse the emigrants for their hostility to one another. What sort of charity shall I feel for the Dukes of Bedford, the Plumbers, the Cokes, and other large lists that I could name, when we meet in exile and beggary in some town on the Continent? My only consolation will be, that their wretchedness, from the greater indulgences which they have always required and enjoyed, will be something sharper than my own. Let them be well drenched with the ingredients of their own cup. My only satisfaction for the draught of this beverage which I shall have to take myself, will be the wry faces which I shall see them make at it.

Farewell. When England becomes too vile or too dangerous to live in and we meet in Siberia, we shall at least have the satisfaction of thinking that we are not the authors of our own calamities. W. W.

—*From the Crewe Papers.*

November 3rd.—News of capture of Dutch ships at Saldanha. Conversation about answer to French Directory. Opinions of Mr. Pitt upon that subject.

4th.—Recorder's report. Cabinet; went thither with Lord Chatham, with whom I had had satisfactory conversation at Queen's House. Cabinet, in which paper produced, in answer to Directory's note to Lord Malmesbury's communication. Recommendation about Duc de Castries to have command of French corps and O'Connell as Adjutant-General to them. House of Commons. Nothing material. Answer from Mr. Pitt about application of preceding night. Went to dine with him: present, Speaker, Lord Hawkesbury, Steele, Elliot, and Long, afterwards Wilberforce.

5th.—Saw Chevalier Almeida.

6th.—After dinner drove to Prince de Léon: Byng, Lady Guildford, Lord Mendip.

7th.—Learnt from Mr. Dundas that, without Council, arrangement made for Portugal. 1800 men, British troops; Stuart to be the general. Draft to Vienna drawn by Mr. Pitt; Lord Grenville being absent on account of Mr. Neville's death.

8*th.*—Went with Mr. Byng to see trees found near Lord Grenville's. Letter to Duke of York recommending Gardiner and Hutchinson for foreign corps in Portugal, with other arrangements, particularly O'Connell. Lord Mulgrave for chief command.

12*th.*—Went to office; saw Delancey; thence to F. O.; thence to dinner with Chancellor, Pitt, Lord Chatham, Speaker, Wilberforce, Dr. Scott, Mr. Corry, Lord Westmoreland, Lord Mornington. Stayed talking to the Chancellor after the rest were gone on the subject of a paper which he had put into my hand relative to Finance.

News of successes on the Rhine. Extraordinary Gazette to come out.

13*th.*—Walked with Lord Hawkesbury up Constitution Hill to Berkeley Square, where called on Lady Anne Bernard.

15*th.*—Letter from M. Saladin mentioning that the small cantons had shown a great zeal to furnish their contingent of 18,000 for the protection of their neutrality. Resolved to shirk all duties, levee, Cabinet, &c. Indulged too long in reading 'Philosophical Transactions.'

16*th.*—Took walk to Putney Common. Came to my own room to tea, and continued reading communications from Jersey relative to Prigent. Timms, the messenger, came from Lord Malmesbury. M. Duverne arrived.

17*th.*—Council. Talked over terms of peace. Wait for writing at length to Lord Malmesbury till accounts shall come from Vienna.

18*th.*—Dinner at Lord Lucan's: present, Lord and Lady Spencer, Lady Caroline Barham, Lady Pembroke. Wrote to P. de Bouillon with short letter enclosed to Puisaye.

19*th.*—Ellis arrived from France. Lady Elliot landed at Weymouth. Letter from Sir Sidney Smith of 9th brought by M. Duverne.

26*th.*—*Oxford.* Saw Dean of Christ Church before I came away; also Winstanley and Mr. Loveday. Got to Beaconsfield by dinner: continued reading by the way Polybius. No additional person but Nagle. Received official report of Austrian successes on the Rhine and in Italy.

27*th.*—Account of capture of Amboyna and Banda.

28*th.*—Meeting of Parliament after the adjournment. State of Ellis's opinions: 'that France, unable and unwilling to propagate its opinions; unable, as having no money, and being no longer able to employ revolutionary measures; unwilling, as being the country of all others that is the most impressed with the mischievous tendency of its own principles—mean nothing but quiet enjoyment of their own constitution.'

29*th.*—Went to Foreign Office. Saw Ellis. Particular conversation with Canning. Wish that there had been greater intercourse: same sentiment had been expressed by Rose: lamented influence acquired by others in consequence rather of habit than deliberate preference. Great superiority of Pitt over Lord Grenville. It seemed a little as if Ellis was acquainted with the subject of it. I went to see a letter from Vienna which had come two or three days ago with answer about ——.

December 1*st.*—Dinner at home: Admiral Christian and General Simcoe. Read two satires of Juvenal. M. Duverne introduced to me by the Duc d'Harcourt.

2*nd.*—Dinner at Huskisson's.

3*rd.*—Conversation with Duverne. More conversation with Canning; though short, to same effect as former. Letters from Lord Malmesbury of 28th ult. Directory seemed to admit basis. Thinks that no stand will be made but about Netherlands. Letters from Naples. Peace not yet ratified; was not signed by Prince of Belmonte, but by approbation of Lord Malmesbury.

5*th.*—Council. Debated whether '*projet*' should be

offered without requiring declaration from them as to Belgium being, or not, an object of treaty.

8th.—Went to House for report of Budget not expecting to stay—warm debate.

10*th.*—Stayed at Fulham all day notwithstanding Council, in which Lord Malmesbury's instructions settled. Wrote letter to Mulgrave. Thought about the business for Wednesday, viz. Austrian remittance, as also that of La Fayette.

13*th.*—Some attendance in the House. The day, I think, of Jekyll's question about employment of the troops at Northampton.

14*th*—Went up late for debate on Austrian remittance; had been employed in thinking on question all morning. Did not speak though the fairest occasion for it was given, and though I am persuaded now it would have answered in every respect. I have done nothing but regret it ever since and with reason; except that it is not reasonable to regret that which cannot be recalled.

16*th.*—Debate on Marquis de la Fayette.

17*th.*—At office pretty early; remained till past three, settling with General Delancey appointments of barrack-masters. Went to House, which sat, and should have presented Bill on Tower Hamlets but it was not ready; King's message about remittance; thence to Foreign Office; thence dinner at Duke of Portland's: present, Chancellor, Lord Cornwallis, Lord Spencer, Lord Chatham, Pitt, Sir Joseph Banks and American minister.

19*th.*—Rode in Hyde Park: saw men practising the new sword exercise. Came away at nine, after presenting the Mutiny Bill. Feel, I am afraid, the effect of London, still more of Westminster, air.

21*st.*—News from Colpoys of the 18th, who had received account of the sailing of the Brest fleet and was going in the track which they were known to have taken.

23rd.—Council on American claims, or aid to Portugal, viz. present of such stores as can be spared, and advance or pledge to purchase others. Saw Sir S. Smith, Duc d'Harcourt, and M. Duverne. Despatch, stating that Lord Malmesbury was coming away.

24th.—Lord Malmesbury's return, having been ordered to quit Paris in forty-eight hours. Papers to be laid before Parliament. Dinner at home. Interruption during the time by writing to Mr. Burke. The Comte d'Andigné called for an answer to Mad^e. de ——. Mention of the other d'Andigné, formerly captain in Regiment de Brie, and now works and maintains himself as a joiner. Lawrence called afterwards; went with him to Foreign Office.

Expressions, τοῦ δεῖνος, that he never believed any account received from a Frenchman; that he had not made up his mind as to the opinion most proper to be supported in France (*i. e.* as seemed to be explained), the opinion most likely to succeed. A strong confirmation in my mind that there was no serious wish for the re-establishment of royalty.

31st.—News of French fleet having been in Bantry Bay. Letters did not leave Cork till the 29th.

1797.

January 2nd.—Council, I think, where it was settled to remit *aux Agens du Roi* 20,000*l.* per month for three months, besides other future and additional allowances. Proposal by me for addition to Puisaye about which nothing settled.

5th.—Note from Duke of Harcourt about state of those dismissed from the Cadres. Letter to Pitt, claiming addition to Puisaye and Frotté.

7th.—Letters from Bantry Bay. The second eight ships still at mouth of bay. Letters from Russia, with refusal of offer, and generally of taking part in the war.

8th.—Had intended to go to Beaconsfield in morning; had ordered the horses for evening. Wish now that I had gone, though certainly I have reason to think that I should not have succeeded. Sat up late reading the 'Old Manor House.'

9th.—Breakfasted at Salt Hill. Tried again, for the first time since the time for my sitting for my picture to Sir Joshua,* the calculation in my head. As far as I recollect now (February 2nd); the numbers were 6824 × 2632 = 17,960,768. The last time but one of my trying anything of the sort, as far at least as I recollect, was upon the same road in 1783.

11th.—St. James's after levee. First time of seeing the

* The portrait of Mr. Windham by Sir Joshua Reynolds is now in the Kensington Gallery. There is a full length portrait of him by Hoppner in St. Andrew's Hall, Norwich, and one by Sir Thomas Lawrence, in University College, Oxford.

King since return of Lord Malmesbury. Dinner at Mr. Dundas': present, Mr. Pitt, Duke of Portland, Lord Liverpool, Lord Spencer, Lord Chatham.

14*th.*—At home all the morning receiving French, viz. MM. de la Boissière, Chapdelaine, La Roche St. André, Le Braux, Potier.

17*th.*—After breakfast went to see the gun at Blackfriars and afterwards engine. Engine works, upon an average, sixteen hours a-day, sixteen strokes a minute, and thirty-two gallons, I think, each stroke. Wrote strong and earnest letter to Mr. Burke in consequence of accounts received.

19*th.*—Set out with Dr. King for Beaconsfield.

20*th.*—Returned with Mr. Burke to town.

24*th.*—Mr. Burke returned to Beaconsfield.

26*th.*—Letters for Puisaye and Prince de Bouillon, to be taken by Boterel, &c.

27*th.*—Boterel, Chatillon and La Saille, set off early in morning for Portsmouth.

30*th.*—George, jun., and Robert, dined here. Had been at the battle between Wood and Bartholomew.

February 1*st.*—Found letters from Prince de Bouillon and Puisaye, enclosing one to Duke of Harcourt and to Chatillon, &c. Went with them to Lord Grenville's whom I saw at his return from St. James's. Wrote letter to Puisaye in answer, and enclosed to Sir P. Parker.

4*th.*—Arrived at Bath between six and seven. At Mr. Burke's, No. 11, North Parade, till bedtime.

5*th.*—Fatal news from army of Italy.* Actions from 9th to 16th January. Dined with Mrs. Burke. Mr. Burke not very well. Have nearly finished Professor Robinson's MS. Have been reading parts of Keill's 'Phy. Sect.'

6*th.*—Called on Mr. Burke; went with him to Wilber-

* Austrian marshals defeated by Buonaparte at Rivoli, January 14th; capitulation of Mantua, February 2nd.

force; did not return till four. Read in book lent by Wilberforce, a Mr. Fuller against Dr. Priestley. Went to North Parade, where finding Mr. B. very well, went to ball to Miss Cholmondeleys.

7*th.*—Stayed at Mr. Burke's till half-past ten, he having had a return of his vomitings. I almost despair. Called again in North Parade. Home: wrote letter to Dutheil.

8*th.*—Walked to Parade before breakfast to enquire after Mr. Burke. Wrote from before two till near four. Again to Parade. Wrote till dressing for the Duchess of York: present, Lady Altamont and Lady M. Howe, Miss Cholmondeley, Duchess of Newcastle, Lord Coleraine, Lords Somerville, Northey, Fitzgerald.

10*th.*—Wrote letter to Lady Asgill. Melancholy fate!

12*th.*—Increase of burthens in consequence of the war; I think, 6,000,000*l.* Opinion about Prince of Wales's succession, confirming Burke's idea.

14*th.*—Conversation with Grenville about state of things, in which he agreed with me.

15*th.*—Dined at Lord Grenville's. Cabinet. Nothing considered but letters from the Prince of Wales about Ireland.

19*th.*—Called on Lord Spencer to talk over Whitbread's motion for Friday.

22*nd.*—Paper communicated by Lord Malmesbury from General Stampfort,* who dates from Brunswick. Speaks of the effects of the French Revolution rendering all other Governments feeble, timid, and indecisive. Recommends, in a memoir written before the Empress's death, a plan of defensive war, occupying the right bank of the Rhine with 120,000, and making incursions and wasting the country opposite. Communication from Mr. Pitt, at dinner at Chancellor's. Lord Grenville of opinion

* A general in the Dutch service, preceptor to the young Prince of Orange, a very able man and an excellent writer.

that the late expedition proves the improbability of success in any similar one. Would not have got to Cork; could not have remained there. No possibility of doing anything by invasion here or in any country that would exert itself. Country only frightened because not taught better. Lord Spencer thinks they would have got to Cork. Lord Liverpool's hint to recommencing hostilities upon them. Saw M. de Gourdeau.

25*th*.—News of descent in Wales.*

26*th*.—To town in morning having heard account of descent in Wales. Account of surrender. Council at Mr. Pitt's, afterwards at Buckingham House.

28*th*.—Debate on notice, I think, of Fox, relative to affairs of Bank.

March 2*nd*.—Fatal news of the arrest of Puisaye which seems but too true.

3*rd*.—Saw M. de la Garde,† who gave me some consolation about M. de Puisaye; principally founded on a letter said to have been written by him on the 18th ult. News of Admiral Jervis's victory on the 14th ult. Debate on Whitbread's motion about Admiralty. Spoke.

4*th*.—Met at Mr. Pitt's on instruction to the Bank. Talk with Canning at the Foreign Office. Thence to Admiralty to examine prisoners from Wales, viz. Tate, Le Brun *alias* Baron de Rochemure.

5*th*.—Saw M. de Williamson to enquire about the M. Rochemure (le Baron de), who had been in the Cadres, and was second in command of the expedition to Wales.

6*th*.—Saw M. de Boterel fils; his report of M. de Rochemure. Office. Duke of Portland's. M. de Boterel again, with account of his father's being landed. Stayed to get his passport and by those means was luckily at

* French force at Fishguard Point.

† La Garde was Secretary-General to the Directory, and communicated the discussions and correspondence of the Government to Maret, to whose party he belonged.

home when M. de P. came. Arrival of M. de Puisaye, accompanied by M. de la Saille et M. Duval. M. de Boterel had remained at Weymouth with L'Abbé Guillo.

8*th*.—Fast-day.

9*th*.—Duke of York's levee at Horse Guards; afterwards to Drawing-room; stayed later than usual talking to Sir R. Calder. Motion relative to public credit.

10*th*.—Motion of Sheridan for paying off the debt to the Bank.

11*th*.—Meant to have gone to Fulham, but could not get away in morning and stayed afterwards to see Sir Gilbert Elliot, who I found was to be at Lord Malmesbury's. Attending at Treasury and Foreign Office to get money.

12*th*.—News of the removal of the Duc de la Vauguyon.

13*th*.—Came to town by one to Mr. Pitt, in consequence of notice. No time to think of the business; Harrison's motion.

14*th*.—Received from Canning 4,000*l*., viz. 3,000*l*. for February and 1,000*l*. for the present month.

15*th*.—On coming home found Lieut. Pierson with letters, &c., from Commodore Nelson. To St. James's late. where went in to King and left Nelson's account of his part of action.* 500*l*. to Prigent for Puisaye, 500*l*. to Frotté.

16*th*.—Breakfasted at Lord Spencer's, expecting to meet Sir G. Elliot and Colonel Drinkwater.

19*th*.—MM. de Belcourt, La Saille, and Boterel to dinner. Council at Chancellor's: letter from Nautical, telling me of the departure of Forestier and Caris. Letter to Mr. Carter to stop them.

21*st*.—Club: Fox, Sir Charles Bunbury. Drove to House of Lords, where had been motion of Lord Moira's about Ireland.

22*nd*.—Saw Lady Spencer first time since her illness.

* The boarding of the Spanish ships 'San Nicolas' and 'San Josef.'

Account of Admiral Hotham and Lord Keith. Lord Mornington had been intended for India; stopped by D.'s (Duke's) objection to the lady. Motion for indemnity at the Bank. Went to Lady Malmesbury's; sat down by Lord M.

23rd.—Fox's motion respecting Ireland.

24th.—Paid 100*l.* to Abbé Guillo for sixteen persons going by Guernsey into France, including 20*l.* for Prigent.

25th.—Rode to Fulham to breakfast; read while there chiefly papers of Addison. Dined at Duke of P.'s with Sir G. Elliot and M. Pozzo di Borgo.

26th.—Called at Lady Spencer's and had long talk. After dinner sorted Puisaye's letters. Learnt from Lady S. history of the Prince of Wales's offers to Lord Fitzwilliam, to Fox, and to Grey; contemptuous answer of the latter. How this communicated? Resolution of the King thereupon relative to Queen. Learnt from Hammond of letters from Vienna, stating the offers made by General Clark* and their honourable rejection of them. The offers were—Restitution of Italian Dominions, Bavaria, and Indemnification for losses on this side the Rhine. The Court of Vienna states only the necessity of a naval force in the Mediterranean and pecuniary succours.

27th.—Debate, I have a notion, about Bank, in which I should have taken part.

30th.—Went into House of Lords, where Lord Oxford's complaint of his protestation not having appeared.

31st.—Apprehensions of Portugal making peace. Menacing language to be held. Reluctance on the part of Mr. P. from fear that if it failed of its effect, matters might be still worse. Idea still discoverable in Mr. D. of foreign acquisition. Despatch from General Stuart marking the deplorable neglect of preparation in their Government. Nothing further gained in respect of naval cooperation in the Adriatic; but promise of squadron of

* Clark, afterwards Duc de Feltre and Minister of War to Napoleon.

frigates. Lord Grenville's opinion as to continuance and duration of war. Resolution to give discharge in full to Royalists. Lord Grenville had seen Frotté; great commendation of him. Proposal to give him sum of money and have done with him. Report on Bank Committee. Fox's argument about second promises: wished to have answered it, but prevented. Council.

April 2nd.—Came up to town by three to meet Mr. Pitt preparatory to Sheridan's motion. Met him and Mr. Dundas on the road. Dined at Sir Charles Bunbury's: present, Duké of Leeds, Dr. Scott, Dr. Wharton, Malone. Note from M. de Brecourt; business of Fruglaye; too late in consequence. Called in way back to Fulham, and sat with him alone till past ten. Received and read before I went to bed his letter to the King.

3rd.—Departure of Frotté for the interior. Council on letter to Vienna in answer to their communication of the rejection of General Clark's offer. Agreed, I think, to offer same terms for 'an exchange' as was before offered for 'Belgium itself.' Measure for finally closing with the Royalists and casting them off, confirmed.

4th.—Stayed all the morning at Fulham preparing for business expected in the House, viz. Sheridan's motion on remittance to Emperor, *i. e.* thinking of that more than of anything else. In riding to town fell in with Ryder, afterwards with Villiers. Felt uncommonly faint and weak. Day in the House very satisfactory. Sheridan's motion: speakers, Sheridan, Pitt, Fox; Sheridan in reply, Sir W. Pulteney.

5th.—Dreadful news from Bath; great and immediate danger. Dinner at home; Lord Pembroke, Douglas, Munday, Sir G. Cornewall, Sir Gilbert Elliot, M. Pozzo di Borgo. Saw for the first time the Comte de Guest, the brother of the Chevalier who had been here when Puisaye was. Army extraordinaries, that had been presented before Christmas. Bank business.

12th.—Regretted not having got Mrs. Crewe to take me to Lady Palmerston's who had written to propose for me to call. In interval of attendance at St. James's saw Elizabeth and Cecilia. 'I honour you for your firmness, &c.'*

15th.—Arrived at Bath about one. Read by the way Apollonius: much satisfaction in it. Invitation from Lady Cork to a breakfast, which she was giving to the officers of the Supplementary Militia. Mr. B. grievously changed since I had last seen him. Lord Hawkesbury here, Wilberforce, and Blanket.

17th.—Account of mutiny at Portsmouth.

18th.—Blanket breakfasted with me: party with Lady Cork to see caisson: inventor's name, Waldon; comes from Lichfield; bold and original invention. Dinner at Lord Cork's. Called on Mr. Burke, where Sir W. Scott, Lawrence, and Dr. Burney, junior, who is on a small tour with his son round by Chepstow. I had found Lawrence and Burney below, and sat with them for some time talking of matters of Greek literature.

21st.—Called on Mr. Burke; found Wilberforce there; walked away with him. Met M. Boisberthelot, with whom had conversation about probable or possible course of things, viz. idea that invasion here might possibly lead in the end to reunion with the Royalists. Mr. Burke showed Wilberforce what he had caused to be extracted from the period of the Succession War, viz. that when the whole trade of the country was not more than six millions, we had expended more than four in the subsidising and maintaining armies upon the Continent. Wilberforce described his own opinion as always having been against the West Indian expeditions and for operations on the coast of France. He seemed, however, to have no adequate ideas of the means existing for the latter pur-

* These were the words the King, George III., addressed to Mr. Windham at this audience. They alluded to his constant opposition to the abortive negotiation for peace.

pose. I could have been glad, therefore, to have had him to dinner some day with M. Boisberthelot. He stated to me strongly the confidence entertained at first of the facility with which the war was to be terminated.

22*nd.*—Lord Hawkesbury called at a little before nine; walked out with him by the pump-room to his door. Day delicious. Meditated on public matters. Read Apollonius. Dined at Marlborough. Contrived floats for caisson.

In this and other conversations Lord Hawkesbury very right in all his ideas as to the errors of the war.

23*rd.*—I slept at Sir Thomas Rich's. Breakfasted partly with him. His idea, that the foundation of mutinies in the navy was laid by Lord Sandwich's method of separating officers from men and removing the men by squads into different ships; when crews were removed, rivalry between ships then destroyed, or rather between crews.

24*th.*—Saw General Forbes: his opinion that the order for withdrawing all British officers from the Black corps is very bad: no other security against great abuse. European troops still best on trying occasions. Mulattoes utterly and universally faithless: about 30,000 in the island,* I understood, males and capable of bearing arms. Thinks the fever accidental and hopes it will not return. Cannot keep the island but by aid of a large part of the natives.

26*th.*—Came to town for levee. Not in with the King. King spoke so little as to give reason to think that some effect produced by the letters from General Stuart complaining of Emigrant Corps. Letters from General Stuart to Mr. Dundas; great reason to think the complaint not true. A more direct avowal from Mr. Fox than ever before of intention to revolutionise the country.

28*th.*—Walked with Lord Cornwallis to George Street,

* The Mauritius.

where met Mrs. Guise. Dressed for Recorder's report; too late, but stayed for council. Subject—the Marriage. Read Wickham's * letters of April 1st; chiefly relative to communications with Baptiste. Strange imprudence of the P. de C. M. Mongaillard.† Proposes remittance of money, 30,000*l.*, of which has advanced part. Conference with General Mack; his idea of the use to be made of his force. Bad opinions and feelings about the Condé army. W. much struck with his manner. Villars (Q. real name) only intermediate between him and Baptiste.

29*th.*—Went with Sir Thomas Frankland to Academy. Great picture, Lawrence's 'Devil.' Pleasant, as I always find that dinner.

30*th.*—Tempted to come up to town; met Speaker and rode backwards and forwards with him. Foreign Office. Good news from Tyrol. Walked away with Canning and Charles Ellis. Got on my horse at Buckingham Gate. Employed, upon recollection, in morning as well as evening, principally in reading Gifford's answer to Erskine.

May 1*st.*—Lord William Bentinck took his seat in this Parliament. Went with Grenville to play; first time, I believe, since '93. Mrs. Siddons' benefit.

The Right Hon. Edmund Burke to R. Troward, Esq.

Bath: May 1, 1797.

Dear Sir,—If I am at all really recovering, it is very slowly and with many drawbacks. I am glad you are pleased with the figures for the monument of our late friend. I thought Hickey's design admirable, and I should think the execution of the gentleman who has undertaken to finish it equal to the original model. As to the epitaph, which I sketched, it was my design to make it plain, grave, and moral. In general

* English minister in Switzerland.

† A political intriguer attached to the army of Prince de Condé; he had been banished from London, under the Alien Act, in 1794.

I prefer epitaphs in prose—you may put more into a line, if that is convenient for the marble. It need not be divided into paragraphs; but the place of division may be supplied by one of those large full points in the middle of the line, after the last letter; as we see done in some ancient monuments. I cannot contrive to shorten what I have wrote more than by the few lines that I have marked; and I am sure that my faculties are not capable of anything better than what I have done. As I ought to do, I have done my best. If anything were to be corrected I was in hopes Mr. Windham would rather have exercised his own judgment than remitted the affair to mine, which is at present very infirm, and certainly no better than it was when I wrote the inscription.

As to the verses, they appear to me to be very spirited; but they are a copy of verses, and not an epitaph. I am in general an enemy to epitaphs in verse; but when they are used they ought not to exceed ten lines at most, and ought rather to resemble some of the fine serious epigrams of Martial than the style of an elegy, to be distinguished by their fine finishing and polish more than for any stretch of fancy or exuberance of thought. I can do nothing towards the correction of these verses. To write a verse is a matter of great labour; to attempt to correct it is still greater; and I am ill-fitted for labour of the slightest kind. Of all this Mr. Wallis, on consulting with Mr. Windham, will be the best judge. You may show him this letter; it is entirely submitted to Mr. Wallis's discretion, but I could wish it a discretion so advised as I propose.

The erection of this monument does honour to Mr. Wallis's friendship, which does not end with the life of its object, but extends to his fame.

I am, with very great regard and esteem, dear Sir,

Your faithful and obliged humble servant,

EDMUND BURKE.

To R. Troward, Esq.

[The preceding letter refers to an inscription for the monument of Garrick, which had been composed by Mr. Burke. This inscription was found to be too long for the tablet and was not adopted; but a copy of it has been preserved amongst Mr. Windham's papers, which enables the editor of this Diary to publish it. It is in the following terms:—

TO THE MEMORY OF DAVID GARRICK,

Whose remains lie interred near the monument of William Shakespeare and close to the body of Samuel Johnson.

He was born at Hereford in the year 1716, and died in London in the year 1779.

Under him the English dramatic representation took a new form; he brought it nearer to the standard of nature, and to the expression of real passion.

Shakespeare was the chosen object of his study: in his action, and in his declamation [inexhaustible] he expressed all the fire, the enthusiasm, the energy, the facility, the endless variety of that great poet. Like him he was equally happy in the tragic and the comic style.

He entered into the true spirit of the poets, because he was himself a poet, and wrote many pieces with elegance and spirit.

He raised the character of his profession to the rank of a liberal art, not only by his talents, but by the regularity and probity of his life and the elegance of his manners. His friendships were sincere, his manners were amiable. He excelled in all relations of domestic and social life. His conversation was gay, cheerful, and ingenious. His wit was without levity, affectation, or malice, and as inoffensive as it was pointed. His society was therefore courted and cultivated by all those of his time who were the most distinguished by their taste and erudition.

His memory will be long honoured by all who are sensible how much a solid, refined, and moral taste, in its public pleasures, contributes to the improvement and glory of a great nation.]

2nd.—Went to Mrs. Siddons', where met Mrs. Twiss.

3rd.—Cabinet dinner at Lord Spencer's; all there but the Chancellor. Lord Cornwallis seemingly impatient of my censure of present mode of firing helter-skelter;

denies that platoon-firing, ever observed in action. Nothing decided but the grounds on which the proceeding should be continued on the Emperor's loan, notwithstanding the news of the preliminaries being signed. It stands at present in a postscript in Moreau's letter. Some talk about Ireland and proposal of Mr. D. for the sending a few more regiments. Notion of Lord Liverpool of bringing things to a crisis; nothing decided. Touched shortly on my idea of changing the system of the war and the necessity that would arise for it—not relished. Lord Grenville's idea, that if the peace with the Emperor concluded, the armies would infallibly be brought in by the Directory to establish a Jacobin system. In that case, continuance of war certain. In the other event, thinks that the Moderate party might be desirous of peace.

4th.—Waked in night, *i. e.* about four o'clock, and lighting a candle, read for about an hour to the end of the 'Electra.' Dressed and went to Drawing-room: Mrs. Coke, Lord Andover, Lady Jerningham, whom I had not seen since her return to town. Lady Inchiquin expected to see masks.

7th.—Went to Canning preparatory to our going together to Addiscombe. Lord and Lady Hawkesbury there and Lord Hervey. Felt particularly pleasant. Read before going to bed with great delight in 'Scotch Ballads.'

8th.—Rode to town in morning. Uncommon benefit from the country. News upon arrival of second mutiny. Would not go down to the House, being so dissatisfied with course decided upon. Dined at home. Called in evening at Lord Spencer's, thence to Lord Malmesbury's, where I found Ellis quite of my opinion.

9th.—Council on mutiny. My opinion as before, that Parliament should set forth the fact of the proceeding or fulfil the promises of the Admiralty, and declare those outlaws who would not return to their duty either immediately or within a certain time. Pitt had originally intended this, but yielded to the other opinion; Lord Grenville decidedly of the same opinion with myself. Would not go down to the House. Company to dinner: Anstruther, Lord Pembroke, Fullarton, Ellis, Lord Winchelsea and afterwards Lawrence.

10*th.*—Council on further proceedings. Despatches, too, had at this time arrived from Sir M. Eden of the 29th ult., still no communication of the particulars of the preliminaries. 'His Imp. Maj.' wished the King to keep all his conquests. Some conversation of this,—more of Ireland, on which I declared my opinion for negotiation combined with force. Lord Howe had been with most, if not all, the Cabinet, at Lord Spencer's overnight: went away to-day after conference with Mr. Pitt.

11*th.*—Council on report of intended mutiny in the Guards to-morrow morning. Though, I think, the thing wholly unlikely, the consequences if they should take place, too dreadful not to be more provided against. There does not seem to be anything to prevent their being masters of the Tower, the Mint, the Palace and the Cabinet. It is many months since I urged to Lord Cornwallis the not leaving all the arms of the country at the Tower. Drove to Lady Malmesbury's, where were Lady C. Bentinck, Lady Ryder and her sister.

13*th.*—Saw Mr. Williams for first time: called in consequence on Wilberforce. His opinions agree with mine as to mode of proceeding in respect of fleet.

16*th.*—Grey's motion for censure.

20*th.*—Meeting at the Duke of York's, with officers, to settle pay and allowances. Saw Dr. Hussey on his return from Ireland.

21*st.*—Came up to town to War Office; afterwards to Duke of York's, to concert further on augmentation to the army.

22nd.—Day of Windsor ball. Went to House and presented Estimates; urged to-day, in conversation with Mr. Pitt, in walking from the House, the making concession and changing the government in Ireland.

The Right Hon. Edmund Burke to R. Troward, Esq.

Bath: May 22, 1797.

My dear Sir,—I am to quit this place to-morrow, having received no benefit, and expecting no further. As to the epitaph, I cannot, upon my plan, and in order to do full justice to the subject, shorten it very considerably. They who like an impassioned style upon monuments will not be pleased with this, whether it be long or short; but for my part I hate all general expressions of admiration, which may as well be applied to one man as another. I think these things in churches, particularly, ought to have a moral turn, and ought to account why it is fit that an actor should have a place in so solemn a temple, among legislators, heroes, saints, and the ornaments of science, erudition, and genius. I think Garrick well entitled to that place, though I think that others of the same profession were not; and the reason ought to be assigned, as in that epitaph I have assigned it. I could wish that Mr. Windham could see this epitaph, together with this, and my last letter to you upon the subject. But, to be sure, it is Mr. Wallis that must finally determine. For my part, I am the more indifferent about everything of the kind, as I do not think that these memorials, nor the temples that contain them, or any of our frail works, can long continue. If you can't get at Mr. Windham (as in the present state I don't wonder that you cannot, for I think he must be nearly heart-broken, as in truth I am), be so good as to hand the papers I speak of to Mr. Woodford, who has the last chance of catching a flying moment of his leisure.

Believe me, my dear Sir,

Your very faithful and obedient servant,

Edmund Burke.

To R. Troward, Esq.

23rd.—Motion for Repeal of Bills. General exposition of Fox's view of things, confirming what I had supposed and referred to a conversation which I recollect particularly to have had with Hare; though also, I think, with Fox.

24th.—Moved resolution in the Committee on Estimates about Augmentation of Pay. (Taken with a sudden absence of recollection.) Fox went in to the King.

28th.—Went with Woodford to Beaconsfield. Long discourse of Mr. B. about the state of the trade with Ireland, which he considers as wholly in favour of that country, that is, as being a trade which they should desire. (The measures with respect to Ireland must be diatetic.) Mode of farming does not admit of their breeding sheep.

31st.—Council in morning. Measure agitated about sending to France: Lord Grenville against, at least in the form proposed: Lord Spencer rather so: Lord C. vehement for: said enough to leave no doubt of my own opinion; an affectation in speaking of it as a thing rather agreed.

June 1st.—Proclamation to be laid before Parliament. News that Duncan was left in Ousely Bay, with only his own ship and Admiral Onslow's. Question a little agitated, whether any regulation to be made about prize-money: I rather brought it forward and inclined to it. Touched again upon measures for securing Purfleet and for raising corps of Chasseurs. Indemnification to subscribers to Loyalty Loan. Spoke on doctrine laid down by Speaker.

2nd.—Proposal for Bill against seducing soldiers. Missed an opportunity of saying a few words.

3rd.—Brought in and read twice, I think, Bill for preventing endeavours to seduce soldiers, &c. As it happened, no discussion, all passed unanimously. After the House was up went with Mrs. Lukin, Mary, and Kitty to the Exhibition and to the wild beasts. Went to Lady Malmesbury's, where stayed till past twelve, later than was wise. In the course of the evening, Ellis's, Lord Granville Leveson, Sneyd, Canning, Mrs. Robinson.

5*th.*—Celebration of birthday. Dined with Duke of Portland: present, Duke of Montrose, Duke of Atholl, Lord Liverpool, Ryder, Grenville, Sir W. Scott, Lord Townshend, Sheriff, Villars.

7*th.*—Went to Texier's; I believe about the fourth time of my having heard him. M^e. Grétery came with Lady Jerningham.

8*th.*—Account received of buoys having been taken up. Answer received from Directory. New message agreed upon and sent. Strong dissatisfaction expressed by Lord Grenville at the delay and neglect of proper measures against the insurgents. It would seem by accounts in papers, that the mutiny at the Nore broke out on the 10th ult. 'Lancaster' crew returned to duty; the acceptance of their submission settled at Admiralty.

9*th.*—Council by desire of Lord Grenville on subject of mutiny. Agreed that instructions should be sent to Admiral Buckner not to accept submission of any ship, so as to imply pardon, without communication with Government. I introduced an opinion that all who had acted as delegates must be excepted from pardon and punished capitally; but did not know, till it was stated, that the number was near thirty. Pressed pointedly the collecting a force of gunboats below the vessels.

10*th.*—Met Grenville and learnt from him the news of the three ships being come in, 'Repulse,' 'Leopard' and 'Ardent,' *i. e.* escaped from the mutineers. Grenville wanted me to go to Admiralty, where Pitt was. News afterwards of the red flag having been taken down in all the ships. Captain Knight and Commissioners arrived. Meeting at Lord Spencer's, in evening, of Pitt, Chancellor, Lord Chatham, and Solicitor-General. Message sent to Dover yesterday, according to Nepean, to bring round a sloop that was there and two gunboats.

11*th.*—Went before breakfast to Admiralty, where saw Captain Knight and Admiral Paisley. Captain Knight's opinion clear, that they could get down, notwithstanding the removal of the buoys: states one method of doing it by going down in succession. Dinner at home. Lieut.-Colonel Williams, Lieut.-Colonel Clinton, jun., Lord Winchelsea, Steele, Cholmondeley.

12*th.*—Trinity House dinner. Calvert, who had been aboard the mutineers, ridiculed the idea of their being able to get down. Sir Phil. Stephens, of the same opinion, observed that colliers came up in the darkest nights. Bromfield, likewise, convinced of the inefficiency of removing buoys, unless vessels are placed to oppose their going out. Clearly of opinion that vessels might be anchored, particularly lime barges, &c., in the swashes, that would ride out in any weather.

13*th.*—Dined at Club. I set Dr. Burney down at Chelsea. He thinks of Sir Ch. Blagden's politics and character as I do. I did very weakly in opposing Lord Lucan's manœuvre in bringing him in.

14*th.*—Cabinet dinner at the Chancellor's; being detained at the House did not come in till the end of the first conversation on the affairs of the mutineers, who have now chiefly surrendered, I think all but three ships. Parker taken and on shore. Council in the morning relative to Portugal, but changed in consequence of an answer from the Directory, accompanied by a passport. They name Lille, not as a matter of option; prescribe the form of treaty, *i. e. Définitif et séparé*; and state the same in the passport. Expression dropped by D. expressive of the same purpose as others, that I have remarked lately from Pitt.

15*th.*—Renewal of Council on French affairs. Complete opposition of opinion. Pitt, Dundas, Chancellor, Lord Cornwallis, Lord Chatham and ultimately Lord Liverpool; on the other side, Lord Grenville, Lord

Spencer, Duke of Portland, myself. Unless we make a general change of system, it is almost indifferent what we do. Lord Grenville observed truly, that we were at a period at which nothing but firmness could save us; that if we were to continue these concessions there was no reason why the Government should exist at the end of a twelvemonth. Council in the evening which I did not attend; lasted till past twelve. *Séance orageuse.**

16*th.*—Went to Admiralty, where conversation with Lady Spencer, from whom learnt history of Cabinet of preceding evening. Lord Spencer afterwards and Grenville: both seem to be, Grenville clearly, for taking first moment of concession in favour of Catholics.

17*th.*—Determined, however, that the Parliament should not be dissolved. Took occasion from that to remark my opinion that its concession in favour of Catholics would be desirable. Law proposed against oaths of secrecy: discussion about it and objection on my part to oaths of allegiance, either for sailors or against those supposed to be coming into Scotland. Urged to Pitt business of Postmaster at Norwich. Should have gone out of town early in the morning, but stayed for Council, supposing it to be for Irish affairs in general, but it was only on business of supposed emigration to Scotland.

19*th.*—Expectation of making a motion on Subalterns.

25*th.*—Rode to breakfast with Grenville; found him strong in support of Lord Grenville's opinion. 'Had not nerves.' Council. Lord G. agreed to consider before he decided, what the prospect was of final agreement or disagreement on the main question. It did not appear to me that the prospect now held out was different at all from what was before understood. In fact it was nothing at all; for it was expressly declared that, sooner than fail, all would be given up. Went away leaving the discussion

* *Vide* Stanhope's Life of Pitt, vol. iii. p. 53.

non fondée. Stayed some time with Canning. Met Cazales, who told me that he had been against the King's proclamation. He is confident that the Directory will not make peace. The King told him that the proclamation that he made was such as it was in consequence of the advice of Charette. He (Cazales) did not believe what Dutheil told him, that the King was in correspondence with Pichegru. Thought there were persons capable of deceiving the King by a forged signature. Character of M. Davarney, *énergie*, *bonne foi*, *sans prétentions.* Clear that nothing should be attempted. Fears imprudence of the Royalists. Leave the Jacobins and the Moderates to fight with one another. Maret engaged in a plot here for seizing the Tower. Bishop d'Autun applied for audience to Lord Grenville: was not received: then made his communication (viz. of Maret's intention) to some one else.

26*th.*—Set off by eleven: read Aristotle with little intermission all the way.

30*th* —Blanket to breakfast. I had rode out before breakfast. Office. Talked afterwards with Huskisson; rode a short distance. Puisaye and Cazales to dinner: sat till near twelve. Cazales' opinion, that in thirty years' time there will be a monarch and *noblesse* in France, if not the present, some others. Puisaye agreed in opinion even as to a less period. Parker executed.

July 2*nd.*—Message from the Directory. Plan in circulation for the reduction of the army of Condé. Lord Grenville contends for the best of the three, at all events for the second.

4*th.*—Rode in Lord Pembroke's riding-house. Sir Richard Strachan confirmed completely my idea about mooring chains: confident that ships would ride there, having rode there himself: should be two pairs more. Thinks there should be five or six vessels, brigs and sloops of war.

5th.—St. James's; too late for levee. Council. Went in to the King: strong opinion in favour of Stuart, not well towards Mulgrave. Pitt told me, at St. James's, of his and Dundas having ascribed to me the pamphlet entitled 'Remarks preparatory to the Issue, &c.' Arrived at Beaconsfield by half-past ten. Cazales there. Did not see Mr. B. that night.

6th.—It was not till a good while after breakfast that I saw Mr. Burke. Dr. Lind was come. There was no doubt in either of the physicians as to the speedy approach of dissolution. Mr. B., when I saw him, which was in the dressing-room of his bed-room above stairs, was in the same possession of his faculties as ever, but very feeble and languid; his voice, however, not much affected, as he observed, *vox et prœterea nihil.* He talked about Dundas's defeat at the Indian House which Woodford had mentioned; but said that it did not signify, as he had a back game and had only to step into the House of Commons. Much of Hastings' and Impey's fortunes had been, he said, in a vessel called the 'Beehive,' which was lost. I have a notion it had been in ingots. He diverted himself with the circumstance of the French Government having seized upon part of Impey's fortune. 'Robbing the robbers.' 'Vainqueurs des Vainqueurs,' &c. I walked at the back of the house meditating on the changes that had taken place. The day was very rainy. After dinner, before I went, I was again introduced to Mr. B. He was gratified, I understood, by my desire to see him. I stayed but a short time. He asked me if I had a print of his son's picture that hung in the room. Mrs. B. had given me one. He observed he was soon going to join him—a remark which Mrs. B. observed was not fair to her. In the morning he had commended Wilberforce's book, observing among other merits that he stated the objections of his adversaries in their full force. He desired me to tell him that he should have written to him upon it if his health would have permitted. Speaking of the late King of Prussia's account to his sister, the Margravine of Bareuth, of the merits of Voltaire, that he was . . . and a good companion, as appeared by the 'Pucelle d'Orleans.' He spoke with horror of the book, as destroying all love of country, and blamed himself for having polluted his imagination by reading it. In both conversations he was either absent, or less quick of hearing, not always answering to what was said. When, in my last conversation, I talked of coming to him again on Sunday, he smiled in a marked manner, expressive, as I thought then, of satisfaction, but, as I now rather think, of belief that he should not last so long. He took my hand at parting, closing his eyes and keeping them shut till I quitted him.

7th.—Prepared to go to Woolwich. Set out with Sir Gilbert and M. Pozzo di Borgo. I went forward on horseback and the latter part of the way with Blanket, in his chaise. Experiment: 1st, all fell short, 4lb. each, 15 elev. Low-gaged ball and two wads in great gun. In 2nd and 3rd, Sadler's seems to have fallen short, and all the rest to have gone home. Rode back the greater part of the way afterwards in chaise with Blanket. Walked with Sir Gilbert Elliot to Somerset House.

8th.—Despatches of 6th from Lord Malmesbury's account of reception at Lisle and exchange of full powers.

9th.—News that the event so long known to be not distant, latterly seeming to be so imminent, had happened, and that that great light of the world, Mr. Burke, was no more! After meditating upon what had happened and what I should do, wrote to Mrs. B.; then went to Duke of Portland's: returned without seeing him.* Called on Sir W. Jerningham without mentioning what had happened. Dined with Sir Gilbert Elliot.

* Letter from Mr. Canning to Mr. Ellis. *Vide* Lord Malmesbury's Diary vol. iii. p. 396.

10*th*.—Went to Duke of Portland's and consulted about proposal. A public funeral.

11*th*.—Came to town in the morning and saw the Speaker, afterwards Mr. Pitt with him. Not successful.

12*th*.—Council upon report of two sailors convicted of serving the enemy; one, in the first instance, left for execution, afterwards changed for Botany Bay. Dinner (Cabinet) at Mr. Pitt's; no business while I stayed. I was called away about eight, by note from Lawrence, who called afterwards and remained with me till past ten.

13*th*.—Day excessively hot; room oppressive. Council, in consequence of letters from Lord Malmesbury. They insisted, as a *sine quâ non*, that none of the conquests of the Republic should be given up. This not resisted, but evaded: wait to see whether the nature of the proposal will bring this into question. They require restitution of satisfaction for ships at Toulon; exemption of Belgium from any charge on account of the loan; surrender of the title of King of France. Lord Malmesbury speaks of these as wholly extravagant. Deliberate opinion from P. that they must be given up. Answer at present not refusing but evading. Hear with surprise, not necessary to consider such things yet.

14*th*.—Company at home: Brocklesby, Malone, Langton, Charles Greville.* Walked with Malone in Park till past 10. In bed before 12, after reading publication sent me by Brand of Mr. White, and part of Grattan's speech.

15*th*.—Day of last offices performed to Burke.

19*th*.—Cabinet on last letters from Lord Malmesbury. They say, that, in consequence of their Secret Articles. nothing can be given from their allies either. This comes

* Charles Greville, son of Fulke Greville, of Wilbury, Wilts, grandson to the fifth Lord Brooke, and brother to Mrs., afterwards Lady Crewe He married, in 1793, the Lady Charlotte Cavendish Bentinck, daughter of William, third Duke of Portland.

as their answer from Paris. Plenipotentiaries affect to be surprised. Talk still of compensations. Probably mean Spanish part of St. Domingo in exchange for Gibraltar. This acknowledgment of the force of their Secret Articles to be a *sine quâ non* to negotiation even.

20th.—Conceived the idea of offering myself for the county, but shall not. Prorogation of Parliament.

22nd.—Dined at Lord Hawkesbury's with Canning. M. Tromelin came by appointment in the evening. Walked to Mrs. Crewe's, thence home, having sent away carriage.

24th.—Took leave of Cazales, who was to set off the same evening. Two methods: first, *guerre civile*; second, gradual change of public opinion. Saw Tryon: gave him his passport. 'Filippo Casino.'

26th.—Some idea that this was the day when I saw Beckwith, the pilot of the 'Grampus,' who confirmed to me completely the insufficiency of the removal of the buoys for preventing the ships from going out. Saw that he did not think that they intended to go out, but they clearly might. Dinner at the Duke of Portland's; Mr. Pitt and Mr. Dundas not there.

27th—Drawing-room; Council afterwards and expected meeting on Monday of Seditious Societies. Saw Prince de Salm. Letters from Lord Malmesbury. Plenipotentiaries wait for counter projects from Paris. French Ministry has been changed: Talleyrand Perigord appointed.

28th.—Recorder's report. Dined with Canning. Saw Nesbit in morning about Prince de Salm. M. Hamelin arrived from Nantes: brought letter from Kersebec.

31st.—Settled to go to Woburn.

August 1st.—Came to town in morning; called on Comte Staremberg.

2nd.—Dinner, I think, at Lady Jerningham's: present, Lally Tollendal, Livarot, the Chevalier, another Frenchman, a tall man, who spoke English. In the evening,

Lord Fitzgerald and M. ——, the missionary to China, thought to be very like me.

5*th*.—Report of Captain Halket of the 'Circe,' founded on account of three fishermen and his own observation, of the Dutch fleet having sailed on the 30th ultimo. Contradicted since.

6*th*.—Walked out as far as Marble Hill, pleasant; met Comte de Jarnac, as I was going down, who lives a few doors from Mrs. Cholmondeley.

8*th*.—Lord Granville Leveson arrived. Opinion that the delay of the Directory's answer promises well, *i. e.* in Cabinet sense. Language of Couthon and Maret, I think, as well as private informant intimates, that the Directory promises to be what is called reasonable.

12*th*.—Dined at home; went afterwards to tea at Symmons'. Found on coming home the narrative of Lord Macartney's Embassy, which began.

11*th*.—Up before seven: walked round the Park.

15*th*.—News arrived by French papers and Lord Malmesbury, of peace made by Portugal. Lord Grenville suspects it to be treachery of Aranjo, who is known to be a Jacobin, acting under his former powers and contrary to his last instructions, which were to repair to Lisle and put himself under the protection of Lord Malmesbury.

16*th*.—Dined with Canning, Hammond, Huskisson and Lord Granville Leveson. Canning clear, that our conduct last August lost Italy. Hammond thinks St. Domingo has cost, in all, four millions. *Mem.*: To see the letter Woronzow promised to show me, containing an offer from Naples of 60,000 men, upon condition of certain pecuniary aid from us. Council to-day on peace of Portugal. Mentioned letter from Bishop of Léon, recommending conveyance of priests. Opinion that they had better not go just at this crisis.

17*th*.—Dined with Chancellor. Conversation about accounts and quantity. Walked away with Canning and

Lord Grenville. Further Council on Portuguese peace. Letter agreed on for interposing to prevent it. Talk of Sir S. Smith's situation. Person recommended by Lord Grenville, a Mr. Plunkee, in room of Swinburne.

20th.—Sadler called; explained to him the purpose of the experiments on porcelain. Went to Symmons' to tea, where I saw his son's translation of 'Soliloquy in Hamlet.'

25th.—All day at Fulham. Chief reading, 'History of European Settlements,' with digressions in consequence into Anson's 'Voyage,' which I had not looked into for a good many years.

29th.—News arrived, but question authenticity, of French peace. It is contained in Paris papers, and pretends to have been received at Paris by telegraph. Telegraph from Deal also pretends that flag of truce was seen off Dover.

30th.—Dined at Canning's: present, Legge [Rev.], Hammond, Lord Lavington, Lord Granville Leveson. Discussion about the case of Las Casas, likely to be arrested at Dover. Hammond thinks that McKenzie has been over to western shore of America.

31st.—Delay now about answer from Holland. Hammond thinks that the Plenipotentiaries are embarrassed: the Directory not wishing peace, know not how, with the earnestness which we have for it, to find means of preventing its taking place.

September 1st.—News of failure off Teneriffe, on the 24th of July.

2nd.—Accounts of disturbances in Scotland, in consequence of the New Militia Bill: *i. e.* further accounts: nine men killed by the rioters.

4th.—Sent letter to Mr. Pitt, with Royalist account.

5th.—Puisaye, whom I had not seen since his dinner with Cazales. Afterwards to Lady Lavington's, where Staremberg* and Madame Staremberg.

* Austrian Minister at London.

6*th*.—General Delancey. Office: Canning: home. Got away not till near seven; had afterwards to stop at Sadler's to finish mould. At Bulstrode by eleven: Lady Charlotte, Lady Mary [Bentinck], Mr. and Mrs. Hussey.*

7*th*.—Breakfasted with the Duke, who was to go to London. Arrived at Beaconsfield before breakfast was over; first time since day after the funeral. Drew Mrs. B. about in the garden chair.

9*th*.—At Warfield before three. Speaker, seeing my horses, had sent up and engaged me to dinner next day. Sleepy during the evening. Remained below talking of India and getting a good deal of information respecting the habits and circumstances of the country, which it is very foolish not to have got before. Received, I think, news of the triumph of the Directory and the New Revolution effected on the morning of the 4th.

12*th*.—Dined at Wallingford; tedious delay; slept part of the way to Oxford; arrived before dark; have not the proper feel about it. Long walk after supper, by moonlight.

13*th*.—Walked about with Dr. Routh,† with whom I had long and pleasant conversation. Reason for accents, that they assist conjecture. Mr. Hay, Dr. Routh and the Vice-Chancellor to dinner.

14*th*.—Called on Winstanley; went with him to his hall. Called on Mr. Loveday. Melchior, who showed us the produce of his Welsh tour, two years ago; much struck with his conversation. Remarkable advantage of a large scale in the representation of scenes such as he had taken. Dinner with the Vice-Chancellor; extremely pleasant; more and more pleased with Vice-Chancellor.

* Mrs. Hussey, daughter of Horatio, second Lord Walpole of Wolterton.

† Dr. Routh, President of Magdalen, Oxford; died 22nd September, 1854, in his 100th year.

‡ Edmund Isham, D.D., Warden of All Souls'.

15*th*.—Dined at Stratford; read on my way thither what remained of publication of Mr. Burke; finished afterwards the treatise on 'Rhet.' (Arist.), and began the 'Poetics.' Did not get to Aston, in consequence of the badness of the roads, till past ten.

17*th*.—Church: Dr. Spencer. Sermon on the Purity of Life. I suspect Dr. Johnson's.

18*th*.—Went to Packington in the chaise; thence to the ground on horseback. Colonel Hugonin had come with me. Day fine; exhibition interesting; scene pleasant. Went into the riding-house before dinner, rode Spanish horse given to Lord Aylesford by Lord Bute. Little grey Hungarian horse. Lawrence, of the veterinary school, there, who says that the sinews of thorough-bred horses are composed of smaller and more numerous fibres than those of others. Length of riding-house, I think, 140 feet by 35 feet.

19*th*.—Went into my room between seven and eight; after tea and till just now have been reading, without interruption, Polybius.

20*th*.—Went to see Soho. What I most remember in way of contrivance is, what they call the parallel motion, by which the action of the beam on the pistons was regulated in the steam-engine and the conical form of wheels, that were to act on each other, to which may be added the suspended bags for skating the pieces of copper. Lord Malmesbury returned to London.

23*rd*.—Oxford by about two. Obliged myself to read political pamphlet, after finishing First Book of Polybius. Called on Winstanley and President of Magdalen. Dined at Benzington uncomfortably. Sent forward to Park Place and found there Lord Malmesbury, as was Lady M.

25*th*.—Borriac, the name, I think, of one of the new Plenipotentiaries, formerly known as the President d'Alco.

26*th.*—In riding over the forest met the King, who was going a hare-hunting. Present: Generals Harcourt and Gwyn, Lord Walsingham, G. Villars. Continued with H. M. till he went towards Windsor. Stated my repentance of measure about the King of Prussia. Many civil things from H. M. as to our agreement and my opinions, qualities, &c. The use to be made of these is as an incitement to deserve them.

27*th.*—Levee: Admiral Nelson invested: could not go in: contrived not to be spoken to.

28*th.*—Drawing-room. Dined, I think, with Mr. Pitt. Present: Lord Malmesbury, Canning, Lord Mornington, Lord Chatham. Pleasant dinner. Council afterwards; in which declaration agreed upon, and solution of papers. Portugal left to negotiate its peace, subject to the conditions that she had proposed.

October 1*st.*—Idle thoughts all morning, except that part when I was meditating speeches not wholly unusefully. Nothing done after coming to town, as I had to call on Canning and settle about going down. Went down with Frederick North, taking box with papers, *i. e.* selected correspondence during the negotiations, in the chaise, which however did not read.

2*nd.*—Croydon Fair. Counted in two miles, seventy-eight carriages, which, supposing me to go twice as fast as they, would give me in that space half the number more than the carriages that were in it at the commencement of the time, which would give 286 for the whole number of the carriages upon the road, or that had been upon the road during the time that I was riding that two miles, viz. $78 \times \frac{2}{3} = 52 \times 5.5 = 286$. Council, in which declaration settled.

3*rd.*—Answer from the Directory to Lord Malmesbury's note, *i. e.* answer from the Commissioners after consulting the Directory.

6*th.*—Dined at the London Tavern with Directors to

meet Lord Mornington;* present, Dundas, Anstruther, Canning, Rose, Huskisson, Sir William Scott, Wellesley, Sir J. Scott.

5*th.*—Went, I have a notion, to riding-house: met Lord Heathfield,† who suggested idea about regulation of King's plates. Council, I think. Answer to the last message: I should have liked it better as at first talked of, with refusal to go back to France, except merely to sign. Conversation after others were gone with Lord Grenville, who expresses wish to see the statement given by me to Mr. P., and agrees as to the improbability of any good settlement in France, except by means of civil war, aided by war from without

7*th.*—Employed in settling papers and accounts, when Puisaye came to talk on the subject of the letter, which he had sent me in the morning relative to L'Orient. Resolved therefore to stay in town and go the next morning to Beaconsfield, that I might talk on the subject the next day with Lord Grenville.

9*th.*—Rode after breakfast to Dropmore for purpose which had very much determined my coming, namely, to confer with Lord Grenville about Puisaye's letter.

11*th.*—Council and audience. Unable, however, to do much, except read Fox's speech at the Westminster meeting: pretty near a direct avowal of intention to subvert the Government. Dinner at Canning's. Read first 'Defence of Emigrants,' then preface to Porson's 'Hecuba.'

13*th.*—News of Admiral Duncan's victory.‡ Inquire into the fact, communicated by Cazales to Puisaye, of a large sum, 14,000*l.*, supposed to be sent from here to La Fayette.

* On his appointment as Governor of Bengal.

† Francis Augustus Eliott, son of the first Lord Heathfield, who defended Gibraltar. He died in 1813.

‡ Camperdown.

14*th*.—Shall go this evening to Salt Hill; the illumination tempts me but I shall not stay for it. Of what value is a victory with counsels such as those by which we are now governed?

16*th*.—During ride to Sunning Hill met Ciciaporci: joined by Fitzpatrick, with whom much free and amicable talk. At Staines, while I waited for chaise, got accounts from Woodford by messenger. The amount of Fitzpatrick's conversation was—that peace could not now be made; the last attempt sincere, but not the former: that Fox was fairly following his own line; that Parliamentary reform would probably lead to a revolution: that either this monarchy or the Republic must fall: that the country was, to be sure, full of wealth, but people would not long continue to part with it; that if war was to be made, Burke's the only rational principle; war in La Vendée certainly a most formidable one. Particularly struck with Burke's statement about this exclusion of the emigrants. In short, I very much doubt whether on any point we think at all differently.

18*th*.—Rode to town by quarter past eleven, after some conversation with the Duke of York whom I met upon the road, and calling for a short time on Puisaye, who informed me of his having seen the Duc de la Trimouille, who made invitations to Puisaye of joining him in what was carrying on. Proper caution of Puisaye. Met Adam by appointment on Desbarres' business; Doyley, Tromelin, who was to set off this evening, meaning to pass by St. Marcon, as I understood. He goes to re-establish the correspondence there. At St. James's in time for the levee. King not over-gracious. Only saw Lord Grenville for a few minutes before his going in to the closet. Could not fix any time for talking to him, as he was going back immediately to Dropmore. Delivered to him copy of Puisaye's letter.

21st.—Rode over Battersea Bridge and across the fields to Blackfriars.

23rd.—Dined at home. Allègre arrived, coming directly to Park Street: has not been in London since his departure with Sir Edward Pellew. Canning, who had just come from Walmer and had wished me to come to dinner.

24th.—Received from Puisaye letter from Etienne, with information about St. Maloes.

26th.—Talked on affairs of Royalists and other smaller matters with the Duc de Harcourt; found from him that the Prince de la Trimouille, whose memorial came in circulation to-day, had not been with the Duc de H——. To Drawing-room. Long conversation with the Princess of Wales, who told me of Miss Hayman's having been dismissed from the child, and of her intention to take her about her (the Princess).

November 1st.—Queen's house at eight. Instead of going to Cockpit went to Fulham. Sorry to find during many parts of the day how much memory, as to what I had been about, deserted me, or rather recollection. I dont know, however, that this was more than in former times. Council chiefly on speech. Consent of Mr. Pitt that Brécourt should draw for 2,000*l.* from the interior and agreement to pay the bonds, with such other advances as should be settled.

2nd.—Council. Portugal's conditional ratification had been stopped by their Ambassador at Lisbon. We, not being able to give any part of the force required, leave them to do as they can. Agree to renew attempt on Spain.

3rd.—Waked early with uneasy thoughts at state of things and with observations that might have been made of what passed overnight. Went to Fulham about half-past six, calling on Dr. Burney, with whom I sat for half an hour. Melancholy image ofpast time.

5th.—Went to Addiscombe: Lord Hawkesbury.

7*th.*—Tierney's motion about the third Secretary.

20*th.*—Bad account, I think, received to-day from Ireland. Insurrection spreading. More counties to be declared in that state. Effect felt of late declaration of the French.

23*rd.*—Rode out to Twickenham and to Richmond, where I called on Penn who was not at home. Met Duke of Clarence who rode back through Richmond Park.

25*th.*—Lord W. Bentinck to breakfast: Sir Horatio Nelson and Lieutenant Pierson, Mudge.

28*th.*—Company at dinner: Chancellor, Lord Minto, Sir Horatio Nelson, Payne, Lord Lavington, Grenville and Cholmondeley.

30*th.*—Council. Regulation agreed upon to be introduced into a Bill about Emigrants. Question relative to American trade. Allow foreign goods in American bottoms from America, not from foreign and hostile islands to neutral ports. Doubtful to English ports. Much talk afterwards about measures of war. Paper from Sir J. Warren though without his name. Orders have been given for new treatment of French prisoners. Letter from France to make it likely that they will come too. Representations of bad treatment of our prisoners, *i. e.* ours in France.

December 2*nd.*—Engagements at office till time to dress for Lord Mendip's: present, Chancellor, Duke of Portland, Lord Clifden and his brother, latterly uncommonly right. Conversation with Admiral Waldegrave. Shocking want of regulation in Newfoundland. Indians, not more than 300, hunted like wild beasts; have only bows and arrows; find their way to —— Island, distant fifteen leagues, even in fog.

3*rd.*—Garshore stated fact about 'Annual Register.' His proposal for 800*l.* a-year to get it on good footing, under care of Gillies, refused by Treasury. Motion of employing Thompson.

4th.—Up to town for debate. Spoke, in consequence of being called up, in some measure, by what was said by Nicholls about agreement with Burke's opinions. Called to order by Wilberforce. Good matter, but not made the most of, and much omitted.

8th.—Found that Nicholls' motion about taxing Ministers was to come. Met Pitt; short talk on motion; spoke pretty well.

9th.—Dined alone. Was preparing to send for Brécourt when he and Allègre called on me. Opera, for first time. Dance of 'Bacchus and Ariadne.' We have advanced to the point of seeing people dance naked.

10th.—Baron de Rolle, I think, with communication of business from Monsieur about recall of Puisaye.

The Right Hon. W. Windham to Captain Lukin.

December 16, 1797.

Dear William,—Your letters of the 27th and 31st October have both reached me to-day; and are the first, as far as I recollect, that have come directly to me, or that I have heard of at all, since your letter to Robert from Madeira, or whatever the island was, where you were so near being surprised by the mutineers. I showed your letter upon that occasion to Admiral Gambier, who had made some civil enquiries after you, and he thought so well of your conduct, as to have communicated the account, as he told me, to some of his colleagues. Before I have an occasion of sending this, I shall know, probably, what orders Lord Spencer has, or purposes to send out. I flatter myself that positive orders for your return are already on their way. Robert, who will probably write by this opportunity, will tell you all that relates to the Parsonage, which is going on very well and the current news of the day. I can only state to you in general, that my opinion of the state of things is not more favourable than at the worst period of any at which you have ever heard it. I do not reckon it among the least calamities of the time—certainly not among those that affect me least—that the world has now lost Mr. Burke. Oh! how much we rue that his counsels were not followed! Oh! how exactly do we see verified all that he has predicted!—though I do not think that, in the course of a few months, perhaps not in many months, any dangerous attacks will be made upon this country. I do not, on that account, see our fate less certain and at no very distant period, if some unlooked-for chance, such as we can now hardly form an imagination of, does not come to supply the utter insufficiency of our own talents and means. Unless some fortunate shift of wind should happen, we are so beset with dangers on all sides, so completely embayed, that it is impossible we can weather the breakers upon either tack.

You will have heard of our rejoicings here and the impression made by Lord Duncan's victory. It was a good work and as well done, I believe, as was possible; but we should not have heard so much of it had it not been *Duncan*. For Lord St. Vincent's victory, the greatest beyond all example in naval annals, not a candle burnt. For the same reason, hardly anything said of Admiral Onslow, though, had Duncan been Onslow, and, *vice versâ*, the whole honour of the victory would have been ascribed to him.

Farewell! I wish you may meet with an enemy's frigate, properly above the 'Thames'' match, in coming home.

Your affectionate uncle,

W. WINDHAM.

17*th*.—Rode to town. Conversation with Hammond, who told me of plans agitated by seditious meetings.

19*th*.—Procession to St. Paul's.*

20*th*.—Office. George Hanger, with a proposal about raising a corps of chasseurs from the Supplementary Militia. Called on Lady Malmesbury; followed to Opera, where I saw a dance about Britannia and Jacobinism.

21*st*.—Dinner at Lord Malmesbury's: present, Lord Pembroke, Lord Minto, Canning, Frere, Lord Leveson Gower, Lord Morpeth, Pelham.

* General Thanksgiving for our naval victories. The King and Parl ment went in grand procession to deposit the colours taken.

1798.

January 4th.—Debate;* second part; ever to be regretted. On returning from the House the overnight, I had settled some points necessary for the next day. In the morning I felt much better than I had done the day before: I revised what I had before purposed, corrected and made additions and before I went to the House, prepared at all points. My infatuation in not speaking exceeds all that I have ever known in myself or could conceive. Upon a review, the circumstance of Mr. Dundas taking the place I wished in the debate, made hardly any difference. Everything was, notwithstanding, as much provided to my wishes as if I had bespoke it. The loss to me is something incalculable and my regret is such that I know not what to do with myself. It breaks my slumbers and makes me incapable of doing anything. My regret arises not merely from what I have lost, but from the distrust excited of the effect of any resolution I can form on any occasion and of the power of acting in the moment, according to any place, however deliberately settled and however conformable to what I shall be sure to think the moment afterwards. All my consolation must be, that the whole of my materials are not thrown away, though I can hardly hope for an opportunity of applying them so well; and next, that the severe penance which I am undergoing for this folly, may have a better effect, than similar penances have had heretofore.

* Debate on trebling the assessed taxes.

5th.—Went home to dine and dress, meaning to be at the House by the time of Tierney making his motion, for the repeal of the clauses for exempting the Royal Family.

7th.—Dinner at Canning's: present, Lord Granville Leveson, Frere, Hammond, I think, and Huskisson.

9th.—Hippisley, Sir James Pulteney and Fullarton to dinner. Subject: The state of the country as to prospect of invasion and means to be taken for defence.

11*th.*—Saw Sir W. Howe. Much impressed with danger he thought force insufficient in '95, when North threatened, by 12,000 men; said so and got rebuked for it. Could not, in his present district, viz. Essex, bring against an enemy who should land at Clayton, or Clacton (near Ipswich river as it would seem), more than 6,000. River Lea ought to be provided with sluices. Thinks there should be much light infantry: present arms as good as any: must endeavour to teach use of bayonet. Great difficulty with light infantry to teach them to disperse. Only three positions—Colchester, Chelmsford, and Brentwood—Lord Petre's, not Warley. Two former would require 25,000 men.

Dined with Sir W. Scott, Speaker, Master of the Rolls, American Minister, Grant, Douglas, Wilberforce. Sat with Sir W. till near twelve. Anecdote: That at the beginning of the war he had stated two methods with respect to treatment of neutrals, as I understood, trading with colonies: one strong, such as used by Lord Chatham; the other mild, that P. had declared explicitly for, in as full tone as ever used by Lord Chatham, adding, that the war could not last more than a year.

12*th.*—Saw Simcoe, both upon subject of Canada and of affairs in general. Simcoe convinced to the full extent that I am, that the war should have been carried on in France—was going to read Turreau—had from the beginning written to Lord Moira; thinks highly of Sir W. Howe. Five thousand times better than Lord C.

Brigadier C. not equally the confidence of the army. News of twelve sail of the line being ready at Brest: twelve sail ordered out in consequence.

13*th.*—Answer to memorial of Haugwitz. Question of P. Frederick. Authority from Pitt to empower Puisaye to draw for 2,000*l.* from interior as part of payment. War Office, in which I explained to Lewis my ideas as to the several salaries, viz.

4,000*l.* . . .	Secy. at War in future.
2,000*l.* . . .	Depy. or 1,800*l.*
1,200*l.* . . .	1st Clerk.
900*l.* . . .	2nd do. 1,000*l.* at present holder.
900*l.* . . .	3rd do.
750*l.* . . .	4th do.
1,500*l.* . . .	Acct. or 1,400*l.*
900*l.* . . .	Ass.
750*l.* . . .	2nd. do.

16*th.*—Nesbitt to breakfast. The drafting the foreign regiments into 60th, a breach in many of them of their capitulation. Drafting unknown in foreign service. Disturbances apprehended on that account at Martinique: he to call there on that account. Had recommended formerly a reduced half-pay for officers of foreign corps. For want of that, disposed to make unfair advantages. Order had been issued by the Secretary of State for drafting Rohan: stopped by his letter, stating it to be contrary to capitulation. Present expense of St. Domingo 1,100,000*l.* Is to make them increase their contribution to 500,000*l.*, otherwise to evacuate. Thinks, with Simcoe, that greater things may be done with as little expense as smaller. Foresees the impossibility of evacuating, as well as horror. Cannot maintain the mere points. Whole force at present of all sorts and colours 13,000, fit for duty about 9,000. Troops on hills near Saremic perfectly healthy. Forbes kept them for three months on board transports. Did not know till now that he was the

Forbes that he had heard of in India. Never has been a good co-operation from the fleet.

February 4th.—Rode: Park crowded: rode with Adair of Flixton. Met Admiral Young and heard his observation about Sir Sidney's *imprudence*; a good preparation for abandoning a man. Went to Mrs. Crewe's: Miss Hayman there.

5*th.*—Saw M. Mallet, who had been sent by the *Agens du Roi* into Normandy. He is a Genevois, a tall genteel man; had been always in the French service.

8*th.*—Got to Marlborough to breakfast. Occupied chiefly by military speculations and thoughts connected with them. Saw Canning. Party in the evening at the Cholmondeley's: Mrs. Lutwyche and her nieces, the Miss Thrales. Much struck with Sophia. Did not break up till near two.

9*th.*—Dinner at Leigh's: Canning, Lord Pembroke, Lord Malmesbury, Abbé Lemon. Ball, I think, at Tower Rooms; the Princess of Orange, I think, there.

16*th.*—Occupied chiefly with military speculations, trying to form ideas of the operations of troops; what I read was in Polybius.

21*st.*—Went to St. James's; saw General Moreshead, whom I engaged to breakfast with me on the Friday following. He makes the order for attack, Hope and Perryn, then Riddel; he vouches for these not having quitted their ground till ten minutes past five. Attack could not have succeeded.

22*nd.*—Saw Delancey, I think, who gave me his map, with plan of distribution of force.

24*th.*—Paper produced by Huskisson, prepared by Sir Charles Grey,* with stations and distances.

* General Sir Charles Grey (afterwards *first* Earl Grey) was appointed, in 1794, to the chief command of the land forces sent, in conjunction with the naval armament under Lord St. Vincent, to reduce the West India Islands, and was nominated to the command of the southern district in England.

25*th*.—Promised by Huskisson a sight of the plan prepared by the Adjutant-General for police of London, in case of invasion; also copy of the paper of stations, prepared by Sir Charles Grey. Nepean showed me scheme of distribution of gunboats; three divisions, viz. Downs, Portsmouth, Plymouth.

28*th*.—Wrote letter to Sir S. Smith. Lord Lilford called to sign writing for Doughty, who had written to me, beginning with 'Dear Sir!' Got to Binfield. Fine moonlight and frost. Thoughts on journey idle and rambling, chiefly on military matters. Cabinet at Duke of Portland's. Understood that question to be brought forward of measures of defence. On this day money to begin to be paid for Bons, out of 10,000*l*. which had been received, I think, the day before. (Query, Date of conference when this was settled?) Nothing said at Council about defence, as I learnt afterwards from Lord Spencer.

March 2*nd*.—Delightful ride, in delightful day, through green roads, through Holyput, I conceive, to Braywick Saw in the paper at Maidenhead an account of the apprehending of O'Connor and the others.

4*th*.—Rode to Uxbridge. Dined at Lord Spencer's: present, Lord and Lady Lavington, James, Sir H. Nelson, Lord Bathurst, I think; Grenville.

5*th*.—Went, I have a notion, to House and heard from Pitt some particulars of the evidence against O'Connor, &c.

6*th*.—Dined with Nepean: present, Trevor, Sir Andrew Hammond, Sir Horatio Nelson, Governor Philips, just arrived from Lord St. Vincent, Governor Bruce, Mr. Preston, of the India House, Lord Keith, Captain Georges. Letters from Lord St. Vincent about Spanish ships with quicksilver ships that had got out of Cadiz. Event agrees with opinion which Sir Horatio Nelson gave on Sunday last.

11*th.*—Prince William to breakfast.

13*th.*—Dined at Club: Lord Spencer, Malone, Courtenay, Dr. Burney, Dr. Fordyce, Langton. Ballot for Canning: one black ball.

15*th.*—Drawing-room. Attended Council in evening. Examination of Benjamin Binns and Galloway.

17*th.*—Dined at Lord Spencer's: Grenville only. Called in morning at Jeffery's and bought small Homer; found him apparently in very good principles. Wrote to Elliot about Pelham, who, I fear, is past hope. Council, in consequence of apprehension of visitors in Ireland. Attended question about suspension of Habeas Corpus, urged by the Chancellor and Lord Grenville; Pitt as usual. My opinion that it might be done, that it would be useful, but that in point of tests I should like to defer it. Question, Whether Sir Francis Burdett would come if sent for, and right in that case of Privy Council?

21*st.*—Debate in House of Lords on Duke of Bedford's motion for removal of Ministers.

29*th.*—Called at George Street. Mary, with whom stayed till twelve, making her sing.

30*th.*—Saw Duke of York. Talk about defence of country. Stated my plan of opening the country for cavalry. Duke rather seemed to like it. Recommended also the abolition of drafting. Duke agreed about danger of landing in Cawsand Bay. Had seen Delancey on same subject in morning. House: Committee on Mr. Dundas's Bill for Driving Country. Conversation with Rose, jun., who is full of apprehensions about the Isle of Wight and the Needles. Called in at Lord Malmesbury's: communication from Lord M. of letter from Duke of Brunswick, with suggestion from Lord M. about Queen of Naples.

31*st.*—Dinner with Canning: Lord Granville Leveson, Frere, &c. Drank too much wine, so as to become sleepy. Straight home and to bed, having been unable to stay out the reading of some humorous verses and letters of Canning, &c. on Legge's going to Cateaton Street.* According to notice of the 29th, a meeting of Cabinet was to have been held to-day, when Dundas was to have communicated a plan for the defence of the country.

April 1st.—Went to Duke of York's office, where talked to Brownrigg, who seems to concur in all my ideas both with respect to the new formation of the Army and to ideas of preparing the country.

2nd.—Important communication from Count Staremberg.

3rd.—Breakfasted with Sir Andrew Hammond. Course of the tides, as I understand, such, that it is half ebb without (*i. e.* without the Isle of Wight) when it is full tide in Portsmouth harbour; that is, that the periods of high and low water are not the same within and without the harbour, but lie alternately. But then I cannot think I understood him rightly on another point, namely, that the tides within and without are always flowing the same way. Debate on Slave Trade. Spoke, being made to do so principally by Canning.

4th.—St. James's, closet. King's opinion that General Stuart's correspondence exceedingly improper; I don't recollect the term. Saw two men brought up by Colonel Rotenburgh. Colonel R. assured me that six days before, when he left the Isle of Wight, the 10th Regiment had not arrived there, nor, as I understood him, was there any other regular regiment but one of about two or three hundred men; no guns but about four, nor any measure of defence taken.

5th.—Went to town by twelve. Cabinet, upon subject

* The Musæ Cateatonienses to which this passage refers are a collection of humorous verses by Mr. Canning on a trifling incident which had excited his mirth and given vent to a boundless exuberance of rhyme. The volume has never been printed, but we believe that it still exists in manuscript at Saltram, the seat of the Earl of Morley, near Plymouth.

of communication mentioned above, that the fleet should be sent—Netherlands only, not in France. Went to the House where expected Alien Bill, and something to be said by Tyrrwhit Jones; put off till after the holidays. Paper given me by Dundas, containing some suggestions on invasion.

8*th.*—Information by Hammond confirming immediate intentions of a descent.

9*th.*—Rode to town: came by Norwood. Very melancholy with thought of our situation. Lord Mayor's dinner. Would have been pleasant but for same thoughts. Sat with Lawrence and Sir William Scott, explaining what I conceive the situation of the country.

10*th.*—Went to Opera, to Mrs. Crewe. Walked home with Canning and stated my opinion on the situation of affairs. Breakfasted at Admiralty. Conversation with Francis.

11*th.*—Rode out before breakfast; met Clinton, sen.; talked about the state of defence of the country; full of apprehensions; deeply impressed with the deficiency of our force in every respect, particularly in the total want of Light Infantry. Council on draft to Vienna, in consequence of communication from Count Staremberg. Does not go far enough, in my opinion, in the terms on which we are willing to engage. Dinner with Lawrence; fell asleep afterwards, in consequence of vexation at not having done at Council, what I intended and what I failed in, I cannot tell how. Duke of York was to settle next day at the city about the regulation of London, so that hitherto, nothing seems to have been done but to prepare loose plan that is at the reading-room.

12*th.*—Up by six, I believe. Vexed to death at this new instance of my not having executed what I had so fully intended, viz. of forcing on some conversation on the state of things. Last night, after setting down Lawrence in St. James's Square, for the purpose of talking with

Francis, went to Mrs. Crewe's, where was only Miss C.; went into the next room and got some sleep; remained there after Mrs. Crewe went to Lady Palmerston's, whither followed. Great drowsiness, the effect of oppression, the effect of discontent. Allègre called to tell me of his expecting Georges and the rest in town.

13*th.*—Saw Colonel Stanley, who communicated to me Bastard's offer for the defence of his country, &c.: not much in it. Went to office to meet Dundas about gun.

15*th.*—Up by seven: had meant to breakfast at St. Leonard's Hill, but felt doubtful, and the arrival of the messenger with letters determined me to stay. Notes from Woodford of conversation with General Georges. Short walk upon the Heath, recalling something of juvenile feel. Read letters of Puisaye and Cholmondeley, and Tinseau's plan of attempt on coast of France, as I came along. Conversation in evening with Lawrence on Irish affairs and what we had talked of in London.

16*th.*—Saw for the first time Georges who left the Morbihan about a month ago and the coast about nine days since: he embarked at St. Maloes.

18*th.*—Council at eleven. Decision to take tardier course, which will not bring the fleet there till 1st of June, before which, I am afraid, the fate of the country in question will be decided. Made attempt to bring on question about state of country, but could not succeed. Have seen since and with some vexation, that I might and ought to have succeeded, so far, at least, as to have made several of the observations that I wished. Dinner at Pitt's.

19*th.*—Conspirators apprehended last night. Talked to Mr. Pitt about prosecuting the printers, who have inserted lists of jury and recommended issuing immediately, orders for arrests.

20*th.*—Came to town by three. Returned from House dissatisfied, but dissatisfied only at my not having been

Helens, Prince of Orange, Lord Trevor. Went to Duchess of Gordon's.

2nd.—Dined with Lord Malmesbury.

3rd.—Dinner at home: Duc de Berri, Duc de Bourbon, &c. Had walked in the morning with Grenville and Lord Grenville in Park. Lord G. said that the letters to Lord St. Vincent had not gone till either the day before or Tuesday, but that a notice to be in readiness had been sent before.

5th. — Lord Liverpool's to dinner. Query, Whether this morning, or morning before, Sir Richard Strachan? whose opinion was that St. Marcon was not sufficiently secured and had doubts also about Jersey. Thought there should be more mooring chains, and for both places more gunboats. Mooring chains complained of as hurting the anchorage for other ships, by entangling with their anchors. Ridicule of our exultation at taking 'L'Hercule.' Doubt whether, if we were defeated constantly, our people would fight at all. Wrote letter to Mr. Dundas, urging measures for defence of St. Marcon, or decision to give it up.

6th.—News of Sir Sidney Smith's having arrived that day.

7th.—Dined with Wickham: met Mallet du Pan for the first time: present, Canning, Frere, Fagel and his brother. Went to Lady Malmesbury's to meet the Duc de Berri.

8th.—Tierney's motion about Lord Onslow.

11th.—Went out with view of breakfasting with Lord Spencer. Met Grenville, who had come from there having been practising sword exercise. Called on Lady Spencer with him, seeing her for first time. Council, on notice from Dundas relative to persons whose offers of service to be accepted. Clear now that there is no general plan settled; the whole idea, the bringing round all the troops possible. Notion that we did not want light troops, because our troops upon the Continent had been victorious, whenever they had been tried against the enemy by themselves.

13*th.*—Guards sailed for Ostend; rather, perhaps, reported to do so; I have not learnt for certain that they did.

15*th.*—Called in my way out of town on Lady Buckinghamshire, whom I had not seen for a long while: told me of what she alluded to when I had last seen her, of something said about me by Lady Anne Bingham, which I don't believe, though it came from Lady Castlereagh and Lady Camden.

16*th.*—Went to Lord Mendip's: observed to him that what the French had rejected in way of able men, (Dumouriez and others) would set up another state, parodying what was said of Sir I. Newton.*

18*th.*—Dined at Lord Lavington's, to meet General Arnold. Called in my way back on Lord Lucan and Grenville. Consulted Grenville on wish that had been expressed by Pitt, I think, in the evening, that in the statements given in to the Committee, no mention should be made of my own plan.

19*th.*—Dined, I think, at Lord Spencer's: Lord Cadogan and Miss Cadogan.

20*th.*—Mail from Vienna. Thugut said to be appointed to new dominions in Italy, to be succeeded by Cobenzal. Account of Sir Richard Strachan having been carried by tide up the Seine and attacked by eleven gunboats, which he beat off.

22*nd.*—News of event of expedition.

* In conversation at this time with Lord Malmesbury, Mr. Pitt observed of Windham—'Nothing can be so well-meaning or so eloquent as he is: his speeches are the finest productions possible of warm imagination and fancy; yet still I must condemn such parts of them as hold out the French nation as the first in point of military and political abilities, and therefore *deservedly* the first in Europe. This part of it is language I strongly repudiate as not correct, and as unbecoming the mouth of any Englishman.'—Stanhope's *Life of Pitt*, vol. ii.

24th.—Read Dumourier; 'Tableau spéculatif.'

26th.—Called on the Duke of York to suggest the question of breaking the 11th Regiment. His idea very wrong, I think, of denying promotion to the officers. Confident that Captain Winthrop was on shore during the action and relied on his authority on that supposition.

27th.—News of duel between Pitt and Tierney. Censure of myself for not having foreseen and spoke to the Speaker about it.

28th.—Went to the play; 'Isabella' and 'Blue Beard.' Mrs. Crewe, Sir George and Lady Beaumont; house thin and performance, in consequence, apparently flat. Sad falling off from what used to be the interest. Came away before the end of farce. Have thought latterly on old subject of Negat. Signs, in consequence of book sent me by Masères, viz. Frend's 'Algebra.'

June 2nd.—News by telegraph that, in Paris papers of 29th, Buonaparte was said to have sailed from Toulon on the 19th, with twelve sail of line and eight frigates. From other accounts I heard that there were also 300 sail of transports. The last accounts from Curtis were that he was off Finisterre on the 15th. Lord St. Vincent not likely to move or detach till he comes, so that if the French are going to Malaga we are probably too late.

6th.—Water party to Greenwich: Lord Somerville, Lady Salisbury, Lady Sutherland, Mrs. Wilmot, Lady Bruce, Lady Charlotte Bruce, Mr. Osborne, Mrs. Fitzherbert, Lord Digby. Obliged to quit Greenwich on account of expected motion of St. John about O'Connor.

7th.—Called on Dr. Burney who related notion that he had found in St. Augustine, I think, of the divisions of a verse corresponding to the relations of the squares on the sides of the hypotenuse, that is to say, that every harmonious verse is divided first into two parts and then one of the divisions divided again into two, so that the square of the half-foot of one of these shall be equal to the sum of the squares of the half-feet in the other two: a most foolish fancy.

9*th.*—Guards to march to-morrow morning to Portsmouth, to embark for Ireland. Cabinet have never yet heard a word of Ireland. Whole number of troops now gone or under orders, according to return from Calvert 6,806 effective.

10*th.*—Dined at Lord Salisbury's: present, Calonne,* Stair, Lady Talbot, &c. No confirmation yet of Waterford news, *i. e.* of defeat of insurgents near Rosse.

11*th.*—Conversation with Arden. St. John's motion, I think, about O'Connor. Spoke — Lord Hawkesbury said well.

12*th.*—Dinner: Wickham and Chevalier Bayard. The latter stayed after Wickham was gone: he did not think well of St. André: not pleased with the conduct of Blankenburgh: appeared to adopt my idea of Puisaye.

13*th.*—Lord Cornwallis declared Lord-Lieutenant.

14*th.*—House. Sheridan's motion on Ireland. Spoke. Opportunity of saying something about Quiberon; that they fired a passing shot, would never lie fairly alongside.

15*th.*—Elliot arrived from Ireland. Debate on Duke of Leinster's motion. Took leave of Abbé Guillo, who was to go in the evening, in company with Georges and others. Georges took with him 3,000*l.*; two for payment of debts engaged for by Puisaye, one for current service.

16*th.*—From illness of horse, have left off riding and walked about without boots; for some reason uncommonly well.

17*th.*—Went after Wickham: found him at Canning's, where Frere. State of news from French papers about Mediterranean fleet.

18*th.*—Drove to Hampstead: pleasant enough. Sir Sidney Smith (who had been expected) came: returned in carriage with us.

* The Ex-Bourbon Minister, then in exile.

20th.—Romel's proposal was for obtaining, through means of certain sous-chefs, the nomination to military commands, garrison and others, of persons well affected. Everything of this sort he described as very much overlooked by the Directory. Third reading of the Militia Bill.

22nd.—Debate on Irish business. Lord G. Cavendish's motion. House very oppressive; anxious, therefore, that I should not be obliged to speak; no call for it. Grant, however, made one, by speaking after debate seemed to have ended and speaking uncommonly well.

23rd.—Saw M. Rehague. A repetition only of former conversation, that all which there was for me to do was to procure pecuniary assistance which I should do as far as I could.

25th.—Office. Dined with Canning, Hammond, Wickham, Canning's cousin. French paper to 22nd. Prospect rather better of Nelson's overtaking him.

26th.—News of action at Vinegar Hill; afterwards recovery of Wexford.

27th.—Levee. Made communication to the King of what was intended. Said all that I had purposed and sufficiently satisfactorily. Conversation with Mr. Pitt, on subject of not calling Cabinet; first time of seeing him since day of debate with Tierney. Walked after tea to Puisaye who walked back with me, settling about Canada.

July 2nd.—Walked to Chelsea through gardens. Took shelter from shower under haystack. Waterman boasting of cruelties practised on seals, under notion of fun. Reproved him, but not enough. Stayed afterwards and made communication to Mrs. Crewe.

8th.—Walked out round by Lincoln's Inn: stopped in returning by Canning, who called to me from window.

10th.—Up between six and seven. Wrote note and sent it to Miss Rich. Wrote some other letters. At Binfield by about half-past ten. Between eleven and twelve went with Cecy and Mrs. B. in chaise to Mr. Wilson's: Mrs. Forest, Mr. Arthur, Margaret and Harriet following in Mr. Wilson's coach. Byng and I walked from Mr. Wilson's to church, whither Cecy came in the chaise.* The solemn ceremony performed, the impression of which, and the vows made during the time, will never, I hope, be effaced from my mind, we went back to the house, from whence about two o'clock we set out for Reigate. It was twelve or near before we arrived.

25*th*.—Ordered spying-glass for Puisaye from Ramsden. Fear that Blanket will be too late and not in force sufficient. Reports from the officers of the frigate lately taken that light transports had been sent to Europe, to the Mauritius, and thence, with some other force, ordered to the Red Sea. Thinks that the expedition from Toulon will very possibly go on, Buonaparte succeeding or not succeeding in giving Nelson the slip.

27*th*.—Mrs. Crewe came from Bulstrode. Ill in the morning. Sat till I was sick and tired at the War Office. Cecy too late. Distress in consequence. Agitated at this first interview with Mrs. Crewe, &c. Day in the end pleasant.

31*st*.—Wanted, as I recollect, to procure a meeting between Puisaye and Wickham, in which they might have conferred on many points, without interruption from the presence of any third person but myself.

August 2*nd*.—Drawing-room. Presentation at dinner: Lady Palmerston, Lady Mary Fordyce, Malone, who came in by chance. Lady M. stayed till late. Cecy, when I came down, had singed her feathers. Slight ill-humour.

12*th*—Dinner at Hampstead. Walked home with President de Frondeville.

18*th*.—Council at one, upon communication from Russia. Agree to it, upon the event of war breaking out again with Austria, but prefer a concert between the three, *i.e.*

* His marriage to Miss Cecilia Forest.

us, Russia, and Austria. In the separate offer to Russia, the whole idea seems to be of employing any force they may furnish against Holland, and, as it stands at present, they will be limited to that object. Idea thrown out by Pitt, of employing them on the coast of France, as I thought, only thrown out; and even that accompanied by what would be perfect destruction to it, the getting possession of the French navy. Talked afterwards with Canning: his opinion much the same as mine, all or none; *i. e.* the country to remain as it is, upon a pure defensive, unless you can have a universal co-operation.

21st.—Went to Lord Spencer, in consequence of the news of Buonaparte's arrival at Alexandria; with him to Pitt's. Not more than an even chance, that there is even an exaggeration in the news. Certain that some part of the army must have arrived, and that the enemy are in possession.

22nd.—Council. Draft changed from what first proposed: whole offer limited to 100,000*l.* per month. This, I think, in case of a coalition. How, in case of separate engagement with R., I don't recollect, except that there was to be an advance of 300,000*l.*, and 50,000*l.* per month to be paid afterwards should peace be made by them with our consent. About 8,000,000*l.* the war expense of Austria; 90*l.* a man about the calculation, as I understand, of a seaman.

24th.—Went to Vauxhall: gala night. Still very few persons and not at all of the sort as formerly.

27th.—News of French descent at Killala.

31st.—Called at Admiralty and told Lord Spencer report from French papers about Nelson, &c. Saw Duke of Portland first time since his accident.

September 1st.—Dined with Lady Buckinghamshire. Sat for some time in garden looking with telescope at Mars, which is nearer the earth than it has been for two hundred years. News of defeat of troops under Lake.

2nd.—Called at Wimbledon where sat with Huskisson, who showed me paper from Eton founded on the idea of expelling the Turks from Europe, in order to enable them to concentrate their force against the French in Egypt.

8th.—News that Nelson had totally failed in his search for Buonaparte and had returned on 19th July to Sicily. He seemed to have been at Alexandria on the 28th.

12th.—It was day of news of French surrender, I think.

15th.—News from Berlin, ultimately from Constantinople, of victory over Buonaparte by the Beys: 8,000 said to be killed, and 2,000 prisoners. The probability (221 probably) that it is not true. Great evidence, however, of the good disposition of the Turks and of the people upon the spot. Enclosed despatch to be returned to Mr. Wickham, marking *secret* on the cover.

21st.—News conveyed the day before by telegraph of sailing of nine or ten ships of war from Brest; supposed to be for Ireland. Came in Paris papers of the 15th.

23rd.—*Felbrigg.*—Long walk after dinner; conducted by Mary and Kitty, out by greenhouse and round by lodge, white gate, new walk and home by corner of Underwood.

24th.—Went to Wolterton. Day delightful. Came home through what I take to be Spurrel's Yard.

26th.—Lady Suffield in morning. Sent message to George Wyndham who had just come into the country. Plague about Byng's dog: out of humour about it when I went to bed.

27th.—Examined with William and Robert in library Norden's and Pocock's account of Aboukir, or Bequières, the place where Nelson is supposed to have had his victory, announced in letter from Mr. Pitt.

28th.—Rode with William and Robert to Aldborough in expectation of cricket match; thence to Gunton, on way to Aylsham.

29th.—Dinner at Kerrison's.

30*th.*—Called on Mr. Pitt, with a view to speaking about business of Clothing.

October 3rd.—Letter of news of Nelson's victory.

4*th.*—Returned from Aylsham. Brought with me M. Tricoville, Conseiller au Parlement de Rouen; modest, humble man, not very intelligent, nor of very elegant manners. I rode, asking his permission for putting Moreton in the chaise.

8*th.*—Rode to Cromer with Cholmondeley and Cecilia. Galloped to Roughton in pursuit of Byng, whom Cecilia was to have accompanied to Sheringham Gap.

The Right Hon. W. Windham to Captain Lukin.

Felbrigg: October 9, 1798.

DEAR WILLIAM,—Lord Spencer, in his answer to my letter, says:—'Lukin's destination remains still open; and if you like it, he shall be attached to the Channel Fleet, which, I believe, in the present state of things, is as well as anything.' My application was, as you described, to be attached to some of the western squadrons. What are your wishes upon this?

So Nelson is only to be a Baron. I am not sure that the decision is not right, on the principle of considering, not merely the merit and importance of the action, but the rank of the commander; but I doubt whether it would have been so had he been *David* Nelson, instead of *Horatio*.

Was there any history as to the 'Culloden's' getting on shore, more than the necessary risk from her being the leading ship? I am supposing the possibility of some want of skill in the 'Mutine;' supposing, what may not have been the fact, that the 'Mutine' was commanded by Capell.

Yours truly, W. W.

15*th.*—Day of race. My only horse Cleopatra.

20*th.*—Rode to Cromer for purpose of meeting Sir W. Howe. Went into Byng's room and wrote long letter to Canning. Intelligence of action seen off the coast of Ireland.

21*st*.—News arrived in London of Sir J. Warren's* victory.

22*nd*.—Day delicious. Rode with Cecy through Aylmerton Field and back by south gate. Greenhouse to gather nosegay.

December 1*st*.—Princess's, with Lord Minto; Duke and Duchess of Leeds there.

9*th*.—Cabinet on Grenville's instructions. Gave my opinion about mention of re-establishment of better government.

18*th*.—Cabinet; I think, Irish affairs; but, perhaps, only question about proceedings with respect to traitors and the appointing a Secret Committee.

20*th*.—Went from the House of Commons, I think, and dined at the Duke of Portland's, where Lord Waterford and son.

24*th*.—Question started by Lord Minto about Porism: made out part before dinner, the remainder before night. First time of such things I don't know when. Very pleasant.

27*th*.—Conversation with Dundas.

29*th*.—Conversation in morning with Lord Minto, on subject, which I am beginning to moot about resignation. Learnt from Elliot that Tithes not to be brought on.

Conversation to-day, or yesterday, I think, with Duke of York about commissions to barrack-masters.

30*th*.—Called on Mr. Pitt, with a view to stating my difficulties about union. Sent in my name, but he was with Rose and Lowndes about the Bill and wished me to call another time. Elliot set off for Ireland. Huskisson strong on dangers of union.

31*st*.—Meeting at Mr. Pitt's at one. Motion about newspapers.

* Capture of Wolfe Tone.

1799.

January 2nd.—Heard from Lewis of nature of Delancey's proposal, as submitted to Duke of York: widely different from what he had talked of to me. Levee. Long conversation with the King. Stated my ideas about Thugut.

4th.—Wrote note to Mr. Pitt, desiring to see him before he should go out of town for any number of days.

5th.—Joined Lord Spencer on Serpentine River, and skated for first time.

6th.—Prince William to breakfast.

10th.—Conversation with Mr. Pitt.

11th.—Chancellor's dinner: present, Mr. Pitt, Attorney and Solicitor-General, Canning, Master of the Rolls.

17th.—Meeting at the Duke of Portland's office about Lord Camelford, in which business finally settled.

20th.—Chapel: first time of my going with Guards. Duke and Duchess of York there.

23rd.—Debate on King's message relative to union.

24th.—Did not arrive at Binfield till near nine. Melancholy with thoughts of Lady Hippisley, whom it was very unlikely I should ever see again.

29th.—Wrote to Speaker, with whom I was to have dined the next day. Stated, in part, opinion about measures.

31st.—Particular incident.

February 1st.—Day of debate on Union.

4th.—*Bath.*—Sat with Lord Howe. In the evening Mr. Vanburgh's, and ball in new rooms. Miss Wroughton at ball, looking like a mummy, dead and dressed. Wrote to Mr. Pitt about deanery at Wells, vacant by the death of the Dean on Saturday night.

6th.—Occupied, as during the preceding part, with things mathematical or physical; partly, also, metaphysical.

7th.—Debate on Union, whether Speaker should leave the chair. Thought at intervals of what I might say: provided something in case of necessity. Spoke—following Sheridan; missed and mismanaged a good many things.

9th.—Dined with Canning.

13th.—Cabinet dinner: all but Dundas, at Lord Westmoreland's.

14th.—Day of the Speaker's curious proceeding in calling to Lord Belgrave. Great regret after I went home, that I had not recollected to take my hat and walk out of the House.

15th.—Proposal communicated to me through Canning of going into the House of Peers. D. no thoughts of going there. Lord G. sure to retire after the war.

22nd.—Saw Pitt about General Georges and the Royalists. He assented to my ideas and wished only a sort of estimate of what the expense might be.

23rd.—Dined with Lord Spencer: only Lord Althorpe and his tutor.

24th.—Talked in morning with Colonel Drinkwater about plan for army.

26th.—Colonel Wood called and showed me his letters to Dundas; proof, that he saw and judged well the expedition to Egypt, from so early as '96.

March 1st.—Debate on Slave Trade. Spoke dully, but plainly, I think, and distinctly. Went to Canning's to supper. Council on Martial Law Bill in Ireland.

4th.—Waked in morning, between six and seven, by

messenger, with account of Grenville's safety. Got up soon after and wrote answer to Canning.

13*th*.—Rode to Devizes. *Hair in cheese.* Story of Colonel Aylett putting soldier in black hole the night of his marriage. Gloomy thoughts before I went to bed on metaphysical matters, final causes, &c.

16*th*.—*Bath*.—Went to Pump Room. Sir G. Bowyer agrees pretty much in ideas of Quiberon as a station. Fleet—as he learns from Admiral Bowen who is here—within an ace of being lost off Caskets: all their sails split and nothing to replace them. Read pamphlet, 'Coalition against France,' written, I think, with considerable force both of thought and expression. Query author? I have an idea of Coombe.

17*th*.—Church. Dr. Rennel preached; manner excellent; discourse exceedingly good.

20*th*.—*Bath*.—Went out with Cecilia so as to meet the Duchess of Newcastle, by appointment at the Pump Room, at one. Home in time to dress and write a few lines to Kitty, now Mrs. Wright, and poor Dr. Neville.

24*th*.—Employed in drawing out the account in 'Adversaria,' containing an explanation for Cecy of the principles of the common arithmetic notation, preparatory to a better understanding of the ordinary rules of arithmetic. Dined at the Duchess of Newcastle's.

26*th*.—Contradictory accounts of operations between the French and Austrian armies at Coira. Letter from Woodford to say that the bad accounts were the true ones, *i. e.* the result unfavourable.

April 1*st*.—Dinner at home. Read all the evening new collection of 'Intercepted Letters,' published to-day.

9*th*.—Letter in answer to Duke of York about arrears. News of actions between Archduke and Jourdan up to 25th ult. French success in Italy and the Grisons—the last from the French papers. Hammond will not believe [illegible] the Queen [illegible] Ireland [illegible]

[illegible] present. Lady [illegible] Leveson. G. [illegible] called at [illegible] Street [illegible]

[illegible] of settlement [illegible] of Austrian [illegible] Ambassador's [illegible] go to Berlin [illegible] war with France. [illegible]—affect to [illegible] which they have [illegible] the purpose.

[illegible] relative to [illegible] with Pitt: present, [illegible] Lord Hawkesbury, Huskisson. [illegible] just enquiring for her [illegible]

25th.—[illegible] measure settled of sending to [illegible] It is hoped that a return may be made, [illegible] in two months.

May 3rd.—Wrote to Mr. Pitt about sending provisional orders to Lord Bridport off Cape Clear. Query: How long since I urged the making provision for the Brest fleet being destined to the southward?

5th. Lord Spencer, as Nepean told me, still confident that the French are going to Ireland.

Despatch, by which it appears that Prussia is [illegible] to join the Coalition

7th.—Dined with Mr. Pitt: Speaker, Canning, Colonel Hope, Villiers. Duchess of York's birthday. Council, in which offer of Prussia accepted and opinion persisted in of employing the 45,000 Russians on the side of Switzerland, also limiting the last demand of those to come from Dantzic to 20,000. Popham goes to-morrow or next day.

8th.—Dinner at home: Staremberg, Woronzow, Circello.

11th.—Dinner at Lord Lavington's: Lady Pembroke, Lord Hugh Seymour, &c.

12th.—Visit to Comte Woronzow, made by appointment last Thursday. Read to me his two despatches strongly urging the Declaration for Monarchy. Fact that Austria had resented our refusal to consent, at the time of the possession of Toulon, to her seizing upon part of the possessions of Sardinia. The answer of the Court of St. Petersburg to the Porte has been that 'they wanted nothing.'

18th.—News by French papers, of failure of junction of the Ferrol ships.

20th.—Duke of Cumberland's ball. Came away with Pitt and Speaker. Letters from Lord St. Vincent at Gibraltar, of the 20th ult., stating that thirteen of his ships were in Tetuan Bay, driven thither by the westerly wind, three off Cadiz. No information had been received by him from England of the intended junction. Counter orders proposed.

21st.—Sir Francis Burdett's business.

22nd.—Called on Mr. Pitt who was gone out. Went to Monsieur. Visit to Monsieur, Baker Street, No. 1.

24th.—Walked round Park with Pitt, Canning and Banks. Only short previous conversation about M. Philippe.

27th.—Stayed in town to attend motion of Lord Belgrave, respecting Sunday newspapers.

28th.—Received account of event of Norwich election. [illegible]

June 4th.—[illegible] Dined at Lord Salisbury's.

5th.—Saw [illegible] at War Office, by appointment. Lady [illegible] in evening.

21st.—[illegible] reviewed Volunteers at their posts.

22nd.—Dinner at Freemasons' Tavern. Volunteers.

25th.—Dinner at home: Lord Holland, Fitzpatrick, Lord [illegible], Bishop of Meath, Sheridan, Charles [illegible]. Account [illegible] either to-day or yesterday by a Mad. de L[illegible] of [illegible].

26th.—Account published about this time of a despatch said to be intercepted from Buonaparte and sent over by Turkish Ambassador. I feel rather inclined to believe it, except as to the numbers killed, which the Turks may have been tempted to [illegible].

28th.—Council on instructions to Lord Minto. French papers giving account of removal of Directors and Sieyes [illegible], confirming the report brought by Madame de ———. Wrote to Long about business of Minorca.

July 3rd.—Debate on Tierney's resolutions. Obliged unexpectedly to speak again on subject of the object of war. Dissatisfied with what I had done, both as not being so well done as it ought, and as I feared its appearing in a lower tone. Lawrence, however, with whom I walked to Sloane Street, said not.

4th.—Dinner at Freemasons' Tavern, given by Prince of Wales. Came away with Lord Camden and Lord Chatham.

7th.—Walked before breakfast: youthful *feel* and recollection. Called on Lord Pembroke: first time of having been at Lodge.

10th.—Talked with Mr. Pitt about business of Coals. Council. Talk only of what should be done about the Netherlands, as respecting Prussia and Austria. Austria [illegible]w manifestly a wish to have them.

14*th*.—Dinner at Princess's. Lord and Lady Lavington, Canning, Frere, Mattocks, Mr. Spencer.

16*th*.—Proposed to Pitt my idea about including Royalists in case of future capitulations for troops not to serve against the Allies. Had begun letter to Lord Grenville to that effect.

17*th*.—Dined at Chancellor's, instead of dining at India House. Came home and read Hannah More.

18*th*.—Spoke for second time about sending orders to commanders in Mediterranean, about furnishing troops in case of attack on Carthagena. I am partly sure I spoke of it so long ago, as when I walked round Birdcage Walk with Pitt and Canning.

20*th*.—Council. Plan of campaign; to prevail, if possible, upon the Austrians to relinquish purpose of going to Mayence; to enter France on the side of Lyons; to propose alterations to Prussia. Query, precise terms? Pitt's idea was for us to reconquer Flanders, and for them to succeed us in Holland. Objection stated by me, that our troops would get entangled in Flanders' war, and never be got away according to the plan professed, to act on the coast of France. Question of secularisation, which Lord G. is desirous, as myself, of staving off.

26*th*.—Speaker's review: day perfectly good. Went with Lord Malmesbury in chaise.

28*th*.—Prayers in the library; read by Miss Harris.

29*th*.—Went late to Mrs. Crewe's to meet Lawrence about Mr. Burke's letters.

30*th*.—Set off for Teston, so as to arrive by dinner. Stopped in the way at Wilderness, Lord Camden's. Fordyce at Teston. Duke of York and Taylor came afterwards; Chancellor before dinner was over.

August 1*st*.—Review at Lord Romney's.*

5*th*.—Long talk with Canning on the plan of operations

* The King reviewed the Kentish Volunteers to the number of 5,000. Seven thousand persons dined in marquees erected on the lawn.

now going forward. Talk with Pitt, either to-day or yesterday, on the proposed plan of operations, and my reasons for regretting it, as compared with that, which would have reserved our strength to be applied to the coast of France. Closet. King very courteous: great commendation of Cecilia. After dinner, George, who had returned since our absence, and now Dean of Wells.

8*th*.—Dined with Duke of Portland: Lady Charlotte and Lady Mary.

11*th*.—Dined with Nepean. Had rode down and rode back. Saw Willot for the first time, where a house had been taken for him and Barthélemy* on Barnes Common. Willot is a little compact man and both in his person and countenance put me much in mind of Lord Carhampton. He talked too much and did not by his conversation give me a very high idea of his talents.

13*th*.—Too late, as I expected to be, for the beginning of the field-day: did not overtake the troops till the point of Sunning Hill. Day remarkably fine. Curious sally of the King against the emigrants and French in general. Condemnation of Dundas's attempts in West Indies and mine at Quiberon. Saw Willot, I think, for last time; he was to go next day or day after.

14*th*.—Called at Dundas's office: found Pitt and Lord Spencer. Measure agreed upon, giving red riband to Sir Sidney Smith. Dined at Lord Grenville's: present, Monsieur, Duc d'Harcourt, Bishop of Arras,† Duc de Laval, Comte d'Escars, Comte de Vaudreuil, Duc de Bourbon, Pitt. Did not break up till twelve.

15*th*.—Conversation with Pitt about Minorca. Council about persons committed. Question again urged by Chancellor relative to Lord Thanet.

16*th*.—Dined at Princess's. Taken down by the Lavingtons and returned with them. Found Canning there, on his way back from Walmer.

* Le Marquis François Barthélemy.

† Mons. de Couzies.

20*th.*—First relief, in conversation with Blane, from apprehension of possibly fatal consequence from ailment. Dinner: Dundas, Master of Rolls, Huskisson, Pelham. Great spirits.

25*th.*—Went to meet Monsieur at Tower. Shot the Bridge for the first time I don't know when.

28*th.*—This day, I think, saw Lord Gower and Lady Sutherland, whom I endeavoured to persuade to be of party at Greenwich.

29*th.*—Day of dining at Greenwich with Monsieur: present, Comte de Vaudreuil, Comte d'Escars, Bishop of Arras, Duc de Mailly, Duc de Laval, Duc d'Harcourt.

September 1*st.*—Saw Monsieur and gave opinion on supposed plan of calling forth the Royalists immediately. Gave my opinion decidedly against it.

10*th.*—*Weymouth.*—Entertainment on board the 'Anson.'

12*th.*—Recollected not till too late, my folly, in not having asked audience of the King. Doubtful whether I should not still do it; but determined against it—perhaps not improperly. Was impatient to get off, that I might be away before the King came upon the esplanade, in which I succeeded. Journey would have been comfortable, if I had not been tormented and depressed, by recollection of my own folly. Sir Sidney Smith's letters and papers. In this and recollection of former visit, which must have been considerably more than twenty years ago, forgot my discomfort.

13*th.*—Up early, as I had been during the time of my absence. Walked round grounds and wrote a long letter or two before breakfast.

14*th.*—Saw Monsieur at Guildford. In town by dinner.

17*th.*—Went only to War Office. Changed things and went to Sir William,* now Lord Howe, at Ordnance.

* General Sir William Howe, brother to the distinguished Admiral, Richard, second Viscount Howe.

Conversation with Lord Howe about arms. No resource but in purchasing arms abroad.

Conversation in morning with Bishop of Arras and Dutheil. Bishop, and apparently Dutheil, disposed to calling out Royalists, previous to any certainty of operation from Allies.

19*th.*—Long conversation, I think, with Lady Spencer,* on state of Cabinet, &c. Mention of what she had heard from Grenville about me and Pitt.

20*th.*—Rowing match. Williams, the larger and fairer man, was first at that time.

21*st.*—Went to Admiralty; Nepean, Elliot, and Lord Castlereagh there, with whom came away. After dinner read till near nine despatches from Vienna and Switzerland. Pitt come to town.

22*nd.*—Council, on question of men to be taken from the militia of Ireland. Conversation with Pitt on state of Cabinet. Walked away with Pitt and Lord Grenville: parted at Green Park; walked on with Pitt to Birdcage Walk, and settled at last to go to his house. Conversation, upon the whole, seemed to me at the time to be pretty well conducted: instances have occurred since, in which it might have been better. When shall I learn to come to occasions of this sort properly prepared?

23*rd.*—Dinner at Pitt's. Certainly a good deal of attention and of a sort pointed to the object complained of.

24*th.*—Draft received of letter to Grenville, containing plan for constitution of Holland.

25*th.*—Dinner at Pitt's. Tired and out of spirits. Pitt seemed to suspect that it was ill-humour.

26*th.*—Council, I think, on plan for constitution of Holland. Principal discourse, however, on communication from Prince of Orange, with overtures from Dutch Directory. My opinion, that I was glad of any prospect

* Lavinia, daughter of the Earl of Lucan; married, 1781, to George John, Earl Spencer.

of being out of the scrape; that it might be so—namely, that the country might fall tolerably easy, but that I doubted it: that we should hardly get to Amsterdam with the loss of less than 10,000 men. One of the stages in the Militia Bill. Short debate. Spoke in answer to Tierney. Thanks to Sir R. Abercrombie, Sir S. Smith, and Adm. Mitchell.

28*th*.—Meeting at Dundas's with Pitt and Lord Grenville, about supplies to the Royalists. Settled that arms should be ordered immediately from abroad, a sum of money advanced and an account rendered of the application of it. Arrangements to be made with the Admiralty, if not for a force to be stationed at Quiberon, at least for a convoy to the vessels now ready. Question started by Pitt, whether my idea of block-house on Houat and Hadic* should not be acted upon. Much disposition to bring the Royalists forward, if I declared against it.

29*th*.—Letters to Duke of Kent and General Hunter. Funeral of Lady Hippisley.

October 1*st*.—Council, at which proposal made for force to be subsidised. I stated and urged my objection that nothing would be left for subsidies to the interior.

4*th*.—I am reading Russell's account of Aleppo. Captain Dumaresque, with letters from Georges and Mons. de Chatillon. In morning called on Monsieur, who, I had found, was to see Pitt at twelve: he had seen Lord Grenville a day or two before.

9*th*.—Meeting of Pitt and Dundas with Lord Spencer about cruising squadron.

12*th*.—House adjourned. Tierney's observations perfectly just. Dinner at Princess's: conversation with Dundas about arrangements for Royalists.

13*th*.—General Gordon to breakfast. Thinks as I do

* The British took possession of three very small islands, Houat, Hadic, and Dumet, that are off Quiberon, and maintained them till the peace of 1802.

about Holland: would be glad to hear that the troops were all back: wonders that no attention had been given to Money's letter. News of action in Holland, preceding the retreat to original position.

18*th.*—Council. Long discussion on course to be taken with respect to Austria. Pitt had stated his opinion in the morning. I am, upon the whole, inclined to try his method. He is persuaded it would have succeeded, if Lord M. had been sent with it six months before he went. Long discussion also about Holland and about future operations in other parts. Question of the three ways in which a force might be made to act against France. Communication from Seville: agree with me that Portugal would only be an impediment. Stated as the only way, but that not desirable, to take possession at once of Cadiz.

21*st.*—Captain Keats to breakfast. Opinion that Quiberon should be a station for the whole fleet. Communication from Brest by vessels stationed and signals.

23*rd.*—Went to the Lavingtons, where was Payne Galway.

26*th.*—Council at eleven. Measure resolved on for offering Sardinia to Austria, on condition of the King of Sardinia being settled in Tuscany: the Grand Duke to have a compensation in the Netherlands. Number of roubles proposed 140,000. I gave a hesitating assent. Had occasion, in the course of the discussion, to renew my objection to the laying out all for foreign force and reserving none for force in the interior.

28*th.*—Dinner at Lord Boringdon's: Lord Morpeth. Went home with Canning, with whom talked of intended measures and found him strong in opposition to them.

29*th.*—Called on Pitt: interruptions by persons who had been appointed. Conversation resumed with Pitt in walk to Lady Chatham's: some impression made.

30*th.*—Council at St. James's. Did not go in to the King. Met Canning, who stopped the coach and urged the necessity of bringing the question of the Royalists to an issue. Drove straight to Dundas, with whom had a conversation. Saw Huskisson, and afterwards Frere. Wrote to Pitt.

31*st.*—Dined and passed the whole evening alone. Employed the whole evening, without intermission, principally in getting in order 'Royalist Journal.' How much to be regretted that I did not keep one upon the present footing when these affairs were going on, some years ago, and continued it in fact to the present time.

November 7*th.*—New plan about Vienna, in consequence of late dispatches; I explained De la Rosière's plan. Business of Royalists talked of: opened by Pitt. Proposal about sending Monsieur to Jersey. I rather argued against. Ended in opinion that he should only write.

8*th.*—Messenger from Vienna. Long report of a conversation with Thugut, in which Thugut presses against us, some facts in our conduct towards Spain and Holland, which it does not seem easy to answer. One sees also, that much of their conduct arises from the suspicion, not very ill founded, of our attempting, with the aid of Russia, to *forcer la main à l'Empereur.*

It appears, too, that with respect to Piedmont and Tuscany, we were, in the dispatches now recalled, going a great deal beyond what the Austrians required.

10*th.*—Walked out with Prof. Coleman, and saw Lord Spencer's new horse from Constantinople.

17*th.*—Called at Foreign Office; thence to Pitt's, whom I saw just before going away. Short conversation about what had happened—not such as I should have made it. Did not cry out against his idea of waiting for public opinion, nor declare sufficiently against idea of listening to proposals.

18*th.*—Letter to Mr. Pitt, to repair the omissions of yesterday.

20*th.*—Levee. Dinner at Lord Macartney's: present,

Monsieur l'Evêque d'Arras, &c. Mentioned to the King the business of the barrack-masters, but did not contrive to propose, as I intended, that the King should talk to the Duke of York upon the subject of the assistant barrack-masters. Very bad conversation of H.M. to-day, at the levee, about the emigrants. Told H.M. what I had urged to Mr. Pitt.

21*st.*—Drawing-room. Dinner at the Prince of Wales': present, Monsieur, Duc de Bourbon, Stadtholder, Hereditary Prince, Duc d'Harcourt, l'Évêque d'Arras, Archevêque de Narbonne, Monsieur de Vitry, Duc de Mortemart, Comte Étienne, Durford, Monsieur de Vaudreuil, Duc de Maillé, Comte d'Éscart, Monsieur de Polignac, Duke of Clarence, Arthur Paget, Sir H. Popham. Did not break up till eleven or past.

22*nd.*—Conversation with Frere who walked to top of Green Park, on my way to call on the Prince of Orange. Had stated to Frere my application of the conduct and character of Æneas.

27*th.*—Council on dispatches to St. Petersburg. It turns out by Wickham's dispatches, that what I thought was not sufficiently provided for, viz. the endeavouring to procure an Austro-Russian force for Suwarrow, was, in his opinion, not to be obtained, if it was even to be desired.

December 1*st.*—Up not early, *i. e.* not till past nine. Left town. I have, for a long while, felt great difficulty in rising of a morning, insomuch that I can hardly help suspecting that it may have some connection—at least latterly and within the period in which it seems to have increased—with what I now experience of a giddiness which comes on, both when I first lie down and when I rise up and in general when I stoop suddenly. It is, I conceive, about ten days since I first experienced this.

6*th.*—Went to Mrs. Crewe's, where Lord Macartney, Dr. Burney, l'Abbé Tressin. M. l'Abbé de Lisle came afterwards. I went away to Madame de Belzunce, who was at home: first of my seeing her since we met at the Hague.

8*th*—Dinner at Princess's: present, Monsieur, Duc de Bourbon, Lady Margaret, Mrs. and Miss Crewe, Chancellor, Comte Woronzow, Comte and Madame Staremberg. Came home with Lady Margaret and Chancellor. Lady M. stayed here till her carriage came.

9*th*.—Dined with Woronzow: only Huskisson there of English.

12*th*.—Council at two, on dispatches from Constantinople. Determination taken to prevent, if possible, Lord Elgin's consent to the permission to Buonaparte, *i. e.* to the army, to evacuate, or if he should have done so to counteract the effects, by sending orders to Lord Keith to force them back again. Stated my sense of the inconveniences on each side and the danger of their becoming another race of Mamelukes; but still hardly inclined to the opinion adopted. Recommended the offer of assistance to the Turks, such as that of ——, &c. &c., of sending to fortify St. Jean d'Acre. Mentioned business of compensations of St. Domingo.

13*th*.—Conversation with Pitt about future operations. Opinion changed in favour of Belleisle, which I stated to be much the case with myself—that we should be prepared in the greatest detail.

18*th*.—Mr. Disney and Robert dined here. Levee, and, I think, closet, &c. Day of Madame Lancaster. Oh! grief of griefs!

28*th*.—Skated for second time: bating the difference in activity, found that I should soon recover what I had lost.

The Right Hon. W. Windham to Captain Lukin.

Park Street, West: December 30, 1799.

Dear William,—I send down by this post a letter to General Georges, which, if it should not go with the Admiralty orders. I may perhaps enclose to you. At any rate, it must be considered as one of the letters making part of the object of the mission, and which the Commander must take charge of. I have mentioned in it what may serve as an introduction, should you happen to fall in his way. Don't venture too far on shore, and get yourself into any scrape. Georges is a plain farmer-like man, and very much of that class. He is such a figure as you might see at an audit, but very intelligent and much to be relied on in all ways. The second in command, too, Mercier, is a very excellent, modest young man. They are both well acquainted with Park Street. I don't know whether Captain Keats thinks less favourably of Chatillon. He is not very wise, but as fine, brave, honourable a chevalier as ever was.

To save Nepean trouble, I enclose my letter to General Georges to you: you will take care that it is understood to be a public letter. You will explain also to Captain Legge that Prigent, mentioned in his instructions, will not be sent this time; but that he will find nearly as good an assistant in Mr. Penhonet; and though no order can be sent for Madame Penhonet, I hope your gallantry amongst you will not leave her behind. You may get her, if she is a pretty woman, to teach you French.

Farewell! Write to me as often as anything occurs.

Yours truly,

W. Windham.

1800

January 1*st.*—Foreign Office: Mr. Pitt and Canning there.

2*nd.*—Council at eleven on Buonaparte's letter: Pitt, Grenville, Spencer, and Camden. Office. Walked with intention of calling on Sir Charles Grey. Changed mind and called on Lord Malmesbury, with whom sat for some ime. Sir George Staunton called: so bad as hardly to be articulate.

26*th.*—Miss Agnes Berry and Miss Seton dined with Cecy.

February 15*th.*—Saw M. Barantin for the first time; he came about Madame de Catnelan.

17*th.*—House. Advance of 500,000*l.* for Subsidies. Spoke. Found, on coming home, Madame de Sigy and her brother, M. de Perpiquet.

March 1*st.*—Dined at Lord Grenville's: present, Monsieur, Duc d'Orléans, and his brothers. Confirmation from French papers of Frotté's death. I had before entertained hopes.

3*rd.*—Dined with P. William.

8*th.*—At a little before nine went to the Opera. Sat in Duchess of Gordon's box. My motive in going having been to join her in hissing a dance, if it had been such as it was before.

9*th.*—Dinner at Blackheath: present, Chancellor, Lords Abercorn, Fortescue, and Lewisham. Ladies Lewisham and Williams, Duchess of Hamilton, Muir, Miss Garth.

11*th.*—Mutiny Bill.

April 2nd.—Discussion with Chancellor on alteration which I had proposed for article about union.

3rd.—Dined at Lord Spencer's: present, Prince of Wales, Admiral Colpoys, Payne, Tyrrwhit, Pitt, Lord Camden, &c.

5th.—Council: Wickham's despatches, sent by a messenger, very much for the purpose of urging the necessity of diversions here. No alteration, however, made in Expedition.

17th.—Business of union put off in consequence of Pitt not being well. Went to House to canvass and to inform myself about Sir W. Pulteney's motion. Unexpected debate. New instance of Speaker calling to another, viz. Solicitor-General. Went out of the House without staying the decision.

18th.—Spoke on business of Sir W. Pulteney: forgot several little particulars and managed some others not well; but what vexes me most is for having forgotten to bring forward the idea of enforcing a different mode of killing animals.

19th.—Walked after Council and told Pitt whom I met with Lord Chatham, of the arrival of Georges; told Pitt also of the letter that would come on the subject of allowances to field officers for horses.

Council: Expedition. Notice that the necessity stated by Sir Charles Stuart of cavalry and the impossibility of having any from Austria and difficulty of sending them from here, made it necessary that the numbers should be confined to those already embarked. Question about course to be pursued in respect to Malta.

20th.—Cecy dined at Princess's, I at Carlton House, Prince not able to dine there.

21st.—Gave notice of measure about mode of killing animals.

22nd.—Talk about Spanish, which the book subscribed for at Broadlands has made me think of beginning.

23*rd.*—Finished letter to Coke who, I am afraid, is ill, as Mrs. Coke is, dangerously. News of death of Admiral Vandeput! I should fear too true. Called on Lord Liverpool, to consult him about business of Speaker, before I should speak to him. Denunciation from Wilberforce of resumption of business about bull-baiting.

26*th.*—Rode to Riding-house: Lord Heathfield there. Satisfaction at what I had said about bull-baiting. Dinner at Duke of Clarence's, where obliged to dine, instead of at the Royal Academy: present, Duc d'Orléans and his brothers, Duc de Bourbon, Comte d'Escars, Duc de Maillé, M. de Vitry, Prince William, Duke of Cumberland, Stadtholder, Lord Moira, Lord Cholmondeley, Lord Liverpool, Lord Leicester,* Sir J. Warren, Lord Harrington and Colonel Dalrymple.

May 1*st.*—Council. Troops not to be sent to Portugal. Distribution of troops here (Bagshot). No one seems to know how the question has been settled.

7*th.*—Levee. Presented Duc de Castries and Baron de Rolle. Sir Charles Stuart and Duc de Mortemart were invited.

10*th.*—Went to Windsor with Douglas: arrived by two: King there at three. Kept talking till four. Sort of solemn admonition about the Catholics.

15*th.*—Night of the King's danger at the play-house. Had been talking after dinner, probably at the very moment when the case happened, of the plea of insanity as an exemption from punishment.

Council. Pitt not there. Agreed to acquiesce in what was proposed by Austria, viz. Sardinia to be put, as it were, in commission till the end of the war; to which commission Lord Grenville thought we had better send only an Ambassador: legations to be given to them; we, not to be parties, but to engage to dispose the Italian

* George Viscount Townshend was created in May, 1784, Earl of Leicester, and in 1787, Marquis Townshend.

powers. Lucca to be taken by them also. Something, I think, to be given from Genoa to Sardinia. Upon these terms engagements not to take place but by concert for a twelvemonth, I think. Declaration only for the restoration of a safe government. Subsidy 2,000,000*l.*, I think, instead of 1,600,000*l.*

16*th.*—Levee. Stood by Lord Westmoreland and talked to the King on the subject of what had passed. He seemed to like our introducing it.

26*th.*—Lady Carnarvon's to meet Princess.

30*th.*—Day of Divorce Bill. Up late. Unusually languid and incapable of exertion. So perplexed between the two things I had to do, viz. the business of the Divorce Bill and motion about Soldiers' Children, that in the state of bodily languor in which I was I could do nothing.

31*st.*—News of Mary's* death! Simpson was breakfasting with me, when opening, just before he went, a letter which, I observed, had the Bath post-mark, though not in Mrs. Lukin's hand, the fatal intelligence was told all at once.

The Right Hon. W. Windham to Captain Lukin.

London: May 31.

Sad, sad news, my dear William, I have to send you; not of a public, but of a private nature, and such as will try your spirits and affect your kind heart more than anything that has yet befallen you. Your poor sister Mary! never will you see her more! never more will she welcome your return, rejoice in your success, and glad the hearts of us all by her gay and amiable manners, and by her kind and virtuous affections! After a long and bad labour, which ended in the death of the child, and after fostering our hopes for some days by an appearance of doing well, she failed all at once, and has left us nothing but to lament the breach thus made in the happiness of the family, to follow her with our regrets, and to console ourselves

* Mary, eldest daughter of the Dean of Wells and Mrs. Lukin.

[illegible]

[illegible] Mrs. [illegible]

[illegible]

[illegible] of poor [illegible] Mary.

The Right Hon. W. Windham to Mrs. Crewe.

Bath: June 3, 1800.

You know probably the melancholy business that has brought us hither. This very morning I have been employed in performing the last sad duties to the memory of poor dear Mrs. Foy, and conveying her remains to the grave. You know, in general, that I had a very lively regard for her. I really loved her as a daughter and not every father has had a daughter attached to him so much, as I believe she was to me. You were not acquainted with all he merits, nor with many captivating parts of understanding and manner, that only developed themselves upon nearer and longer acquaintance. Her death has thrown a shade over many parts in the prospects of life that were before full of brightness and hope. As if all was to be melancholy upon our arrival here, the answer I received upon a message sent to enquire after Mrs. Coke,* was that she had died a few hours before. I do not mention this loss as coming in competition with the other; but it involves in it much, that one had been in the habit of contemplating with satisfaction, and from which, at different times, part of my own happiness had been derived. Our stay here cannot be long—I fear not longer than Friday or Saturday. There is business in the House which it is necessary that I should attend. I could otherwise spend a week or more here with great satisfaction, with great pleasure indeed, but for the melancholy which the occasion of our coming throws over all one's thoughts. Bath has a charm to me which owes nothing to its condition as a public place and to which the company, in fact, would be a hindrance. I like the place itself, the idea which it inspires and the recollections which it recalls. It is accordingly on that account, as well as from the greater beauty of the scenery and greater facility of enjoying it, infinitely pleasanter to one in summer than in winter. Mrs. W. is better for the journey, though worse for the strong regret she feels for Mary, whom she was very fond of, and the sympathy which she has for the loss of Mrs. Lukin, who, however, from the extreme anxiety that she had felt about Mrs. Foy, while her

* Mrs. Coke, daughter of James Dutton, father of the first Lord Sherborne. Married Thomas William Coke of Holkham, created, 1837, Earl of Leicester.

fate was in suspense, finds herself now in a state of repose, that, aided by her own strength of mind and habits of piety, enables her to come to the aid of poor Mr. Foy, who, having suffered himself to be before more sanguine, is more struck down with the blow now that it has happened. His conduct has very much confirmed the opinion that we had before conceived of him, and embittered the sense one has of the happiness that he and Mrs. Foy might have enjoyed together. Farewell!

Yours ever affectionately,

W. WINDHAM.

June 4.

P.S.—My letter not having been in time for the post yesterday, I open it just to say that I have received your notes and thank you for them. We shall hardly be back in time to dine with you on Sunday.

16*th.*—Lady Willoughby in the evening.

23*rd.*—Catholic business. Spoke at length.

The Right Hon. W. Windham to Earl Spencer.

June 25, 1800.

MY DEAR LORD,—I hear that the proverb is verified, that misfortunes do not come single, and that you have received some bad news at the Admiralty. I conclude it is of the failure of the attempt under Maitland. Will you have the goodness to let me have a line? One is so 'supped full of horrors,' that a little more or less, bating the loss of individuals, cannot make much difference. I could have wished, however, that we had happened to have stood clear of this blast, except by the share we must have in its consequences.

Yours truly,

W. WINDHAM.

Eleven o'clock, Wednesday evening.

July 5*th.*—Breakfasted at Chiswick.

6*th.*—Dinner at Windsor.

11*th.*—Showed to Duke of Portland letter of 9th of May from Pitt. Report of Treason Bill and suggestion thrown out of change of law.

12*th.*—Saw Bishop of Arras and settled with him for visit of Pichegru in evening: he and Tinseau came. Details of battle of Marengo.

14*th.*—Frogmore fête.

15*th.*—Up at seven; out a little after eight; on the ground, viz. the Obelisk, by nine. King not come. Armies manœuvring: ended in position on high range of hills. Prince of Wales there and Duke of Cumberland. Kept by King.

16*th.*—Council, of which the result was, I understand, that Lord Malmesbury was to concur in negotiation for general peace if Austria insisted upon it, but on no account to consent to an armistice.

17*th.*—Entertainment at Lodge and review in the morning at Winkfield Plain. Congratulation of the King that I had not been at Council of day before. If peace to be made, Grenville to be the person. In the evening the King told me of his having chosen a primate: as Mr. Pitt would not, he had!

18*th.*—Late in getting to town. Day of Austrian Subsidy. Ready to speak, but not dissatisfied upon the whole that I did not, as I felt flat and heavy and should hardly have spoken well. P. did not seem to wish me to do so: he probably knew of Canning's intention.

27*th.*—Large concourse upon the Terrace (Windsor). Cecy drank tea with the Queen: the men were with the Equerries.

28*th.*—By royal command, went to field-day instead of to the Eton Speeches. Lord Palmerston and his son there. Arrived not quite in time. Rode a great deal with the King. When I came back, no horses to be had. Stayed necessarily to dinner. Had gone round by Staines, principally with a view of calling on the Duc d'Harcourt, who is, I fear, in a very declining state. Saw the Duchess of H. and Duchess of Mortemart, for the first time.

August 1*st.*—Rowing match. The name of the first man

[illegible] as in the [illegible] thence arise [illegible] but is liable to [illegible]

* The present Vis[illegible] de Redcliffe.

16*th*.—Went through Newbury to Andover, where we dined; thence with four horses to Wilton, where we arrived between nine and ten.

17*th*.—Church in the morning. Hot weather still continues. Got up early in morning and looked out of window. The beer at Andover had given me the heartburn and took off from my satisfaction: the scene and the recollections would otherwise have been a source of considerable pleasure. C. vexed that we did not go with the Malmesburys.

18*th*.—Arrived at Weymouth by half-past three. Had taken four horses for the last two stages. Malmesburys and the King sailing. Missed the King upon the Parade, who from what he said seemed to have expected to meet me.*

20*th*.—Malmesbury went.

The Right Hon. W. Windham to the Hon. Mrs. Byng.

Weymouth: August 22, 1800.

Here we are breakfasting at the hotel, and looking out upon the beach where you used to figure, if I mistake not, attended by your Major Yorkes and other gallants. Poor Malone, too, who by an unfortunate Irish stare, not at all belonging to his character, lost the favour of a woman who might have made him happy, and probably herself too. We came here on Monday from Wilton, where we stayed a day, and where we found Lord

* The following passage from Lord Malmesbury's Diaries explains the important objects for which the King had commanded Mr. Windham's attendance at Weymouth:—

'I was told this evening by Pelham that His Majesty had for a long time since been dissatisfied with Pitt's, and particularly Lord Grenville's, "authoritative manners" towards him, and that an alteration in his Ministry had been often in his mind; that it was with this view he had sent for Windham and myself in August last to Weymouth; that he meant Windham should be his First Minister, and I have the seals for the Foreign Department. The ill success of the Austrians, the proposals brought forward by Pitt, through Otto, perplexed the King, and diverted his attention from his purpose; and Windham also, by his odd and unacquiescent manner, did not encourage His Majesty in his views.'—Vol. iv. p. 23.

luct, any more than he could urge a man to fight if he himself did not feel the necessity. News by the French papers of the new convention made by the Emperor for the purpose of prolonging the armistice for forty-five days and with the condition of giving up the fortress of Ulm, Philipsburgh, and Ingoldstadt.

29*th.*—Confirmation of the account of the Emperor of Russia having laid on the embargo and also of his having taken it off.

November 1*st.*—Cobenzal's letter from Luneville.

11*th.*—Day of Parliament meeting. No call for speaking, unless possibly for one moment, when Nicholl began his old attack about Bellum Internecinum, a pupil of Burke's, &c. which would have let me in very advantageously for all I have thought of saying to him, some time or other, upon that subject. But I felt not in temper to make that sort of reply, nor, as it appeared to me, the House either, and I can hardly now say that I judged wrong. The debate would have ended, but that Grey brought out the speech, which he had come prepared with, but which circumstances had put aside.

The Right Hon W. Windham to Mrs. Crewe.

November 16, 1800.

The aspect of affairs is not good; but there does not appear any immediate prospect of peace—the blessings of peace—and that being the case there is still hope. In war a thousand things may happen, but peace once made, the power of Buonaparte seems certainly fixed, and I know not then how we are to escape. Everything is, however, very bad: one Emperor mad, another weak and pusillanimous; the King of Prussia governed by narrow, selfish, and short-sighted counsels: no vigour, no energy, no greatness of plan, but in the French, and they accordingly govern everything. Nothing is so clear to me, as that a small portion of the soul of Mr. Burke, infused into the counsels of countries and among others of our own, would have rescued the world from this dreadful state long ago. You are very good in excusing that part of our silence which took place at Weymouth. Though there was much from there that I wished often to write to you about, because I thought you would like to hear of royal tittle-tattle, yet the life we lived made it almost impossible. You cannot conceive anything so strange and so unsuited, as it would seem, both to me and Mrs. W.; yet, we really did not dislike it; the extreme graciousness of the King and Queen, and the extraordinary amiableness of all the Princesses, made everything but the hurry of it uncommonly pleasing, and has given me an interest about them that marks our visit there as an epoch in one's life. It was not for want of thinking of you—if you could suspect such a thing—that I did not write, for in my rides with His Majesty we had a great deal of conversation about you.

Yours faithfully, W. W.

—*From the Crewe Papers.*

December 2nd.—Council on questions relative to New Privy Council, whether must be considered as *ipso facto* dissolved; whether this Privy Council to have general jurisdiction. Doubt now about the 'Britanniarum'—the King dislikes it.*

3rd.—Dinner at London Tavern; India Company given to Lord Nelson. Sat between Dundas and Lord Macartney.

9th.—I had spoke in the House and though rising without embarrassment and no distrust of myself, somehow or other got confused and bewildered and in consequence prolix. It was in answer to what Sheridan had advanced of the right of the poor to relief. The instance vexed me, as proving that I was less sure of myself than I supposed. I feared also misrepresentation in the newspapers, which, however, did not take place.

14th.—Called by appointment on Monsieur, who wants details of measures to be taken about army of Condé.

* These questions arose out of the recent Union of Great Britain and Ireland.

23rd.—Drove to Malone's, not having heard anything of them since the day but one before. He had got down-stairs and thought his leg much better. Historical and antiquarian anecdotes. Gentlemen of the Long Robe as opposed to those of the Short Robe. Speaker smoking.

26th.—Day of hearing of William's appointment to the ship 'Doris.'

27th.—Dined at Hammond's. Met Mr. Mackenzie, the person who had travelled to the N. W. coast of America. Present: Huskisson, G. Ellis.

1801.

January 1*st.*—Malone ill with his leg.

4*th.*—Went to see Cook in 'Macbeth' in Lord Chesterfield's box.

February 6*th.*—Dined at Lord Spencer's: present, Grenville, Admiral Young, Lady A. Bingham. Went in the evening to Sir William Scott's. This the occasion, I think, of my speaking to him about expected changes.

7*th.*—Dined at the Speaker's, Mr. Addington.

18*th.*—I went in the morning to Buckingham House: probably interview with the King.

22*nd.*—Dined at Canning's. Payne* called and left note, founded on some dictation from the Prince of Wales.

28*th.*—Cecilia called for the first time to make enquiry after the King.

March 18*th.*—Day of receiving news of Mr. Congreve's death.

The Right Hon. W. Windham to Captain Lukin.

Felbrigg: October 17, 1801.

Dear William,—I perfectly approve of your getting into Parliament, if you can. I had thought of the thing before. What anybody is to do in Parliament, hereafter, I don't know. We are all going fast down the gulf-stream, and shall never stop, I fear, till, with the rest of Europe, we fall under the universal empire of the great Republic. We have signed and sealed; and, as Dogberry, I think, says, 'shall never be our own man again.' I really think there is an end of us.

* Commonly called Jack Payne, and a favourite of the Prince of Wales.

We leave this, the day after to-morrow, in order that I may have some days to look about me before the meeting of Parliament. I have had but little enjoyment here. The state of the country perfectly weighs upon my spirits. Love to all.

Yours affectionately,

W. W.

P.S.—I should rejoice in your bull-baiting if I could rejoice in anything. They have taken their motto well. I defy a person to attack bull-baiting and to defend hunting.

October 25*th.*—Dined at home alone. Cecy at Disney's. Prince William with me till five.

November 4*th.*—Debate * on Report of Preliminaries: spoke.

24*th.*—Canning and Pitt here in the morning.

* Debate was on the Peace of Amiens, when Mr. Windham spoke.

[illegible]

[illegible] —[illegible] Day of Election.

[illegible]—[illegible] and meaning to [illegible] [illegible] Mr. Canning's. Pitt [illegible] [illegible] afterwards.

[illegible] —[illegible] were Mr. Luttrell and L[illegible] [illegible]

[illegible] —[illegible] Commons and proved [illegible] [illegible] and saw Mrs. Glover.* I w[illegible] [illegible] who thinks about [illegible] [illegible] Day of C[illegible] [illegible] Slave Trade. This day, I think I [illegible] with Allegre.

[illegible] —[illegible] past twelve in [illegible], which I [illegible] [illegible]

[illegible] —[illegible] I think, when Byng br[illegible] [illegible] of Mrs. Byng's illness. Went off for Hill[illegible] [illegible] arrive till near eleven. Mrs. B[illegible] [illegible] see her that night.

2[illegible] —Mrs. Byng [illegible] pain and in good spirits, but required to be [illegible]. Passed the day at Cockburn's. I [illegible] read Churchill, which I found among Sir James's books; part of the 'Ghost,' and the 'Conference,' which last I had read—when quite young—before one of the times of my being at Bristol with my mother. Great facility of versification and style and occasionally considerable force of expression; some good strokes too

* Celebrated actress.

of character, but in general, I think, tiresome reading—a great proportion of words to meaning.

31*st.*—Not up till nine. Delayed dressing in consequence of taking up Heliodorus. Saw Robert, who has been elected at Magdalene, afterwards Wyatt, about Felbrigg.

August 1*st.*—Continued to read Heliodorus, with no other interruption than that of a walk of half an hour or more upon the leads, when thought of political matter. Returned to Heliodorus, and continued reading till two. After dinner C. and I walked in Mall and Green Park. Crowds of people: gave me pleasant feel of former times.

2*nd.*—In the evening Cobbett, who showed me letter from Swede and Georges, who called to tell me of the state in which his officers were. Nothing advanced but 25*l.* from Sir H. Dalrymple, without waiting for authority. Great good-will in general from Sir H.; much the contrary from General Gordon. Wishes for a sum. Three or four years. Does not allow a much longer term for the fate of this country. Evidently has in view some change, which he thinks must take place in France, and for which he wishes his officers to be at liberty.

3*rd.*—Went by appointment to Lawrence.

4*th.*—Went to see the 'Invisible Girl.' Conversation in coming back with Cobbett, whom I had called upon; so that not at home till four.

30*th.*—Found letter from Cobbett, stating his having set off for Southampton, in consequence of the reports of the arrests of the persons at Jersey and here.

September 2*nd.*—Georges assured me that there were none of the persons now in question who were chargeable with any act done since the Peace but one, and that was a person, who in coming away had been attacked by two gensdarmes and had killed one in his own defence. The act that might most have been complained of, viz. the putting to death a person who had been seized and kept in custody, with a view of obtaining money—had been committed by persons who were actually here before the Peace was signed.

7th.—Saw Comte Boterel and M. de St. Victor. Did not know the latter till his name was mentioned. Miserable distress: must try to get him something to enable him to go to France. Saw Sir John Warren, who has promised to give me a narrative of the proceedings at Elba, and summary of what he has drawn up about Quiberon.

8th. — Levee. Confidential communication from Addington. Froud there in his new capacity, *i. e.* in consequence of the new arrangement respecting the King.

15th.—Conversation with Pelham, who has quieted me about the inference to be drawn from the infamous paragraph in the 'True Briton.'

18th.—Cecy went to Binfield. Lawrence and I accompanied them to Dropmore: followed Lord Grenville to Stoke Park, where he was with the yeomanry.

21st.—Duke's opinion about Fox's visit to Paris not very different from mine: Prince of Wales's opinion about it.

26th.—Sheridan's explicit disapprobation of journey to Paris: many reasons for wishing to go there himself, but would not: did not wish to have received any civility which might interfere with his manner of speaking of Buonaparte.

October 3rd.—Chief reading during my stay here (Billingbear) has been Congreve's 'Comedies,' all of which I have read through: perfectly answer Johnson's description of them, 'Intrigue was plot,' &c. I read, moreover, first part of 'Peregrine Pickle:' not at all tempted to read on.

7th.—Drawing-room: much talk with the Princesses: Lord St. Helens there.

10th.—Rode to Fawkener's at Hampstead: Duc de Lorges and Madame de Villefort; the latter I had never seen before. Rode back: fine moonlight: less enjoyment of it from necessary attention to my horse.

12*th*.—Went to play: Kemble as 'Falstaff.'

14*th*.—At Hammond's, where I dined; Canning, Leigh, and Lord Boringdon, who is going abroad into Normandy and thence to Spain. Walked away with Canning and Leigh. Accompanied them to Albemarle Street, thence walked by myself in square till past eleven.

15*th*.—Returned to proposition which I had made out, I think, after I had gone to bed.

November 4*th*.—Sent letter to Addington about Louisiana, written the day before.

7th.—Called on Paul Johnson. Sent over to William and Anne upon the chance of Colonel Metzner, who came just as dinner was upon table. He had been aide-de-camp with Lord M. to Knyphausen. The loss at Bunker's Hill was a thousand: I include killed and wounded.

8th.—Day of inspection. Numbers present, 86, exclusive of three serjeants. Rode part of the way with Colonel Metzner to put him in the road to Barningham; turned off beyond Gresham, thence by Beacon and the valleys home.

11th.—Went to Norwich by dinner. Saw in going part of Mr. Harbord's company.

[illegible]

[illegible] pleasant [illegible] what [illegible] desire, [illegible] But a word that [illegible] I [illegible] yesterday as I [illegible] think contrary to what I [illegible] expected previously, that the son of Lord Chatham's family physician, will submit to take the Blue Ribbon and a Peerage. I give him this description, not as considering it to be any reproach to him, but as a further proof of what the Peerage has become of late years. Addington will infallibly be the Minister of the King's confidence. For my own individual impression, and I suppose for that of others on our side, I like it much; it makes the game clear and neat. The division of parties and politics is made as it ought to be: Mr. P. and the persons of his creation, pure and unmixed, on one side, and all the rest of the public men on the other. We have all the authors and actors in the Peace of Amiens now together, and so I hope they will continue till the great crash comes, which may make things set off again upon new principles. This, I think, is as much as can reasonably be expected on public matters. For private—Mrs. W. and I are are both very sorry for the death of Lord Rosslyn, who, whatever faults might belong to him, was a friendly, kindly-disposed man, and one whom I liked to associate with. He had an enjoyment of life that imparted enjoyment to others, as well as a variety of knowledge and experience that rendered his conversation interesting and instructive. His death will be felt by our Duke—as you call him—with whom he had been in perfect health a few hours only before his death, and who is, I fear, himself very far from being so well as one could wish. I hope there is no truth in the report of his going to have a pension.

Farewell! When are we to see you in town?

W. W.

—*From the Crewe Papers.*

7th.—Learnt from Grenville that Addington is to be Peer and President, an Earl it is said; Lord Mulgrave to be Foreign Secretary and Ward, Under-Secretary: but a story that the King objected, *i. e.* to Mulgrave, and the reason supposed to be, the hostility they had both shown to Addington. Mulgrave supposed only to hold the place for Lord Wellesley. Query: What is to be kept for Mulgrave in reserve? The Duke of P. to succeed to the Duchy; the Blue Ribbons to be, Lord Winchelsea, Lord Dartmouth, Lord Abercorn, and, it is supposed, Addington. Singular

[illegible]

[illegible]

[illegible] Fox, Elliot, [illegible] Lord Carysfort [illegible] Lord [illegible]

[illegible]

14th.—[illegible] Lord Moira's: Fox, Lord Grenville, Lord [illegible], Lord Carlisle, T. Grenville, [illegible]. Conversation chiefly on Prince's affairs. [illegible] Lord Moira, Fox, Calcraft, [illegible] not being originally [illegible]

15th.—Day of Parliament meeting. No division. Besides the mover and seconder, viz. Dillon and Charles Adams, none spoke but Fox, Pitt, and myself. The opinion given by F. was, that our answer to the overture of Buonaparte should not have been conditional, *i. e.* subject to a communication with the Continental Powers, but absolute. I slurred over the question, only observing that the account of our prospects from the Continent would have been more satisfactory, if more detailed and pointed.

16*th.*—Levee: great crowd: did not get to speak to the King.

18*th.*—Birthday. Spoken to by the Queen: did not get to the King. Cecilia in white, with gold and fur: head dress very becoming; looking well.

21*th.*—In the morning, after conversation with the

Prince of Wales, went, agreeable to his desire, to Fox. Elliot walked with me and Sheridan came in. Day of communication from Lord St. Vincent, of the 'Naval Papers,' and of communication from P. of Wales relative to supposed purpose in Pitt of resigning and taking a lead in favour of the Catholic Bill.

26th.—Day of talking to Canning on business of Lord Hawkesbury. Walked in Leicester Fields.

31st.—Went, according to arrangement, with Elliot and Grenville to play: Master Betty in 'Frederick.' Lord Spencer, who had been shooting at Osterley, came afterwards. Liked Master B. better than before, but still inclined to my former opinion: his action certainly very graceful, except now and then that he is a little tottering on his legs and his recitation just, but his countenance not expressive; his voice neither powerful nor pleasing.

February 1st.—Went to the House to enquire about papers; Woodford had called and walked part of the way. Pitt gave notice of some financial business, supposed to be preliminary to an idea of going out.

Lord William Bentinck to the Right Hon. W. Windham.

Fort St. George: February 5, 1805.

My dear Sir,—I had the pleasure of receiving a letter from you by Mr. Marsh, and you may be assured, that I shall feel the greatest satisfaction in having it in my power, to contribute to the comfort or advantage of his stay in India.

I am sorry that the new administration is not a stronger one. I do not approve of so many honourable and constitutional characters sticking by Fox, who deserted the Constitution in its utmost need. You observe, *Si non errasset, fecerat ille minus.* The first part of that verse has been alone accomplished. I do believe his principles are sound at the bottom. I was brought up with feelings of love and admiration for him. I do still respect him very much. But my judgment, and more particularly my veneration for Mr. Burke, prevents me from not condemning his past conduct with all my heart and soul. Before I could excuse; I must be satisfied that his opinions have undergone a thorough reform.

Believe me, with the most sincere regard and esteem,

My dear Sir, very faithfully yours,

W. BENTINCK.

8*th*.—Motion for leave for suspension of Habeas Corpus Act: spoke.

12*th*.—Day of Spanish papers. Did not speak. A...

13*th*.—Lord Folkestone called before I had breakfasted, and urged the going down to the Report. I was then all despair and rejected the proposal without consideration, as I did what occurred afterwards when I was walking about the streets with Elliot. Elliot and I called on Malone. We met several people, asking whether we meant to come down to the Report. Fox and Grey, with whom I had come home the night before, or rather in the morning, had never seemed to conceive the idea

21*st*.—Day of my motion.* Spoke, I am afraid, three hours and a half: 'o'erflowing but not full.'

22*nd*.—Supped at Lady Harrington's. Not unpleasant. Moore sang and Lord Barrymore. Mrs. Fitzherbert, Lady de Clifford, Lord Moira, Sir John Warren, two young

* 'It was on the 23rd June of the previous year, that Fox brought forward his motion for the defence of the country. The Attorney-General (the Hon. Spencer Perceval) rose, to the defence of the different parts of their military measures that had been attacked. Perceval took a much more judicious view of the debate, and treated the motion as if it had been in terms for the dismissal of Ministers. This was the true mode of treating it, if he could have executed his idea with skill; but his want of talent drove him to violence and extreme personality, so as to betray the fury and despair of his friends, or rather their convulsions in death. His personal abuse of Fox and Windham was vulgar and gross in the extreme. But we in the gallery were much indebted to him, for it produced a masterly speech from each in their very different styles. Windham repelled the personality, chiefly by the contrast of his own manner, with great fire, but perfect temper, a very polite contempt and exquisite wit; he spoke not more than ten minutes, but he refreshed one's mind from all the bad feelings that Perceval had given us.—Vide *Memoirs of Francis Horner*, vol. i p. 249.

Russians—one, a Madame Visihoff, I think very pretty, uncommonly pretty mouth. Prince at supper: came away in his carriage about two.

The Right Hon. W. Windham to Captain Lukin.

March 9, 1805.

Dear William,—You will have probably guessed, from the result of the proceedings of last night, that there will be no further call for applications to Lord Melville, whose office, of First Lord of the Admiralty, is at this moment in all likelihood at an end. Though one may be sorry for him personally, as one may in the case of a malefactor going to execution, yet one can never regret, for long together, at the termination of power raised by such means as his and employed in such a way. It is a severe reverse, but a most merited one and absolutely necessary, if the Government and Parliament were to hope to retain any character. It is a separate piece of good fortune that the Admiralty is to be taken out of hands that would soon have given us a Scotch navy.

Yours truly,

W. W.

March 17*th*.—Dinner at Lord Derby's: Prince. I sat between Fox and Grey; Grenville and Sheridan just below.

23*rd*.—Dined at Lord Carnarvon's to meet the Prince.

April 8*th*.—Dined early and went to the House. Day of decision against Lord Melville.

May 26*th*.—Dinner at Duke of Bedford's: present, Fox, Grey, Sheridan, Elliot, Lord Derby, Fitzpatrick, Erskine. Had not resolution to go to Mrs. Kemble's party.

27*th*.—Dressed and went to play. Mrs. Siddons in 'Zara.' Had not seen her for years: impression of her excellence not less than formerly. Came back and went with Cecy to Lady L. Manners' and Lady Spencer's.

31*st*.—Heard of death of Sir W. Pulteney and Paley. Went to Mr. Boddington's: present, Mr. Sharpe, Lord H. Petty, Ward, I think; Lady Cockburn, Mrs. Hibbert, Mrs. Opie, Mr. Rogers.

June 4th.—Went in the evening to Lady Lambert's masquerade in Argyle Street. Came away early, or at least earlier than I should otherwise have done, with a view to going with Lord Albemarle, &c. to the fight.

5th.—Went to the fight with Lord Albemarle, Fitzpatrick, Grey and John Ponsonby: young Belcher and Ryan; the former victorious; place, near Shepperton.

10th.—Cecy, Julia and I dined at Hampstead. Met there Littleton, W. Spencer, Luttrell, Rogers, H. Greville.

20th.—I went to Royal Asylum to meet the King. Day of Grey's motion to prorogue Parliament. The number of children in the Asylum at this time—boys, 462; girls, 230; total, 692.

July 8th.—Dined at Lord Melbourne's: Prince there: present, Lord Egremont, William, and Frederick, George Lamb, Dr. Burney, Lord Cowper, Horner.

11th.—Day of second motion about Captain Wright.*

12th.—Dined at Lord Carlisle's: present, Duchess of Rutland, Crawfurd, Elliot.

14th.—Dined at Osterley to meet the Prince of Wales: present, Ponsonby, Lord A. Hamilton, Sir John Shelley.

20th.—Day of fight at Blackwater: Horner, Ward, J. Ponsonby and Kinnaird. The combatants were to have been, Pearce (the Chicken) and Gully; T. Belcher and Dutch Sam; Ryan and Caleb Baldwin: but the fight that actually took place was between Cribb and Nicholls, with a *petite pièce* between a Jew and a jackass-driver.

We did not get to Osterley, where Ponsonby and I were to sleep, till half-past eleven. Horner and Ward went on; Kinnaird had turned off to St. Ann's Hill.

21st.—Came to town in the morning with Lord and Lady Villiers and Lady F. Ponsonby. They set me down in Pall Mall, having to go to Phillip's.

* Wright, accused of conspiracy and detained as a prisoner of war to the end of 1805. He died in the Temple; his death had been attributed to the French Government, but it had no interest in this catastrophe.

25*th.*—Article in the 'Morning Chronicle,' stating coroner's verdict on the man who fought (Dillon).

27*th.*—Day of dining with Adair, on occasion of his marriage.

31*st.*—Went to Duke of Gloucester's. Day of arrival of first news from Sir Robert Calder.

August 2nd.—Long talk with Rogers, while sheltering ourselves from a shower.

3*rd.*—Took Lord M. to Holland House. Went late, in consequence of visit from P. William, and staying to write letter to Lord Buckingham*. Present: Lord Minto, Horner, a Mr. Murray, a Scotch lawyer, Mr. Elmsley, Mr. Allen, the person who travelled with Lord H., Mr. Phillimore, M. ——, the late Russian Minister at Madrid, translator of 'School for Scandal,' Lord H. Petty, Lord A. Hamilton.

4*th.*—Began accounts. No interruptions but by call from Lord Minto, who brought me MS. translation of a Spanish tract on 'Popular Amusements,' promised me yesterday by Lord Holland. Talked of affairs—gloomy presages. He thinks that there is a great deal of disaffection still lurking in the higher orders. Sees no hopes in peace. Opinion that great changes may take place even in three or four years.

5*th.*—I dined at Lord Cowper's: present, Lord and Lady Melbourne, Robison, Hopner, Fred. Lamb, Grenville. Called for by Lady Melbourne to go to Vauxhall, according to agreement: very pleasant. Afterwards supped at Melbourne House: less pleasant, because late. Should have done better, perhaps, to go home, as Grenville did. Lady Elizabeth Monck and her husband there.

8*th.*—Called on Sir Sidney Smith, having to re-deliver to him the papers relative to Capt. W., with short introduction which I had sketched out. Saw, for the first time, Mr. Clive, who was with him on account of the hurt in his shin. Learnt some more about naval tactics, and his 1024 (32 × 32) positions, which, I suspect, should be 16 × 32 sq. I dined with Lord Cowper. Duke of Gloucester going on well.

13*th.*—Set off for Stowe.* Arrived in good time. Prince not to come till Thursday.

23*rd.*—Got up about five o'clock. Sat for an hour reading 'Life of Davila,' but obliged to go to bed by failure of eyes, which hardly allowed me to go on.

September 3*rd.*—Up not till quarter past eight, though awake before. Went down and dressed. Came up till chaise ready. Quitted door at about 18 min. before ten: arrived at Hayes 36 min. past eleven; time 1 h. 54 min. Rate 5·2 miles per hour, putting distance to Hayes at 11. Quitted Hayes 19 min. past one; stay, 1 h. 54 min.; arrived in Pall Mall at 10 min. before four; time 2 h. 31 min. Rate, putting distance at 14, 5·6 miles per hour. Average, 5·4 miles; *i. e.* less than 5½ per hour, putting the whole at 25 miles, *i. e.* while going.

8*th.*—Up betimes, *i. e.* before eight. Went out and saw Monsieur. Considers the M. M. as having no intention whatever of bringing forward the Royal cause, but is of opinion that it would be highly desirable. Might be useful in case of success and no risk of its being prejudicial. Considers himself as having intelligences in France which might do much in case of external aid. Dined at Lord Hollånd's: took Lord Minto: only Lord Duncannon, Lord Lorn and Mr. Allen. Lady H. gave me some prints of bull-fights.

9*th.*—Went to Temple. Various calls, in hopes of meeting Lord Nelson.

10*th.*—Soon after breakfast went out to call on Lord Nelson, meaning to go on to Sir Sidney. Went with him to Dr. Pitcairne, then called on Lord N. again.

11*th.*—Lord Nelson called. Conversation with him.

* Grand fête at Stowe. Prince of Wales, accompanied by Mr. Fox.

His ideas about operations in Mediterranean: observation that Belleisle would, even now, be the best object. Total condemnation of West Indian captures.

13*th.*—Employed, if I recollect, in going on with tract on Neg. Signs.

14*th.*—Met Jackson as I was returning from Temple, and gave him directions about enquiries to be made. Found Lord Minto was going to Holland House, and settled to go together, and finally to stay all night.

15*th.*—In the morning met Baron Graham and had long conversation with him; and fortunate, as he dissuaded me from speaking or writing to Le Blanc.

18*th.*—Dined at Holland House; Lord Minto could not go—Elliot in his stead: present, Duke of Devonshire, Lady Georgiana Morpeth (Lord M. prevented by gout), Mr. Scarlett, whom I had met at Ward's and did not know again, Mr. Marsh, Lord Lorn, Monk Lewis. Lady H. unwell, and retired for latter part of dinner; back in evening; *à la gamba.*

19*th.*—Proceeded to Lord Macartney's, where sat some time. Dutens* came in.

27*th.*—Began letter to Pozzo di Borgo, in answer to one received from him near a twelvemonth ago.

October 17*th.*—C. and I dined alone. Great worry about message from Queen.

This night the first of my reading for any length of time with spectacles. It was a pair lent me by Mrs. Byng.

20*th.*—Dined at Princess's: present, Monsieur, Duc de Berri, Prince de Condé, Duc de Bourbon, M. de Rulhière, le Comte d'Escars, Lady Sheffield, Miss Cholmondeley, Mr. W. Lock, and Mr. J. Angerstein. When the Prince left, the Princess made a sign for us to stay, when small supper was brought, which kept us till twelve.

November 3*rd.*—Lady Scott called and told us that

* Dutens, known as the author of 'Mémoires d'un Voyageur qui se répose.'

Sir William was expected to dinner. Sent over at night to know if there were any news to confirm or contradict the last most alarming accounts, among which were that of Mack's capitulation. Sir W. had dined the night before at Pitt's. His answer was, that nothing was known but what had come from Boulogne; that Pitt was in great spirits, sanguine about assistance from Prussia, French would be in great peril, &c. &c. General Moore and Lord Keith had dined there. Expedition going to Hanover.

4th.—Confirmation of Mack's surrender: extermination of his army, possibly, by this time, of the whole of the Austrian force.

6th.—The account of Lord Nelson's death and victory.

11th.—News in the morning of Sir Richard Strachan's action and capture of four ships of the line.

20th.—Took into room with me 'Edinburgh Review;' article, 'Southey's Madoc.' Differ with reviewers and admire it.

December 20th.—Dined at Holland House; only Fox, Mrs. Fox and Lord Archibald Hamilton, who was just come from Scotland.

26th.—Made out from recollection of what was shown me so many years ago (in the year 1772) by Israel Lyons, the demonstration of that odd property of the multiples of nine, that the sum of their digits shall always be nine, or some multiple of nine.

Made out also, this or the following day, what I had some time ago settled, but had forgot again, as a mode of drawing two figures, answering to the definition commonly given of similar figures yet not similar.

Thucyd. lib. iii. sect. 84:—

ἀπαιδευσίᾳ ὀργῆς ἐκφερόμενοι.

The interpreters take it as ἀπαιδεύτῳ ὀργῇ, and translate it 'immani indignatione,' I think erroneously.

1806.

January 9th.—Day of Nelson's funeral. At Grosvenor Gate by half-past eight. In St. James's Park. Lord H. Petty came to the coach window: walked in the Mall with him. Lord Holland and Fox. Continued with them for the remainder of the day. Sat at church between Fox and Sir W. Scott. Not impressed throughout so much as I ought. Attention disturbed with the cold.

19*th.*—Reading of the amendment too tame and flat, altogether below the occasion. Grey came in before the meeting separated. Present: Francis Lord Henry Petty, Grenville, Whitbread, Sheridan, Calcraft. I stayed for some time to read amendment that had been proposed by Lord Holland, which was in much better style. The only word which we got inserted was 'unexampled.' Dinner at Lord Grenville's.

20*th.*—Increasing rumours of the dangerous state of Pitt. Called in on Lord Buckingham*; learnt from him what had been proposed between him and Gren. and Lord Grenville, and which Grenville and I had before in part concurred in, of declining the debate the next day. Called at Carlton House in consequence of directions given by Prince on birthday. Lord Melbourne there, who told me of his bargain for 2,000 guineas for remainder of term for Leominster.

27*th.*—Day of motion for monument (to Pitt). Had slept at the Stamp Office. Message from Carlton House by Sheridan, just before I went to the House; took

[illegible]

[illegible] suggestions were made respecting the mode of admitting Lord Ellenborough, and [illegible] of Mansfield's answer.

[illegible] —Saw [illegible] early and desired him to go to St. James's Place and urge his objections, which he did to Lady Spencer. After seeing him went there myself and had conversation with Lady S., in which I left her my proxy. Went thence to Fox, from whom I learnt that the point of proposing Lord Ellenborough for the Cabinet, as I now understand it, even in the case of Mansfield's not accepting, was considered as agreed upon.

though certainly not so stated. But Fox having mentioned in his note to Lord Grenville, written when I was by, that I had not understood the point to be settled (so I collect), and having likewise failed to make an appointment with Lord Sidmouth, nothing was done. Fox went to Prince of Wales in consequence of a message, and I went with him to the door. It was then, I think, I went back to St. James's Place and saw Lord Spencer, who rather thought that the point above mentioned respecting Lord Ellenborough, had been considered as settled and that, though retaining all his former objections, nothing could now be done. When we met, finding that no meeting had taken place with Lord Sidmouth, I stated in substance, and I think in terms, that the transaction was still in our hands, and was *res integra.* I particularly stated also, that in the new proceeding of an offer of the Chancellorship to Lord Ellenborough, the refusal of Mansfield having in the meanwhile been received, I think, this morning, the offer would be most likely to succeed, if made *not simpliciter*, but coupled with the circumstance that Lord Sidmouth ought then, if he pleased, have a seat in the Cabinet, stating this to be a suggestion against my own wishes. Lord Grenville and Fox accordingly set off in a carriage of Lord Spencer's to make the offer, I marking my dissent from it to the last, as appeared by what passed on Grey's remark upon my shaking my head. There the meeting broke up—Fox and Lord Grenville setting off to make the proposition, Chancellorship *simpliciter* or Chancellorship with a seat in the Cabinet for Lord Sidmouth. Dinner at Lord George Cavendish's. In the evening, found that what had been agreed to was the present arrangement. My dissatisfaction and perplexity at this as strong as possible, but I foolishly did not say, as I ought to have done, that the case being perfectly new, I must take till the next morning.

31*st.*—Went to Elliot at nine. Proceeded to Lord

Spencer's and from thence to Lord Grenville's, an authorised to state on the part of Lord Spencer much th same as I had to say for myself. Met Lord Wellesley a Lord Grenville's.

February 5*th.*—Day of receiving the Seals.* Kin rather kind. Short conversation: nothing on business.

6*th.*—Drawing-room. Queen most ungracious. En quired after Mrs. Hopwood,† not a word about Mrs. W. Her look not favourable to Lord Grenville, nor to La Spencer: the same I understand to Lady Buckingham.

7*th.*—Went to Lord Buckingham's about St. Vincen &c.: settled for Sir William Young to be named Dominica for the present. King particularly graci Did not much like the appointment, particularly whe mentioned Lord B. But I dwelt principally upon m long acquaintance with Sir W. Young and good opini of him. Went to office. Doubt suggested as to pr priety of what was proposed of sending so large a prop tion of force expected from the Continent to Irela 50,000 men (including regulars and militia), which it supposed that would produce; being thought too mu for Ireland at present. Saw Sullivan.

9*th.*—Went to Foreign Office, for the first time, pr bably, since Peace of Amiens: found both Fox, L Grenville and Lord Spencer talking of affairs of Irela Cabinet to meet to-morrow, and wish that I could c prepared with account of what had been done or c trived by way of defence by late Government; ha written in consequence to Coke. Sheridan and Mrs. F came in.

10*th.*—Cabinet: Lord Grenville, Lord Spencer, L

* In the Administration formed by Lord Grenville on the death of M Pitt, which was known as the Cabinet of 'All the Talents,' Mr. Wind accepted the office of Secretary of State for War and the Colonies, wh he held until the dissolution of that Government on March 25, 1807.

† Honourable Cecilia Byng.

Ioira, Lord Henry Petty, Fox, Grey and myself: Lord idmouth. Agreed to the Repeal of the Parish Bill. Question of Sicily broached; Minorca also. Conversation then about military arrangements,* on which perfect greement, I think, on all parts, from Lord Moira.†

14*th*.—Amyot called: much information from him on Volunteers. Curious history of Cabinet to-day on Irish ffairs at Carlton House, of which Lord Moira had incientally given me notice, and not inadvertently, perhaps, n the morning. I had not been enough struck with it, so nuch as even he (Lord Moira) had let out respecting it.

15*th*.—Cabinet dinner at Lord Grenville's. Lord Fitzwilliam there for the first time. Fox touched upon subect of bringing forward, first, the Repeal of the Parish Bill; stopped by me, I think, without sufficiently marking the sacrifice we were making. Strong and general opinion that notice of some motion ought to be given mmediately; repeated as we were going home by Lord Sidmouth. Not checked properly by me, as it must now be.

16*th*.—Had got up in the night and written letter to Lord Buckingham*, which Elliot wished me not to send. Saw Francis with message for my attending the Prince of Wales.

* The military arrangements here referred to probably related to the plan or limiting the duration of service, in which Mr. Windham took a strong nterest. The subject is adverted to in the following passage from Lord Holland's Memoirs:—The prominent features of the Session were, a pertinacious opposition on a few unimportant subjects, the plan of limiting the duration of Military Services, and the measures preliminary to the African Slave Trade. With respect to the first, the plan was disagreeable to the King and the Duke of York, and the author of it, Mr. Windham, was popular neither in the Parliaments nor in the country. The principle of it had been often recommended in Parliament. Mr. Windham, however, had the honour of pressing it more effectually on public attention, of reducing it to a system, and illustrating its advantages with all the fertility, keenness, and felicity of his abundant genius and exquisite art.—*Lord Holland on the Whig Parliament*, vol. i.

† Master-General of the Ordnance.

[illegible] Duke of York [illegible]

[illegible] He ma[illegible] without any [illegible]

[illegible] reconciled in s[illegible]

[illegible] *the opinion which* I afterwards gave, on [illegible] part which probably struck him as most exceptionable, viz. the 'Detenus.'

29*th*.—Long paper from the King; Cabinet in consequence. Dinner at Lord Sidmouth's: only Grey and Lord Spencer absent. Note, which had been prepared at Cabinet, sent to the King; extraordinary delay in copying it, and strong exemplification of my fatal inability to do anything in certain states of body.

Sir Arthur Wellesley to the Right Hon. W. Windham.

14, Clifford Street: May 7, 1806.

Sir,—The enclosed letter was sent to me by Captain Malcolm of His Majesty's ship the 'Donegal,' with a desire that I should deliver it to you, and under the notion that I might take the liberty of urging you to grant the request which it contains. I cannot, however, venture to do more than to forward you the letter, and as an excuse for so doing, I will shortly state the claims which, in my opinion, Captain Malcolm has upon the public. This officer was for many years the captain of the ship in which Admiral Rainiers' flag was flying, and on his return from the East Indies at the conclusion of the last war, he was, upon the breaking out of this war, appointed captain of the 'Royal Sovereign' and sent to the Mediterranean. When Sir Richard Richerton's flag was removed to that ship, he was appointed captain of the 'Donegal.'

He accompanied Lord Nelson in his pursuit of the French fleet to the West Indies, and upon his return, although he was detached from the fleet on the day of the battle of Trafalgar, he on the following day took the 'Rayo,' of 110 guns, and in the course of the gale of wind which succeeded that engagement, he saved and had in his ship, not less than 1,800 persons, besides her ship's company. He afterwards returned to the West Indies with Sir John Duckworth and was in the action at St. Domingo, in which the 'Donegal' took the ship offered to her. In returning to Europe, the 'Brave,' one of the prizes, was lost in a gale of wind, and Captain Malcolm had the good fortune to save the whole of the ship's company, passengers, &c. The gentleman who has written you the enclosed letter is his brother-in-law, and only requests you to judge from the recital which I have above given of

Captain Malcolm's services, whether he is justified in desiring that I should deliver it and I am justified in transmitting it for your perusal.

I have the honour to be, Sir,

Your most obedient, humble servant,

ARTHUR WELLESLEY.

June 7th.—Dined at Lord Carnarvon's, to meet the Princess, when learnt from her Royal Highness what was the occasion of their meeting.

8*th.*—Dined at Blackheath: present, Monsieur, Prince de Condé, Duc de Bourbon, M. de Puysegur, Lord Harrington, Lord Howick, Lord Henry Petty, Lord Minto, Lord Mount Edgecombe, Vansittart, Lord Carysfort, Lord Petersham, Lord Carnarvon, Lord Robert Spencer, Lady Anna Maria,* Lady Sheffield.

24*th.*—Letters received from Sir Home Popham to the same effect as some received the day before by the Duke of York from Sir David Baird. Duke of Gloucester showed letter which he had received from the Duke of York, stating King's pleasure that he should remain in the north-western district.

July 3rd.—Sent off to Jean Marie. Message through Crawfurd, having called and not found the Duke of York, that more than two thousand would probably be wanted for Buenos Ayres.

24*th.*—Went in evening to Lady Crewe's. Saw Pamela† there for the first time, since meeting her at Paradise's.

25*th.*—Letters from Lord W. (Howe), of the 20th and 21st, stating that Russian peace was signed. Cabinet in consequence; also in evening. Communication in the meantime from Comte Stragonoff of treaty. Extraordinary particulars stated. Short letter sent off immediately to Petersburg.

* Lady Anna Maria Holroyd; married, 1796, Sir John Stanley, afterwards Lord Stanley of Alderley.

† Adopted daughter of Madame de Genlis.

29th.—First meeting on report about Princess.

30th.—King came to town.

August 14*th.*—Dinner at Mansion House, on occasion of Mr. Erskine's departure for America.

15*th.*—Long conversation with Dumourier on subject not communicated to me by colleagues.

The Bishop of Norwich (Dr. Bathurst) to the Right Hon. W. Windham.

Norwich: September 1, 1806.

The University of Oxford can, in my opinion, never elect any man as their representative in Parliament who is, in every point of view, so well qualified as yourself. I have most certainly always thought, and I always said this, and had I a hundred votes, they should be at your service. With respect to the canvass, which is unfortunately going on in the county of Norfolk, my professional situation and some peculiar circumstances (with the nature of which it is not worth while to trouble you) make it advisable for me not to take any part, notwithstanding my personal regard for Mr. Coke, the obligations I am under to him, and the very high respect which I have for his character. As far as you are concerned, allow me to say, and I say it with great truth, that, if eminent talents and unblemished integrity be passports to success, you cannot fail of it. My eldest son hath a vote, and more than a month since he promised, I know, to support Mr. Coke in the first instance and afterwards to assist Mr. Wodehouse, who is connected with my family. It was not then known that Sir Jacob Astley intended to decline the contest. What part my son would have taken, had he been acquainted with your design of offering yourself a candidate, I really do not know, but I do know that he agrees with me in thinking very highly of you.

I am, Sir,

With sincere respect and regard, yours, &c.,

H. Norwich.

September 12*th.*—Message by telegraph that Buenos Ayres taken.

17*th.*—Went to Duke of York; explained a mistake he had been under. Discussion about making new battalions of men who refused to enter for general service. Had named Burke—not for the Cape, but for Crawfurd. New instruction to be drawn for Auchmuty and Beresford. Saw M. Paravicini on the subject of Walcheren.

30*th.*—Received letter from Sir G. Shee, saying that the 17th Dragoons were only then embarking. The order for the embarkation of the 17th must have been given within a day or two at latest of the receipt of the account of the battle of Maida.

October 5*th.*—Discussion with Grenville at Admiralty about Crawfurd's expedition.

November 25*th.*—Dinner at Lord Grenville's: Grenville and Sir Arthur Wellesley. Had seen the latter in the morning.

30*th.*—Consultation in Cabinet on Lord Howick's proposal respecting France. I had seen in the morning Mons. Guillerie and Monsieur. Had read General Dumourier's plan and Tinseau a day or two ago.

December 5*th.*—Long conversation with M. Guillerie: 'History of Georges and Puisaye.' No design against Puisaye's life. He, as an ecclesiastic, could not have signed the order. Georges had no option, for reasons not to be disclosed. No conscription now carried into effect. Little taxation. M. de St. Hilaire, *sans prétentions et sans grade militaire.* Wants M. Guiche or Kishe to go with Prigent, in order to go where his command is, viz. near St. Brieux: is a close friend of M. de St. Hilaire. Their wish for money, 4,000*l.* or so.

7*th.*—Saw De Moutier, after an absence of ten years: just escaped from Prussia. Saw Puisaye, first time for many months, a year perhaps or more. Heard part of his plan; settled details with Prigent.

8*th.*—Saw Lord Valentia for first time. General outline of Egypt. Saw Le Chevalier St. Ange; second time of seeing him; real name, St. Hubert. Mean to speak to Lord Howick about sending money to Strani, at Patras, to counteract the influence of the French consul at Corune, with the Mainotes.

17*th.*—Cabinet dinner at Lord Spencer's: business of Princess of Wales. I had in part stated my opinion a day or two before.

18*th.*—Saw the Duke de Lorges, by desire of Lord Moira, about a man whom he wanted to send to Bordeaux. Wanted to send a thousand pound or two there, having nobody to confide it to there, but his sister.

23*rd.*—Minute finally settled about Princess of Wales.

27*th.*—Minute ultimately sent to the Chancellor, in order to its being transmitted to the King, the same night.

29*th.*—Day of decision to send order to Beresford to stop the troops. Assented coldly. Should have pointedly dissented.

1807.

January 2*nd.*—News from Lord Strangford of repor recapture of Buenos Ayres.

3*rd.*—Saw Mr. MacDonnell of Glengarry, with proposal for raising a Highland brigade. Council great plan of finance stated.

7*th.*—Lord Erskine had written, and was to see M Berney next morning, respecting a re-acceptance of services of Puisaye. Saw Lord Minto about bu expected to come on, about his brother's appointmen a West Indian government. Dinner at Lord Gren The whole time till twelve o'clock, occupied with sion, about loan or subsidy to Russia, and with that general question of old or new world.

Went to see Monsieur, who had left town for L Paget's early in the morning. Purpose of going to k what passed.

12*th.*—Among letters sent, a second to Lord Gren stating that Crawfurd's allowances were nothing but 1,000*l.* outfit.

13*th.*—Arrived at Thetford between ten and ele From paper in 'Monthly Review' I got on mathema subjects and resumed consideration of Negative S retracing former reasonings after a little time very sa factorily: found much enjoyment in it.

15*th.*—Letter from Sir J. Cockburn, confirming more detail Grenville's account of Buenos Ayres, sta his having seen Lord St. Vincent, and settled the ma for the departure of Ermilly, Kirch, and St. Ange. Our extra recruiting had amounted to thirty-five.

17th.—Saw Sir J. Cockburn upon arrival in London, who stated to me his conversation with Monsieur and Monsieur's wish to see me this evening, if possible. Prevented by Cabinet, which I found fixed for nine o'clock. Sir James dined here with Lady Cockburn. Desperately sleepy after dinner: cured only by quantities of tea. Conversation with Lord Howick before dinner, on subject of the reconciliation with Puisaye.

23rd.—Wrote to Lord Howick about Tinseau's project against Toulon. Proposed writing for provisional orders to Petersburg. Plan to be sent to General Fox by next packet.

25th. — Last Cabinet on Princess of Wales. Official news of recapture of Buenos Ayres. Occupation of Maldorado. Cabinet, upon news from Continent, and discussion of plans to be pursued for general conduct of war. Mention by me of state of Caraccas and probability of their being lost, if means not taken to prevent it.

27th.—No suggestion, but that of raising foreign troops in the north of Germany, and of landing a large force, even without purpose of co-operation at Havre or the Cotentin.

29th.—Finance plan proposed by Lord Henry (Petty). Lord Castlereagh made his motion, which I had previously agreed to, for army returns.

February 1st.—Cabinet at Lord Spencer's, he not being well. Lord Grenville did not come till late; Lord Howick gone; Lord Holland and Lord Fitzwilliam not there; former unwell, and I fear latter too. Mentioned necessity of an officer for Buenos Ayres, and suggested Stuart, who is just returned from Mediterranean. Sir G. Prevost, proposed by Lord Grenville; Whitelock, by Leveson Gower.*

* The unfortunate termination of the expedition to Buenos Ayres under General Whitelock, gives a peculiar interest to this passage. Mr. Windham,

8*th.*—Took leave of Lord Minto, who set off this evening. The chances certainly not great that we shall ever meet again.

11*th.*—Wrote private letter to Lord Minto, on subject of preparation of troops for Wellesley, and the general question of Sepoys.

12*th.*—Council at Lord Grenville's in the evening, on this and on King's answer to minute, respecting the admission of Catholic officers. Buenos Ayres again. Long paper read by Lord Howick as to what he should feel it necessary to state as his opinions, in opposition to operations in distant parts for colonial advantages. The same as I ought to have drawn up last war.

13*th.*—Wrote letter to Major General Gower, intimating his intended appointment, and desiring him without mentioning it to come to town.

14*th.*—Dinner; dined at Lord Spencer's; first time since leaving office. Present: Lord Lauderdale, Grey and Lady Harriet Cavendish. Lord Holland prevented by gout: called in there in evening

20*th.*—Account received of Prigent's having landed: was so unwell that the surgeon of the ship dissuaded him from the attempt.

24*th.*—Sent letters to Lord Grenville, stating my views about Lord Rosslyn to succeed Whitelock. Mentioned case of Canadian Fencibles.

26*th.*—Received letters from Captain Durham of the 14th, giving an account of Kirche having been safely landed on the 7th.

27*th.*—Went to House for first time for a long while. Gave opinion on slave trade, referring to intention of speaking more at length on future occasion.

April 18*th.*—Election at Charter House. Dr. Stone

who had prepared the expedition, wished to give the command of it to Sir John Stuart, or to General Crawfurd; but was overruled by the Duke of York.

elected. Order excluding from admission as a poor brother any one who should have been a menial servant within five years. First time of my attending or of having been in the Charter House. News of Hudson's* death! Too late on return to answer Browne's letter; tried, but tired, and could not write it in time.

Company to dinner: Fitzpatrick, Lord Crewe, Sheridan, Courtenay, Lawrence, Sir A. Piggot, Sir Philip Francis, Lord Robert Spencer.

19*th.*—Dinner at Lord Morpeth's: Lord Howick, Crevy, Tierney, Lord Kensington.

20*th.*—Sent letter to Lord Castlereagh. Private letter from Lord Hutchinson. Dined with Duke of Gloucester: present, Monsieur, &c., Lord H. Petty, Lord Cholmondeley, Fawkener. Went from thence to Lord Carnarvon's.

22*nd.*—Answer sent to Carr, junior, of Runton, about land of his to be given to Johnson (Rev. P.).

27*th.*—Saw Macdonald of the 8th Foot (formerly of 25th), who came for papers which he had sent me on the effect of Penal Catholic Laws in army and navy. Wrote to Duke of Northumberland, dated overnight.

May 5*th.* — Received letter from Lord Fitzwilliam, stating that I might go without delay to Higham Ferrars. Wrote to Tierney, desiring him to withdraw me from lottery with a view to reserve my money for other chances. Answer from him explaining why I could not.

[In October 1806, after six days' polling, Mr. Windham was returned for the representation of Norfolk by the votes of 3,722 freeholders, having a majority over Mr. Wodehouse of 365. Owing to an election incident, the particulars of which form the subject of the following letter to the Chancellor, a petition for *treating* was got up against Coke and Windham in the ensuing Parliament, and the election declared to be void. Mr. Windham was

* Of Norwich.

then returned by Lord Fitzwilliam for the borough of Higham Ferrars.]

Right Hon. W. W. to the Lord Chancellor (*Lord Erskine*).

Pall Mall: Jan. 30, 1807.

MY DEAR LORD,—All that you tell me of Coke's having ridiculed Mrs. Berney, referring, as it would seem, to something previous to the election, is wholly out of my knowledge, and unquestionably is not less so out of my belief. It is not, as you know, at all in Coke's manner to ridicule anyone. I could not name a man who has less of the habit or less of the disposition.

With respect to anything that passed *at* the election, the only share, as I can vouch, which she had in it, was that of endeavouring to prevent it; as my only share was that of endeavour to carry his wishes into execution. We had both heard the thing loosely talked of (I had at least) without giving heed to it, or supposing that anything was to happen in consequence, nor did I know to the contrary, till Coke came to me one morning, as we were going to the hill, desiring that I would ride to such an inn, to stop what he had just been told was going on there. I went to the place, but finding nothing of the sort, nor anyone to give me any information, returned towards the hill and thought no more of the matter. So little, in fact, was I prepared for what happened, that I was really taken in by it, and when the carriage appeared, conceived for some time that it was the same we had been accustomed to. I did not find my mistake till I saw something of unusual tumult, and going then into the crowd, was endeavouring to stop the people who were brutally throwing stones. The carriage drove off and then ended the matter. I went up to the Sheriff's room.

Whatever hostility Mrs. B. may have conceived against Mr. Coke or against me for other causes, or how far she may think it right or advantageous to pursue it in the present mode, are points that I can say nothing to; but unquestionably upon the subject immediately referred to, the facts are as I have stated.

This I am bound to say in respect to Mr. Coke and it is

only the truth as respecting myself.—Yours, my dear Lord, with great truth and regard, W. W.

P.S.—I recollect perfectly that Coke gave as the reason of his anxiety to stop what he understood to be preparing, the obligations he had formerly received from the Berney family.

6*th*.—Up by half-past four. Not away till half-past seven. Horses had been waiting, I fear, from till before six. Vexatious provocation at Hatfield, which I could not entirely get off my mind during the whole of the remainder of the journey. Arrived at Higham at half-past seven.

9*th*.—Great civility of landlord at Thorney. Called at Wisbeach on Metcalfe. Arrived at Holkham by three: only Coke there.

June 19*th*.—*London*.—Dined with Sir P. Francis: present, Dukes of Bedford, Devonshire; Lord Fitzwilliam, Lord W. Russell, Lord R. Spencer, Lord Cowper. Pleasant dinner.

The Right Hon. W. Windham to Captain Lukin.

Pall Mall: September 5, 1807.

DEAR WILLIAM,—I have a choice opportunity of writing to you in the return of Mr. Hopner; as I received indeed from him the latest and at the same time the earliest account of you. I feel very doubtful and very anxious for the result of your operations, though Hopner seems to think that the whole will be settled by the time that he returns. If it is, the cause must be either the want of provisions and water, or that the inhabitants cannot submit to the injury to be done to the town; for the works seem to be such as must, for a considerable time, enable a force however weak to hold out against a strong one. But success itself will bring with it no satisfaction. I cannot feel that the accomplishment of all we look for is an equivalent either for the risk that will have been run, or for the certain discredit that we shall have incurred, and ill-will that we shall have excited. Buonaparte's designs upon England will not turn upon his having or not the Danish fleet. Our proceedings in the case of Portugal, though such as I never ceased to regret from the moment almost of my having consented to them, we not without being a thousand degrees so exceptionable as the, and ended accordingly in a way which produced neither repr nor ill-will. Had the worst happened, our conduct could well have been charged as having anything in it unjust or irregular.

Though I am writing from Pall Mall, I am preparing diligently for getting into Norfolk, where everything leads to wish that we may soon be. One cause of delay, hitherto will not disapprove, viz. that I am correcting some of speeches on military matters and hope to publish them afterwards in a form still more corrected. All well, when I heard, which was in fact this morning.

Farewell! You will let us hear from you at your lei. When the fleet returns, we will endeavour to join you off Cro or at Yarmouth.

Yours affectionately,

W. WINDHAM.

September 14*th*.—Sworn to secret service before B. Graham. Story of the Lion (Lord Malmesbury) at Vi.

15*th*.—Saw Colonel Crawfurd and Sir S. Auchm. C. thinks that none of the columns, except, per. Auchmuty's, completely accomplished their object. considers them as having so far accomplished it, as have gone through the town, but to have failed for want of instruction, observing that there was no on the spot to direct. Lumley fell back on Auchm. marching along on the side of the river, after he passed the town. Hint, as Gordon had before s that there was considerable want of arrangement pre to the attack and during the march. No prev pressure, in consequence of the difficulty about supp. He (Auchmuty) had contracted for beef at a dollar for ox; bread sufficiently abundant. His posts had n been insulted, though many of them far detached. S cessful sally, soon after Whitelocke's arrival, from garri of Colma de Sacramente.

October 5*th*.—In the evening, took up for about an hour a volume of Gibbon. First reading of the sort for a long while. Effect very beneficial.

18*th*.—Volunteers out for the first time.

21*st*.—A. Hudson came. I was riding in the park on the Arabian.

26*th*.—Holkham. Went to Warham after shooters. Party to garden. Rode home by the Obelisk wood. Whole very pleasant. On account of the weather at the beginning of the day, the shooting not in the park. 186 head of game only killed. N.B. Rabbits included.

27*th*.—Day rather cold and rainy. Augusta did not ride. Rather regretted it, when Miss Blackwell and I fell in with the shooters. Quantity killed, as we learnt afterwards:—

Hares	262
Pheasants	65
Rabbits	166
Partridges	15
Woodcocks	8
Total	516

28*th*.—Rode round the plantations. This evening or last, 'faro,' besides music. Play, I understand, not high.

November 1*st*.—Went to Aylmerton and rode in wood, examining plantations and making ride useful therefore, as well as beneficial.

Notice in evening of William's arrival from Yarmouth. Anne and he had walked over in the evening, when we found that A. Hudson had come with them.

2*nd*.—Rode in morning with Cecilia to Wolterton, and back by Hanworth. Had met in going out William and Anne, who had been walking to see their grazing grounds. All the family of Lukins dined here to-day, except, I think, the Dean. Girls, *i. e.* Anne and Sally, stayed the night.

3*rd.*—Arrived at Houghton. Opera. The Italians, Spagnoletti, the two singers. Company in the house: Sir John and Lady Shelley, Lord and Lady Ponsonby, Lord Erskine, Lord and Lady Anson, General Keppel, Wilbraham, G. Walpole, Mr. and Mrs. Panton, Miss Wood, Com. Durfort, Churchill, Coke, Miss Blackwell, and Upton.

24*th.*—Made visit to Johnson Gay; first time, by-the-bye, of my ever being in Saxthorpe. Fell in with a soldier, James Brown, in General Turner's company of 3rd Guards, who had been at Copenhagen, and was going to see a sister at P——. Remarkable circumstance that though he had been enlisted only four years and a half, he had totally lost his Norfolk accent, and in the 3rd Guards had got a Scotch one.

26*th.*—Day uncommonly fine. South wind and a bright sun. Long time spent in the park and plantation with gardener.

1808.

February 6th.—Men dinner: present, Lord Henry (Petty), Frankland, Grattan, Sharp, Boddington, Elliot, Lawrence, Ward, Tierney, Rogers, Brougham,* G. Ponsonby, Horner. Cecilia dined upstairs.

10*th.*—Dined at Princess's.

20*th.*—Odd improvement seen even in present instance of the manner in making such preparations. Lucy† singing: very pleasant: sat up till past one o'clock.

March 1st.—Day, I think, of report on Army Estimates; if so, day on which the first intimation was given of an intention to attack the military system of last year, and this intimation was not given spontaneously, but wrung out by observations, with a view of rendering the attempt more difficult, should any such be intended. Lord Castlereagh then said, that in fairness he ought to state that there was an intention of introducing something connected with the subject. I don't recollect how he expresses it in the Mutiny Bill. Upon my asking whether it was to be merely prospective, he and Perceval both answered in the affirmative.

12*th.*—Dined at Whitbread's to meet Princess.

14*th.*—Day, I think, of third reading of Mutiny Bill. Sadly unprepared and out of speaking when I went to the House, but recovered while there and did pretty well.

* Lord Brougham talks of meeting Mr. Windham 'at the age of near sixty,' he says, 'with spirits always the most youthful of the party.'

† Honourable Lucy Byng, married the Rev. John Lukin.

What was said, was said with some impression; but much omitted that might have been introduced with advantage, even under the restraint imposed of not speaking very long.

19*th.*—Not up till eleven. Fell to work immediately to complete 'Protest,' if possible, before two o'clock, when Lord Holland was to deliver it in. Sent it to him by half-past one. He left word, in calling, that he liked it very much; but I don't find that it was delivered in, though House of Lords, I see, met.

20*th.*—Read with Cecilia a good deal of 'Marmion,' the new poem of Sir Walter Scott, which I like. Sent my excuse to Sharp, whose motion about Copenhagen comes on to-morrow.

April 26*th.*—Have read, since I have been here, about thirty pages in the Bipont edition of Thucydides; the part, the latter part of the second book, containing the funeral oration by Pericles; passage at the close showing, in common with so many others, the retired character required of women:—*Καὶ ἧς ἂν ἐπ' ἐλάχιστον ἀρετῆς πέρι ἢ ψόγου ἐν τοῖς ἄρσεσι κλέος ᾖ,*

A correction might be proposed of ἧς, but I should propose '*οἷς*,' not as being used for *αἷς*, though that might be suspected, on the same analogy as the Attics are disposed to use in their adjectives ὃς for ἣ; but in the sense *οἷς* for ἐφ' *οἷς*, in respect of, in point of. I looked also one evening into Prideaux's 'Connections.' Recalled some passages in Homer which I had forgotten, particularly the *αὐτὰρ ἐπεὶ μέγα τόξον.* But my chief employment was, and I am sorry to say a fruitless one, the renewed attempt at solving the problem which I met with in the work of M[e]. Agnesi.

May 10*th.*—Day of battle between Gully and Gregson.

14*th.*—Received and transmitted to Cooke, letter from Dorothy Merchant, to whom I had given a passage to Botany Bay, where she hoped to establish herself as teacher of a school. She states, beef, mutton, and pork, 2*s.* per pound, tea 30*s.*, sugar (brown) 6*s.*, butter 7*s.* Dated, Sydney, Oct. 18th, 1807.

July 2nd.—Wimbledon: breakfast. Spanish deputies at the breakfast: Moterosa de Vega; first time of my seeing them.

11*th.*—News from Spain good, though, as it turned out, less than supposed. Very difficult to say what the event will be. I am afraid that if I were compelled to decide under a penalty, that could leave no consideration but of that which was most probable, I should be obliged to declare for their failure.

12*th.*—Went with Elliot to Holland House. In the evening, Sidney Smith and Abercrombie. Slept in yellow room upstairs, where prints of 'Bull Feast.' North-east quarter. Very pleasant room, but very hot.

13*th.*—Came up to town with General Fox: mentioned to him, though with great precaution, what I had heard about Lord Ch. He, as well as I, was quite incredulous of it. At dinner, Lord Lauderdale, Lord Tweedale, Duke of Argyle. Lord Tweedale has notion of going to Spain; not very well settled and discouraged by Lauderdale, who says, there will be fighting enough here:

16*th.*—Came up to town by water, Miss Winder's boat. A large Dutchman there, who had been at Ceylon, knew Sir G. Staunton and his son; had been on board the 'Swedish Indiaman that had been wrecked on the Goodwin Sands,' in 1798: a most scandalous business seemingly, and this man with the rest shamefully plundered. Went to dinner at Ward's: Rogers, Lord Ponsonby, Lord Cowper, Lord Morpeth.

18*th.*—Stayed at Holland House for the night.

19*th.*—Did not come down till breakfast ready. Mind, alert and active. Remained in library till carriage ready, when I came up to town with Lord and Lady Holland and Charles. Lord H.'s epigram upon him, the Latinity of

'Musam studuisse. Sunt qui te musam impensè studuisse negârunt.' It has, I find, an accusative in the sense of *cuperes valde amare.* Sir Gilbert Affleck died last night. Lady A. was at Holland House, but I did not see her.

August 8*th.*—Went with party from Lady Melbourne's to Vauxhall.

10*th.*—Dined with Lord Cowper: present, Lord and Lady Melbourne, Duke of Devonshire, Lady Elizabeth Forster and Madlle St. Jule, Ward and Lord Palmerston.

11*th.*—Went in evening with H. Elliot to Blackheath. Duchess of Brunswick's birthday. News of 27th ult. from Madrid, stating that the French were withdrawing. Princess danced with St. Leger, Puysegur, and Lord Rivers. Lady Salisbury and her daughters there. News of 27th ult. from Madrid, stating that the French were withdrawing.

13*th.*—In the evening read principally papers in the 'Adventurer' and Rogers' 'Pleasures of Memory;' thought less of the papers in the 'Adventurer' than I had done formerly, *i. e.* forty years ago or more, and less than I had been led to expect of Rogers. Went to bed about one, after beginning Spanish grammar.

14*th.*—At Thetford by nine. Had just got my papers out, when Mingay came over. Could have wished him away, but conversation upon the whole not unpleasant. Told me of his having seen, as a child, my father lay in state in this very room. Nearly half-past ten when he left me. Resumed, in coming along, the subject, long laid aside, of Neg. Signs.

17*th.*—*Norwich.* Dinner with Grand Jury. Good deal of conversation, not unpleasant. Manners on each side as they should be. In evening, ball. Tried Lady Caroline* with a little view to reconciliation, but scarcely enough to make the trial a fair one. A new beauty, a

* Lord Caroline Hobart (Lady Suffield) took a very active part in the politics of the country.

Miss Jones, a niece to the Dean, very modest and well-mannered, as well as very handsome.

18*th.*—Called on Coke to show him what was proposed. Walked with him afterwards and called on Dr. Lubbock, Dr. Beevor and John Taylor. Saw the last: much changed since I had seen him before. Neither of the other two visible. Dr. L. in the last stage. Marked examples on all sides of the rapid progress of life and of the little time that is probably remaining to oneself! I have observed, too, this time, more than I have happened to note before, the decrease of people whom I remember, or who remember me. 'Gazette' with details of victory over Dupont,* &c. Dinner went off as well as could be hoped, or as was necessary. Nothing could have been mended, but that I might have compressed into still fewer words my thanks for my health being drank. Pleasant walk afterwards, *i. e.* in Market Place; same as I remember formerly in Taylor's garden.

20*th.*—Stopped at Aylsham. Poor Adey fast declining. It is thus, I fear, that I shall go. Stopped at Ingworth and saw premises. Greatly struck at arrival at Felbrigg with the silence and the solitude: carried my thoughts far back, particularly to a time when I remember to have come over from Dereham. Drank tea, walked over to Parsonage and saw Mrs. W. Lukin.

30*th.*—Search in Blackstone and Goldsmith's 'History;' much struck with style of latter; deserving, I think, to be more talked of.

September 6*th.* — Called at —— and told Mrs. —— that she must be *heig'ned.*† It was then about ten, or a little after. I should suppose that my nose fell of itself a-bleeding and continued so long, thought it necessary to send to Earle.‡ Went to bed a little before two. Nose

* Battle of Baylen, July 19th, 1808.

† Provincialism for raising price or rent.

‡ Earle, medical practitioner, well known and much respected at Cromer.

plugged up with lint and directions how to proceed, in case bleeding should recommence. Necessary, he thought, that some one should sit up: Mary Bean the person and very attentive. Released her from her attendance about five.

7th.—From motion in getting up and causing back to be rubbed for lumbago, a further escape of blood from the mouth. Discharge through the nose continued apparently through the whole day.

8th.—I had found myself yesterday more sensible to cold than usual, insomuch that I changed from nankeen pantaloons, and in the evening ordered for the first time, a fire. It seems to have been owing to the blood that I had lost, which Mr. Earle, to my surprise, estimated at two pounds, *i.e.* thirty-two ounces.

9th.—Tremendous visit from G. Wyndham; it commenced not long after I had done breakfast and was prolonged by successive showers till two o'clock. Meant very kindly as an enquiry how I did, but very bad in its effects.

10th.—Stopped in coming home at the cottages of Stamp and Buck: fine specimens of the manners of the poor.

16th.—Left Newmarket after breakfast by ten. At Chesterford heard report of news; said to be excellent, but without particulars. Feasted upon the hopes of what I should meet at Hockrill. Alas! *quanti de spe decidi!* it was the news of the convention with Junot. *There never was surely such a proceeding in the history of wars or negotiations.* There is no bearing the thought of it. What with this and with pain from lumbago, little pleasure through whole of the day's journey.

20th.—Dined at Holland House: Ward, M. Lewis, and Marquis de Romana, whom Lord H. had engaged on purpose. He had landed at Yarmouth only on the 17th or thereabouts. Little short, black man, something between Lord H. Petty and Sir R. Barclay: pleasant, natural, lively, and unaffected.

24th.—Fatal news received of the death of Captain Herbert. Mrs. B. called in the morning before I was dressed. Kept it from Cecilia. Poor Charles H.,* for whom I had begun to feel a growing kindness, but still more to be lamented Biddy!

25th.—Went by appointment to the Duc d'Angoulême, whom I had not seen since the year 1794: saw him and Duc de Berri, No. 39, George Street, Portman Square. Called on Monsieur in returning. Went in to Duke of Queensberry, whom I saw at his window; full of life, but very difficult to communicate with and greatly declined in bodily powers: decline of late rapidly marked, like setting sun.

October 5th.—Dined at Holland House: Lady Affleck, Mrs. Fox, and Miss Willoughby; Sydney Smith, just returned from Edinburgh, Lord Henry Petty, who had come to town to take leave of them, Ward and Lushington. Learnt from Lord H. in confidence that there was a great deal of dissatisfaction among the Spaniards at the delay in sending them horses.

8th.—Went to Holland House: didn't fail to enjoy myself, though with a considerable degree of uneasiness: violent pain every time I attempted to move.

15th.—In the morning saw Ferguson (Major-General); satisfied by him both of the general merit of Sir Arthur Wellesley † and of the main points of his case in the present instance. Excellent arrangement for ensuring supply of provisions; had sufficient for seventeen days at the time. Grand scheme of course to be observed with the reinforcements; certainly overruled as to the renewal

* Charles, second son of the Earl of Carnarvon, accidentally drowned; married Bridget, daughter of fifth Viscount Torrington.

† In very early days Mr. Windham was a great admirer of the Duke of Wellington, and foresaw the great military genius he afterwards displayed. In the House of Commons he defended him on all occasions, and especially when heavily attacked after the Battle of Talavera.

of the action and plan of marching forward previously. Clinton supposed to be the person who determined Sir Harry.* Every reason for supposing Sir Hew† to be all that I can easily suppose him to be. Wrote to the Duc d'Avéry.

19*th.*—In the evening heard from Dr. Blane that Sir W. Scott was returned; sending off a note, was lucky enough to bring him. Curious accounts of French oppressions and exactions; thinks of the Convention as is done here; favours Sir Harry; rather inclined to give credit to statement of Sir Hew; states some particulars well deserving of consideration on the temper and feelings of the army; disapproves answer to City address.

25*th.*—Battle at Moulsey; Gregson and Cribb, Cropley and Belcher (Th.); a new performer, Powell and Dogherty. The last-named in each pair the victors, though in the last two victories disputed. First good beginning that has been made on treatise, so necessary to be begun and concluded on 'Neg. Sign;' striking example how much in matters of this sort power comes with exertion.

November 3*rd.*—For the last three days, I think, have made no progress in dissertation, at least on paper, though I have thought continually upon the subject and not without advantage. The time not occupied by walks which I have taken latterly and with the repose in consequence, which was sometimes necessary, was employed in letter-writing, which has happily kept me in a state of freedom from arrears that is quite unusual and not more unusual than pleasant.

21*st.*—After tea went into room and found a confirmation of what I have always experienced, that capacity for employment comes with the employment; even at times seeming at the outset most unpromising.

28*th.*—Went over to Jeffery's; stayed talking with him

* Sir Harry Burrard. † Sir Hew Dalrymple.

till six. Mr. Fox's work, he tells me, goes off now very heavily. It could hardly be otherwise; not enough of it. Diligently and well employed, partly on dissertation and partly in making calculation about estate offered at Beckham.

December 2nd.—Felt at breakfast something of weakness in right arm, which, combined with sensation in leg on same side, not quite pleasant; from a short time after rheumatism had left back and descended into leg and thigh, a sort of tingling and pricking there, as when limb has been asleep.

After dinner, Mr. Disney* and Mr. Frazer came, on their return from attending the funeral of poor Captain Herbert at the place of family interment, near Highclere. The gloom which they brought with them and which continued for some time, cleared away by degrees, and their presence then added something to the cheerfulness of the evening.

4th.—Arrived at Bath a little after three. Went immediately on arriving to Mrs. Guise; far better than I had expected, meaning as to immediate suffering, though possibly not as to final danger. Dined at hotel. Walked in evening to Mrs. Guise with Cecilia. On the moment of our arrival met, with great surprise as also much to my satisfaction, Ward, who had just come on his way from Falmouth.

6th.—Met at Pump General Ramsay, who has lately come from living with Elliot at Minto; much conversation on Spanish affairs, which we had the further means of continuing by his coming to breakfast with us. Before he went Hippisley called, who had had a letter from his correspondent at Plymouth, announcing that there was upon the road worse news than any that had yet been received. What he meant relates probably to the news

* Married Augusta, sister to Mrs. Windham.

[illegible]

[illegible] Waldegrave.

20*th*.—After dinner slept only for a few minutes, afterwards 'Vicar of Wakefield,' which we just completed by supper and bedtime; a most absurd book, with hardly anything to carry it through but the name of the author, or to reconcile the reader to it but the catastrophe giving such full measure of happiness to the good, and such proper punishment to the wicked and worthless. Tiresome disputations, false opinions, uninteresting digressions, improbable incidents, nothing perfectly right, even where it cannot be said to be violently wrong; the very humour being little more than a good attempt and never being quite successful.

31*st*.—According to state paper, the force now in Spain is:—

Baird's infantry . .	12,000
Ordered from Portugal ditto	25,000
Ditto, cavalry . .	1,200
From England, ditto .	2,300
Total .	40,500

To which it is supposed, that, without any exertion, might have been added:—

Remaining force in Portugal	9,500
From Sicily . . .	10,000
Total .	19,500
Making in all . .	60,000

But, with exertion, it is supposed from 2,000 to 5,000 cavalry might have been added, and with greater exertion, 8,000 or 10,000 more; and if militia had been taken, such a force as would have made up the whole to the amount of 95,000.

Busset, the messenger, left Salamanca on the 26th of November, at which time Moore was there with not less than 17,000. Left Astorga on the 28th; Baird there and when joined by the cavalry and some infantry that had fallen back on Ponteferrada and Villafranca, would amount to 16,000. According to Lord William Bentinck, the French had received reinforcements previous to the 10th November, to the amount of 48,000. According to Mr. G. Leith's account, the army under Blake beaten, in consequence of the bad conduct of the officers in the new levies; the conduct of the men excellent; they would have stayed and been cut to pieces if their officers had not run away.

Calculation of the French force gives reason to think that on the 1st of Nov. 1808, they had of the army properly French about 610,000, with about 110,000 auxiliaries, making in all 720,000; this is exclusive of invalids, national guards, gensdarmerie, &c.: the last-mentioned, which are of the nature of heavy cavalry, supposed to be not less than 10,000 and not bad troops. An Austrian paper, in paper communicated from Austrian Government, made the French force at the commencement of the war, in 1805, 509,024, exclusive of auxiliaries, and 15,000 Imperial Guards. Difficult to conceive that with this the armies at Eylau and Friedberg should have been so small.

Old statistical calculation confines military establishments to 1 in 100 on the population (whole population, I conclude). In Great Britain, taking army and navy, supposed 1 in 30; in France, 1 in 40 on whole population, supposing 35,000,000, would give 900,000.

An intercepted dispatch states the reinforcements coming, to be 66,000 infantry and 8,000 cavalry, which, with the troops there, and Junot's and Dupont's army, would make the whole number allotted to Spain about 200,000.

1809.

January 8th.—Went to Abbey; sat in corporation pew; reader, a Mr. Williams, a young man who read naturally and unaffectedly and Mr. Richards, who preached a very excellent sermon and such as showed in the writer powers much above the common run. After church, long with General Ramsay, talking over the late Spanish news brought by Captain Wodehouse or Wyndham, and containing the account of Moore's second retreat, when in consequence of the approach, real or supposed, of Buonaparte, he gave up the design of attacking Soult.

Dinner at Sir W. Jerningham's: Madame Catalani and her husband. Madame C. very gay, good-humoured and unoffending. A little of the courtezan manners, but not more than was consistent with the idea of her being, what I understand she is, a very well behaved woman. No harm in her husband.

The Right Hon. W. Windham to Mrs. Crewe.

Bath: Jan. 21, 1809.

The campaign is begun in Parliament, and I am receiving the reports here without being a partaker in the action. It has so rarely happened to me to be absent on the day of the meeting of Parliament, or indeed during any part of the sittings, that I hardly know myself in my new situation. Till the battle was actually begun and the sound had reached us, I felt very composed, and perhaps even comfortable, at being exempt from the necessity of taking any part since the arrival of the papers. To-day I feel a little uneasy and restless, like an old dragoon horse at the sound of a trumpet. W. W.

—*From the Crewe Papers.*

24*th*.—News from Plymouth, brought by Lord Paget, of the embarkation of the army, the previous action and the death of General Moore.

25*th*.—Saw Major Palmer, who came away with the dispatches; seems to disapprove of language about Spaniards, yet joins in it in detail; general disapprobation of Moore, but questions rigour in enforcing regulations about baggage. French perfectly kept in awe by our cavalry. General sense of superiority in our whole army.

February 19*th*.—Nearly the whole time from breakfast till Mr. Legge's coming down, employed in reading Cobbett. More thoroughly wicked and mischievous than almost any that has appeared yet.

27*th*.—Lawrence's death. Died last night.

March 1*st*.—Employed during the morning in running about, partly with a view to the business of the Enclosure of Antingham, and partly to that of the Mutiny Bill.

4*th*.—At home till near three; was going out when Colonel Walker called by appointment, and explained more in detail the operation performed by his regiment, the 50th, in the battle of Vimiera.

20*th*.—The Duke of York's resignation.

21*st*.—To-day or yesterday card from Whitbread to dine with him on Sunday next: cannot go, being to dine with the Princess.

22*nd*.—Dined at home with C., Mrs. Cholm[y], Julia, and Mrs. Duntye: fact of her having been bitten by a dog of Lady Deerhurst's, a day or two before, and fortitude in having the piece cut out.

26*th*.—Went out, I have a notion, during the morning with Cecilia. Dinner at Princess's. Took Elliot and Lord Henry. Unwell when at Princess's. Got away in time to go in for a short time to Lady Stafford's. Monsieur there, who talked to me about the business of Puisaye. I had seen Allègre before upon the same business, and stated to him that I thought Puisaye unjustifiable in the letter produced, *Si veut le Roi, si veut, &c.* I said the same to Monsieur, but in other respects professed to take no part.

April 4th.—Felbrigg.—Fell in with Paul Johnson; called on Clark of the Row; employed afterwards in looking over plantations.

5th.—G. Walpole * believes his brother to be at Wolterton; has not heard: fears something of paralytic affection: opinion given formerly by Warren as to the probability of such attack in the family, derived from grandmother. Lord John had had such attack when only thirty: last but one when in the House of Commons, preparing to speak against Pitt's Austrian Loan, as I understood. Talk about affairs in Spain: thinks highly of Moore; little of Wellesley. Approves greatly of my plan of campaign. Rode out afterwards, examining plantations. Wind came round to the south, but colder than ever. Lofty tree behind woodyard, which William thinks would make topmast, and if equal in quality to Norway timber would be worth 200*l.*

9th.—On going down soon after breakfast, led on by the fine weather (the first day that has felt like spring) to take walk round in the wood; first up the eastern side of the wood, then to the west; crossed into Savannah, back by round wood, examining as I went and making memorandum which I must not fail to set down.

21st.—Not back to House of Lords till a few minutes after Grey had begun.† Stayed till end of his speech, which lasted for four hours: very good, went through the whole subject, disposing the parts in good order, and treating them severally in a clear, luminous and

* General the Honourable George Walpole. Born in 1758, and died in 1831.

† Earl Grey's speech on the 21st April, 1809, was on the conduct of the campaign in Spain and Portugal.

as it is now called! Quantity of electricity as the surface, intensity as the number of plates. This in the case of imperfect conductors, but in the case of perfect, both quantity and intensity, as I understand, as the surface. Explanation of thunder (viz. the noise) and waterspouts. His idea that the firing practised by ships only calculated to produce effect by the passage of ball: common opinion that it is the concussion, and accordingly, as I have been told, guns not shotted.

23*rd*.—Walked out a little; afterwards read a little in Thucydides: less at a loss than I might have expected.

26*th*.—Not quite inattentive during morning, in thinking of business that was to come on, but not so diligent as I might have been. Walked for a time in Green Park. Order of speeches: Sir J. Newport, W. Smith, then, I think, Sir Francis B., Fuller, Wilberforce, myself.* Certainly did not bring out well what had long been in my mind, and felt throughout I was speaking ill, which contributed no doubt to make me do so. Succeeded, however, by force of matter; for I am quite sure my execution was less good than usual. Success, however, as vouched by others' judgments, greater than usual.

28*th*.—Up not long after eight. Rode to Blane, and got answer: he does not advise more laudanum, but diluting liquor. Hippisley with this new dreadful charge against Woodford, which his restless and prying curiosity had poked out, and which his malice will propagate.

June 15*th*.—Day of rejecting Cruelty Bill. I had been riding in the morning and went to the House without returning home. Sir F. Burdett stated his creed. Had some thoughts of rising after him, but determined in the negative, I believe rightly. The only speech that it would have been good to make, was such as would have contained a short and neat summary of the general absurdity of his proposal.

* Mr. Windham spoke on Curwen's Reform Bill.

16*th.*—Rode, I suppose. Dined at Rogers: Lord and Lady Charlemont, Elliot, Horner. Went afterwards to Lady Orford's, having before gone with Cecilia to Lady Keith's. Not home till broad daylight. Air painful to the chest in coming home, but did not, as it happened, catch cold. Acquaintance made here with a Mr. Curzon, who, if his political opinions continue, a man to be cultivated.

19*th.*—Had written a letter to William about Sheringham business.

22*nd.*—Dined at Lord Harrowby's, first time: present, Lord and Lady Morpeth, Mr. Vernon, Lord Granville Leveson (Secretary of War), Canning, Adderley, Baron Trip, Lady Harriet Cavendish.*

25*th.*—Hoped to be up soon, but from sleeping in the evening, did not get well to sleep. Breakfasted below. Read 'Edinburgh Review;' afterwards, for first time, after I know not what interval, a little Greek, viz. Plut. 'Phocian;' the same, I think, as recommended so many years since by Fox and which put me first on reading 'Plutarch's Lives.'

28*th.*—Same as day before. One of these days saw old Saunderson, Mrs. Drake's instructor; he is a Lincolnshire man, bred a tailor: first book that gave him taste for mathematics, Leadbeater, I think. Knew Lawson, of whom he speaks as a good geometer, but not a man of much invention. Wildbore, who, like Lawson, was a clergyman, he seemed to consider as a very first-rate man. Masères he seemed to estimate truly: for Hutton expressed considerable respect. Mrs. D. he spoke of as one of his most diligent scholars: no great opinion of female powers in that way. He read with Lord R. Spencer and with one of the Miss Bouveries.

30*th.*—I certainly feel a decay of strength since last year.

* Lady Harriet Cavendish, afterwards Countess Granville.

July 8th.—Refused Berry's carriage and got drenched. Fire at North's. Not home till a little before four. Should have broken open presses.

16th.—Read papers, and last number but one of Cob. A little in the Milton: Licence for universal printing: and in Thucydides. βραγχὸς βήξ.

23rd.—Confirmation of bad news and account of Cobbett's trial for false imprisonment, &c. Some hopes still entertained, that victory of Buonaparte not conclusive. Expedition not yet clearly off.

The Right Hon. William Windham to Captain Lukin.

Beaconsfield: July 23, 1809.

Dear William,—I hold to my purpose of going to the Assizes, and shall accordingly leave this for town to-morrow. Terrible news this from Germany, though the learned in London, I understand, at least those about the offices, do not consider the battle was one of those decisive ones that leaves nothing to be afterwards hoped. There is nothing to me in the event that at all comes unexpectedly, however it may be to be lamented. The most discouraging consideration is the dreadful inferiority of talents that there appears always to be on the side of the Austrians. Why is Buonaparte to be able to pass the Danube before the Archduke is apprised of what he is about? I cannot think that this would have happened the other way. Our expedition, I conceive, to be a most injudicious one, whatever be the event. My idea is that the whole should have been sent to Spain, so as not to leave Buonaparte, when he has settled the Austrian business, to begin, as he did last year, on the banks of the Ebro, but to have driven the whole of the French force out of the peninsula. With a view, even to a respite from invasion, the total clearance of Spain would have been of more importance than the destruction of all the vessels and arsenals in the Scheldt, should we even accomplish that object. If I had been tempted to any other object, it would have been with a view to remote and contingent consequences, the capture of Belleisle, the troops being to proceed afterwards to Spain.

I have written to Hudson, to state my intention of being at the Assizes and to know whether he could give me a bed.

Yours affectionately,

W. W.

My cold is better; but another of the poor men who were hurt at the fire (one of them is dead) is, I fear, in a bad way. They went into the house not only after I had left it, but after I was gone home.

24*th.*—Awake by half-past eight, up by nine. Read a little this morning in Lord Bolingbroke's 'Study of History.' What extreme foppery! yet what can one point out as proofs?

28*th.*—Employed pretty constantly all day, but not altogether, on business preparatory to going, *i.e.* on things that could not be done with equal advantage afterwards, nor altogether in a manner conformable to the last improved methods. The greatest want, is a want of methodical recollection, and next to that, the want of a right selection, so as to ensure always a priority of those objects which suffer by postponements.

August 3*rd.*—Visit to Cossey.

4*th.*—*Felbrigg.*—Dined with the Hudsons: William and Mrs. L. only, with William, junr.

5*th.*—Little William taken to school.

6*th.*—Rode out. The shoots in the part of the plantation in the north-west, which was cut this spring, do not seem to be vigorous, neither from the trees that remain, nor from the stubs. I fear they may have been chilled.

7*th.*—Between twelve and one William came over, who had returned yesterday. Walked with him first about the house, giving directions to carpenters; then out of doors, looking at horses and plantations. Time not altogether wasted.

9*th.*—Walked a little before breakfast with Hoste, and

learnt from him some facts about killing animals. Some butchers, he says, have a way of breaking the necks of sheep when they kill them: they may be killed, as I understand, by the spine. A common way of killing fowl to cut them in the mouth, leaving them then, of course, to bleed to death: he cuts their heads off.

10*th.*—*Holkham.*—Long ride in the morning with Coke. Sheep fly-bitten. Threshing machine. Am to get from Coke some cuttings of French willows, sea buckthorn, and evergreen oak; forgot to ask him the principal properties of the last named.

11*th.*—Up at six; stopped to speak to Coke and to urge the necessity of not neglecting the sort of fever which is hanging about him. Set out before the chaise and stopped at Langton's, to suggest the necessity of his urging the same advice. Whole way to Holt employed in attempts on problem.

I have been looking over books in the book-case, where the Dionysius stands, Stow's 'Chronicle and Survey of London.'

> By wisdom, truth, and heed was he,
> Advanced an alderman to be.

First chapter also of that most absurd dogmatical and offensive book, 'The Divine Legation Demonstrated.'

14*th.*—Read in library; for first time, in Swift's* 'Ode to Athenian Society.' Not in good state to judge, but thought it but heavy, though not worse perhaps than odes generally are. Mem.: to read it again.

16*th.*—Day of 'Gazette' arriving, with news of Wellesley's victory† of 28th of July. Substance of it received in letter from Amyot on my return last night. I rode a

* 'As when the deluge first began to fall.'

† Battle of Talavera.

little before breakfast, to P. Johnson's, who, with his wife, was at home; had examined in our way the new plantations, riding down Springdale.

22*nd.*—Morning fine. Rode to plantation, on Aylmerton Common, and examined with Nicholls what had been done there. Instead of all thinning and none on outside, it should have been more thinning in middle, but a little throughout. Time of year wrong, too: thinning in autumn gives the evil without the benefit. Back to breakfast not till a little past nine. Dean, at my desire, has begun examination of old letters; some curious: have found narrative of 'Tour to Glaciers.' Box of papers sent upstairs, in which the Dean has since found many curious particulars.

September 13*th.*—Began a letter to Lord Holland, who seems to have come back from Spain.

22*nd.*—Went out and settled situation for cottages, and examined and determined about Swift's grove, viz. to take it down, all but a few oaks, and to replace it by young plants. Home by Marble Hill.

24*th.*—Walked about with A. Hudson and William; by walk and consequent fatigue morning very much lost. Half asleep when time for going to Aylsham, where agreed that we were to dine. Dinner not unpleasant.

30*th.*—At home all morning, with no interruption but a call from Earle. It was at a time when I had wearied myself with writing, and for relaxation was indulging myself in reading 'Irene.' Sent over to Aylmerton party to dine here.

October 9*th.*—*London.*—Met Lord Bessborough and Fitzpatrick, who proposed my dining at Holland House: dined there accordingly; Lord Bessborough calling for me. In the carriage was Lord Thanet, whom I had hardly been in company with before: much to be liked, as far as can be so judged.

At dinner, Lamb and Lady Caroline, Horner, who

had just come from the west, those before named and Curran, who reminded me of a former introduction at Burke's, with some little dissatisfaction that I did not remember it.

26*th.*—Evening of going to Duchess of Brunswick's.

29*th.*—Called at Lord Spencer's, but found at gate Lady S. gone; thence to Lord Sidmouth; he has been to Dropmore; means to keep himself aloof; cannot support present people; cannot help in a Ministry; that if they enter triumphantly, must be the more obliged to support the Catholics. Does not believe my speculation, that Lord Wellesley will come in as first Lord and Canning in his old place. My belief is founded on what I have learnt to-day from Legge of the language of Lord St. Helens, who is quite satisfied that Canning is a most ill-used man.*

November 10*th.*—Read a little in Arist. 'Polit.' before I went to bed.

12*th.*—Not up till twenty minutes past nine. Rode to Holland House; met Lord Derby; found Scarlet at Holland House and rode back with him. Asked to stay and meet T. Grenville and Tierney.

17*th.*—Dined at Duke of Brunswick's. I went with H.R.H. to play. Sat down by Lord H. Fitzgerald. Rode to Holland House and walked with Lord Holland to farm, where I saw Spanish mules.

23*rd.*—Slept in carriage going to Holland House. Dinner upon table: present, Duke of Argyle, Lamb and Lady Caroline, Lushington, Sir R. Wilson, Stuart (from Spain), Lady Affleck, Lord R. Fitzgerald.

24*th.*—Went up for a short time into library, and read

* In consequence of differences in the Cabinet between Lord Castlereagh and Mr. Canning, then Foreign Minister, he resigned that office on the 7th September; Lord Castlereagh followed his example, and on the 22nd September a duel took place between them. Lord Wellesley, then in Spain, was sent for, and received the seals of the Foreign Department on the 6th December.

in 'Oration of Lysias.' Difference between ὑβρίζειν τινά and ὑβρίζειν εἰς τινα.

December 5th.—In the evening read poem of 'Talavera,' ascribed to Croker. Afterwards, when upstairs, Mrs. Montagu's 'Letters,' which think very highly of; one of their chief merits is *series juncturaque.* Nothing can be more easy and natural than the manner in which the thoughts rise one out of the other, even where the thoughts may appear rather forced, nor is the expression ever harsh or laboured. I see but little to object to in the thoughts themselves; but nothing can be more natural or graceful than the manner in which they are put together. The flow of her style is not less natural, because it is fully charged with shining particles, and sparkles as it flows.

19*th.*—Dr. Ferris, since I have been here, has lent me a treatise of Dr. Vincent's, on the Origin of the Greek verb, which seems to be ingenious. As far as I can collect from the little I have read, the theory seems to be, that the verb arises from the combination of the substantive and the verb εω, being the general expression for motion, that is, action. He sent over at the same time Mrs. Galando's 'Letters;' a foolish slander, as it seems, against Mrs. Siddons.

1810.

January 6th.—Day of receiving news of the death of poor G. Wyndham,* who died on the night of the 2nd, or, more correctly, on the morning of the 3rd.

11th.—Went to see, with Mr. Disney and Colonel Burke, Mr. Davis's collection of pictures. 'Head of Christ,' by Leonardo da Vinci, which had been in the possession of Troward. I should conceive this to be the first in the collection. Its merits would consist in the beauty of the countenance and a strong expression given to a countenance perfectly quiescent.

The Right Hon. W. Windham to Captain Lukin.

Pall Mall: January 20, 1810.

Dear William,—At the same time that I got your letter announcing the death of poor G. Wyndham, I got one from Sir Jacob Astley. I heard the news with very considerable concern, and shall long feel to miss G. Wyndham. He was a friendly, well-disposed man, who never offended and often pleased. In all cases where liking and preference were alone concerned, he was always disposed to side with me, and would have done, I dare say, for me as much as he would for anyone. How much in any case that might have been I have no means of knowing, but whether it was more or less, one owes something to the preference, and it is always pleasant to have as a neighbour a person so disposed; and whether the feeling was that of pure, unmixed kindness, or from his interest and consideration, in virtue of the

* Died suddenly in the night, at Melton Constable, the seat of Sir Jacob Astley.

name and family connection, as in some degree united with mine, I shall feel that a great blank is made by his death in the system of Felbrigg life.

With best love to Anne from Mrs. W. and myself,

Yours affectionately,

W. W.

26*th.*—Day on which majority obtained against the Ministry on question of Lord Porchester's motion to resolve an enquiry; spoke a little—not on the general subject, but on the mere question of waiting or not for papers.

29*th.*—Letter brought by Amyot and Cutler, announcing Mrs. Guise's death! I had been out to Lord Grey's to meet Jerningham, but came too late, having sat up overnight. I, coming back, fell in with George Cockburn, who was on his way to me in consequence of note from me enquiring about some circumstances at Walcheren. Could not attend much to what he said, and excused myself accordingly. I wish she could have lived! How one feels now that the opportunity one had of seeing and being with her were not turned to the best account. It is satisfactory, however, to have seen her so recently, and to have parted with such marks of kindness, but still without sufficient impression upon my mind that one was seeing her possibly for the last time.

February 1*st.*—Not out in morning. Thanks voted to Lord Wellington.* Spoke, not so well as I ought, but tolerably. First speech from Vernon, a very striking performance. 'Envy might drive the colour from his cheek;' viz. Whitbread and Lord F. I was sorry to see so much talent applied to such bad notions. Sat up reading Shakespeare.

2*nd.*—Drove in the coach with Cecilia to Lord Fitzwilliam's, whom I found at home and talked with about Catholics and the course to be pursued in case of mes-

* After the battle of Talavera.

sage from the King; and afterwards to Lord Grenville's, who stated what the view was respecting the Catholic petition.

13*th.*—Saw Wright, having met him in Braid's shop, and proposed to him to walk with me to my house. He there admitted, to the fullest extent and without hesitation, that all the expressions dwelt upon by Cobbett, 'of the impressions made upon the gallery,' 'way of standing,' &c., were his words and not mine, and that I never asked him a question upon such subjects.

14*th.*—Dined, by appointment, at Lord Holland's: present, Lord Morpeth, Lady Georgiana, Lord and Lady Boringdon* (first time of seeing Lady B. since her marriage), Tierney and Lord Archibald Hamilton.

17*th.*—Called on Sir P. Francis, who was at home, and with whom I had much discourse on subject of speech, which he had read and seemed to like. His criticism on a part to be examined and guarded against, should there be really any room to mistake.

18*th.*—Dined at Lord Cholmondeley's: present, Duke of Gloucester, Duke of Bedford, Lords Stafford, Grenville, Ponsonby, Gower, Cowper, Holland, Lauderdale, Whitbread and Tierney.

22*nd.*—Went into House of Lords to hear Grey on presenting the Catholic Bill; stayed for a little while to hear Lord Wellesley on Portuguese Subsidy.

25*th.*—Dined at Lord Spencer's: present, Grenville, Lord Morpeth and Lady Georgiana, Lord Granville Leveson and Lady Harriet Cavendish, Ward, Lord and Lady Ponsonby.

26*th.*—Army estimates. Spoke after Huskisson. Well satisfied, not because anything very good in what I said, but from a feel of power in myself in saying it. Found

* Lady Boringdon, afterwards Countess of Morley, so well known in society for her wit and amiable qualities.

printed paper from Basil Montagu and sat up writing notes to detect its sophistry.

27*th*.—Went on with Basil Montagu, a most shallow reasoner. Walked out at a little after twelve and calling on Lord Holland, walked with him up Constitution Hill into Hyde Park, his horses following, till it was time for him to return. Pleasant conversation on many topics; he does not violently dissent from notions expressed in printed speech.

March 3*rd*.—I went to the Opera; went first into H.R.H. box, then to Lady Harrowby's, and finally, for a very short time, into Melbourne's, who I found had some quarrel with me about politics; I did not understand or do not recollect very well what, but I suppose about the printers. Saw in going away Lady Asgill, who is still handsome, though she has lost more of her beauty than of her coquetry.

10*th*.—Called at Lord Holland's; Grey there, and Brougham. Something odd in Grey's manner. Had written note to Lord Aberdeen, with whom I was to dine; dined there: Lord Morpeth and Lady Georgiana, Lord and Lady Cowper, M. Berry, Lords Holland and Lauderdale.

18*th*.—At home again during morning, except quite late, when I called at Lord Holland's. Lord Holland as usual; Lady Holland something wrong, I think. Talk of Romilly's pamphlet. Much surprise on Lord Holland's part, as it seemed, as well as with my lady, that I should think it sophistical.

25*th*.—Dinner at Lord Granville Leveson's: Lord and Lady Morpeth, Canning, Huskisson, Lord and Lady Aberdeen, Lady M. Hamilton (no conversation with her), Mary Berry, by whom I sat.

26*th*.—Question. First day, I think, of Walcheren.

29*th*.—Early dinner. House. Had fixed myself for speaking, and felt in particular good state for it; prepared to get up after Canning, but Speaker called to Whitbread. At home, I suppose, between two and three.

30th.—Day of concluding debate on Walcheren question. Went out in morning and got some facts from Lord Rosslyn. Very feeble from continuance of diarrhœa, and could not at all collect my thoughts for what I was to do. Better after I had been some time in the House. Got up at the time wished; circumstances of call at the same time for Brougham. Spoke, as I understand from Hippisley, for two hours. Successful beyond any instance that I can remember, I mean of myself. Less pleased than I should have been if there had been less chance in it, if what was said had been more distinctly on my mind beforehand.

April 4th.—Reserved myself for dinner of Opposition at Thatched House. Only W. Smith and Sheridan. How many years since I met Sheridan at a dinner, except possibly in very large company!

6th.—Walked to the House. House in committee, and could not wait to move paper. Met Coleman and Becket, who were only going to serve warrant on Sir F. Burdett. Talked afterwards with Lord Harrowby, and to Ryder and Lord Liverpool, whom we met. Did not like to stay and consult with them.

7th.—Went late with Sir J. Cockburn and Robert to Albemarle Street. Found Life Guards in Piccadilly hunted by, and hunting, the mob. Houses lighted, and good deal of disturbance there, and in the streets adjoining on the north side.

9th.—Meeting at one o'clock at Lord Grenville's, for the purpose of settling, if we could, what should be done in the House. Could come to no agreement. Terrible disposition to yield to popular opinion, and to give up the House of Commons.

10th.—Sorry to find that Lord Grey still hangs on notions of reform. Elliot called and agreed to dine here. Did not get to House till towards close of Anstruther's speech, which was foolishly received by the boys. Per-

[illegible]

[illegible] May [illegible]

[illegible] I am sorry [illegible] tell you that sentence is just [illegible] a very severe operation, no trifling [illegible] the consequence of a hurt which I got [illegible] Of this, however, you must say nothing.

Yours affectionately,

W. W.

12*th*.—Walked out. Omitted foolishly to enquire at St. James's Church, otherwise should have learnt that there was to be an administration of the Sacrament at seven, which would just have suited me, as besides the privacy, I could have gone then before I took any physic.

13*th*.—Sorry that, for want of earlier enquiry, I had missed the Sacrament at St. James's at seven o'clock. Remedied the loss by writing to Fisher, and afterwards going, when I received it in his room in company only with Mrs. Fisher. Blane in evening, and Wilson; which last dissuaded me the operation; Elliot afterwards. Not convinced by Wilson, as he has no hopes to give of evil stopping or being removed.

FELBRIGG PARSONAGE.

APPENDIX.

The two following Letters were addressed by General Dumourier to Mr. Windham when he held the office of Secretary of State for War and the Colonies in 1806.

NOTE SUR LE MEXIQUE.

12 juin 1806.

Dans la note que j'ai envoyée à Mr Fox, de Stralsund, le 22 avril, sur la continuation de la guerre de terre et de mer, voyez le paragraphe intitulé *Mexique :*

'Le coup le plus terrible que l'Angleterre puisse porter à Buonaparte est de séparer les possessions espagnoles de leur métropole, non pas en tentant follement de se les asservir, mais en y plaçant une dynastie qui les garantisse également, et de l'indépendance américaine et de l'influence, ou du joug, de la France. Toutes les pertes, toutes les gênes que Buonaparte parviendra à faire supporter au commerce et aux manufactures anglaises en Europe seront réparées au centuple par la création d'une nouvelle puissance, alliée nécessaire de l'Angleterre, et qui, par ses consommations, dépendrait de son commerce et de ses manufactures.

'Le projet d'arracher le Mexique à la monarchie espagnole ne doit point être envisagé comme une conception dévastatrice et de haine contre cette monarchie. C'est un acte de prévoyance digne du gouvernement d'une nation profonde et réfléchie. Les progrès de la population et de la culture de la Louisiane, depuis son union avec les États-Unis, annoncent l'invasion prochaine du Mexique, dès que les nouveaux établissements qui s'étendent déjà à la droite du Mississipi dans les riches plaines des Cenis se répandront jusqu'au Rio del Norte. Alors, les frontières du nouveau Mexique seront bientôt franchies par les aventuriers américains, à moins que le Mexique n'ait un souverain résidant sur les lieux, qui puisse rassembler sur les mêmes frontières des forces indigènes bien conduites. Toutes les nations de l'Europe

[illegible]

[illegible]

[illegible] sa patrie. Tel est [illegible] paraît avoir mis trop de confiance et protégeant [illegible] avançant l'argent [illegible] projet, sans en avoir examiné les conséquences.

Depuis trois ans on ménageait l'Espagne, et on rejettait toute proposition de tenter quelqu'entreprise contre les Indes espagnoles, d'abord dans [illegible] calculé d'amener par ces égards la cour de Madrid à une exacte neutralité, peut-être aussi faute de plans, enfin par égard pour la Russie, qui exigeait, disait-on, que l'Angleterre respectât les possessions de l'Amérique espagnole, vraisemblablement par jalousie sur la navigation de la Mer du Sud. Cette condescendance pour la politique russe est une faiblesse qui n'aurait pu être excusable que dans le cas où on eût eu lieu d'espérer, par l'influence de la Russie, de ramener la cour de Madrid, non-seulement à une neutralité exacte mais à une jonction de ses forces à celles du Portugal, de la Russie et de l'Angleterre, pour fermer les Pyrénées aux Français et s'affranchir du joug de Buonaparte.

Comme cet espoir, s'il a eu lieu, a été totalement illusoire, la condescendance pour la protection accordée par la Russie à l'Espagne est déplacée, surtout dans le moment où cette cour paraît abandonner les plans vigoureux qu'elle avait adoptés, se rapprocher de la France par la Prusse, ne présenter à l'avenir qu'une médiation dangereuse, et ne respirer que la paix. Une pareille politique ne mérite plus des ménagements désavantageux, et l'Angleterre rentre dans tous ses droits de nuire à Buonaparte, en arrachant à l'Espagne ses possessions, d'où il tire tout l'or qu'il emploie contre l'Angleterre.

Mais si le précédent Ministère a commis l'erreur de se laisser lier les bras sur cet article par la cour de Pétersbourg, quelle inconséquence n'a-t-il pas commise en protégeant les projets révolutionnaires d'un aventurier ? La Russie jetera les hauts cris sur cette expédition, et il n'y a pas d'excuse à donner de la part de l'Angleterre ; car Miranda a fait ses propositions au gouvernement anglais ; c'est de Londres qu'il est parti, c'est de Londres qu'il a emporté au moins 600 livres sterling pour faire son armement. On aura beau nier cette mission qu'on croit très-secrète, la cour de Russie doit la regarder comme un grief, et ne tardera pas à en porter des plaintes auxquelles on n'aura rien à répondre.

Mais cette expédition est en elle-même nuisible, et c'est la seule manière de révolutionner les Indes espagnoles qu'on ne devait pas tenter. Miranda, parti d'Angleterre avec de l'argent, est allé faire à New-York un armement composé d'Américains ; son plan est fondé sur des principes démocratiques ; c'est pour les États-Unis qu'il travaille. S'il réussit, non-seulement cette révolution sera démocratique, mais elle sera américaine. Parité de principes, liaisons de commerce, secours prompts, tout l'attache à l'Amérique; tout le rend dépendant des États-Unis, et c'est au moment où on est en contestation avec ces Etats, où peut-être on est menacé d'une rupture par rapport aux violences commises contre l'Etat de New-York,* qu'on s'est suscité ce nouveau sujet de querelle, qu'on ouvre cette nouvelle carrière à l'ambition des États-Unis.

Dans quelle partie se fait cette expédition? Dans le point le plus rapproché de la Grenade, de Tabago et de la Trinidad. Si elle réussit, l'amélioration de ces trois colonies, la liberté de leur commerce, seront dans la dépendance d'un aventurier démocrate, dont l'intérêt est d'attirer les Américains, et qui aura sur son flanc gauche l'appui de Curaçao, d'où il recevra les secours des Français et des Hollandais, qui l'exciteront et l'appuieront contre l'Angleterre.

D'après la connaissance des principes personnels de cet aventurier, des circonstances et du lieu de son départ, du choix du point de son débarquement, des dangereux résultats de sa réussite, le Ministère présent serait aussi blâmable que le précédent, s'il laissait opérer cette révolution, que pour l'intérêt de l'Angleterre il doit étouffer dans sa naissance. En même tems qu'il doit, par ses escadres, fermer à Miranda toute communication avec les États-Unis et intercepter tous les secours du Congrès et de Curaçao, en lui enlevant l'Ile de la Marguerite et l'enfermant dans la province de Caracas: en même tems il doit opposer le plus promptement possible, dans un autre point de ce continent, aux principes révolutionnaires démocratiques qu'il aura déjà répandus, des principes révolutionnaires royalistes qui remplissent le même but de séparer ces colonies de la métropole, séparation qui est inévitable, qui est commencée depuis l'expédition de Miranda, et qu'il faut diriger, puisqu'elle est entamée.

Les habitans des Indes espagnoles n'ont point du tout un caractère analogue à une révolution démocratique. Attachés à leur religion et à leurs usages, ils ont un dévouement particulier pour le gouvernement monarchique, qui seul leur convient, qui seul peut rallier les quatre castes qui composent leur population. Espagnols naturels, Espagnols créoles, Indiens et Noirs, ou sang-mêlé.

* Ces violences ne sont pas injustes, elles sont conformes au droit de la mer mais elles sont envenimées par l'inimitié du président Jefferson.

Aveuglés par leur haine contre le gouvernement de la métropole, il est possible qu'ils embrassent avec fureur les moyens qu'un aventurier démocrate pourrait leur présenter: alors ils tomberaient dans tous les malheurs de l'anarchie. Mais, si on leur pré·ente un prince de la maison de Bourbon, qui ait des droits à les gouverner, et que ce prince, s'engageant à résider parmi eux, leur offre la perspective d'une royauté indigène et d'une existence nationale, alors leur amour-propre naturel, qui anime également les quatre castes, les ramènera sur-le-champ à leur caractère, à leurs principes, leur fera abhorrer l'anarchie démocratique et l'aventurier qui leur apporte ce funeste présent, et les ralliera sous les étendards d'un roi légitime, d'un sang qu'ils chérissent, et autour d'un trône dont la splendeur flattera leur vanité.

C'est dans le Mexique même qu'il faut présenter un prince de la maison de Bourbon, qui ne soit ni de la branche espagnole, ni de la branche française ayant un droit direct à la couronne de France. Ce prince doit être connu d'avance par sa bravoure et ses talents; il doit savoir la langue espagnole, il doit avoir déjà passé les mers, être acclimaté, dans la force de l'âge, n'être point étranger aux Américains espagnols. Toutes ces qualités se trouvent réunies dans le duc d'Orléans, qui, en outre, a aux yeux de la nation anglaise le mérite de s'être accoutumé depuis cinq ans aux mœurs, aux usages, à la langue du pays, qui lui donne un asyle honorable, qui est aimé et estimé du Roi, du Prince, de la famille royale et de toute la nation.

Son caractère moral, sa probité délicate, ses connaissances étendues, la valeur brillante qu'il a déployée à la guerre, sa constance dans l'adversité, toutes ses qualités naturelles et acquises lui donnent un droit incontestable au choix du gouvernement anglais pour aller fonder un royaume en Amérique, qui assure à l'Angleterre un allié solide et nécessaire, et un débouché certain pour son commerce et ses manufactures. Mon amitié pour ce prince respectable ne m'aveugle pas, et si j'en connaissais un plus propre à remplir ce but, je le proposerais sans balancer.

Aucun prince n'est plus en état que lui de réunir les esprits des différents habitans de l'Amérique espagnole sous une royauté sage, indépendante de l'Espagne, de détruire les idées démocratiques propagées par l'aventurier Miranda, d'anéantir son parti, de former une armée indigène pour s'opposer aux progrès des

Américains dans le Golfe du Mexique, d'aider l'Angleterre à chasser les Hollandais de Curaçao, les Français des Antilles. L'Angleterre peut compter sur la solidité de son alliance, parce-que ses liens politiques seront encore plus forts que sa reconnaissance.

Ses droits à occuper le nouveau royaume du Mexique sont aussi réels que ceux de la branche espagnole de Bourbon. Dès que la politique nouvelle, occasionnée par la révolution française, oblige à démembrer ces états d'outre-mer de la monarchie espagnole, comme on a séparé par la guerre de la succession l'hérédité de la France de celle de l'Espagne, il est le plus proche héritier par Anne d'Autriche de cette partie de la succession de Charles-Quint, dont le même principe politique exclut nécessairement la branche aînée des Bourbons, à cause de son droit direct à la couronne de France.

On ne peut pas craindre l'éventualité de l'extinction de cette branche aînée, soutenue par quatre princes, dont l'aîné (Louis XVIII) est le seul qui ait une femme hors d'âge, dont le second (Monsieur) est veuf, le troisième (le duc d'Angoulême) a une jeune épouse, le quatrième (le duc de Berry) a 29 ans, et peut être marié.

Cependant, pour tout prévoir dans une affaire de cette importance, on peut prendre d'avance des mesures sur le cas de cette éventualité, comme on l'a fait par le traité d'Utrecht, en stipulant que, dans le cas où la couronne de France reviendrait par droit de succession au duc d'Orléans devenu roi du Mexique, il serait engagé à remettre ce dernier royaume à un de ses frères, ou de ses collatéraux, de manière à ce que dans aucun tems ces deux couronnes ne pussent être réunies sur une même tête.

Quant à l'exécution de cette entreprise, le duc d'Orléans est le plus propre de tous les princes à en diriger toutes les parties et tous les mouvements dans le plus grand détail, si le gouvernement faisait d'avance un traité éventuel avec lui et mettait à sa disposition une somme de 500,000 livres sterling, avec la faculté de rassembler une force armée de 6000 hommes prise soit parmi les Écossais et Irlandais catholiques, soit parmi les Italiens, Espagnols, Portugais ou autres étrangers qu'il pourrait attacher à sa fortune. Son point de rassemblement, d'entrepôt et de départ pourrait être une des Antilles à son choix. Le prétexte de l'armement pourrait être l'attaque de la Martinique, ou de Cuba, ou de Porto-Rico, pour masquer le plus longtems possible le vrai but de l'expédition.

'Ce prince, ayant passé dix-huit mois à la Havane, a certainement combiné d'avance tous les moyens de pénétrer dans le Mexique; il connaît le fort et le faible de cet empire, ainsi que les dispositions de ses habitans, et on peut s'en rapporter avec confiance au plan qu'il tracera, et que lui seul en Europe est en état d'exécuter, tant par ses talents, sa naissance, sa vigueur personnelle, que par le secours des mêmes qualités de ses deux frères, de leur liaison intime avec l'Angleterre, de leur habitude à braver les dangers, et surtout de leur union, qui de ces trois têtes n'en fait qu'une, et présente trois successeurs pour achever l'entreprise, en cas qu'il arrivât malheur à l'un d'eux dans son exécution.

En adoptant ce plan, l'Angleterre aussi aura fait un roi, aura révolutionné le globe d'une manière plus glorieuse et plus utile que Buonaparte, auquel elle aura porté un coup terrible, en lui enlevant les trésors du Nouveau-Monde, et laissant à sa charge la nation espagnole, dont une partie émigrera pour aller retrouver la liberté dans une nouvelle monarchie. Quant à la cour de Madrid, on parviendra peut-être à la ramener à une politique saine et vigoureuse par l'espoir qu'on lui fera entrevoir de lui réserver ses possessions du Pérou, du Chili et de Buenos-Ayres, à condition qu'elle secouera avec énergie le joug de Buonaparte, et s'alliera solidement avec l'Angleterre et le Portugal.

La Russie, par la mollesse de sa politique, a perdu le droit d'intervenir dans la disposition du sort de l'Amérique espagnole. Le gouvernement anglais n'a aucune obligation de lui annoncer ses projets à cet égard, puisque les liens qui étaient le prétexte de sa condescendance se relâchent de jour en jour, et changent la nature des obligations mutuelles. Cependant, pour guérir sa jalousie et diminuer l'ombrage qu'elle pourrait prendre de la création de ce nouvel État sur la Mer du Sud, il sera possible, lorsque l'expédition sera en train, et pas plus tôt, d'entrer en négociation avec le cabinet de Pétersbourg, pour lui démontrer que son intérêt sur cette mer étant purement commerciel, et vu la nature ingrate de ses ports situés au nord-est de son empire ne pouvant fournir qu'une navigation très-bornée, son plus grand avantage est que toutes les côtes de l'ouest du continent américain espagnol soient vivifiées par un gouvernement solide et par un souverain résidant sur ce continent.

L'étendue naturelle de ce nouvel empire, que l'Angleterre peut fonder en Amérique sous le nom de royaume du Mexique, doit comprendre toute la bande des côtes du golphe de ce nom, depuis le Rio del Norte, au nord, jusqu'à la Guyane hollandaise au sud, ainsi que toutes les îles de ce golphe appartenantes à l'Espagne, à l'exception de Cuba qui sera cédée à l'Angleterre, et peut-être de Porto-Rico, pour faire le prix d'une alliance étroite avec le Danemark, en cas qu'on réussisse à ramener la Russie à des principes énergiques et à former la ligue du Nord. C'est ainsi que l'Angleterre peut lier les intérêts des deux hémisphères, et réunir à son avantage contre l'ennemi commun les puissances les plus séparées par leur distance géographique.

Gunnersbury Lodge, near Acton, Middlesex : 27 juin 1806.

MONSIEUR,

Vous êtes mon ministre, et je vous dois toutes les idées que me suggère mon dévouement sincère à l'Angleterre. Longtems avant que vous fussiez à la tête du département auquel je suis attaché, ma confiance vous rendait le même hommage, et j'avais soumis à vos lumières une partie de mes travaux.

J'ai eu l'honneur de vous envoyer le 12 une note générale sur la continuation de la guerre; je l'avais fait passer à Mr Fox, de Stralsund, par la voie du ministre anglais. Voici deux notes détaillées que j'ai faites depuis ma conférence avec Mr Fox sur deux paragraphes de la note générale, *Sardaigne* et *Mexique*. Mon opinion est que les négociations ne doivent point arrêter l'activité de la guerre, qu'il faut au contraire se presser d'acquérir des objets d'échange et de compensation. Buonaparte vous donne un exemple très-bon à suivre: il se dépêche de faire son frère roi de Hollande; il presse le siége de Gaëte, il menace les Iles Ioniennes; il fait des progrès en Dalmatie; il excite contre vous les États-Unis; il expédie à tout moment de nouvelles escadres pour vous faire du mal partout, autant qu'il peut.

Le seul moyen d'égaliser les négociations est de déployer toutes vos ressources sans perdre de tems. Certainement trois grandes opérations dépendent uniquement de vous seuls, malgré la défection de vos alliés du continent.

1° Dans l'Inde, aller prendre et détruire de fond en comble Batavia, car vous ne devez plus aucun ménagement aux Hollandais, puisque leurs colonies sont devenues la propriété de la famille de Buonaparte, et prendre les Iles de France et de Bourbon. Sans ces deux opérations, vous perdrez l'Inde sous peu d'années;

2° Faire un roi du Mexique: par cette opération acquérir un allié puissant qui, par la suite, contienne les États-Unis, vous aide à chasser des Antilles les Français et les Hollandais, vous assure un débouché pour vos manufactures, et vous dédommage au centuple des gênes qu'elles éprouvent en Europe. Par cette expédition, aussi solide que brillante, aussi facile que lucrative, vous acquerrez, sans tirer un coup de fusil, la domination du Golfe du Mexique par la possession de la Havane, celle de la Mer du Sud par celle de Manille, que le nouveau roi du Mexique vous cédera pour le prix de son exaltation; vous ne pouvez les acquérir que par ce moyen, en profitant des circonstances, qui ne se représenteront jamais et qui tourneront contre vous, si vous les laissez échapper. Le commerce des deux mers sera dans vos mains, les richesses métalliques de l'Amérique espagnole arriveront en Angleterre, vous en priverez l'Espagne et Buonaparte, et cette révolution numéraire changera la face politique de l'Europe;

3° Créer une puissance navale sarde, dépendante de vous, qui coupera la communication par mer entre la France, l'Italie et l'Espagne, qui menacera toujours sa puissance en Italie en soutenant la Sicile et Malte, et qui arrêtera ses projets du Levant. Cette création inquièterait sa possession du midi de l'Italie, et la rendrait en tout tems précaire et dangereuse.

Tels sont les plans qui m'ont occupé pendant mon voyage et depuis mon retour. Je ne crains point d'être indiscret ou importun en les proposant: 1° parceque le Ministère actuel est trop fort par ses talents et son énergie pour ne pas les prendre en considération, les discuter mûrement, et s'occuper sans retard de leur exécution, s'il les adopte. Quoique étranger, je ne crains ni préjugé national, ni jalousie de la part des hommes qui nous gouvernent. 2° Parcequ'ils ne contrarient en rien vos négociations, puisque vous êtes toujours en activité d'hostilités, et que cet état de guerre, dont profite sans interruption Buonaparte sur les deux hémisphères, ne vous permet pas de stagnation, ou de suspension, dans la conduite de votre guerre.

Quant à la paix, je la crois plus *infaisable* que jamais depuis la création du royaume de Hollande et l'élévation du cardinal Fesch à la dignité d'Electeur archichancelier de l'empire d'Allemagne. Attendez ce qu'en penseront les puissances du continent: tant pis pour elles si, tout en prévoyant les funestes conséquences de ces deux nouveaux actes, elles se laissent entraîner à la paix par leur pusillanimité ou par la corruption de leurs ministres. Vous n'avez besoin d'aucun allié pour exécuter les trois plans proposés, et ils vous reviendront en foule quand vous aurez réussi.

J'ai presque envie de finir ma lettre comme Diderot commence un de ses livres: *Jeune homme, prends et lis.* Vous connaissez le tendre et respectueux attachement de votre serviteur,

DUMOURIER.

The Right Hon. W. Windham to Major-General Sir John Stuart, &c. &c.

Downing Street: 15th Sept. 1806.

SIR,—I have received and laid before the King your despatch of the 6th of July, containing an account of the brilliant and decisive victory obtained by the troops under your command, on the 4th of the same month, over the French forces in Calabria, and exhibiting to the world a new and convincing proof, in addition to so many others, that whenever the armies of this country are placed in circumstances fairly to try their strength with the enemy, the result is never different from that which marks so invariably the progress of His Majesty's arms in every instance of naval combat.

It is not possible for me to express in terms too strong the satisfaction felt by His Majesty at the whole of the proceedings of that day, in which every one appears to have vied with another in the discharge of their respective duties, and where the result of the whole has been such an accession of glory to the British arms, as cannot fail to produce the most beneficial effects at the present moment, and to become a source of just and honourable pride to the inhabitants of these islands as long as the country shall endure. The judgment with which the whole of the enterprise was planned and conducted is considered by His Majesty as not less deserving of his commendation, than the vigour and determination with which it was carried into execution; and it is no small consolation to His Majesty's mind that the same superior valour and discipline which contributed so directly to ensure the victory, have rendered the loss comparatively small among the brave troops by whom these qualities were so eminently displayed.

Conformably to the sentiments thus expressed, I am happy in having to state to you, that while the whole of the army will partake of His Majesty's thanks for the strikingly meritorious conduct observed by every one on this memorable occasion, it is His Majesty's gracious intention that the officers commanding corps (a list of whom you will accordingly send over), should enjoy the privilege of bearing a medal commemorating the service for which it was given, and similar to those granted to the army in Egypt; and that for yourself should be reserved the honourable distinction of the Order of the Bath, joined to such pecuniary reward as Parliament, on the recommendation of His Majesty, may be dispoed to grant, in further proof of the high sense entertained of your merit, and of the eminent service which you have rendered to your country.

I lament to think that, in the midst of services thus glorious, and which have received from His Majesty such unqualified approbation, there should be any proceeding, though of a different nature, which His Majesty cannot regard with equal favour, but in which he is persuaded, nevertheless, that you have been actuated by motives not less meritorious than those which have governed your conduct in every other instance.

The proceeding to which I allude is that of the proclamation issued in your name to the inhabitants of Calabria, which, besides the objection to be made to it, should it be construed by any one as pledging the faith of this country to the protection of the Calabrians to an indefinite extent, and in all circumstances, is one that ought on no account to have been issued, but with the sanction and authority of His Majesty's Minister resident at the time in Sicily, and accredited to His Sicilian Majesty, and whose exclusive province it was to decide upon and direct all measures involving, like the present, matters of great political delicacy and importance.

While, however, I am directed by His Majesty thus to point out to you the irregularity into which you have been inadvertently betrayed, I am happy in being permitted to say that His Majesty is pleased to consider it as ascribable wholly to an error in judgment, and as not tending in any degree to efface the sense entertained by His Majesty of the merit and value of your services in all other respects, nor to vary His Majesty's intention of conferring upon you those signal marks of his royal favour, which I have already had the satisfaction of stating to you.

I am, &c.

(Signed) W. WINDHAM.

INDEX.

PRINTED BY SPOTTISWOODE AND CO., NEW-STREET SQUARE, LONDON

CPSIA information can be obtained
at www.ICGtesting.com
Printed in the USA
BVHW012228010120
568339BV00011B/1227/P